Praise for *The 7 Habits of Highly Effective People*
by Stephen R. Covey

"Dr. Stephen R. Covey's *The 7 Habits of Highly Effective People* is as relevant and timely today as it was when it was first published 25 years ago. Whether you lead a large organization in a Fortune 500 company or are just getting started in business, the principles discussed in *The 7 Habits of Highly Effective People* provide enduring and universal truths for effective, values-based leadership. *The 7 Habits* is a must read for anyone who seeks to understand how to inspire and motivate others. It remains one of the most important business books of our time."

—KEVIN TURNER, COO of Microsoft Corporation

"Fundamentals are the key to success. Stephen Covey is a master of them. Buy his book, but most important, use it!"

—ANTHONY ROBBINS, author of *Unlimited Power*
and *Awaken the Giant Within*

"The lessons outlined in *The 7 Habits of Highly Effective People* are an important guide to success. This book is one of the top-selling books of all-time for a reason. The success I've had in swimming and in life is credited to a similar proactive, goal-setting approach—*Dream, Plan, Reach*. Through my Foundation's programing, we recognize the power of dreams and stress the importance of executing a detailed plan to propel you toward your goals."

—MICHAEL PHELPS, Olympic Swimmer, Gold Medalist

"The 7 Habits have taught me profound truths that transcend because they are based on principles. They have helped me see what I cannot see. In every situation I can use the principles and paradigms associated with each habit, think over and reset the north direction of my life."

—JUAN NINO, Project Management, Global Auditor
& Project Start Up Lead, Halliburton, Mexico

"Let's forget the content of his books. Or the gazillions of copies *The 7 Habits of Highly Effective People*, or any of his others books for that matter, has sold around the world. Let's forget his memorable seminars—and his business success. One simply cannot pay tribute to Stephen Covey without saying at the outset that he was a lovely human being. I will say, unequivocally, that Stephen expected the best of all of us—and he provided us with straightforward tools and advice to help us get from here to a better there. In short, I will miss Stephen. He stirred my better angels, as he did for millions of others in truly every corner of the world."

—TOM PETERS, author of *The Little Big Things: 163 Ways to Pursue Excellence* and coauthor of *In Search of Excellence*

"The company launched the 7 Habits program in 2001 to align all the Mary Kay China people under one set of values and principles. The 7 Habits help us to think, to set priorities, to work with each other and to live our lives. In the last twelve years, our people continue to expand its cycle of influence, involving our family members, the independent sales force, and business partners. The people's effectiveness has a great impact on the top and bottom lines. As a result, the company was named 'the Best Employer' for the last ten years and became 'the #1 cosmetics brand in sales in China' in 2012."

—PAUL MAK, President, Mary Kay, Greater China

"Stephen R. Covey opened the world's eyes, once again, to the power of basic human truths—take responsibility for your life, create your destiny, seek mutual benefit and understanding, and be abundant and always service-oriented. When we do so, we not only change our own lives, but we change the world, because of who we are. Stephen Covey will truly be remembered and known in history and by future generations not only for his 7 Habits, but for his own personal commitment to family love and contribution to community. He was a great example to the two of us and to our family. His was a life well-lived."

—GOVERNOR MITT ROMNEY AND FIRST LADY ANN ROMNEY

"Twenty-five years after it first appeared, the wisdom of *The 7 Habits of Highly Effective People* is more relevant than ever before. On an individual level, people are burning out, and on a collective level we are burning up the planet. So, Dr. Covey's emphasis on self-renewal and his understanding that leadership and creativity require us to tap into our own physical, mental, and spiritual resources, are exactly what we need in this moment."

—ARIANNA HUFFINGTON, Chair, President, and
Editor-in-Chief, The Huffington Post Media Group

"The *7 Habits of Highly Effective People* brings people together in an organization. It blends inherent local wisdom with an organization's culture so that it becomes a distinct culture by which the institution is differentiated. *The 7 Habits* is an enabler to 'walk' the 'talk.' It's a tool to build a culture of trust and a contributive spirit that emanates good corporate governance. It engages and unleashes employees to be interdependently objective, honest, and perceptive to new ideas, and to work within the system to form the best institution in the market. Life is a duty and is a continuing search to build a contributive life and to give the best. *The 7 Habits* helps to build sensitivity, to recognize the potential of people for self-development. It contains principles and universal values applicable for everyone and can be pragmatically applied to deliver a sincere contribution and to leave a legacy."

—MRS. GUNARNI SOEWORO, Independent Commissioner,
PT Bank Mandiri (Persero) Tbk, Indonesia

"We've always tried to live our lives trying to make a positive difference for others and Dr. Covey definitely made a difference in our lives. It's rare when you admire someone not only for his incredible business sense and leadership abilities, but for who he truly is as a man. We were blessed to see his true human nature was centered in kindness, generosity, and a respect for others. These characteristics are what define a true leader, someone whose legacy will continue to inspire, lead, and guide well beyond his time. We are honored and blessed to have been fortunate enough to spend time with this inspirational man and will continue to try to live by the principles he taught in his beloved *7 Habits* book."

—KARL AND KAY MALONE, Retired NBA Player and Wife

"Stephen Covey has been my mentor–role model for many years. He has written a foreword for my two bestselling books *You Can Make It Happen: A Nine-Step Plan for Success* and *Identity: Your Passport to Success*. I admire him for being able to walk the walk and talk the talk and having the best organizational and leadership content in our field of study. He has been an inspiration to me personally and I treasure my time spent with him especially in my early years. I think of him when I need inspiration regarding my work. Stephen was an extraordinary individual with an extraordinary family. Even though he has left this earth his spirit and teaching will always be with us. It's a pleasure to be able to support his philosophy and his truth. There is only one Stephen Covey."

—STEDMAN GRAHAM, Chairman and CEO
of S. Graham & Associates

"*The 7 Habits* of Stephen Covey has been the start of a life-changing journey for me and for the thousands of people who were part of the businesses that I was privileged to lead. There is no doubt in my mind that the world and its many institutions have become a better place to be because of the wisdom that Stephen has spread. Our lives and our organizations have become happier and more productive. It's up to us to pass on his legacy!"

—TEX GUNNING, CEO TNT Nederland B.V., The Netherlands

"I have learned so much from Stephen Covey over the years that every time I sit down to write, I'm worried about subconscious plagiarism! *The 7 Habits* is not pop psychology or trendy self-help. It is solid wisdom and sound principles."

—RICHARD M. EYRE, author of *Life Balance*
and *Teaching Your Children Values*

"Covey is hot and getting hotter."

—*BusinessWeek*

"*The 7 Habits of Highly Effective People* is a good book I recommend to everybody. The content is built into our company's program for talent development. It helps us to be clearer about our objective and provide the effective approach to get there."

—HANK XU, CEO of Bank of Communication
Pacific Credit Card Center, Singapore

"Stephen R. Covey's book *The 7 Habits* has had a major impact on my life and work as a director of various public organizations in mental health care, in child welfare, and at the Department of Justice. *The 7 Habits* has been the basis of a positive change of culture in these organizations. This has resulted in more focus and greater cooperation and has led to better business results.

As a professor, I have seen the life-changing impact it has had on students and their academic development. During my lectures I use various elements of *The 7 Habits*. At the universities where I teach, these lectures are highly rated by professionals and students.

Above all, the personal encounters I had with Stephen R. Covey were memorable, inspiring, and refreshing. It was a great honor to have met Stephen R. Covey."

—GABRIËL ANTHONIO, PhD, Chairman of the Board of
Youth Care Friesland, Professor in Leadership & Change
Management at Stenden University, The Netherlands

"This book contains the kind of penetrating truth about human nature that is usually found only in fiction. At the end, you will feel not only that you know Covey, but also that he knows you."

—ORSON SCOTT CARD, author of *Ender's Game*,
winner of the Hugo and Nebula Awards

"Many of us perform the 7 Habits in varying degrees. But, Stephen arranged the habits in a compact and systematic manner that can be learned by all. We had success when implementing and cascading the 7 Habits with several thousand people because they were practical and beneficial in our day-to-day activities. I am definitely a supporter and try to be a practitioner. I am not saying I am there yet, but I am trying, because it makes sense: Sharpen the Saw, Begin with the End in Mind, Put First Things First. The 7 Habits make sense and can become a handy reference for anyone. They will live on, not just today, but also tomorrow."

—ARWIN RASYID, President Director, Bank CIMB Niaga, Indonesia

"With all the responsibilities and demands of time, travel, work, and families placed upon us in today's competitive world, it's a big plus to have Stephen Covey's *The 7 Habits of Highly Effective People* to refer to."

—MARIE OSMOND, author of *The Key Is Love:
My Mother's Wisdom, A Daughter's Gratitude*

"*The 7 Habits* encompasses timeless principles that can help guide any company toward success."

—TONY HSIEH, *New York Times* bestselling author of
*Delivering Happiness* and CEO of Zappos.com, Inc.

"We have been working under the influence of the 7 Habits for more than twenty years, applying them in personal and professional areas of our lives. As the habits have been extended throughout the company, the employees' engagement has increased, since they value that the organization cares about them and their families, making a notable impact in their lives. As an innovative company, we consider technology a fundamental tool for living the 7 Habits; at this time we are using a digital version of the solution. Our recruitment procedures and performance evaluations are based on considerations of *The 7 Habits* and it is having an impact on our operations in Mexico, Colombia, Peru, and Central America."

—JOSE RICARDO MANSILLA PAETAU, President of
the Board of Directors, GRUPO PIT, Guatemala

"I first read Dr. Stephen Covey's book *The 7 Habits of Highly Effective People* in 1990, just before my first hospital command. I used the book to develop common understanding for discussions of change management and continuous improvement in every assignment over the next twenty years leading to my selection as the Air Force Surgeon General 2009–2012. In 2008, I met Dr. Covey when he visited the Chairman of the Joint Chiefs at the Pentagon. I told him of the extraordinary impact of his writings dating back to 1993 when my senior staff at Mountain Home AFB attended his "Seven Habits Seminar" and subsequently built the first ten-bed Expeditionary Hospital. These hospitals became the mainstay for casualty care in Afghanistan and Iraq for the USAF over ten years of war. In 2001, his teachings helped me shape the development of new concepts in air evacuation. This evacuation system delivered over 90,000 casualties (nearly 10,000 being the most severely injured of the war) safely home over ten years of conflict, with only four not surviving the transport. Following our conversation at the Pentagon, Dr. Covey sent me a leadership stick that remains one of my most treasured possessions, but it was he who was the true leader of leaders. Dr. Covey's incredibly intuitive *7 Habits of Highly Effective People* provided the common understanding and language to visualize what needed to be done to build the most effective trauma system the world has ever known."

—CHARLES B. GREEN, Lieutenant General, MD, MPH,
Retired Surgeon General, U.S. Air Force


"Stephen Covey's pathbreaking book continues to guide and inspire millions. It persuasively shows them that developing personal effectiveness can guide them on the road to happiness and help them lead the changes that will make the world a better place."

—ROSABETH MOSS KANTER, PhD, Arbuckle Professor,
Harvard Business School Chair and Director;
Harvard University Advanced Leadership Initiative;
bestselling author of *Confidence* and *SuperCorp*

"In person or through the words of *The 7 Habits*, Stephen Covey shaped my professional and business life. As a military leader, I found that 'beginning with the end in mind' helped ensure mission success despite the complexity of a problem. Today, working with some of our nation's highest-need students and the urban educators teaching them, I constantly revisit Stephen's guidance to 'listen and seek first to understand.' So basic and yet so influential; I continue to be shaped by Stephen's work as I attempt to practice these not-so-simple 7 Habits and share his work with those around me."

—JOHN SCANLAN II, CAPTAIN, USNR, CFO
Cleveland Metropolitan School District

"*The 7 Habits* was for me a breakthrough in the way of looking at myself and other people. Am I proactive? Do I know my target? Are my priorities right? All these simple questions again and again, every day, changed my way of thinking and behaving. I sincerely think that Stephen Covey made me a better person. And far more important, he made me a better coach."

—JOËL SCHOLS, Cofounder Newtel nv, Belgium

"When I think of Steve Covey, I imagine him smiling as he hears the words, 'Well done, my good and faithful servant.' An important reason Steve deserves such praise is *The 7 Habits of Highly Effective People*. This book's lessons are as meaningful today, if not more so, than they were when Steve first penned them 25 years ago. *The 7 Habits* continues to be a must read—and a must reread."

—KEN BLANCHARD, PhD, coauthor of
*The One Minute Manager* and *Leading at a Higher Level*

"Around 20 years ago I was introduced to this book in a seminar held for executives in Jakarta. From that time onward, I am certain that *7 Habits* is compulsory for me personally, for my family, and for the people in the organization that I lead. I uphold this consistently up to now. I am grateful that Stephen Covey left this valuable legacy for all of us."

—TP RACHMAT, President Director,
TP Triputra Investindo Raya, Indonesia

"*7 Habits of Highly Effective People* has had an impact on the lives of literally millions of readers across the world for 25 years. The blueprint it has provided for principled living and leadership is a timeless message that has never been more important. Integrity, character, hard work, and honorable determination are so vividly displayed throughout the pages of this book and are interwoven in all of the lessons taught—inspiring greater success and achievement."

—SENATOR ORRIN G. HATCH

"One of the greatest habits you can develop is to learn and internalize the wisdom of Stephen Covey. He lived what he said and this book can help you live, permanently, in the 'Winner's Circle.' "

—DR. DENIS WAITLEY, author of *The Psychology of Winning*

"We are very fortunate to have brought the 7 Habits program in-house. The impact was tremendous—especially in helping us recover so quickly from the devastating Thailand flood in 2011."

—DR. SAMPAN SILAPANAD, Vice President,
Magnetic Head Operations, Western Digital, Thailand

"For me, the greatest lesson of *The 7 Habits* is that effectiveness is truly a habit. Win the private victories over yourself each day, as Dr. Covey teaches in his landmark book, and eventually, you'll win the big ones. As the oldest woman ever to compete in Olympic swimming, I've found that reaching small daily goals is the key to achieving bigger goals—even our greatest hopes and dreams."

—DARA TORRES, Olympic Swimmer, Gold Medalist

"*The 7 Habits* has been on my favorite business book list for the past quarter century. It's the one business book that spills over onto my favorite 'any category' book. Its lessons are life lessons worthy of 24/7 consideration."

—JOEL PETERSON, Chairman of the Board, Jet Blue

"Orbicon has collaborated with FranklinCovey for five years. The result is a firm with 'Good Habits.' *The 7 Habits of Highly Effective People* provided the management team with a common language and self-leadership skills. And most important, it strengthened our business culture. The mind-set embedded in *The 7 Habits* has subsequently been strengthened by training in Helping Clients Succeed, which has given us new standards for our relations with clients and other partners. As our participants frequently say: 'You can say a lot about this training—but it works!'"

—JESPER NYBO ANDERSEN, CEO, Orbicon, Denmark

"Good-bye, Dale Carnegie. Stephen Covey has had a profound influence on my life. His principles are powerful. They work. Buy this book. Read it, and as you live the principles your life will be enriched."

—ROBERT C. ALLEN, author of *Creating Wealth* and *Nothing Down*

"This book has the gift of being simple without being simplistic."

—M. SCOTT PECK, author of *The Road Less Traveled*

"After the 7 Habits training sessions, we could really witness improvements in the ability of our employees to work together and this is exactly what we wanted. The fact that we have continued the training over the years shows that we think it's still worth it. The benefits in terms of personal development, better relations among employees, and better efficiency in working across borders are so important for the success of an international corporation like Georg Fischer, with companies on all continents."

—YVES SERRA, CEO, Georg Fischer AG, Schaffhausen, Switzerland

"In large corporations and elementary schools alike, Stephen Covey has reshaped the way we think about how we live our lives and the way we lead others. The influence this book has had on students across the world will be felt for decades to come. This is an anniversary that deserves celebration!"

—DANIEL DOMENECH, Executive Director AASA,
The School Superintendents Association

"In the 7 *Habits* book, Stephen Covey provides us with a pattern for living our lives with integrity and honor, and for giving service to others. We are inspired to achieve our greatest desires in life, when we apply and practice what the book teaches. Thank you, Stephen, for a life well lived. You have left us with a legacy that will long be remembered."

—STEVE YOUNG, NFL Hall of Famer and Super Bowl MVP

"I am reading it with profit. . . . It is most thoughtful and enlightening."

—NORMAN VINCENT PEALE, author of *The Power of Positive Thinking*

"*The 7 Habits of Highly Effective People* is a formidable legacy left by Stephen Covey. It provides a simple, principle-based framework to help individuals face their private and public challenges successfully. I am the CEO of a large K-12 Education Company, and we are now offering *The 7 Habits* in an adapted format to thousands of elementary and middle school students in association with FranklinCovey. Watching the academic and behavioral improvements among the students we serve with the program is one of the most rewarding professional experiences I have ever had."

—MANOEL AMORIM, President and CEO of Abril Educação, Brazil

"Happily, this book has advised and encouraged us for 25 years. Now, I encourage us to be loyal and supportive for another 25 years."

—MAYA ANGELOU

"I've never known any teacher or mentor on improving personal effectiveness to generate such an overwhelmingly positive reaction . . . this book captures beautifully Stephen's philosophy of principles. I think anyone reading it will quickly understand the enormous reaction I and others have had to Dr. Covey's teachings."

—JOHN PEPPER, Former President, P&G

"There are very few business books that are essential reading for anyone who wants to make a difference. This is one of the great ones."

—SETH GODIN, author of *The Icarus Deception*

"*The 7 Habits of Highly Effective People* is a landmark achievement that has touched the lives of millions of people and has helped businesses, churches, and families worldwide. It has also had a special place in my own life. Knowing the principles has helped me embrace major paradigm shifts to help others. I miss Dr. Covey, but know he will live on to help others for generations to come."

—DR. DANIEL G. AMEN, MD, author of
*Change Your Brain, Change Your Life*

"This book, *The 7 Habits of Highly Effective People*, opened the eyes of the world to a liberating truth: that our mind-sets play strange tricks on us. We are poor if we think we are poor. Dr. Covey taught that the key to changing our lives is to change that mind-set about ourselves—to realize that we are each incalculably rich in potential and possibilities."

—MUHAMMAD YUNUS, Nobel Peace Prize Winner, 2006

"In AP Pension, we have used *The 7 Habits of Highly Effective People* since 2007 to achieve competitive strength by improving our effectiveness. Our output per staff has doubled in this period. We now have a common culture, values, goals, and language—and this has given us execution power to focus externally on clients and not internally on ourselves. *The 7 Habits of Highly Effective People* is the most durable investment AP Pension has made."

—SØREN DAL THOMSEN, CEO of AP Pension, Denmark

"Many years ago after completing my MBA, I had the opportunity to read *The 7 Habits of Highly Effective People* by Dr. Stephen R. Covey. The book was insightful and outstanding and has had a profound influence on my leadership style, career, and life. The principles and approach outlined have helped me lead teams in growth-oriented, entrepreneurial, and global enterprises. Leadership awards and accolades earned were due to the insights and teachings from Dr. Covey. The principles applied across cultures and made me a better leader, mentor, and spouse."

—MICHAEL FUNG, retired CFO, Walmart U.S.

"Ten years ago I attended a seminar where Dr. Covey taught the 7 Habits to a large audience of adults, mostly corporate leaders. As I looked around the room and saw how engaged everyone was, I couldn't help but think, 'Why wait until people are adults to teach them these skills?' Soon afterward we began teaching the 7 Habits at our school, first to staff and then to students—even five-year-olds. The influence it has had on our school over the past decade has been amazing. In my 36 years in education, I have never seen anything have such an impact on student achievement, teacher retention, and parent satisfaction. It thrills me that students are now learning these same powerful habits in schools across the globe through *The Leader in Me*."

—MURIEL THOMAS SUMMERS, Principal,
A.B. Combs Elementary School

"*The 7 Habits* is more than a book: It is the legacy of a great teacher who lived the life he wrote about. Dr. Stephen R. Covey's convictions came from principles and experience. I am grateful for this man, but I will not miss him. He will continue to be with me every day, through the things that he taught."

—CLAYTON CHRISTENSEN, Professor, Harvard Business School, and
author of *The Innovator's Dilemma* and *How Will You Measure Your Life?*

"Self-improvement has been a secular religion in America even before Independence. It's a critical reason why we became the greatest economy in the world. Stephen Covey's classic, *The 7 Habits of Highly Effective People*, epitomizes this very American characteristic. I and countless others have referred to his book time and time again. It will be used for generations to come. Ben Franklin, who was the first to popularize ways to live better and to achieve success, would have been immensely impressed with Covey's masterpiece."

—STEVE FORBES, Chairman and Editor-in-Chief, Forbes Media

"Stephen Covey influenced thousands in the U.S. Navy, starting with me. Growing and developing leaders is our business, with life and death implications. The *7 Habits* taught us to think anew, taking on challenges new to each of us and vital for the defense of our nation. His work impacted a generation of leaders in our Navy and helped me lead our Navy in the days following 9/11. I will never forget him sitting around the dinner table with a group of my leadership team sharing ideas for making the Navy a better place to be. He changed our lives forever!"

—ADMIRAL VERN CLARK, U.S. Navy, Retired

"I almost never recommend business or self-help books. But, *The 7 Habits of Highly Effective People* is one of those rare exceptions—in fact, I rate the book a 10 and highly recommend it to business associates, family members, and friends. I am especially pleased to have been associated with Stephen Covey and his team and appreciate their important contributions to the world of business."

—FRED REICHHELD, Bain Fellow, author of *The Ultimate Question*

"It is my honor to endorse the book that has touched my life in the most profound way—*The Seven Habits of Highly Effective People*. I am overjoyed and filled with gratitude when I think of Stephen's legacy in my life, from understanding that the only solid center in my life are principles, to one of his amazing quotes that guides my human struggle: 'Whenever you see the problem out there, THAT is the problem.' This book gave me a roadmap for a principled centered human experience that I have been using since I discovered it 13 years ago. As I experience and try to integrate these principles into my life, I go back to the book and amaze myself evermore for its profound teachings. I am amazed by how little I understood many of these principles five years ago, and I am sure I will say the same thing in five years! I consider Stephen to be one of my most important mentors in life, even though I saw him only a couple of times and spent only a little time with him. I will never forget his way of affirming me and others. Truly one of the most amazing teachers of the last century, how lucky are we who have experienced him through the *7 Habits*.

The warmest regards and the deepest gratitude to you, his family, for making his legacy transcend and inspire the generations to come."

—JUAN BONIFASI, CEO Grupo Entero, Guatemala

"Stephen Covey's *7 Habits of Highly Effective People* has given tremendous guidance to the Marriott organization as we've managed associates in 74 countries. His insights have helped us achieve breakthrough leadership for hospitality excellence."

—J. W. MARRIOTT, JR., Chairman and CEO
of Marriott International, Inc.

"No person lasts forever, but books and ideas can endure. Stephen R. Covey's life is done, but his work is not. It continues, right here in this book as alive today as when first written."

—JIM COLLINS

# 7 The HABITS of HIGHLY EFFECTIVE PEOPLE

*Powerful Lessons in Personal Change*

## Stephen R. Covey

**SIMON &
SCHUSTER**

London · New York · Sydney · Toronto · New Delhi

A CBS COMPANY

First published in Great Britain by Simon & Schuster UK Ltd, 1989

This edition published by Simon & Schuster UK Ltd 2013
A CBS COMPANY

17

Simon & Schuster UK Ltd
1st Floor
222 Gray's Inn Road
London WC1X 8HB

www.simonandschuster.co.uk

Simon & Schuster Australia, Sydney
Simon & Schuster India, New Delhi

*Designed by Irving Perkins Associates.*

Excerpt of 'Little Giddings' from Four Quartets, copyright 1943 by T.S. Elliot and renewed
1971 by Esme Valerie Eliot, reprinted by permission of Harcourt Brace Jovanovich, Inc.

A CIP catalogue record for this book is available from the British Library

ISBN TPB: 978-1-47112-939-1
ISBN PB: 978-1-47113-182-0

Printed and bound in India by Replika Press Pvt. Ltd.

# ACKNOWLEDGMENTS

Interdependence is a higher value than independence.

This work is a synergistic product of many minds. It began in the middle seventies as I was reviewing 200 years of success literature as part of a doctoral program. I am grateful for the inspiration and wisdom of many thinkers and for the trans-generational sources and roots of this wisdom.

I am also grateful for many students, friends, and colleagues at Brigham Young University and the Covey Leadership Center and for thousands of adults, parents, youth, executives, teachers, and other clients who have tested this material and have given feedback and encouragement. The material and arrangement has slowly evolved and has imbued those who have been sincerely and deeply immersed in it with the conviction that the Seven Habits represent a holistic, integrated approach to personal and interpersonal effectiveness, and that, more than in the individual habits themselves, the real key lies in the relationship among them and in how they are sequenced.

For the development and production of the book itself I feel a deep sense of gratitude:

—to Sandra and to each of our children and their spouses for living lives of integrity and service and for supporting my many travels and involvements outside the home. It's easy to teach principles loved ones live.

—to my brother John for his constant love, interest, insights and purity of soul.

—to the happy memory of my father.

—to my mother for her devotion to her more than 87 living descendants and for her constant demonstrations of love.

—to my dear friends and colleagues in the business, especially:

—to Bill Marre, Ron McMillan, and Lex Watterson for feedback, encouragement, editorial suggestions, and production help.

—to Brad Anderson, who at great personal sacrifice for over a year, developed a Seven Habits video-based development program. Under his leadership this material has been tested and refined and is being implemented by thousands of people across a broad range of organizations. Almost without exception, after initial exposure to this material, our clients desire to make it available to greater numbers of employees, underscoring our confidence that it "works."

—to Bob Thele for helping to create a system for our firm that gave me the peace of mind to enable me to really focus on the book.

—to David Conley for communicating the value and power of the Seven Habits to hundreds of business organizations so that my colleagues, Blaine Lee, Roice Krueger, Roger Merrill and Al Switzler, and I have the constant opportunity to share ideas in a large variety of settings.

—to my proactive literary agent Jan Miller, and my "can do" associate Greg Link and his assistant Stephanni Smith and Raleen Beckham Wahlin for their creative and courageous marketing leadership.

—to my Simon & Schuster editor Bob Asahina for his professional competence and project leadership, for his many excellent suggestions and for helping me to better understand the difference between writing and speaking.

—to my earlier devoted assistants Shirley and Heather Smith and to my present assistant Marilyn Andrews for a level of loyalty which is truly uncommon.

—to our Executive Excellence magazine editor Ken Shelton for his editing of the first manuscript years ago, for helping refine and test the material in several contexts, and for his integrity and sense of quality.

—to Rebecca Merrill for her invaluable editing and production assistance, for her inner commitment to the material, and for her skill, sensitivity, and carefulness in fulfilling that commitment, and to her husband, Roger, for his wise, synergistic help.

—and to Kay Swim and her son, Gaylord, for their much appreciated vision which contributed to our organization's rapid growth.

To my colleagues,
empowered
and empowering

# 7 The HABITS of HIGHLY EFFECTIVE PEOPLE

# Contents

# Foreword to the 25th Anniversary Edition of Stephen Covey's *The 7 Habits of Highly Effective People*

I first met Stephen Covey in 2001, when he asked for a meeting to talk about ideas. After a warm greeting—his enveloping handshake feeling like the comfortable leather of a softball glove that you've worn a thousand times—we settled into a conversation that lasted two hours. Stephen began by asking questions, lots of questions. Here sat a master teacher, one of the most influential thinkers of the day, and he wanted to learn from someone twenty-five years his junior.

As the conversation opened an opportunity for me to exercise my own curiosity, I began, "How did you come up with the ideas in *The 7 Habits*?"

"I didn't," he responded.

"What do you mean?" I asked. "You wrote the book."

"Yes, I wrote the book, but the principles were known long before me." He continued, "They are more like natural laws. All I did was put them together, to synthesize them for people."

That's when I began to understand why this work has had such an impact. Covey had spent more than three decades studying, practicing, teaching, and refining what he ultimately distilled into these pages. He did not seek credit for the principles; he sought to teach the principles, to make them accessible. He saw creating the 7 Habits not primarily as a means to his own success, but as an act of service.

When Bob Whitman, chief executive of FranklinCovey, called to ask if I would consider writing a foreword for the 25th anniversary edition of *The 7 Habits of Highly Effective People*, I responded first by rereading the entire book; I'd read it shortly after its initial publication in 1989, and it was a gift to reengage with its message. I also wanted to recalibrate: what makes it an enduring classic? I see four factors that contributed to its rarefied stature:

1. Covey created a "user interface" organized into a coherent conceptual framework, made highly accessible by Covey's strong writing;
2. Covey focused on timeless principles, not on mere techniques or momentary fads;
3. Covey wrote primarily about *building character*, not about "achieving success"—and thereby helped people become not just more effective individuals, but better leaders;
4. Covey himself was a Level 5 teacher, humble about his own shortcomings, yet determined to share widely what he'd learned.

Stephen Covey was a master synthesizer. I think of what he did for personal effectiveness as analogous to what the graphical user interface did for personal computers. Prior to Apple and Microsoft, few people could harness computers to their daily lives; there was no easily accessible user interface—there were no mouse pointers, friendly icons, or overlapping windows on a screen, let alone a touch screen. But with the Macintosh and then Windows, the mass of people could finally tap the power of the microchip behind the screen. Similarly, there had been hundreds of years of accumulated wisdom about personal effectiveness, from Benjamin Franklin to Peter Drucker, but it was never assembled into one coherent, user-friendly framework. Covey created a standard operating system—the "Windows"—for personal effectiveness, and he made it easy to use. He proved to be a very fine writer, a master of short stories and conceptual wordplay. I will never forget the story in Chapter 1 about the man on the subway who could not control his screaming kids (and the point it makes), nor will I ever forget the lighthouse or the wrong jungle or the analogy of the golden eggs. Some of his conceptual wrapping paper worked exceptionally well, being both descriptive of a concept, and at the same time prescriptive in its application. "Win/Win or No Deal." "Seek First to Understand, Then to Be Understood." "Begin with the End in Mind." "Put First Things First." He made the ideas even more accessible by using personal life-struggles and stories—raising children, building a marriage, dealing with friends—to teach the habits and build muscle fiber for living them. The ideas embedded in the framework are timeless. They are *principles*. This is why they work, and why they speak to people in all age groups around the globe. In a world of change, disruption, chaos, and relentless uncertainty, people crave an anchor point, a set of constructs to give them guidance in the face of turbulence. Covey believed that timeless principles do indeed exist, and that the search for them is not folly, but wisdom. He rejected the view of those who shout from the rooftops, "There is nothing sacred, nothing enduring, nothing durable to build upon in this ever-changing landscape! Everything is new! Nothing from the past applies!"

My own research quest has focused on the question, "What makes a great company tick—why do some companies make the leap from good to great (while others don't), why do some become built to last (while others fall), and why do some thrive in chaos?" One of our key findings is the idea of "Preserve the Core / Stimulate Progress"; no enterprise can become or remain truly great without a core set of principles to preserve, to build upon, to serve as an anchor, to provide guidance in the face of an ever-changing world. At the same time, no company can remain great without stimulating progress—change, renewal, improvement, and the pursuit of BHAGs (Big Hairy Audacious Goals). When you blend these two together—Preserve the Core *AND* Stimulate Progress—you get a magical dialectic that keeps a company or organization vibrant over time. Covey found a similar pattern in personal effectiveness: first build upon a strong core of principles that are not open for continuous change; at the same time, be relentless in the quest for improvement and continuous self-renewal. This dialectic enables an individual to retain a rock-solid foundation and attain sustained growth for a lifetime.

But I think the most important aspect of *The 7 Habits*—what makes it not just practical, but profound—is its emphasis on *building character* rather than "attaining success." There is no effectiveness without discipline, and there is no discipline without character. While writing this foreword, I'm in the midst of finishing a two-year journey as the class of 1951 Chair for the Study of Leadership at the United States Military Academy at West Point. I've come to a personal belief that a key ingredient in the West Point recipe is the idea that great leadership begins first with character—that leadership is primarily a function of who you *are*, for this is the foundation for everything you do. How do you build leaders? You first build character. And that is why I see the 7 Habits as not just about personal effectiveness, but about leadership development.

As I reflect upon some of the exceptional leaders I've studied in my research, I'm struck by how Covey's principles are manifested in many of their stories. Let me focus on one of my favorite cases, Bill Gates. It's become fashionable in recent years to attribute the outsize success of someone like Bill Gates to luck, to being in the right place at the right time. But if you think about it, this argument falls apart. When *Popular Electronics* put the Altair computer on its cover, announcing the advent of the first-ever personal computer, Bill Gates teamed up with Paul Allen to launch a software company and write the BASIC programming language for the Altair. Yes, Gates was at just the right moment with programming skills, but so were other people—students in computer science and electrical engineering at schools like Cal Tech, MIT, and Stanford; seasoned engineers at technology companies like IBM, Xerox, and HP; and scientists in government research laboratories. *Thousands* of people could've done what Bill Gates did at that moment, *but they didn't.* Gates *acted* upon the moment. He dropped out of Harvard, moved to Albuquerque (where the Altair was based), and wrote computer code day and night. It was not the luck of being at the right moment in history that separated Bill Gates, but his *proactive response* to being at the right moment (*Habit 1: Be Proactive*).

As Microsoft grew into a successful company, Gates expanded his objectives, guided by a very big idea: a computer on every desk. Later, Gates and his wife created the Bill & Melinda Gates Foundation, with huge goals, such as eradicating malaria from the face of the Earth. As he put it in his 2007 Harvard commencement speech, "For Melinda and for me, the challenge is the same: how can we do the most good for the greatest number with the resources we have" (*Habit 2: Begin with the End in Mind*).

True discipline means channeling our best hours into first-order objectives, and that means being a nonconformist in the best sense. "Everyone" might say finishing Harvard should be the most important task for a young Bill Gates. Instead, he aligned his efforts with his mission, despite any disapproving glances from well-meaning people. As he built Microsoft, he poured his energies into two overriding objectives: getting the best people and executing on a few big software bets; everything else was secondary. When Gates first met Warren Buffett at a dinner, the host asked all those at the table what they saw as the single most important factor in their journey through life. As Alice Schroeder related in her book *The Snowball*, both Gates and Buffett gave the same one-word answer: "Focus." (*Habit 3: Put First Things First*).

Gates's relationship to the fourth habit (*Habit 4: Think Win/Win*) is a bit more complicated. At first glance, Gates would appear to be a win/lose character, a fierce combatant who so feared how easily a company's flanks could be turned that he wrote a "nightmare" memo laying out scenarios of how Microsoft could lose. In the race for industry standards, there would be only a small set of big winners, and a lot of losers, and Gates had no intention of Microsoft's being anything less than one of the big winners. But a closer look reveals that he was masterful at assembling complementary forces into a coalition. To achieve his big dream, Gates understood that Microsoft would need to complement its strengths with the strengths of others: Intel with its microprocessors, and personal computer manufacturers such as IBM and Dell. He also shared equity, so that when Microsoft won, Microsoft people would win as well. And he displayed a remarkable ability to complement his personal strengths with the strengths of others, especially his longtime business alter ego, Steve Ballmer; Gates and Ballmer accomplished much more by working together than they ever could alone; 1 + 1 is much larger than 2. (*Habit 6: Synergize*).

As Gates moved to social impact with the Foundation, he did not step forth saying, "I've been successful in business, so I already know how to achieve social impact." Quite the opposite; he brought a relentless curiosity, a quest to gain understanding. He pushed with questions, trying to get a handle on the science and methods needed to solve some of the most intractable problems, ending one exchange with a friend with a comment along the lines of "I need to learn more about phosphates." (*Habit 5: Seek First to Understand, Then to Be Understood.*) And, finally, I'm struck by how Gates renewed. Even during the most intense years building Microsoft, he periodically set aside an entire week to unplug for reading and reflection, a Think Week. He also developed a penchant for reading biographies; at one point he told Brent Schlender of *Fortune*, "It's amazing how some people develop during their lives"—a lesson Gates looks to have taken as a mantra for his own life (*Habit 7: Sharpen the Saw.*)

Gates is a fabulous case, but I could have used others. I could have highlighted Wendy Kopp, who founded Teach For America with the idea to inspire hundreds of thousands of college graduates to serve at least two years teaching children in our most underserved schools, with the ultimate aim to create an indomitable social force to radically improve K–12 education (*Be Proactive; Begin with the End in Mind*). Or I could have used Steve Jobs living in a house without furniture, too busy creating insanely great products to get around to seemingly unimportant activities like buying a kitchen table or a sofa (*Put First Things First*). Or Herb Kelleher of Southwest Airlines, who created a win/win culture between management and labor, with everyone uniting together after 9/11 to keep its thirty years of consecutive profitability intact while also keeping intact every single job (*Think Win/Win*). Or even Winston Churchill, who took naps throughout the Second World War, thereby giving himself "two mornings" every day (*Sharpen the Saw*).

I do not mean to imply that the 7 Habits map one-for-one to building a great company. The principles in *Good to Great* and *Built to Last*, for example, and the principles in *The 7 Habits of Highly Effective People* are complementary, but distinct. Covey set out to write a book, not on building great organizations, but on achieving great personal effectiveness. Still, organizations are composed of people, and the more effective those people, the stronger the organization. And I do suspect that those who live the 7 Habits perhaps have a higher likelihood of becoming Level 5 leaders, those rare transformational figures I wrote so much about in *Good to Great*. Level 5 leaders display a paradoxical combination of personal humility and professional will, channeling their energy, drive, creativity, and discipline into something larger and more enduring than themselves. They're ambitious, to be sure, but for a purpose beyond themselves, be it building a great company, changing the world, or achieving some great object that's ultimately not about them. One of the most important variables in whether an enterprise remains great lies in a simple question: what is the *truth* about the inner motivations, character, and ambition of those who hold power? Their true, internal motivations *will absolutely* show up in their decisions and actions—if not immediately, then over time, and certainly under duress—no matter what they say or how they pose. And thus, we return full circle to a central tenet of Covey's framework: build inner character first— private victory before public victory.

And that brings me to Stephen Covey himself as a Level 5 teacher. Throughout his rather miraculous career, he displayed a disarming humility about his impact and influence, combined with an indomitable will to help people grasp the ideas. He genuinely believed the world would be a better place if people lived the 7 Habits, and that belief shines through these pages. As a Level 5 teacher, Stephen Covey did his human best to live what he taught. He said that he personally struggled most with Habit 5 ("Seek First to Understand, Then to Be Understood"). There is a great irony in this, as he first went on a multi-decade intellectual journey to gain understanding, before he wrote the book. He was first and foremost a learner who became a teacher, then a teacher who learned to write, and in so doing made his teachings enduring. In Habit 2, Stephen challenges us to envision our own funeral, and consider, "What would you like each of the speakers to say about you and your life? . . . What character would you like them to have seen in you? What contributions, what achievements would you want them to remember?" I suspect he would be very pleased with how it turned out for him.

No person lasts forever, but books and ideas can endure. When you engage with these pages, you will be engaging with Stephen Covey at the peak of his powers. You can feel him reaching out from the text to say "Here, I really believe this, let me help you— I want you to *get* this, to learn from it, I want you to grow, to be better, to contribute more, to make a life that matters." His life is done, but his work is not. It continues, right here in this book, as alive today as when first written. *The 7 Habits of Highly Effective People* is twenty-five years young, off to a very strong start indeed.

—Jim Collins
Boulder, Colorado
July 2013

# A COVEY FAMILY TRIBUTE TO A HIGHLY EFFECTIVE FATHER

There is no doubt that our father's habit of "sharpening the saw" ultimately saved a life that day in Montana. Growing up, we often saw him doing what he called "winning the daily private victory" early in the morning by meditating, reading his scriptures, and exercising. That particular afternoon he was quietly reading on the beach while enjoying the beautiful view of the lake when he heard a faint cry, "Help me!" Using the binoculars he always seemed to carry with him to search for wildlife, he zoomed in on a fisherman's float tube out in the lake. Someone was desperately hanging on to the edge, about to fall into the ice-cold water.

Quickly, our father jumped onto his Jet Ski and reached the tube, where he found a heavily intoxicated man. He pulled him onto his Jet Ski and brought him back to shore. He then searched for the man's family at a nearby campground and found they were totally unaware he was even missing, as they had been drinking as well. A few years later, the man he rescued related this story to a large group, claiming it was a turning point in his life. Unaware of who had rescued him that day, he was grateful that someone had cared enough to hear his cry and save him.

This incident is symbolic of our father, Stephen R. Covey, who was a type of "lifeline" not only to his posterity of nine children and fifty-four grandchildren, but also to a multitude of people and organizations who have been inspired and forever changed by *The 7 Habits of Highly Effective People*. He always acknowledged he didn't invent these habits, as they were based on universal principles or natural laws, such as responsibility, integrity, abundance, and renewal. But he also believed that "common sense isn't always common practice." And thus, he devoted his life to getting his message to as many people as possible.

After his passing in July 2012, our family realized the scope and magnitude of his lifelong mission to "unleash human potential."

We were overwhelmed by the thousands of emails, letters, notes, visits, and calls from people all over the world who wanted to share their own personal stories of how he similarly threw them a lifeline and rescued them from such things as a life without purpose, being an ineffective leader of a company, a failing marriage, a damaged relationship, or overcoming an abusive upbringing. Over and over, we heard experiences of how our father had the unique ability to affirm the one while also literally inspiring millions with his principle-centered approach to living.

Dad was a "man for all seasons" and lived with integrity. Throughout the years, he had many opportunities to train world leaders and heads of state and considered it a great privilege and responsibility. Once during a discussion, when everyone in the group was criticizing the then current U.S. president, he remained noticeably silent. When asked why he hadn't joined in the melee, he simply responded, "I may have the chance to influence him someday; and if I do, I don't want to be a hypocrite." Several months later, this same president called Dad, said he had just finished reading *The 7 Habits of Highly Effective People* for the second time, and asked if Dad could personally train him in applying the principles. By the end of his life Dad had met with thirty-one heads of state including four presidents of the United States.

Our father never taught anything without striving to live it first. This was especially true of the 7 Habits, which he researched and developed over many years, well before the book was published. He was the master of being "proactive," and much to our vexation while growing up, we were never allowed to make excuses or blame our circumstances, friends, or teachers for our problems. We were simply taught to "make it happen" or "choose another response." Luckily, our mother allowed us to be victims and blame other people on occasion; she provided a healthy balance to our father!

Dad's "R and I" (resourcefulness and initiative), as he called it, was legendary. Once he was stuck in a traffic jam due to construction and was in jeopardy of missing his plane. He decided he couldn't wait anymore and instructed the cab driver that he was exiting the cab to redirect traffic so their lane could start moving and to pick him up down the road. The cab driver was stunned. "You can't do that," he said, to which Dad gleefully responded, "Watch me!" He got out and directed the traffic so that his lane began moving again (along with honks and cheers from cars in his lane); his cab driver picked him up, and he made his flight.

Our family knew him as unpretentious and uninhibited, often carrying on full conversations with strangers while wearing fake buck teeth or outrageous wigs to cover his trademark bald head so he could be incognito. One time he was asked to leave a golf course because he got bored with golfing and started an enormous water fight with a friend. We cringed when we got trapped in an elevator with him, knowing that within seconds he would turn and face the other passengers (violating their personal space), and with a big smile on his face cheerfully say, "You may have wondered why I called this short meeting!" and then laugh hysterically at his own joke.

We learned not to care so much what others thought and to just enjoy his fun-loving personality. He was famous for his power naps. Frequently, he would scrunch up his jacket and put on his eye mask and take short naps to renew himself in the most unusual places, including stores, movie theaters, airports, trains, under park benches, or wherever and whenever he could find a little space and time. His enthusiasm was contagious and he taught us to live with a "carpe diem" (seize the day) mentality and to "suck the marrow out of life," as he loved to say.

He was always somewhat surprised and embarrassed by his professional success, and remained humble and unaffected by his fame. He simply saw himself as a steward of the great work he was doing, always giving credit to others and to God. He was never ashamed of his values and his faith and believed that if God was at the center of your life, everything else would find its proper place. He taught us that in the long run, the only way to enduring success as an individual or an organization is to live in accordance with timeless principles.

Our father tried really hard to walk the talk and practice what he preached, and he often apologized to us when he'd fall short, saying things like, "Son, I'm so sorry that I lost my temper with you," or "Darling, that was unkind of me. What can I do to make it up to you?" People frequently ask us what it was like growing up with him, as if he couldn't possibly be as good as he seemed. Although he was by no means perfect and struggled with such things as being patient while waiting in traffic jams or while Mom got ready, there wasn't a discernible gap between what he taught and how he lived. He was who you thought and hoped he would be. Perhaps the greatest compliment we can pay our father is this: as good as he was in public as an author and teacher, he was even better in private as a husband and father. And we loved him for that consistency.

We all knew that Dad would rather spend time with his family than with anyone else, and he proved it by how he managed his time and put "first things first." Though he traveled a lot under many demands on his time, he rarely missed anything really important to us, like a birthday or a basketball game, sometimes planning up to two years in advance. He continually made deposits into each of our "emotional bank accounts" with one-on-one dates and modeled that "in relationships, the little things are the big things." He was the master of teaching moments and would apply true principles to whatever we were dealing with, encouraging us to make decisions based on our values and not how we felt in the moment. He taught by example that "life is a mission and not a career," and that we could find true happiness by serving others.

Dad adored our mother, Sandra, and had a remarkable relationship with her for fifty-six years. A few times a week, they had a ritual of connecting with each other—they would take a ride on a Honda motorbike, driving slowly enough to "talk it over" while they enjoyed the scenery and just being together. They called each other on the phone two or three times a day, even when he was out of town. They discussed everything under the sun from politics to great books to raising kids, and Dad valued her opinion more than anyone else's. He was a deep thinker and had a tendency to be too theoretical. Mom was an excellent sounding board and would help him simplify and make his material practical, saying, "Oh, Stephen, this is way too complicated. No one knows what you're even talking about. Keep it simple and tell more stories." He loved the feedback! Now with children of our own, we marvel at their win-win relationship and reflect on how they enjoyed such a happy life together.

Dad had a beautiful definition of leadership: he taught that *leadership is communicating others' worth and potential so clearly that they are inspired to see it in themselves*. Right after our father passed away, a man who had grown up under very rough circumstances relayed this message, which encompasses what he really was about: "I want your family to know that I still have the twenty-minute affirmation tape he made for me thirty years ago, where among other things he told me that God loved me, that I would go to college, and that I would have a family of my own one day. I've listened to it all the time over the past thirty years, and I've accomplished everything he saw in me. I'm not who I am without him. Thank you!"

At this significant anniversary of *The 7 Habits of Highly Effective People*, and amid the accolades and the millions of lives and thousands of organizations this book has influenced, the Stephen R. Covey family children wish to pay tribute to a "highly effective" family man. Just as he rescued a drowning man years ago, we trust that his life and words will continue to extend similar lifelines to you and your family, to your team and organization, and to countless other people and causes. Given the turbulent world in which we find ourselves today, we believe the timeless principles of the 7 Habits are more relevant than ever before and that the message and impact of the 7 Habits is only just beginning.

We will always be grateful for such a great father and "Papa," as the grandkids liked to call him. His legacy now lives in us and in all those who have been influenced by his magnificent spirit and inspiring teachings, to live lives of integrity, to contribute and make a difference in the world, and to rise to the greatness that lies within each of us.

Sincerely,
The Stephen R. Covey children:
Cynthia, Maria, Stephen, Sean,
David, Catherine, Colleen,
Jenny, and Joshua

# FOREWORD TO THE 2004 EDITION

The world has changed dramatically since *The 7 Habits of Highly Effective People* was first published. Life is more complex, more stressful, more demanding. We have transitioned from the Industrial Age into the Information / Knowledge Worker Age—with all of its profound consequences. We face challenges and problems in our personal lives, our families, and our organization's unimagined even one and two decades ago. These challenges are not only of a new order of magnitude, they are altogether different in kind.

These sweeping changes in society and rumbling shifts in the digitized global marketplace give rise to a very important question—one I'm asked fairly often: "Are The 7 Habits of Highly Effective People still relevant *today*?" And for that matter, "Will they be relevant ten, twenty, fifty, one hundred years from now?" My answer: the greater the change and more difficult our challenges, the *more* relevant the habits become. The reason: our problems and pain are universal and increasing, and the solutions to the problems are and always will be based upon universal, timeless, self-evident *principles* common to every enduring, prospering society throughout history. I did not invent them and take no credit for them. I've simply identified and organized them into a sequential framework.

One of the most profound learnings of my life is this: if you want to achieve your highest aspirations and overcome your greatest challenges, *identify and apply the principle or natural law that governs the results you seek. How* we apply a principle will vary greatly and will be determined by our unique strengths, talents, and creativity, but, ultimately, success in any endeavor is always derived from acting in harmony with the principles to which the success is tied.

Many people do not think this way, at least consciously. In fact, you will increasingly find that *principled* solutions stand in stark contrast to the common practices and thinking of our popular culture. Allow me to illustrate this contrast with a few of the most common human challenges we face.

*Fear and insecurity.* So many people today are gripped with a sense of fear. They fear for the future. They feel vulnerable in the workplace. They are afraid of losing their jobs and their ability to provide for their families. This vulnerability often fosters a resignation to riskless living and to co-dependency with others at work and at home. Our culture's common response to this problem is to become more and more independent. "I'm going to focus on 'me and mine.' I'll do my job, do it well, and get on to my real joys off the job." Independence is an important, even vital, value and achievement. The problem is, we live in an *interdependent* reality, and our most important accomplishments require interdependency skills well beyond our present abilities.

*"I want it now."* People want things and want them now. "I want money. I want a nice, big house, a nice car, the biggest and best entertainment center. I want it all and I deserve it." Though today's "credit card" society makes it easy to "get now and pay later," economic realities eventually set in, and we are reminded, sometimes painfully, that our purchases cannot outstrip our ongoing ability to produce. Pretending otherwise is unsustainable. The demands of interest are unrelenting and unforgiving. Even working hard is not enough. With the dizzying rate of change in technology and increasing competition driven by the globalization of markets and technology, we must not only be educated, we must constantly re-educate and reinvent ourselves. We must develop our minds and continually sharpen and invest in the development of our competencies to avoid becoming obsolete. At work, the bosses drive results, and for good reason. Competition is fierce; survival is at stake. The need to produce *today* is today's reality and represents the demands of capital, but the real mantra of success is sustainability and growth. You may be able to meet your quarterly numbers, but the real question is, are you making the necessary investment that will sustain and increase that success one, five, and ten years from now? Our culture and Wall Street scream for results *today*. But the principle of *balancing* the need to meet today's demands with the need to invest in the capabilities that will produce tomorrow's success is unavoidable. The same is true of your health, your marriage, your family relationships, and your community needs.

*Blame and victimism.* Wherever you find a problem, you will usually find the finger-pointing of blame. Society is addicted to playing the victim. "If only my boss wasn't such a controlling idiot . . . If only I hadn't been born so poor . . . If only I lived in a better place . . . If only I hadn't inherited such a temper from my dad . . . If only my kids weren't so rebellious . . . If only the other department didn't mess up orders all the time . . . If only we weren't in such a declining industry . . . If only our people weren't so lazy and without drive . . . If only my wife was more understanding . . . If only . . . If only." Blaming everyone and everything else for our problems and challenges may be the norm and may provide temporary relief from the pain, but it also chains us to these very problems. Show me someone who is humble enough to accept and take *responsibility* for his or her circumstances and courageous enough to take whatever *initiative* is necessary to creatively work his or her way through or around these challenges, and I'll show you the supreme power of choice.

*Hopelessness.* The children of blame are cynicism and hopelessness. When we succumb to believing that we are victims of our circumstances and yield to the plight of determinism, we lose hope, we lose drive, and we settle into resignation and stagnation. "I am a pawn, a puppet, a cog in the wheel and can do nothing about it. Just tell me what to do." So many bright, talented people feel this and suffer the broad range of discouragement and depression that follows. The survival response of popular culture is cynicism—"just lower your expectations of life to the point that you aren't disappointed by anyone or anything." The contrasting principle of growth and hope throughout history is the discovery that "I am the creative force of my life."

*Lack of life balance.* Life in our cell phone society is increasingly complex, demanding, stressful, and absolutely exhausting. For all our efforts to manage our time, do more, be more, and achieve greater efficiency through the wonders of modern technology, why is it we increasingly find ourselves in the "thick of thin things"—subordinating health, family, integrity, and many of the things that matter most to our work? The problem is not our work, which is the sustaining engine of life. It's not the complexity or change. The problem is that our modern culture says, "go in earlier, stay later, be more efficient, live with the sacrifice for now"—but the truth is that balance and peace of mind are not produced by these; they follow the person who develops a clear sense of his or her highest priorities and who lives with focus and integrity toward them.

*"What's in it for me?"* Our culture teaches us that if we want something in life, we have to "look out for number one." It says, "Life is a game, a race, a competition, and you better win it." Schoolmates, work colleagues, even family members are seen as competitors—the more they win, the less there is for you. Of course we try to appear generous and cheer for others' successes, but inwardly, privately, so many of us are eating our hearts out when others achieve. Many of the great things in the history of our civilization have been achieved by the independent will of a determined soul. But the greatest opportunities and boundless accomplishments of the Knowledge Worker Age are reserved for those who master the art of "we." True greatness will be achieved through the abundant mind that works selflessly—*with* mutual respect, *for* mutual benefit.

*The hunger to be understood.* Few needs of the human heart are greater than the need to be understood—to have a voice that is heard, respected, and valued—to have influence. Most believe that the key to influence is communication—getting your point across clearly and speaking persuasively. In fact, if you think about it, don't you find that, while others are speaking to you, instead of really listening to understand, you are often busy preparing your response? The real beginning of influence comes as others sense *you* are being influenced by *them*—when they feel understood by you—that you have listened deeply and sincerely, and that you are open. But most people are too vulnerable emotionally to listen deeply—to suspend their agenda long enough to focus on understanding before they communicate their own ideas. Our culture cries out for, even demands, understanding and influence. However, the principle of influence is governed by mutual understanding born of the commitment of at least one person to deep listening first.

*Conflict and differences.* People share so much in common, yet are so magnificently different. They think differently; they have different and sometimes competing values, motivations, and objectives. Conflicts naturally arise out of these differences. Society's competitive approach to resolving the conflict and differences tends to center on "winning as much as you can." Though much good has come from the skillful art of *compromise*, where both sides give on their positions until an acceptable middle point is reached, neither side ends up truly pleased. What a waste to have differences drive people to the lowest common denominator between them! What a waste to fail to unleash the principle of *creative cooperation* in developing solutions to problems that are better than either party's original notion!

*Personal stagnation.* Human nature is four dimensional—body, mind, heart, and spirit. Consider the differences and fruits of the two approaches:

### BODY:
*Cultural tendency:* maintain lifestyle; treat health problems with surgery and medication.
*Principle:* prevent diseases and problems by aligning lifestyle to be in harmony with established, universally accepted principles of health.

### MIND:
*Culture:* watch television, "entertain me."
*Principle:* read broadly and deeply, continuous education.

### HEART:
*Culture:* use relationships with others to forward your personal, selfish interests.
*Principle:* deep, respectful listening and serving others brings greatest fulfillment and joy.

### SPIRIT:
*Culture:* succumb to growing secularism and cynicism
*Principle:* recognize that the source of our basic need for meaning and of the positive things we seek in life is *principles*—which natural laws I personally believe have their source in God.

I invite you to keep both these universal challenges and your own unique needs and challenges in mind. As you do, you will find enduring solutions and direction. You will also find the contrast between the popular culture's approach and the timeless, principled approach of the ages will become more and more evident.

\*    \*    \*

On a final personal note, I want to repeat a question I constantly pose in my teaching: How many on their deathbeds wished they'd spent more time at the office—or watching TV? The answer is, No one. They think about their loved ones, their families, and those they have served.

Even the great psychologist Abraham Maslow, at the end of his life, put the happiness and fulfillment and contributions of his posterity ahead of his self-actualization (the top need of his famous "need hierarchy"). He called it self-transcendence.

This is so true with me. By far the greatest and most satisfying impact of the principles embodied in the 7 Habits comes out of the lives of my children and grandchildren.

For example, my nineteen-year-old granddaughter, Shannon, was "drawn" to serve the orphans of Romania and wrote Sandra and me of an epiphany one day after a little sick child threw up on her and then reached out for a hug. In that moment, Shannon inwardly resolved "I don't want to live a selfish life anymore. I must spend my life in service." As of this writing she has returned to Romania and is still serving the people.

All of our children are married and, with their spouses, have developed principle-based mission statements focused on service. To see them live these mission statements gives us joy in our posterity.

As you now commence reading *The 7 Habits of Highly Effective People*, I also promise you an exciting learning adventure. *Share* with your loved ones what you are learning. And most important, *start applying* what you are learning. Remember, to learn and not to *do* is really not to learn. To know and not to *do* is really not to know.

I have personally found living the 7 Habits a constant struggle—primarily because the better you get, the very nature of the challenge changes, just like skiing, playing golf, tennis, or any sport does. Because I sincerely work and struggle every day at living these principle-embodied habits, I warmly join you in this adventure.

—Stephen R. Covey

*Part One*

# PARADIGMS
## and PRINCIPLES

# INSIDE-OUT

*There is no real excellence in all this world
which can be separated from right living.*

DAVID STARR JORDAN

IN MORE THAN 25 YEARS of working with people in business, university, and marriage and family settings, I have come in contact with many individuals who have achieved an incredible degree of outward success, but have found themselves struggling with an inner hunger, a deep need for personal congruency and effectiveness and for healthy, growing relationships with other people.

I suspect some of the problems they have shared with me may be familiar to you.

*I've set and met my career goals and I'm having tremendous professional success. But it's cost me my personal and family life. I don't know my wife and children anymore. I'm not even sure I know myself and what's really important to me. I've had to ask myself—is it worth it?*

*I've started a new diet—for the fifth time this year. I know I'm overweight, and I really want to change. I read all the new information, I set goals, I get myself all psyched up with a positive mental attitude and tell myself I can do it. But I don't. After a few weeks, I fizzle. I just can't seem to keep a promise I make to myself.*

*I've taken course after course on effective management training. I expect a lot out of my employees and I work hard to be friendly toward them and to treat them right. But I don't feel any loyalty from them. I think if I were home sick for a day, they'd spend most of their time gabbing at the water fountain. Why can't I train them to be independent and responsible—or find employees who can be?*

*My teenage son is rebellious and on drugs. No matter what I try, he won't listen to me. What can I do?*

*There's so much to do. And there's never enough time. I feel pressured and hassled all day, every day, seven days a week. I've attended time management seminars and I've tried half a dozen different planning systems. They've helped some, but I still don't feel I'm living the happy, productive, peaceful life I want to live.*

*I want to teach my children the value of work. But to get them to do anything, I have to supervise every move . . . and put up with complaining every step of the way. It's so much easier to do it myself. Why can't children do their work cheerfully and without being reminded?*

*I'm busy—really busy. But sometimes I wonder if what I'm doing will make any difference in the long run. I'd really like to think there was meaning in my life, that somehow things were different because I was here.*

*I see my friends or relatives achieve some degree of success or receive some recognition, and I smile and congratulate them enthusiastically. But inside, I'm eating my heart out. Why do I feel this way?*

*I have a forceful personality. I know, in almost any interaction, I can control the outcome. Most of the time, I can even do it by influencing others to come up with the solution I want. I think through each situation and I really feel the ideas I come up with are usually the best for everyone. But I feel uneasy. I always wonder what other people really think of me and my ideas.*

*My marriage has gone flat. We don't fight or anything; we just don't love each other anymore. We've gone to counseling; we've tried a number of things, but we just can't seem to rekindle the feeling we used to have.*

These are deep problems, painful problems—problems that quick fix approaches can't solve.

A few years ago, my wife Sandra and I were struggling with this kind of concern. One of our sons was having a very difficult time in school. He was doing poorly academically; he didn't even know how to follow the instructions on the tests, let alone do well on them. Socially he was immature, often embarrassing those closest to him. Athletically, he was small, skinny, and uncoordinated— swinging his baseball bat, for example, almost before the ball was even pitched. Others would laugh at him.

Sandra and I were consumed with a desire to help him. We felt that if "success" were important in any area of life, it was supremely important in our role as parents. So we worked on our attitudes and behavior toward him and we tried to work on his. We attempted to psych him up using positive mental attitude techniques. "Come on, son! You can do it! We know you can. Put your hands a little higher on the bat and keep your eye on the ball. Don't swing till it gets close to you." And if he did a little better, we would go to great lengths to reinforce him. "That's good, son, keep it up."

When others laughed, we reprimanded them. "Leave him alone. Get off his back. He's just learning." And our son would cry and insist that he'd never be any good and that he didn't like baseball anyway.

Nothing we did seemed to help, and we were really worried. We could see the effect this was having on his self-esteem. We tried to be encouraging and helpful and positive, but after repeated failure, we finally drew back and tried to look at the situation on a different level.

At this time in my professional role I was involved in leadership development work with various clients throughout the country. In that capacity I was preparing bimonthly programs on the subject of communication and perception for IBM's Executive Development Program participants.

As I researched and prepared these presentations, I became particularly interested in how perceptions are formed, how they govern the way we see, and how the way we see governs how we behave. This led me to a study of expectancy theory and self-fulfilling prophecies or the "Pygmalion effect," and to a realization of how deeply imbedded our perceptions are. It taught me that we must look *at* the lens through which we see the world, as well as at the world we see, and that the lens itself shapes how we interpret the world.

As Sandra and I talked about the concepts I was teaching at IBM and about our own situation, we began to realize that what we were doing to help our son was not in harmony with the way we really *saw* him. When we honestly examined our deepest feelings, we realized that our perception was that he was basically inadequate, somehow "behind." No matter how much we worked on our attitude and behavior, our efforts were ineffective because, despite our actions and our words, what we really communicated to him was, "You aren't capable. You have to be protected."

We began to realize that if we wanted to change the situation, we first had to change ourselves. And to change ourselves effectively, we first had to change our perceptions.

## THE PERSONALITY AND CHARACTER ETHICS

At the same time, in addition to my research on perception, I was also deeply immersed in an in-depth study of the success literature published in the United States since 1776. I was reading or scanning literally hundreds of books, articles, and essays in fields such as self-improvement, popular psychology, and self-help. At my fingertips was the sum and substance of what a free and democratic people considered to be the keys to successful living.

As my study took me back through 200 years of writing about success, I noticed a startling pattern emerging in the content of the literature. Because of our own pain, and because of similar pain I had seen in the lives and relationships of many people I had worked with through the years, I began to feel more and more that much of the success literature of the past 50 years was superficial. It was filled with social image consciousness, techniques and quick fixes—with social Band-Aids and aspirin that addressed acute problems and sometimes even appeared to solve them temporarily, but left the underlying chronic problems untouched to fester and resurface time and again.

In stark contrast, almost all the literature in the first 150 years or so focused on what could be called the *Character Ethic* as the foundation of success—things like integrity, humility, fidelity, temperance, courage, justice, patience, industry, simplicity, modesty, and the Golden Rule. Benjamin Franklin's autobiography is representative of that literature. It is, basically, the story of one man's effort to integrate certain principles and habits deep within his nature.

The Character Ethic taught that there are basic principles of effective living, and that people can only experience true success and enduring happiness as they learn and integrate these principles into their basic character.

But shortly after World War I the basic view of success shifted from the Character Ethic to what we might call the *Personality*

*Ethic.* Success became more a function of personality, of public image, of attitudes and behaviors, skills and techniques, that lubricate the processes of human interaction. This Personality Ethic essentially took two paths: one was human and public relations techniques, and the other was positive mental attitude (PMA). Some of this philosophy was expressed in inspiring and sometimes valid maxims such as "Your attitude determines your altitude," "Smiling wins more friends than frowning," and "Whatever the mind of man can conceive and believe it can achieve."

Other parts of the personality approach were clearly manipulative, even deceptive, encouraging people to use techniques to get other people to like them, or to fake interest in the hobbies of others to get out of them what they wanted, or to use the "power look," or to intimidate their way through life.

Some of this literature acknowledged character as an ingredient of success, but tended to compartmentalize it rather than recognize it as foundational and catalytic. Reference to the Character Ethic became mostly lip service; the basic thrust was quick-fix influence techniques, power strategies, communication skills, and positive attitudes.

This Personality Ethic, I began to realize, was the subconscious source of the solutions Sandra and I were attempting to use with our son. As I thought more deeply about the difference between the Personality and Character Ethics, I realized that Sandra and I had been getting social mileage out of our children's good behavior, and, in our eyes, this son simply didn't measure up. Our *image* of ourselves, and our role as good, caring parents, was even deeper than our *image* of our son and perhaps influenced it. There was a lot more wrapped up in *the way we were seeing* and handling the problem than our concern for our son's welfare.

As Sandra and I talked, we became painfully aware of the powerful influence of our own character and motives and of our perception of him. We knew that social comparison motives were out of harmony with our deeper values and could lead to conditional love and eventually to our son's lessened sense of self-worth. So we determined to focus our efforts on *us*—not on our techniques, but on our deepest motives and our perception of him. Instead of trying to change him, we tried to stand apart—to separate *us* from *him*—and to sense his identity, individuality, separateness, and worth.

Through deep thought and the exercise of faith and prayer,

we began to *see* our son in terms of his own uniqueness. We *saw* within him layers and layers of potential that would be realized at his own pace and speed. We decided to relax and get out of his way and let his own personality emerge. We *saw* our natural role as being to affirm, enjoy, and value him. We also conscientiously worked on our motives and cultivated internal sources of security so that our own feelings of worth were not dependent on our children's "acceptable" behavior.

As we loosened up our old perception of our son and developed value-based motives, new feelings began to emerge. We found ourselves enjoying him instead of comparing or judging him. We stopped trying to clone him in our own image or measure him against social expectations. We stopped trying to kindly, positively manipulate him into an acceptable social mold. Because we saw him as fundamentally adequate and able to cope with life, we stopped protecting him against the ridicule of others.

He had been nurtured on this protection, so he went through some withdrawal pains, which he expressed and which we accepted, but did not necessarily respond to. "We don't need to protect you," was the unspoken message. "You're fundamentally okay."

As the weeks and months passed, he began to feel a quiet confidence and affirmed himself. He began to blossom, at his own pace and speed. He became outstanding as measured by standard social criteria—academically, socially and athletically—at a rapid clip, far beyond the so-called natural developmental process. As the years passed, he was elected to several student body leadership positions, developed into an all-state athlete and started bringing home straight A report cards. He developed an engaging and guileless personality that has enabled him to relate in non-threatening ways to all kinds of people.

Sandra and I believe that our son's "socially impressive" accomplishments were more a serendipitous expression of the feelings he had about himself than merely a response to social reward. This was an amazing experience for Sandra and me, and a very instructional one in dealing with our other children and in other roles as well. It brought to our awareness on a very personal level the vital difference between the Personality Ethic and the Character Ethic of success. The Psalmist expressed our conviction well: "Search your own heart with all diligence for out of it flow the issues of life."

## PRIMARY AND SECONDARY GREATNESS

My experience with my son, my study of perception and my reading of the success literature coalesced to create one of those "Aha!" experiences in life when suddenly things click into place. I was suddenly able to see the powerful impact of the Personality Ethic and to clearly understand those subtle, often consciously unidentified discrepancies between what I knew to be true—some things I had been taught many years ago as a child and things that were deep in my own inner sense of value—and the quick fix philosophies that surrounded me every day. I understood at a deeper level why, as I had worked through the years with people from all walks of life, I had found that the things I was teaching and knew to be effective were often at variance with these popular voices.

I am not suggesting that elements of the Personality Ethic—personality growth, communication skill training, and education in the field of influence strategies and positive thinking—are not beneficial, in fact sometimes essential for success. I believe they are. But these are secondary, not primary traits. Perhaps, in utilizing our human capacity to build on the foundation of generations before us, we have inadvertently become so focused on our own building that we have forgotten the foundation that holds it up; or in reaping for so long where we have not sown, perhaps we have forgotten the need to sow.

If I try to use human influence strategies and tactics of how to get other people to do what I want, to work better, to be more motivated, to like me and each other—while my character is fundamentally flawed, marked by duplicity and insincerity—then, in the long run, I cannot be successful. My duplicity will breed distrust, and everything I do—even using so-called good human relations techniques—will be perceived as manipulative. It simply makes no difference how good the rhetoric is or even how good the intentions are; if there is little or no trust, there is no foundation for permanent success. Only basic goodness gives life to technique.

To focus on technique is like cramming your way through school. You sometimes get by, perhaps even get good grades, but if you don't pay the price day in and day out, you never achieve true mastery of the subjects you study or develop an educated mind.

Did you ever consider how ridiculous it would be to try to cram on a farm—to forget to plant in the spring, play all summer and then cram in the fall to bring in the harvest? The farm is a natural system. The price must be paid and the process followed. You always reap what you sow; there is no shortcut.

This principle is also true, ultimately, in human behavior, in human relationships. They, too, are natural systems based on the law of the harvest. In the short run, in an artificial social system such as school, you may be able to get by if you learn how to manipulate the man-made rules, to "play the game." In most one-shot or short-lived human interactions, you can use the Personality Ethic to get by and to make favorable impressions through charm and skill and pretending to be interested in other people's hobbies. You can pick up quick, easy techniques that may work in short-term situations. But secondary traits alone have no permanent worth in long-term relationships. Eventually, if there isn't deep integrity and fundamental character strength, the challenges of life will cause true motives to surface and human relationship failure will replace short-term success.

Many people with secondary greatness—that is, social recognition for their talents—lack primary greatness or goodness in their character. Sooner or later, you'll see this in every long-term relationship they have, whether it is with a business associate, a spouse, a friend, or a teenage child going through an identity crisis. It is character that communicates most eloquently. As Emerson once put it, "What you are shouts so loudly in my ears I cannot hear what you say."

There are, of course, situations where people have character strength but they lack communication skills, and that undoubtedly affects the quality of relationships as well. But the effects are still secondary.

In the last analysis, what we *are* communicates far more eloquently than anything we *say* or *do*. We all know it. There are people we trust absolutely because we know their character. Whether they're eloquent or not, whether they have the human relations techniques or not, we trust them, and we work successfully with them.

In the words of William George Jordan, "Into the hands of every individual is given a marvelous power for good or evil—the silent, unconscious, unseen influence of his life. This is simply the constant radiation of what man really is, not what he pretends to be."

## THE POWER OF A PARADIGM

The 7 Habits of Highly Effective People embody many of the fundamental principles of human effectiveness. These habits are basic; they are primary. They represent the internalization of correct principles upon which enduring happiness and success are based.

But before we can really understand these Seven Habits, we need to understand our own "paradigms" and how to make a "paradigm shift."

Both the Character Ethic and the Personality Ethic are examples of social paradigms. The word *paradigm* comes from the Greek. It was originally a scientific term, and is more commonly used today to mean a model, theory, perception, assumption, or frame of reference. In the more general sense, it's the way we "see" the world—not in terms of our visual sense of sight, but in terms of perceiving, understanding, interpreting.

For our purposes, a simple way to understand paradigms is to see them as maps. We all know that "the map is not the territory." A map is simply an explanation of certain aspects of the territory. That's exactly what a paradigm is. It is a theory, an explanation, or model of something else.

Suppose you wanted to arrive at a specific location in central Chicago. A street map of the city would be a great help to you in reaching your destination. But suppose you were given the wrong map. Through a printing error, the map labeled "Chicago" was actually a map of Detroit. Can you imagine the frustration, the ineffectiveness of trying to reach your destination?

You might work on your *behavior*—you could try harder, be more diligent, double your speed. But your efforts would only succeed in getting you to the wrong place faster.

You might work on your *attitude*—you could think more positively. You still wouldn't get to the right place, but perhaps you wouldn't care. Your attitude would be so positive, you'd be happy wherever you were.

The point is, you'd still be lost. The fundamental problem has nothing to do with your behavior or your attitude. It has everything to do with having a wrong map.

If you have the right map of Chicago, *then* diligence becomes important, and when you encounter frustrating obstacles along the way, *then* attitude can make a real difference. But the first and most important requirement is the accuracy of the map.

Each of us has many, many maps in our head, which can be divided into two main categories: maps of *the way things are*, or *realities*, and maps of *the way things should be*, or *values*. We interpret everything we experience through these mental maps. We seldom question their accuracy; we're usually even unaware that we have them. We simply *assume* that the way we see things is the way they really are or the way they should be.

And our attitudes and behaviors grow out of those assumptions. The way we see things is the source of the way we think and the way we act.

Before going any further, I invite you to have an intellectual and emotional experience. Take a few seconds and just look at the picture on the opposite page.

Now look at the picture on page 34 and carefully describe what you see.

Do you see a woman? How old would you say she is? What does she look like? What is she wearing? In what kind of roles do you see her?

You probably would describe the woman in the second picture to be about 25 years old—very lovely, rather fashionable with a petite nose and a demure presence. If you were a single man you might like to take her out. If you were in retailing, you might hire her as a fashion model.

But what if I were to tell you that you're wrong? What if I said this picture is of a woman in her 60's or 70's who looks sad, has a huge nose, and is certainly no model. She's someone you probably would help across the street.

Who's right? Look at the picture again. Can you see the old woman? If you can't, keep trying. Can you see her big hook nose? Her shawl?

If you and I were talking face to face, we could discuss the picture. You could describe what you see to me, and I could talk to you about what I see. We could continue to communicate until you clearly showed me what you see in the picture and I clearly showed you what I see.

Because we can't do that, turn to page 53 and study the picture there and then look at this picture again. Can you see the old woman now? It's important that you see her before you continue reading.

I first encountered this exercise many years ago at the Harvard Business School. The instructor was using it to demonstrate clearly

and eloquently that two people can see the same thing, disagree, and yet both be right. It's not logical; it's psychological.

He brought into the room a stack of large cards, half of which had the image of the young woman you saw on page 33, and the other half of which had the image of the old woman on page 53.

He passed them out to the class, the picture of the young woman to one side of the room and the picture of the old woman to the other. He asked us to look at the cards, concentrate on them for about ten seconds and then pass them back in. He then projected upon the screen the picture you saw on page 34 combining both images and asked the class to describe what they saw. Almost every person in that class who had first seen the young woman's image on a card saw the young woman in the picture. And almost every person who had first seen the old woman's image on a card saw an old woman in the picture.

The professor then asked one student to explain what he saw to a student on the opposite side of the room. As they talked back and forth, communication problems flared up.

"What do you mean, 'old lady'? She couldn't be more than 20 or 22 years old!"

"Oh, come on. You have to be joking. She's 70—could be pushing 80!"

"What's the matter with you? Are you blind? This lady is young, good looking. I'd like to take her out. She's lovely."

"Lovely? She's an old hag."

The arguments went back and forth, each person sure of, and adamant in, his or her position. All of this occurred in spite of one exceedingly important advantage the students had—most of them knew early in the demonstration that another point of view did, in fact, exist—something many of us would never admit. Nevertheless, at first, only a few students really tried to see this picture from another frame of reference.

After a period of futile communication, one student went up to the screen and pointed to a line on the drawing. "There is the young woman's necklace." The other one said, "No, that is the old woman's mouth." Gradually, they began to calmly discuss specific points of difference, and finally one student, and then another, experienced sudden recognition when the images of both came into focus. Through continued calm, respectful, and specific communication, each of us in the room was finally able to see the other point of view. But when we looked away and then back, most of us would immediately see the image we had been conditioned to see in the ten-second period of time.

I frequently use this perception demonstration in working with people and organizations because it yields so many deep insights into both personal and interpersonal effectiveness. It shows, first of all, how powerfully conditioning affects our perceptions, our paradigms. If ten seconds can have that kind of impact on the way we see things, what about the conditioning of a lifetime? The influences in our lives—family, school, church, work environment, friends, associates, and current social paradigms such as the Personality Ethic—all have made their silent unconscious impact on us and help shape our frame of reference, our paradigms, our maps.

It also shows that these paradigms are the source of our attitudes and behaviors. We cannot act with integrity outside of them. We simply cannot maintain wholeness if we talk and walk differently than we see. If you were among the 90 percent who typically see the young woman in the composite picture when conditioned to do so, you undoubtedly found it difficult to think in terms of having to help her cross the street. Both your *attitude* about her and your *behavior* toward her had to be congruent with the way you *saw* her.

This brings into focus one of the basic flaws of the Personality Ethic. To try to change outward attitudes and behaviors does very little good in the long run if we fail to examine the basic paradigms from which those attitudes and behaviors flow.

This perception demonstration also shows how powerfully our paradigms affect the way we interact with other people. As clearly and objectively as we think we see things, we begin to realize that others see them differently from their own apparently equally clear and objective point of view. "Where we stand depends on where we sit."

Each of us tends to think we see things as they are, that we are *objective*. But this is not the case. We see the world, not as *it is*, but as *we are*—or, as we are conditioned to see it. When we open our mouths to describe what we see, we in effect describe ourselves, our perceptions, our paradigms. When other people disagree with us, we immediately think something is wrong with them. But, as the demonstration shows, sincere, clearheaded people see things differently, each looking through the unique lens of experience.

This does not mean that there are no facts. In the demonstration, two individuals who initially have been influenced by different conditioning pictures look at the third picture together. They are now both looking at the same identical facts—black lines and white spaces—and they would both acknowledge these as facts. But each person's interpretation of these facts represents prior experiences, and the facts have no meaning whatsoever apart from the interpretation.

The more aware we are of our basic paradigms, maps, or assumptions, and the extent to which we have been influenced by our experience, the more we can take responsibility for those paradigms, examine them, test them against reality, listen to others and be open to their perceptions, thereby getting a larger picture and a far more objective view.

## THE POWER OF A PARADIGM SHIFT

Perhaps the most important insight to be gained from the perception demonstration is in the area of paradigm shifting, what we might call the "Aha!" experience when someone finally "sees" the composite picture in another way. The more bound a person is by the initial perception, the more powerful the "Aha!" experience is. It's as though a light were suddenly turned on inside.

The term *paradigm shift* was introduced by Thomas Kuhn in his highly influential landmark book, *The Structure of Scientific Revolutions*. Kuhn shows how almost every significant breakthrough in the field of scientific endeavor is first a break with tradition, with old ways of thinking, with old paradigms.

For Ptolemy, the great Egyptian astronomer, the earth was the center of the universe. But Copernicus created a paradigm shift, and a great deal of resistance and persecution as well, by placing the sun at the center. Suddenly, everything took on a different interpretation.

The Newtonian model of physics was a clockwork paradigm and is still the basis of modern engineering. But it was partial, incomplete. The scientific world was revolutionized by the Einsteinian paradigm, the relativity paradigm, which had much higher predictive and explanatory value.

Until the germ theory was developed, a high percentage of women and children died during childbirth, and no one could understand why. In military skirmishes, more men were dying from small wounds and diseases than from the major traumas on the front lines. But as soon as the germ theory was developed, a whole new paradigm, a better, improved way of understanding what was happening, made dramatic, significant medical improvement possible.

The United States today is the fruit of a paradigm shift. The traditional concept of government for centuries had been a monarchy, the divine right of kings. Then a different paradigm was developed—government of the people, by the people, and for the people. And a constitutional democracy was born, unleashing tremendous human energy and ingenuity, and creating a standard of living, of freedom and liberty, of influence and hope unequaled in the history of the world.

Not all paradigm shifts are in positive directions. As we have observed, the shift from the Character Ethic to the Personality Ethic has drawn us away from the very roots that nourish true success and happiness.

But whether they shift us in positive or negative directions, whether they are instantaneous or developmental, paradigm shifts move us from one way of seeing the world to another. And those shifts create powerful change. Our paradigms, correct or incorrect, are the sources of our attitudes and behaviors, and ultimately our relationships with others.

I remember a mini-paradigm shift I experienced one Sunday morning on a subway in New York. People were sitting quietly— some reading newspapers, some lost in thought, some resting with their eyes closed. It was a calm, peaceful scene.

Then suddenly, a man and his children entered the subway car. The children were so loud and rambunctious that instantly the whole climate changed.

The man sat down next to me and closed his eyes, apparently oblivious to the situation. The children were yelling back and forth, throwing things, even grabbing people's papers. It was very disturbing. And yet, the man sitting next to me did nothing.

It was difficult not to feel irritated. I could not believe that he could be so insensitive as to let his children run wild like that and do nothing about it, taking no responsibility at all. It was easy to see that everyone else on the subway felt irritated, too. So finally, with what I felt was unusual patience and restraint, I turned to him and said, "Sir, your children are really disturbing a lot of people. I wonder if you couldn't control them a little more?"

The man lifted his gaze as if to come to a consciousness of the situation for the first time and said softly, "Oh, you're right. I guess I should do something about it. We just came from the hospital where their mother died about an hour ago. I don't know what to think, and I guess they don't know how to handle it either."

Can you imagine what I felt at that moment? My paradigm shifted. Suddenly I *saw* things differently, and because I *saw* differently, I *thought* differently, I *felt* differently, I *behaved* differently. My irritation vanished. I didn't have to worry about controlling my attitude or my behavior; my heart was filled with the man's pain. Feelings of sympathy and compassion flowed freely. "Your wife just died? Oh, I'm so sorry! Can you tell me about it? What can I do to help?" Everything changed in an instant.

Many people experience a similar fundamental shift in thinking when they face a life-threatening crisis and suddenly see their priorities in a different light, or when they suddenly step into a new role, such as that of husband or wife, parent or grandparent, manager or leader.

We could spend weeks, months, even years laboring with the Personality Ethic trying to change our attitudes and behaviors and not even begin to approach the phenomenon of change that occurs spontaneously when we see things differently.

It becomes obvious that if we want to make relatively minor changes in our lives, we can perhaps appropriately focus on our attitudes and behaviors. But if we want to make significant, quantum change, we need to work on our basic paradigms.

In the words of Thoreau, "For every thousand hacking at the leaves of evil, there is one striking at the root." We can only achieve quantum improvements in our lives as we quit hacking at the leaves of attitude and behavior and get to work on the root, the paradigms from which our attitudes and behaviors flow.

## SEEING AND BEING

Of course, not all paradigm shifts are instantaneous. Unlike my instant insight on the subway, the paradigm-shifting experience Sandra and I had with our son was a slow, difficult, and deliberate process. The approach we had first taken with him was the out-growth of years of conditioning and experience in the Personality Ethic. It was the result of deeper paradigms we held about our own success as parents as well as the measure of success of our children. And it was not until we changed those basic paradigms, until we saw things differently, that we were able to create quantum change in ourselves and in the situation.

In order to *see* our son differently, Sandra and I had to *be* differently. Our new paradigm was created as we invested in the growth and development of our own character.

Paradigms are inseparable from character. *Being* is *seeing* in the human dimension. And what we *see* is highly interrelated to what we *are*. We can't go very far to change our seeing without simultaneously changing our being, and vice versa.

Even in my apparently instantaneous paradigm-shifting experience that morning on the subway, my change of vision was a result of—and limited by—my basic character.

I'm sure there are people who, even suddenly understanding the true situation, would have felt no more than a twinge of regret or vague guilt as they continued to sit in embarrassed silence beside the grieving, confused man. On the other hand, I am equally certain there are people who would have been far more sensitive in the first place, who may have recognized that a deeper problem existed and reached out to understand and help before I did.

Paradigms are powerful because they create the lens through which we see the world. The power of a paradigm shift is the essential power of quantum change, whether that shift is an instantaneous or a slow and deliberate process.

## THE PRINCIPLE-CENTERED PARADIGM

The Character Ethic is based on the fundamental idea that there are *principles* that govern human effectiveness—natural laws in the human dimension that are just as real, just as unchanging and unarguably "there" as laws such as gravity are in the physical dimension.

An idea of the reality—and the impact—of these principles can be captured in another paradigm-shifting experience as told by Frank Koch in *Proceedings*, the magazine of the Naval Institute.

> Two battleships assigned to the training squadron had been at sea on maneuvers in heavy weather for several days. I was serving on the lead battleship and was on watch on the bridge as night fell.

The visibility was poor with patchy fog, so the captain remained on the bridge keeping an eye on all activities.

Shortly after dark, the lookout on the wing of the bridge reported, "Light, bearing on the starboard bow."

"Is it steady or moving astern?" the captain called out.

Lookout replied, "Steady, captain," which meant we were on a dangerous collision course with that ship.

The captain then called to the signalman, "Signal that ship: We are on a collision course, advise you change course 20 degrees."

Back came a signal, "Advisable for you to change course 20 degrees."

The captain said, "Send, I'm a captain, change course 20 degrees."

"I'm a seaman second class," came the reply. "You had better change course 20 degrees."

By that time, the captain was furious. He spat out, "Send, I'm a battleship. Change course 20 degrees."

Back came the flashing light, "I'm a lighthouse."

We changed course.

The paradigm shift experienced by the captain—and by us as we read this account—puts the situation in a totally different light. We can see a reality that is superseded by his limited perception—a reality that is as critical for us to understand in our daily lives as it was for the captain in the fog.

Principles are like lighthouses. They are natural laws that cannot be broken. As Cecil B. DeMille observed of the principles contained in his monumental movie, *The Ten Commandments*, "It is impossible for us to break the law. We can only break ourselves against the law."

While individuals may look at their own lives and interactions in terms of paradigms or maps emerging out of their experience and conditioning, these maps are not the territory. They are a "subjective reality," only an attempt to describe the territory.

The "objective reality," or the territory itself, is composed of "lighthouse" principles that govern human growth and happiness—natural laws that are woven into the fabric of every civilized society throughout history and comprise the roots of every family and institution that has endured and prospered. The degree to which our mental maps accurately describe the territory does not alter its existence.

The reality of such principles or natural laws becomes obvious to anyone who thinks deeply and examines the cycles of social history. These principles surface time and time again, and the degree to which people in a society recognize and live in harmony with them moves them toward either survival and stability or disintegration and destruction.

The principles I am referring to are not esoteric, mysterious, or "religious" ideas. There is not one principle taught in this book that is unique to any specific faith or religion, including my own. These principles are a part of most every major enduring religion, as well as enduring social philosophies and ethical systems. They are self-evident and can easily be validated by any individual. It's almost as if these principles or natural laws are part of the human condition, part of the human consciousness, part of the human conscience. They seem to exist in all human beings, regardless of social conditioning and loyalty to them, even though they might be submerged or numbed by such conditions or disloyalty.

I am referring, for example, to the principle of *fairness*, out of which our whole concept of equity and justice is developed. Little children seem to have an innate sense of the idea of fairness even apart from opposite conditioning experiences. There are vast differences in how fairness is defined and achieved, but there is almost universal awareness of the idea.

Other examples would include *integrity* and *honesty*. They create the foundation of trust which is essential to cooperation and long-term personal and interpersonal growth.

Another principle is *human dignity*. The basic concept in the United States Declaration of Independence bespeaks this value or principle. "We hold these truths to be self-evident, that all men are created equal, that they are endowed by their Creator with certain unalienable Rights, that among these are Life, Liberty, and the pursuit of Happiness."

Another principle is *service*, or the idea of making a contribution. Another is *quality* or *excellence*.

There is the principle of *potential*, the idea that we are embryonic and can grow and develop and release more and more potential, develop more and more talents. Highly related to *potential* is the principle of *growth*—the process of releasing potential and developing talents, with the accompanying need for principles such as *patience, nurturance,* and *encouragement*.

Principles are not *practices*. A practice is a specific activity or action. A practice that works in one circumstance will not necessarily work in another, as parents who have tried to raise a second child exactly like they did the first can readily attest.

While practices are situationally specific, principles are deep, fundamental truths that have universal application. They apply to individuals, to marriages, to families, to private and public organizations of every kind. When these truths are internalized into habits, they empower people to create a wide variety of practices to deal with different situations.

Principles are not *values*. A gang of thieves can share values, but they are in violation of the fundamental principles we're talking about. Principles are the territory. Values are maps. When we value correct principles, we have truth—a knowledge of things as they are.

Principles are guidelines for human conduct that are proven to have enduring, permanent value. They're fundamental. They're essentially unarguable because they are self-evident. One way to quickly grasp the self-evident nature of principles is to simply consider the absurdity of attempting to live an effective life based on their opposites. I doubt that anyone would seriously consider unfairness, deceit, baseness, uselessness, mediocrity, or degeneration to be a solid foundation for lasting happiness and success. Although people may argue about how these principles are defined or manifested or achieved, there seems to be an innate consciousness and awareness that they exist.

The more closely our maps or paradigms are aligned with these principles or natural laws, the more accurate and functional they will be. Correct maps will infinitely impact our personal and interpersonal effectiveness far more than any amount of effort expended on changing our attitudes and behaviors.

## Principles of Growth and Change

The glitter of the Personality Ethic, the massive appeal, is that there is some quick and easy way to achieve quality of life—personal effectiveness and rich, deep relationships with other people—without going through the natural process of work and growth that makes it possible.

It's symbol without substance. It's the "get rich quick" scheme promising "wealth without work." And it might even appear to succeed—but the schemer remains.

The Personality Ethic is illusory and deceptive. And trying to get high quality results with its techniques and quick fixes is just about as effective as trying to get to some place in Chicago using a map of Detroit.

In the words of Erich Fromm, an astute observer of the roots and fruits of the Personality Ethic:

> Today we come across an individual who behaves like an automaton, who does not know or understand himself, and the only person that he knows is the person that he is supposed to be, whose meaningless chatter has replaced communicative speech, whose synthetic smile has replaced genuine laughter, and whose sense of dull despair has taken the place of genuine pain. Two statements may be said concerning this individual. One is that he suffers from defects of spontaneity and individuality which may seem to be incurable. At the same time it may be said of him he does not differ essentially from the millions of the rest of us who walk upon this earth.

In all of life, there are sequential stages of growth and development. A child learns to turn over, to sit up, to crawl, and then to walk and run. Each step is important and each one takes time. No step can be skipped.

This is true in all phases of life, in all areas of development, whether it be learning to play the piano or communicate effectively with a working associate. It is true with individuals, with marriages, with families, and with organizations.

We know and accept this fact or principle of *process* in the area of physical things, but to understand it in emotional areas, in human relations, and even in the area of personal character is less common and more difficult. And even if we understand it, to accept it and to live in harmony with it are even less common and more difficult. Consequently, we sometimes look for a shortcut, expecting to be able to skip some of these vital steps in order to save time and effort and still reap the desired result.

But what happens when we attempt to shortcut a natural process in our growth and development? If you are only an average tennis player but decide to play at a higher level in order to make a better impression, what will result? Would positive thinking alone enable you to compete effectively against a professional?

What if you were to lead your friends to believe you could play

the piano at concert hall level while your actual present skill was
that of a beginner?

The answers are obvious. It is simply impossible to violate, ignore, or shortcut this development process. It is contrary to nature,
and attempting to seek such a shortcut only results in disappointment and frustration.

On a ten-point scale, if I am at level two in any field, and desire
to move to level five, I must first take the step toward level three.
"A thousand-mile journey begins with the first step" and can only
be taken one step at a time.

If you don't let a teacher know at what level you are—by asking a question, or revealing your ignorance—you will not learn
or grow. You cannot pretend for long, for you will eventually be
found out. Admission of ignorance is often the first step in our
education. Thoreau taught, "How can we remember our ignorance,
which our growth requires, when we are using our knowledge all
the time?"

I recall one occasion when two young women, daughters of a
friend of mine, came to me tearfully, complaining about their father's harshness and lack of understanding. They were afraid to
open up with their parents for fear of the consequences. And yet
they desperately needed their parents' love, understanding, and
guidance.

I talked with the father and found that he was intellectually
aware of what was happening. But while he admitted he had a
temper problem, he refused to take responsibility for it and to
honestly accept the fact that his emotional development level was
low. It was more than his pride could swallow to take the first step
toward change.

To relate effectively with a wife, a husband, children, friends,
or working associates, we must learn to listen. And this requires
emotional strength. Listening involves patience, openness, and the
desire to understand—highly developed qualities of character. It's
so much easier to operate from a low emotional level and to give
high-level advice.

Our level of development is fairly obvious with tennis or piano
playing, where it is impossible to pretend. But it is not so obvious
in the areas of character and emotional development. We can
"pose" and "put on" for a stranger or an associate. We can pretend.
And for a while we can get by with it—at least in public. We might
even deceive ourselves. Yet I believe that most of us know the

truth of what we really are inside; and I think many of those we live with and work with do as well.

I have seen the consequences of attempting to shortcut this natural process of growth often in the business world, where executives attempt to "buy" a new culture of improved productivity, quality, morale, and customer service with strong speeches, smile training, and external interventions, or through mergers, acquisitions, and friendly or unfriendly takeovers. But they ignore the low-trust climate produced by such manipulations. When these methods don't work, they look for other Personality Ethic techniques that will—all the time ignoring and violating the natural principles and processes on which a high-trust culture is based.

I remember violating this principle myself as a father many years ago. One day I returned home to my little girl's third-year birthday party to find her in the corner of the front room, defiantly clutching all of her presents, unwilling to let the other children play with them. The first thing I noticed was several parents in the room witnessing this selfish display. I was embarrassed, and doubly so because at the time I was teaching university classes in human relations. And I knew, or at least felt, the expectation of these parents.

The atmosphere in the room was really charged—the children were crowding around my little daughter with their hands out, asking to play with the presents they had just given, and my daughter was adamantly refusing. I said to myself, "Certainly I should teach my daughter to share. The value of sharing is one of the most basic things we believe in."

So I first tried a simple request. "Honey, would you please share with your friends the toys they've given you?"

"No," she replied flatly.

My second method was to use a little reasoning. "Honey, if you learn to share your toys with them when they are at your home, then when you go to their homes they will share their toys with you."

Again, the immediate reply was "No!"

I was becoming a little more embarrassed, for it was evident I was having no influence. The third method was bribery. Very softly I said, "Honey, if you share, I've got a special surprise for you. I'll give you a piece of gum."

"I don't want gum!" she exploded.

Now I was becoming exasperated. For my fourth attempt, I resorted to fear and threat. "Unless you share, you will be in real trouble!"

"I don't care!" she cried. "These are my things. I don't have to share!"

Finally, I resorted to force. I merely took some of the toys and gave them to the other kids. "Here, kids, play with these."

Perhaps my daughter needed the experience of possessing the things before she could give them. (In fact, unless I possess something, can I ever really give it?) She needed me as her father to have a higher level of emotional maturity to give her that experience.

But at that moment, I valued the opinion those parents had of me more than the growth and development of my child and our relationship together. I simply made an initial judgment that I was right; she should share, and she was wrong in not doing so.

Perhaps I superimposed a higher-level expectation on her simply because on my own scale I was at a lower level. I was unable or unwilling to give *patience* or *understanding*, so I expected her to give *things*. In an attempt to compensate for my deficiency, I *borrowed strength* from my position and authority and forced her to do what I wanted her to do.

But borrowing strength builds weakness. It builds weakness in the borrower because it reinforces dependence on external factors to get things done. It builds weakness in the person forced to acquiesce, stunting the development of independent reasoning, growth, and internal discipline. And finally, it builds weakness in the relationship. Fear replaces cooperation, and both people involved become more arbitrary and defensive.

And what happens when the source of borrowed strength—be it superior size or physical strength, position, authority, credentials, status symbols, appearance, or past achievements—changes or is no longer there?

Had I been more mature, I could have relied on my own intrinsic strength—my understanding of sharing and of growth and my capacity to love and nurture—and allowed my daughter to make a free choice as to whether she wanted to share or not to share. Perhaps after attempting to reason with her, I could have turned the attention of the children to an interesting game, taking all that emotional pressure off my child. I've learned that once children gain a sense of real possession, they share very naturally, freely, and spontaneously.

My experience has been that there are times to teach and times not to teach. When relationships are strained and the air charged with emotion, an attempt to teach is often perceived as a form of judgment and rejection. But to take the child alone, quietly, when the relationship is good and to discuss the teaching or the value seems to have much greater impact. It may have been that the emotional maturity to do that was beyond my level of patience and internal control at the time.

Perhaps a sense of possessing needs to come before a sense of genuine sharing. Many people who give mechanically or refuse to give and share in their marriages and families may never have experienced what it means to possess themselves, their own sense of identity and self-worth. Really helping our children grow may involve being patient enough to allow them the sense of possession as well as being wise enough to teach them the value of giving and providing the example ourselves.

## The Way We *See* the Problem *Is* the Problem

People are intrigued when they see good things happening in the lives of individuals, families, and organizations that are based on solid principles. They admire such personal strength and maturity, such family unity and teamwork, such adaptive synergistic organizational culture.

And their immediate request is very revealing of their basic paradigm. "How do you do it? Teach me the techniques." What they're really saying is, "Give me some quick fix advice or solution that will relieve the pain in my own situation."

They will find people who will meet their wants and teach these things; and for a short time, skills and techniques may appear to work. They may eliminate some of the cosmetic or acute problems through social aspirin and Band-Aids.

But the underlying chronic condition remains, and eventually new acute symptoms will appear. The more people are into quick fix and focus on the acute problems and pain, the more that very approach contributes to the underlying chronic condition.

The way we see the problem *is* the problem.

Look again at some of the concerns that introduced this chapter, and at the impact of Personality Ethic thinking.

*I've taken course after course on effective management training. I expect a lot out of my employees and I work hard to be friendly toward them and to treat them right. But I don't feel any loyalty from them. I think if I were home sick for a day, they'd spend most of their time gabbing at the water fountain. Why can't I train them to be independent and responsible—or find employees who can be?*

The Personality Ethic tells me I could take some kind of dramatic action—shake things up, make heads roll—that would make my employees shape up and appreciate what they have. Or that I could find some motivational training program that would get them committed. Or even that I could hire new people that would do a better job.

But is it possible that under that apparently disloyal behavior, these employees question whether I really act in their best interest? Do they feel like I'm treating them as mechanical objects? Is there some truth to that?

Deep inside, is that really the way I see them? Is there a chance the way I look at the people who work for me is part of the problem?

*There's so much to do. And there's never enough time. I feel pressured and hassled all day, every day, seven days a week. I've attended time management seminars and I've tried half a dozen different planning systems. They've helped some, but I still don't feel I'm living the happy, productive, peaceful life I want to live.*

The Personality Ethic tells me there must be something out there—some new planner or seminar that will help me handle all these pressures in a more efficient way.

But is there a chance that *efficiency* is not the answer? Is getting more things done in less time going to make a difference—or will it just increase the pace at which I react to the people and circumstances that seem to control my life?

Could there be something I need to see in a deeper, more fundamental way—some paradigm within myself that affects the way I see my time, my life, and my own nature?

*My marriage has gone flat. We don't fight or anything; we just don't love each other anymore. We've gone to counseling; we've tried a number of things, but we just can't seem to rekindle the feeling we used to have.*

The Personality Ethic tells me there must be some new book or some seminar where people get all their feelings out that would help my wife understand me better. Or maybe that it's useless, and only a new relationship will provide the love I need.

But is it possible that my spouse isn't the real problem? Could I be empowering my spouse's weaknesses and making my life a function of the way I'm treated?

Do I have some basic paradigm about my spouse, about marriage, about what love really is, that is feeding the problem?

Can you see how fundamentally the paradigms of the Personality Ethic affect the very way we see our problems as well as the way we attempt to solve them?

Whether people see it or not, many are becoming disillusioned with the empty promises of the Personality Ethic. As I travel around the country and work with organizations, I find that long-term thinking executives are simply turned off by psych up psychology and "motivational" speakers who have nothing more to share than entertaining stories mingled with platitudes.

They want substance; they want process. They want more than aspirin and Band-Aids. They want to solve the chronic underlying problems and focus on the principles that bring long-term results.

## A NEW LEVEL OF THINKING

Albert Einstein observed, "The significant problems we face cannot be solved at the same level of thinking we were at when we created them."

As we look around us and within us and recognize the problems created as we live and interact within the Personality Ethic, we begin to realize that these are deep, fundamental problems that cannot be solved on the superficial level on which they were created.

We need a new level, a deeper level of thinking—a paradigm based on the principles that accurately describe the territory of effective human being and interacting—to solve these deep concerns.

This new level of thinking is what *The 7 Habits of Highly Effective People* is about. It's a principle-centered, character-based, "inside-out" approach to personal and interpersonal effectiveness.

"Inside-out" means to start first with self; even more fundamentally, to start with the most *inside* part of self—with your paradigms, your character, and your motives.

It says if you want to *have* a happy marriage, *be* the kind of person who generates positive energy and sidesteps negative energy rather than empowering it. If you want to *have* a more pleasant, cooperative teenager, *be* a more understanding, empathic, consistent, loving parent. If you want to *have* more freedom, more latitude in your job, *be* a more responsible, a more helpful, a more contributing employee. If you want to be trusted, *be* trustworthy. If you want the secondary greatness of recognized talent, focus first on primary greatness of character.

The inside-out approach says that private victories precede public victories, that making and keeping promises to ourselves precedes making and keeping promises to others. It says it is futile to put personality ahead of character, to try to improve relationships with others before improving ourselves.

Inside-out is a process—a continuing process of renewal based on the natural laws that govern human growth and progress. It's an upward spiral of growth that leads to progressively higher forms of responsible independence and effective interdependence.

I have had the opportunity to work with many people—wonderful people, talented people, people who deeply want to achieve happiness and success, people who are searching, people who are hurting. I've worked with business executives, college students, church and civic groups, families and marriage partners. And in all of my experience, I have never seen lasting solutions to problems, lasting happiness and success, that came from the outside in.

What I have seen result from the outside-in paradigm is unhappy people who feel victimized and immobilized, who focus on the weaknesses of other people and the circumstances they feel are responsible for their own stagnant situation. I've seen unhappy marriages where each spouse wants the other to change, where each is confessing the other's "sins," where each is trying to shape up the other. I've seen labor-management disputes where people spend tremendous amounts of time and energy trying to create legislation that would force people to act as though the foundation of trust were really there.

Members of our family have lived in three of the "hottest" spots on earth—South Africa, Israel, and Ireland—and I believe the source of the continuing problems in each of these places has been the dominant social paradigm of outside-in. Each involved group is convinced the problem is "out there" and if "they" (meaning others) would "shape up" or suddenly "ship out" of existence, the problem would be solved.

Inside-out is a dramatic paradigm shift for most people, largely because of the powerful impact of conditioning and the current social paradigm of the Personality Ethic.

But from my own experience—both personal and in working with thousands of other people—and from careful examination of successful individuals and societies throughout history, I am persuaded that many of the principles embodied in the Seven Habits are already deep within us, in our conscience and our common sense. To recognize and develop them and to use them in meeting our deepest concerns, we need to think differently, to shift our paradigms to a new, deeper, "inside-out" level.

As we sincerely seek to understand and integrate these principles into our lives, I am convinced we will discover and rediscover the truth of T. S. Eliot's observation:

> *We must not cease from exploration and the end of all our exploring will be to arrive where we began and to know the place for the first time.*

# THE 7 HABITS—
## AN OVERVIEW

*We are what we repeatedly do.*
*Excellence, then, is not an act, but a habit.*

ARISTOTLE

OUR CHARACTER, BASICALLY, is a composite of our habits. "Sow a thought, reap an action; sow an action, reap a habit; sow a habit, reap a character; sow a character, reap a destiny," the maxim goes.

Habits are powerful factors in our lives. Because they are consistent, often unconscious patterns, they constantly, daily, express our character and produce our effectiveness . . . or ineffectiveness.

As Horace Mann, the great educator, once said, "Habits are like a cable. We weave a strand of it every day and soon it cannot be broken." I personally do not agree with the last part of his expression. I know they can be broken. Habits can be learned and unlearned. But I also know it isn't a quick fix. It involves a process and a tremendous commitment.

Those of us who watched the lunar voyage of Apollo 11 were transfixed as we saw the first men walk on the moon and return to earth. Superlatives such as "fantastic" and "incredible" were inadequate to describe those eventful days. But to get there, those astronauts literally had to break out of the tremendous gravity pull of the earth. More energy was spent in the first few minutes of lift-off, in the first few miles of travel, than was used over the next several days to travel half a million miles.

Habits, too, have tremendous gravity pull—more than most people realize or would admit. Breaking deeply imbedded habitual tendencies such as procrastination, impatience, criticalness, or selfishness that violate basic principles of human effectiveness involves more than a little willpower and a few minor changes in our lives. "Lift off" takes a tremendous effort, but once we break out of the gravity pull, our freedom takes on a whole new dimension.

Like any natural force, gravity pull can work with us or against us. The gravity pull of some of our habits may currently be keeping us from going where we want to go. But it is also gravity pull that keeps our world together, that keeps the planets in their orbits and our universe in order. It is a powerful force, and if we use it effectively, we can use the gravity pull of habit to create the cohesiveness and order necessary to establish effectiveness in our lives.

## "Habits" Defined

For our purposes, we will define a habit as the intersection of *knowledge*, *skill*, and *desire*.

Knowledge is the theoretical paradigm, the *what to do* and the *why*. Skill is the *how to do*. And desire is the motivation, the *want to do*. In order to make something a habit in our lives, we have to have all three.

I may be ineffective in my interactions with my work associates, my spouse, or my children because I constantly tell them what I think, but I never really listen to them. Unless I search out correct principles of human interaction, I may not even *know* I need to listen.

Even if I do know that in order to interact effectively with others I really need to listen to them, I may not have the skill. I may not know *how* to really listen deeply to another human being.

But knowing I need to listen and knowing how to listen is not enough. Unless I *want* to listen, unless I have the desire, it won't be a habit in my life. Creating a habit requires work in all three dimensions.

The being/seeing change is an upward process—being changing seeing, which in turn changes being, and so forth, as we move in an upward spiral of growth. By working on knowledge, skill, and desire, we can break through to new levels of personal and interpersonal effectiveness as we break with old paradigms that may have been a source of pseudo-security for years.

It's sometimes a painful process. It's a change that has to be motivated by a higher purpose, by the willingness to subordinate what you think you want now for what you want later. But this process produces happiness, "the object and design of our existence." Happiness can be defined, in part at least, as the fruit of the desire and ability to sacrifice what we want *now* for what we want *eventually*.

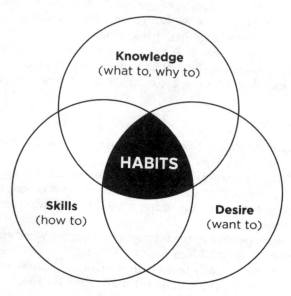

**EFFECTIVE HABITS**
*Internalized principles and patterns of behavior*

## THE MATURITY CONTINUUM

The Seven Habits are not a set of separate or piecemeal psych-up formulas. In harmony with the natural laws of growth, they provide an incremental, sequential, highly integrated approach to the development of personal and interpersonal effectiveness. They move us progressively on a Maturity Continuum from *dependence* to *independence* to *interdependence*.

We each begin life as an infant, totally *dependent* on others. We are directed, nurtured, and sustained by others. Without this nurturing, we would only live for a few hours or a few days at the most.

Then gradually, over the ensuing months and years, we become more and more *independent*—physically, mentally, emotionally, and financially—until eventually we can essentially take care of ourselves, becoming inner-directed and self-reliant.

As we continue to grow and mature, we become increasingly aware that all of nature is *interdependent*, that there is an ecological system that governs nature, including society. We further discover that the higher reaches of our nature have to do with our relationships with others—that human life also is interdependent.

Our growth from infancy to adulthood is in accordance with natural law. And there are many dimensions to growth. Reaching our full physical maturity, for example, does not necessarily assure us of simultaneous emotional or mental maturity. On the other hand, a person's physical dependence does not mean that he or she is mentally or emotionally immature.

On the maturity continuum, *dependence* is the paradigm of *you*—*you* take care of me; *you* come through for me; *you* didn't come through; I blame *you* for the results.

*Independence* is the paradigm of *I*—*I* can do it; *I* am responsible; *I* am self-reliant; *I* can choose.

*Interdependence* is the paradigm of *we*—*we* can do it; *we* can cooperate; *we* can combine our talents and abilities and create something greater together.

Dependent people need others to get what they want. Independent people can get what they want through their own effort. Interdependent people combine their own efforts with the efforts of others to achieve their greatest success.

If I were physically dependent—paralyzed or disabled or limited in some physical way—I would need you to help me. If I were emotionally dependent, my sense of worth and security would come from your opinion of me. If you didn't like me, it could be devastating. If I were intellectually dependent, I would count on you to do my thinking for me, to think through the issues and problems of my life.

If I were independent, physically, I could pretty well make it on my own. Mentally, I could think my own thoughts, I could move from one level of abstraction to another. I could think creatively and analytically and organize and express my thoughts in understandable ways. Emotionally, I would be validated from within. I would be inner directed. My sense of worth would not be a function of being liked or treated well.

It's easy to see that independence is much more mature than

dependence. Independence is a major achievement in and of itself. But independence is not supreme.

Nevertheless, the current social paradigm enthrones independence. It is the avowed goal of many individuals and social movements. Most of the self-improvement material puts independence on a pedestal, as though communication, teamwork, and cooperation were lesser values.

But much of our current emphasis on independence is a reaction to dependence—to having others control us, define us, use us, and manipulate us.

The little-understood concept of interdependence appears to many to smack of dependence, and therefore, we find people, often for selfish reasons, leaving their marriages, abandoning their children, and forsaking all kinds of social responsibility—all in the name of independence.

The kind of reaction that results in people "throwing off their shackles," becoming "liberated," "asserting themselves," and "doing their own thing" often reveals more fundamental dependencies that cannot be run away from because they are internal rather than external—dependencies such as letting the weaknesses of other people ruin our emotional lives or feeling victimized by people and events out of our control.

Of course, we may need to change our circumstances. But the dependence problem is a personal maturity issue that has little to do with circumstances. Even with better circumstances, immaturity and dependence often persist.

True independence of character empowers us to act rather than be acted upon. It frees us from our dependence on circumstances and other people and is a worthy, liberating goal. But it is not the ultimate goal in effective living.

. Independent thinking alone is not suited to interdependent reality. Independent people who do not have the maturity to think and act interdependently may be good individual producers, but they won't be good leaders or team players. They're not coming from the paradigm of interdependence necessary to succeed in marriage, family, or organizational reality.

Life is, by nature, highly interdependent. To try to achieve maximum effectiveness through independence is like trying to play tennis with a golf club—the tool is not suited to the reality.

Interdependence is a far more mature, more advanced concept.

If I am physically interdependent, I am self-reliant and capable, but I also realize that you and I working together can accomplish far more than, even at my best, I could accomplish alone. If I am emotionally interdependent, I derive a great sense of worth within myself, but I also recognize the need for love, for giving, and for receiving love from others. If I am intellectually interdependent, I realize that I need the best thinking of other people to join with my own.

As an interdependent person, I have the opportunity to share myself deeply, meaningfully, with others, and I have access to the vast resources and potential of other human beings.

Interdependence is a choice only independent people can make. Dependent people cannot choose to become interdependent. They don't have the character to do it; they don't own enough of themselves.

That's why Habits 1, 2, and 3 in the following chapters deal with self-mastery. They move a person from dependence to independence. They are the "Private Victories," the essence of character growth. *Private victories precede public victories.* You can't invert that process any more than you can harvest a crop before you plant it. It's inside-out.

As you become truly independent, you have the foundation for effective interdependence. You have the character base from which you can effectively work on the more personality-oriented "Public Victories" of teamwork, cooperation, and communication in Habits 4, 5, and 6.

That does not mean you have to be perfect in Habits 1, 2, and 3 before working on Habits 4, 5, and 6. Understanding the sequence will help you manage your growth more effectively, but I'm not suggesting that you put yourself in isolation for several years until you fully develop Habits 1, 2, and 3.

As part of an interdependent world, you have to relate to that world every day. But the acute problems of that world can easily obscure the chronic character causes. Understanding how what you are impacts every interdependent interaction will help you to focus your efforts sequentially, in harmony with the natural laws of growth.

Habit 7 is the habit of renewal—a regular, balanced renewal of the four basic dimensions of life. It circles and embodies all the other habits. It is the habit of continuous improvement that creates

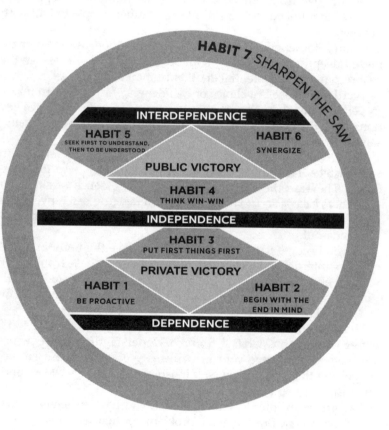

the upward spiral of growth that lifts you to new levels of under-standing and living each of the habits as you come around to them on a progressively higher plane.*

The diagram on the preceding page is a visual representation of the sequence and the interdependence of the Seven Habits, and will be used throughout this book as we explore both the sequen-tial relationship between the habits and also their synergy—how, in relating to each other, they create bold new forms of each other that add even more to their value. Each concept or habit will be highlighted as it is introduced.

## EFFECTIVENESS DEFINED

The Seven Habits are habits of *effectiveness*. Because they are based on principles, they bring the maximum long-term beneficial results possible. They become the basis of a person's character, creating an empowering center of correct maps from which an in-dividual can effectively solve problems, maximize opportunities, and continually learn and integrate other principles in an upward spiral of growth.

They are also habits of effectiveness because they are based on a paradigm of effectiveness that is in harmony with a natural law, a principle I call the "P/PC Balance," which many people break themselves against. This principle can be easily understood by re-membering Aesop's fable of the goose and the golden egg.

This fable is the story of a poor farmer who one day discovers in the nest of his pet goose a glittering golden egg. At first, he thinks it must be some kind of trick. But as he starts to throw the egg aside, he has second thoughts and takes it in to be appraised instead.

The egg is pure gold! The farmer can't believe his good fortune. He becomes even more incredulous the following day when the experience is repeated. Day after day, he awakens to rush to the nest and find another golden egg. He becomes fabulously wealthy; it all seems too good to be true.

But with his increasing wealth comes greed and impatience. Un-able to wait day after day for the golden eggs, the farmer decides he will kill the goose and get them all at once. But when he opens

---

* To see how effective you are—where your strengths lie and how you can improve—take the Personal Effectiveness Quotient (PEQ) at www.7HabitsPEQ.com.

the goose, he finds it empty. There are no golden eggs—and now there is no way to get any more. The farmer has destroyed the goose that produced them.

I suggest that within this fable is a natural law, a principle—the basic definition of effectiveness. Most people see effectiveness from the golden egg paradigm: the more you produce, the more you do, the more effective you are.

But as the story shows, true effectiveness is a function of two things: what is produced (the golden eggs) and the producing asset or capacity to produce (the goose).

If you adopt a pattern of life that focuses on golden eggs and neglects the goose, you will soon be without the asset that produces golden eggs. On the other hand, if you only take care of the goose with no aim toward the golden eggs, you soon won't have the wherewithal to feed yourself or the goose.

Effectiveness lies in the balance—what I call the P/PC Balance. P stands for *production* of desired results, the golden eggs. PC stands for *production capability*, the ability or asset that produces the golden eggs.

## THREE KINDS OF ASSETS

Basically, there are three kinds of assets: physical, financial, and human. Let's look at each one in turn.

A few years ago, I purchased a *physical asset*—a power lawnmower. I used it over and over again without doing anything to maintain it. The mower worked well for two seasons, but then it began to break down. When I tried to revive it with service' and sharpening, I discovered the engine had lost over half its original power capacity. It was essentially worthless.

Had I invested in PC—in preserving and maintaining the asset—I would still be enjoying its P—the mowed lawn. As it was, I had to spend far more time and money replacing the mower than I ever would have spent, had I maintained it. It simply wasn't effective.

In our quest for short-term returns, or results, we often ruin a prized physical asset—a car, a computer, a washer or dryer, even our body or our environment. Keeping P and PC in balance makes a tremendous difference in the effective use of physical assets.

It also powerfully impacts the effective use of *financial* assets. How often do people confuse principal with interest? Have you ever invaded principal to increase your standard of living, to get more golden eggs? The decreasing principal has decreasing power to produce interest or income. And the dwindling capital becomes smaller and smaller until it no longer supplies even basic needs.

Our most important financial asset is our own capacity to earn. If we don't continually invest in improving our own PC, we severely limit our options. We're locked into our present situation, running scared of our corporation or our boss's opinion of us, economically dependent and defensive. Again, it simply isn't effective.

In the *human* area, the P/PC Balance is equally fundamental, but even more important, because people control physical and financial assets.

When two people in a marriage are more concerned about getting the golden eggs, the benefits, than they are in preserving the relationship that makes them possible, they often become insensitive and inconsiderate, neglecting the little kindnesses and courtesies so important to a deep relationship. They begin to use control levers to manipulate each other, to focus on their own needs, to justify their own position and look for evidence to show the wrongness of the other person. The love, the richness, the softness and spontaneity begin to deteriorate. The goose gets sicker day by day.

And what about a parent's relationship with a child? When children are little, they are very dependent, very vulnerable. It becomes so easy to neglect the PC work—the training, the communicating, the relating, the listening. It's easy to take advantage, to manipulate, to get what you want the way you want it—right now! You're bigger, you're smarter, and you're *right!* So why not just tell them what to do? If necessary, yell at them, intimidate them, insist on your way.

Or you can indulge them. You can go for the golden egg of popularity, of pleasing them, giving them their way all the time. Then they grow up without any internal sense of standards or expectations, without a personal commitment to being disciplined or responsible.

Either way—authoritarian or permissive—you have the golden egg mentality. You want to have your way or you want to be liked. But what happens, meantime, to the goose? What sense of responsibility, of self-discipline, of confidence in the ability to make good choices or achieve important goals is a child going to have a few years down the road? And what about your relationship? When he reaches those critical teenage years, the identity crises, will he know from his experience with you that you will listen without judging, that you really, deeply care about him as a person, that you can be trusted, no matter what? Will the relationship be strong enough for you to reach him, to communicate with him, to influence him?

Suppose you want your daughter to have a clean room—that's P, production, the golden egg. And suppose you want her to clean it—that's PC, production capability. Your daughter is the goose, the asset, that produces the golden egg.

If you have P and PC in balance, she cleans the room cheerfully, without being reminded, because she is committed and has the discipline to stay with the commitment. She is a valuable asset, a goose that can produce golden eggs.

But if your paradigm is focused on production, on getting the room clean, you might find yourself nagging her to do it. You might even escalate your efforts to threatening or yelling, and in your desire to get the golden egg, you undermine the health and welfare of the goose.

Let me share with you an interesting PC experience I had with one of my daughters. We were planning a private date, which is something I enjoy regularly with each of my children. We find that the anticipation of the date is as satisfying as the realization.

So I approached my daughter and said, "Honey, tonight's your night. What do you want to do?"

"Oh, Dad, that's okay," she replied.

"No, really," I said. "What would you like to do?"

"Well," she finally said, "what I want to do, you don't really want to do."

"Really, honey," I said earnestly, "I want to do it. No matter what, it's your choice."

"I want to go see *Star Wars*," she replied. "But I know you don't like *Star Wars*. You slept through it before. You don't like these fantasy movies. That's okay, Dad."

"No, honey, if that's what you'd like to do, I'd like to do it."

"Dad, don't worry about it. We don't always have to have this date." She paused and then added, "But you know why you don't like *Star Wars*? It's because you don't understand the philosophy and training of a Jedi Knight."

"What?"

"You know the things you teach, Dad? Those are the same things that go into the training of a Jedi Knight."

"Really? Let's go to *Star Wars!*"

And we did. She sat next to me and gave me the paradigm. I became her student, her learner. It was totally fascinating. I could begin to see out of a new paradigm the whole way a Jedi Knight's basic philosophy in training is manifested in different circumstances.

That experience was not a planned P experience; it was the serendipitous fruit of a PC investment. It was bonding and very satisfying. But we enjoyed golden eggs, too, as the goose—the quality of the relationship—was significantly fed.

## ORGANIZATIONAL PC

One of the immensely valuable aspects of any correct principle is that it is valid and applicable in a wide variety of circumstances. Throughout this book, I would like to share with you some of the ways in which these principles apply to organizations, including families, as well as to individuals.

When people fail to respect the P/PC Balance in their use of physical assets in organizations, they decrease organizational effectiveness and often leave others with dying geese.

For example, a person in charge of a physical asset, such as a machine, may be eager to make a good impression on his superiors. Perhaps the company is in a rapid growth stage and promotions are coming fast. So he produces at optimum levels—no downtime, no maintenance. He runs the machine day and night. The production is phenomenal, costs are down, and profits skyrocket. Within a short time, he's promoted. Golden eggs!

But suppose you are his successor on the job. You inherit a very sick goose, a machine that, by this time, is rusted and starts to break down. You have to invest heavily in downtime and maintenance. Costs skyrocket; profits nose-dive. And who gets blamed for the loss of golden eggs? You do. Your predecessor liquidated the asset, but the accounting system only reported unit production, costs, and profit.

The P/PC Balance is particularly important as it applies to the human assets of an organization—the customers and the employees.

I know of a restaurant that served a fantastic clam chowder and was packed with customers every day at lunchtime. Then the business was sold, and the new owner focused on golden eggs—he decided to water down the chowder. For about a month, with costs down and revenues constant, profits zoomed. But little by little, the customers began to disappear. Trust was gone, and business dwindled to almost nothing. The new owner tried desperately to reclaim it, but he had neglected the customers, violated their trust, and lost the asset of customer loyalty. There was no more goose to produce the golden egg.

There are organizations that talk a lot about the customer and then completely neglect the people that deal with the customer—the employees. The PC principle is to *always treat your employees exactly as you want them to treat your best customers.*

You can buy a person's hand, but you can't buy his heart. His heart is where his enthusiasm, his loyalty is. You can buy his back, but you can't buy his brain. That's where his creativity is, his ingenuity, his resourcefulness.

PC work is treating employees as volunteers just as you treat customers as volunteers, because that's what they are. They volunteer the best part—their hearts and minds.

I was in a group once where someone asked, "How do you shape up lazy and incompetent employees?" One man responded, "Drop hand grenades!" Several others cheered that kind of macho management talk, that "shape up or ship out" supervision approach.

But another person in the group asked, "Who picks up the pieces?"

"No pieces."

"Well, why don't you do that to your customers?" the other man replied. "Just say, 'Listen, if you're not interested in buying, you can just ship out of this place.' "

He said, "You can't do that to customers."

"Well, how come you can do it to employees?"

"Because they're in your employ."

"I see. Are your employees devoted to you? Do they work hard? How's the turnover?"

"Are you kidding? You can't find good people these days. There's too much turnover, absenteeism, moonlighting. People just don't care anymore."

*    *    *

That focus on golden eggs—that attitude, that paradigm—is totally inadequate to tap into the powerful energies of the mind and heart of another person. A short-term bottom line is important, but it isn't all-important.

Effectiveness lies in the balance. Excessive focus on P results in ruined health, worn-out machines, depleted bank accounts, and broken relationships. Too much focus on PC is like a person who runs three or four hours a day, bragging about the extra ten years of life it creates, unaware he's spending them running. Or a person endlessly going to school, never producing, living on other people's golden eggs—the eternal student syndrome.

To maintain the P/PC Balance, the balance between the golden egg (production) and the health and welfare of the goose (production capability) is often a difficult judgment call. But I suggest it is the very essence of effectiveness. It balances short term with long term. It balances going for the grade and paying the price to get an education. It balances the desire to have a room clean and the building of a relationship in which the child is internally committed to do it—cheerfully, willingly, without external supervision.

It's a principle you can see validated in your own life when you burn the candle at both ends to get more golden eggs and wind up sick or exhausted, unable to produce any at all; or when you get a good night's sleep and wake up ready to produce throughout the day.

You can see it when you press to get your own way with someone and somehow feel an emptiness in the relationship; or when you really take time to invest in a relationship and you find the desire and ability to work together, to communicate, takes a quantum leap.

The P/PC Balance is the very essence of effectiveness. It's validated in every arena of life. We can work with it or against it, but it's there. It's a lighthouse. It's the definition and paradigm of effectiveness upon which the Seven Habits in this book are based.

## How to Use This Book

Before we begin work on the Seven Habits of Highly Effective People, I would like to suggest two paradigm shifts that will greatly increase the value you will receive from this material.

First, I would recommend that you not "see" this material as a book, in the sense that it is something to read once and put on a shelf.

You may choose to read it completely through once for a sense of the whole. But the material is designed to be a companion in the continual process of change and growth. It is organized incrementally and with suggestions for application at the end of each habit so that you can study and focus on any particular habit as you are ready.

As you progress to deeper levels of understanding and implementation, you can go back time and again to the principles contained in each habit and work to expand your knowledge, skill, and desire.

Second, I would suggest that you shift your paradigm of your own involvement in this material from the role of learner to that of teacher. Take an inside-out approach, and read with the purpose in mind of sharing or discussing what you learn with someone else within 48 hours after you learn it.

If you had known, for example, that you would be teaching the material on the P/PC Balance principle to someone else within 48 hours, would it have made a difference in your reading experience? Try it now as you read the final section in this chapter. Read as though you are going to teach it to your spouse, your child, a business associate, or a friend today or tomorrow, while it is still fresh, and notice the difference in your mental and emotional process.

I guarantee that if you approach the material in each of the following chapters in this way, you will not only better remember what you read, but your perspective will be expanded, your understanding deepened, and your motivation to apply the material increased.

In addition, as you openly, honestly share what you're learning with others, you may be surprised to find that negative labels or perceptions others may have of you tend to disappear. Those you teach will see you as a changing, growing person, and will be more inclined to be helpful and supportive as you work, perhaps together, to integrate the Seven Habits into your lives.

## What You Can Expect

In the last analysis, as Marilyn Ferguson observed, "No one can persuade another to change. Each of us guards a gate of change that can only be opened from the inside. We cannot open the gate of another, either by argument or by emotional appeal."

If you decide to open your "gate of change" to really understand and live the principles embodied in the Seven Habits, I feel comfortable in assuring you several positive things will happen.

First, your growth will be *evolutionary*, but the net effect will be *revolutionary*. Would you not agree that the P/PC Balance principle alone, if fully lived, would transform most individuals and organizations?

The net effect of opening the "gate of change" to the first three habits—the habits of Private Victory—will be significantly increased self-confidence. You will come to know yourself in a deeper, more meaningful way—your nature, your deepest values and your unique contribution capacity. As you live your values, your sense of identity, integrity, control, and inner-directedness will infuse you with both exhilaration and peace. You will define yourself from within, rather than by people's opinions or by comparisons to others. "Wrong" and "right" will have little to do with being found out.

Ironically, you'll find that as you care less about what others think of you, you will care more about what others think of themselves and their worlds, including their relationship with you. You'll no longer build your emotional life on other people's weaknesses. In addition, you'll find it easier and more desirable to change because there is something—some core deep within—that is essentially changeless.

As you open yourself to the next three habits—the habits of Public Victory—you will discover and unleash both the desire and the resources to heal and rebuild important relationships that have deteriorated, or even broken. Good relationships will improve—become deeper, more solid, more creative, and more adventuresome.

The seventh habit, if deeply internalized, will renew the first six and will make you truly independent and capable of effective interdependence. Through it, you can charge your own batteries.

Whatever your present situation, I assure you that you are not your habits. You can replace old patterns of self-defeating behavior with new patterns, new habits of effectiveness, happiness, and trust-based relationships.

With genuine caring, I encourage you to open the gate of change and growth as you study these habits. Be patient with yourself. Self-growth is tender; it's holy ground. There's no greater investment.

It's obviously not a quick fix. But I assure you, you will feel benefits and see immediate payoffs that will be encouraging. In the words of Thomas Paine, "That which we obtain too easily, we esteem too lightly. It is dearness only which gives everything its value. Heaven knows how to put a proper price on its goods."

*Part Two*

# PRIVATE VICTORY

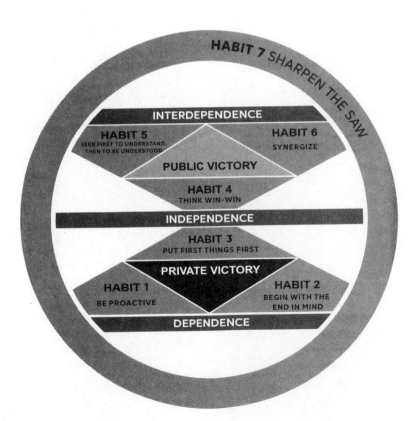

# HABIT 1:
## BE PROACTIVE

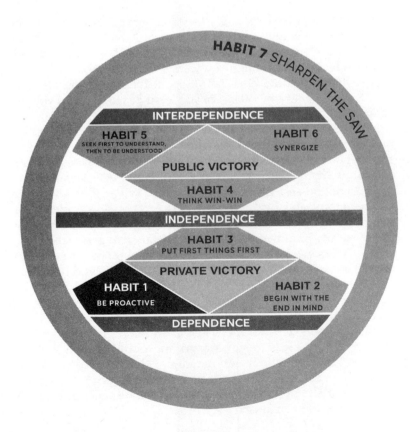

# Principles of Personal Vision

*I know of no more encouraging fact*
*than the unquestionable ability of man*
*to elevate his life by conscious endeavor.*

HENRY DAVID THOREAU

A s YOU READ THIS BOOK, try to stand apart from yourself. Try to project your consciousness upward into a corner of the room and see yourself, in your mind's eye, reading. Can you look at yourself almost as though you were someone else?

Now try something else. Think about the mood you are now in. Can you identify it? What are you feeling? How would you describe your present mental state?

Now think for a minute about how your mind is working. Is it quick and alert? Do you sense that you are torn between doing this mental exercise and evaluating the point to be made out of it?

Your ability to do what you just did is uniquely human. Animals do not possess this ability. We call it "self-awareness" or the ability to think about your very thought process. This is the reason why man has dominion over all things in the world and why he can make significant advances from generation to generation.

This is why we can evaluate and learn from others' experiences as well as our own. This is also why we can make and break our habits.

We are not our feelings. We are not our moods. We are not even our thoughts. The very fact that we can think about these things separates us from them and from the animal world. Self-awareness enables us to stand apart and examine even the way we "see" ourselves—our self-paradigm, the most fundamental paradigm of effectiveness. It affects not only our attitudes and behaviors, but also how we see other people. It becomes our map of the basic nature of mankind.

In fact, until we take how we see ourselves (and how we see others) into account, we will be unable to understand how others see and feel about themselves and their world. Unaware, we will project our intentions on their behavior and call ourselves objective.

This significantly limits our personal potential and our ability to relate to others as well. But because of the unique human capacity of self-awareness, we can examine our paradigms to determine whether they are reality- or principle-based or if they are a function of conditioning and conditions.

## THE SOCIAL MIRROR

If the only vision we have of ourselves comes from the social mirror—from the current social paradigm and from the opinions, perceptions, and paradigms of the people around us—our view of ourselves is like the reflection in the crazy mirror room at the carnival.

"You're never on time."

"Why can't you ever keep things in order?"

"You must be an artist!"

"You eat like a horse!"

"I can't believe you won!"

"This is so simple. Why can't you understand?"

These visions are disjointed and out of proportion. They are often more projections than reflections, projecting the concerns and character weaknesses of people giving the input rather than accurately reflecting what we are.

The reflection of the current social paradigm tells us we are largely determined by conditioning and conditions. While we have acknowledged the tremendous power of conditioning in our lives, to say that we are *determined* by it, that we have no control over that influence, creates quite a different map.

There are actually three social maps—three theories of determinism widely accepted, independently or in combination, to explain the nature of man. *Genetic determinism* basically says your grandparents did it to you. That's why you have such a temper. Your grandparents had short tempers and it's in your DNA. It just goes through the generations and you inherited it. In addition, you're Irish, and that's the nature of Irish people.

*Psychic determinism* basically says your parents did it to you. Your upbringing, your childhood experience essentially laid out your personal tendencies and your character structure. That's why you're afraid to be in front of a group. It's the way your parents brought you up. You feel terribly guilty if you make a mistake because you "remember" deep inside the emotional scripting when you were very vulnerable and tender and dependent. You "remember" the emotional punishment, the rejection, the comparison with somebody else when you didn't perform as well as expected.

*Environmental determinism* basically says your boss is doing it to you—or your spouse, or that bratty teenager, or your economic situation, or national policies. Someone or something in your environment is responsible for your situation.

Each of these maps is based on the stimulus/response theory we most often think of in connection with Pavlov's experiments with dogs. The basic idea is that we are conditioned to respond in a particular way to a particular stimulus.

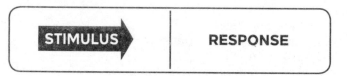

How accurately and functionally do these deterministic maps describe the territory? How clearly do these mirrors reflect the true nature of man? Do they become self-fulfilling prophecies? Are they based on principles we can validate within ourselves?

## Between Stimulus and Response

In answer to those questions, let me share with you the catalytic story of Victor Frankl.

Frankl was a determinist raised in the tradition of Freudian psychology, which postulates that whatever happens to you as a child shapes your character and personality and basically governs your whole life. The limits and parameters of your life are set, and, basically, you can't do much about it.

Frankl was also a psychiatrist and a Jew. He was imprisoned in the death camps of Nazi Germany, where he experienced things that were so repugnant to our sense of decency that we shudder to even repeat them.

His parents, his brother, and his wife died in the camps or were sent to the gas ovens. Except for his sister, his entire family perished. Frankl himself suffered torture and innumerable indignities, never knowing from one moment to the next if his path would lead to the ovens or if he would be among the "saved" who would remove the bodies or shovel out the ashes of those so fated.

One day, naked and alone in a small room, he began to become aware of what he later called "the last of the human freedoms"—the freedom his Nazi captors could not take away. They could control his entire environment, they could do what they wanted to his body, but Victor Frankl himself was a self-aware being who could look as an observer at his very involvement. His basic identity was intact. *He could decide within himself how all of this was going to affect him.* Between what happened to him, or the stimulus, and his response to it, was his freedom or power to choose that response.

In the midst of his experiences, Frankl would project himself into different circumstances, such as lecturing to his students after his release from the death camps. He would describe himself in the classroom, in his mind's eye, and give his students the lessons he was learning during his very torture.

Through a series of such disciplines—mental, emotional, and moral, principally using memory and imagination—he exercised his small, embryonic freedom until it grew larger and larger, until he had more freedom than his Nazi captors. They had more *liberty*, more options to choose from in their environment; but he had more *freedom*, more internal power to exercise his options. He became an inspiration to those around him, even to some of the guards. He helped others find meaning in their suffering and dignity in their prison existence.

In the midst of the most degrading circumstances imaginable, Frankl used the human endowment of self-awareness to discover a fundamental principle about the nature of man: *Between stimulus and response, man has the freedom to choose.*

Within the freedom to choose are those endowments that make us uniquely human. In addition to *self-awareness*, we have *imagination*—the ability to create in our minds beyond our present reality. We have *conscience*—a deep inner awareness of right and wrong, of the principles that govern our behavior, and a sense of the degree to which our thoughts and actions are in harmony with them. And we have *independent will*—the ability to act based on our self-awareness, free of all other influences.

Even the most intelligent animals have none of these endowments. To use a computer metaphor, they are programmed by instinct and/or training. They can be trained to be responsible, but they can't take responsibility for that training; in other words, they can't direct it. They can't change the programming. They're not even aware of it.

But because of our unique human endowments, we can write new programs for ourselves totally apart from our instincts and training. This is why an animal's capacity is relatively limited and man's is unlimited. But if we live like animals, out of our own instincts and conditioning and conditions, out of our collective memory, we too will be limited.

The deterministic paradigm comes primarily from the study of animals—rats, monkeys, pigeons, dogs—and neurotic and psychotic people. While this may meet certain criteria of some researchers because it seems measurable and predictable, the history of mankind and our own self-awareness tell us that this map doesn't describe the territory at all!

Our unique human endowments lift us above the animal world. The extent to which we exercise and develop these endowments empowers us to fulfill our uniquely human potential. Between stimulus and response is our greatest power—the freedom to choose.

## "Proactivity" Defined

In discovering the basic principle of the nature of man, Frankl described an accurate self-map from which he began to develop the first and most basic habit of a highly effective person in any environment, the habit of *proactivity*.

While the word *proactivity* is now fairly common in management literature, it is a word you won't find in most dictionaries. It means more than merely taking initiative. It means that as human beings, we are responsible for our own lives. Our behavior is a function of our decisions, not our conditions. We can subordinate feelings to values. We have the initiative and the responsibility to make things happen.

Look at the word *responsibility*—"response-ability"—the ability to choose your response. Highly proactive people recognize that responsibility. They do not blame circumstances, conditions, or conditioning for their behavior. Their behavior is a product of their own conscious choice, based on values, rather than a product of their conditions, based on feeling.

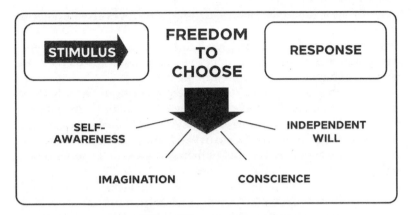

## PROACTIVE MODEL

Because we are, by nature, proactive, if our lives are a function of conditioning and conditions, it is because we have, by conscious decision or by default, chosen to empower those things to control us.

In making such a choice, we become *reactive*. Reactive people are often affected by their physical environment. If the weather is good, they feel good. If it isn't, it affects their attitude and their performance. Proactive people can carry their own weather with them. Whether it rains or shines makes no difference to them. They are value driven; and if their value is to produce good quality work, it isn't a function of whether the weather is conducive to it or not.

Reactive people are also affected by their social environment, by the "social weather." When people treat them well, they feel well; when people don't, they become defensive or protective. Reactive people build their emotional lives around the behavior of others, empowering the weaknesses of other people to control them.

The ability to subordinate an impulse to a value is the essence of the proactive person. Reactive people are driven by feelings, by circumstances, by conditions, by their environment. Proactive people are driven by values—carefully thought about, selected and internalized values.

Proactive people are still influenced by external stimuli, whether physical, social, or psychological. But their response to the stimuli, conscious or unconscious, is a value-based choice or response.

As Eleanor Roosevelt observed, "No one can hurt you without your consent." In the words of Gandhi, "They cannot take away our self respect if we do not give it to them." It is our willing permission, our consent to what happens to us, that hurts us far more than what happens to us in the first place.

I admit this is very hard to accept emotionally, especially if we have had years and years of explaining our misery in the name of circumstance or someone else's behavior. But until a person can say deeply and honestly, "I am what I am today because of the choices I made yesterday," that person cannot say, "I choose otherwise."

Once in Sacramento when I was speaking on the subject of proactivity, a woman in the audience stood up in the middle of my presentation and started talking excitedly. It was a large audience, and as a number of people turned to look at her, she suddenly became aware of what she was doing, grew embarrassed and sat back down. But she seemed to find it difficult to restrain herself and started talking to the people around her. She seemed so happy.

I could hardly wait for a break to find out what had happened. When it finally came, I immediately went to her and asked if she would be willing to share her experience.

"You just can't imagine what's happened to me!" she exclaimed. "I'm a full-time nurse to the most miserable, ungrateful man you can possibly imagine. Nothing I do is good enough for him. He never expresses appreciation; he hardly even acknowledges me. He constantly harps at me and finds fault with everything I do. This man has made my life miserable and I often take my frustration out on my family. The other nurses feel the same way. We almost pray for his demise.

"And for you to have the gall to stand up there and suggest that nothing can hurt me, that no one can hurt me without my consent, and that I have chosen my own emotional life of being miserable—well, there was just no way I could buy into that.

"But I kept thinking about it. I really went inside myself and began to ask, 'Do I have the power to choose my response?'

"When I finally realized that I do have that power, when I swallowed that bitter pill and realized that I had chosen to be miserable, I also realized that I could choose not to be miserable.

"At that moment I stood up. I felt as though I was being let out of San Quentin. I wanted to yell to the whole world, 'I am free! I am let out of prison! No longer am I going to be controlled by the treatment of some person.' "

It's not what happens to us, but our response to what happens to us that hurts us. Of course, things can hurt us physically or economically and can cause sorrow. But our character, our basic identity, does not have to be hurt at all. In fact, our most difficult experiences become the crucibles that forge our character and develop the internal powers, the freedom to handle difficult circumstances in the future and to inspire others to do so as well.

Frankl is one of many who have been able to develop the personal freedom in difficult circumstances to lift and inspire others. The autobiographical accounts of Vietnam prisoners of war provide additional persuasive testimony of the transforming power of such personal freedom and the effect of the responsible use of that freedom on the prison culture and on the prisoners, both then and now.

We have all known individuals in very difficult circumstances, perhaps with a terminal illness or a severe physical handicap, who maintain magnificent emotional strength. How inspired we are by their integrity! Nothing has a greater, longer lasting impression upon another person than the awareness that someone has transcended suffering, has transcended circumstance, and is embodying and expressing a value that inspires and ennobles and lifts life.

One of the most inspiring times Sandra and I have ever had took place over a four-year period with a dear friend of ours named Carol, who had a wasting cancer disease. She had been one of Sandra's bridesmaids, and they had been best friends for over 25 years.

When Carol was in the very last stages of the disease, Sandra spent time at her bedside helping her write her personal history. She returned from those protracted and difficult sessions almost transfixed by admiration for her friend's courage and her desire to write special messages to be given to her children at different stages in their lives.

Carol would take as little pain-killing medication as possible, so that she had full access to her mental and emotional faculties. Then she would whisper into a tape recorder or to Sandra directly as she took notes. Carol was so proactive, so brave, and so concerned about others that she became an enormous source of inspiration to many people around her.

I'll never forget the experience of looking deeply into Carol's eyes the day before she passed away and sensing out of that deep hollowed agony a person of tremendous intrinsic worth. I could see in her eyes a life of character, contribution, and service as well as love and concern and appreciation.

Many times over the years, I have asked groups of people how many have ever experienced being in the presence of a dying individual who had a magnificent attitude and communicated love and compassion and served in unmatchable ways to the very end. Usually, about one-fourth of the audience respond in the affirmative. I then ask how many of them will never forget these individuals—how many were transformed, at least temporarily, by the inspiration of such courage, and were deeply moved and motivated to more noble acts of service and compassion. The same people respond again, almost inevitably.

Victor Frankl suggests that there are three central values in life—the experiential, or that which happens to us; the creative, or that which we bring into existence; and the attitudinal, or our response in difficult circumstances such as terminal illness.

My own experience with people confirms the point Frankl makes—that the highest of the three values is attitudinal, in the paradigm or reframing sense. In other words, what matters most is how we *respond* to what we experience in life.

Difficult circumstances often create paradigm shifts, whole new frames of reference by which people see the world and themselves and others in it, and what life is asking of them. Their larger perspective reflects the attitudinal values that lift and inspire us all.

## TAKING THE INITIATIVE

Our basic nature is to act, and not be acted upon. As well as enabling us to choose our response to particular circumstances, this empowers us to create circumstances.

Taking initiative does not mean being pushy, obnoxious, or aggressive. It does mean recognizing our responsibility to make things happen.

Over the years, I have frequently counseled people who wanted better jobs to show more initiative—to take interest and aptitude tests, to study the industry, even the specific problems the organizations they are interested in are facing, and then to develop an effective presentation showing how their abilities can help solve the organization's problem. It's called "solution selling," and is a key paradigm in business success.

The response is usually agreement—most people can see how powerfully such an approach would affect their opportunities for employment or advancement. But many of them fail to take the necessary steps, the initiative, to make it happen.

"I don't know where to go to take the interest and aptitude tests."

"How do I study industry and organizational problems? No one wants to help me."

"I don't have any idea how to make an effective presentation."

Many people wait for something to happen or someone to take care of them. But people who end up with the good jobs are the proactive ones who are solutions to problems, not problems themselves, who seize the initiative to do whatever is necessary, consistent with correct principles, to get the job done.

Whenever someone in our family, even one of the younger children, takes an irresponsible position and waits for someone else to make things happen or provide a solution, we tell them, "Use your R and I!" (resourcefulness and initiative). In fact, often before we can say it, they answer their own complaints, "I know— use my R and I!"

Holding people to the responsible course is not demeaning; it is affirming. Proactivity is part of human nature, and, although the proactive muscles may be dormant, they are there. By respecting the proactive nature of other people, we provide them with at least one clear, undistorted reflection from the social mirror.

Of course, the maturity level of the individual has to be taken into account. We can't expect high creative cooperation from those who are deep into emotional dependence. But we can, at least, affirm their basic nature and create an atmosphere where people can seize opportunities and solve problems in an increasingly self-reliant way.

## ACT OR BE ACTED UPON

The difference between people who exercise initiative and those who don't is literally the difference between night and day. I'm not talking about a 25 to 50 percent difference in effectiveness; I'm talking about a 5000-plus percent difference, particularly if they are smart, aware, and sensitive to others.

It takes initiative to create the P/PC Balance of effectiveness in your life. It takes initiative to develop the Seven Habits. As you study the other six habits, you will see that each depends on the development of your proactive muscles. Each puts the responsibility on you to act. If you wait to be acted upon, you *will* be acted upon. And growth and opportunity consequences attend either road.

At one time I worked with a group of people in the home improvement industry, representatives from twenty different organizations who met quarterly to share their numbers and problems in an uninhibited way.

This was during a time of heavy recession, and the negative impact on this particular industry was even heavier than on the economy in general. These people were fairly discouraged as we began.

The first day, our discussion question was "What's happening to us? What's the stimulus?" Many things were happening. The environmental pressures were powerful. There was widespread unemployment, and many of these people were laying off friends just to maintain the viability of their enterprises. By the end of the day, everyone was even more discouraged.

The second day, we addressed the question, "What's going to happen in the future?" We studied environmental trends with the underlying reactive assumption that those things would create their future. By the end of the second day, we were even more depressed. Things were going to get worse before they got better, and everyone knew it.

So on the third day, we decided to focus on the proactive question, "What is *our* response? What are *we* going to do? How can *we* exercise initiative in this situation?" In the morning we talked about managing and reducing costs. In the afternoon we discussed increasing market share. We brainstormed both areas, then concentrated on several very practical, very doable things. A new spirit of excitement, hope, and proactive awareness concluded the meetings.

At the very end of the third day, we summarized the results of the conference in a three-part answer to the question, "How's business?"

Part one: What's happening to us is not good, and the trends suggest that it will get worse before it gets better.

Part two: But what we are causing to happen is very good, for we are better managing and reducing our costs and increasing our market share.

Part three: Therefore, business is better than ever.

Now what would a reactive mind say to that? "Oh, come on. Face facts. You can only carry this positive thinking and self-psych approach so far. Sooner or later you have to face reality."

But that's the difference between positive thinking and proactivity. We did face reality. We faced the reality of the current circumstance and of future projections. But we also faced the reality that we had the power to choose a positive response to those circumstances and projections. Not facing reality would have been to accept the idea that what's happening in our environment had to determine us.

Businesses, community groups, organizations of every kind—including families—can be proactive. They can combine the creativity and resourcefulness of proactive individuals to create a proactive culture within the organization. The organization does not have to be at the mercy of the environment; it can take the initiative to accomplish the shared values and purposes of the individuals involved.

## LISTENING TO OUR LANGUAGE

Because our attitudes and behaviors flow out of our paradigms, if we use our self-awareness to examine them, we can often see in them the nature of our underlying maps. Our language, for example, is a very real indicator of the degree to which we see ourselves as proactive people.

The language of reactive people absolves them of responsibility.

"That's me. That's just the way I am." *I am determined. There's nothing I can do about it.*

"He makes me so mad!" *I'm not responsible. My emotional life is governed by something outside my control.*

"I can't do that. I just don't have the time." *Something outside me—limited time—is controlling me.*

"If only my wife were more patient." *Someone else's behavior is limiting my effectiveness.*

"I have to do it." *Circumstances or other people are forcing me to do what I do. I'm not free to choose my own actions.*

| REACTIVE LANGUAGE | PROACTIVE LANGUAGE |
| --- | --- |
| There's nothing I can do. | Let's look at our alternatives. |
| That's just the way I am. | I can choose a different approach. |
| He makes me so mad. | I control my own feelings. |
| They won't allow that. | I can create an effective presentation. |
| I have to do that. | I will choose an appropriate response. |
| I can't. | I choose. |
| I must. | I prefer. |
| If only. | I will. |

That language comes from a basic paradigm of determinism. And the whole spirit of it is the transfer of responsibility. *I am not responsible, not able to choose my response.*

One time a student asked me, "Will you excuse me from class? I have to go on a tennis trip."

"You *have* to go, or you *choose* to go?" I asked.

"I really *have* to," he exclaimed.

"What will happen if you don't?"

"Why, they'll kick me off the team."

"How would you like that consequence?"

"I wouldn't."

"In other words, you *choose* to go because you want the consequence of staying on the team. What will happen if you miss my class?"

"I don't know."

"Think hard. What do you think would be the natural consequence of not coming to class?"

"You wouldn't kick me out, would you?"

"That would be a social consequence. That would be artificial. If you don't participate on the tennis team, you don't play. That's natural. But if you don't come to class, what would be the natural consequence?"

"I guess I'll miss the learning."

"That's right. So you have to weigh that consequence against the other consequence and make a choice. I know if it were me, I'd choose to go on the tennis trip. But never say you *have* to do anything."

"I *choose* to go on the tennis trip," he meekly replied.
"And miss my class?" I replied in mock disbelief.

A serious problem with reactive language is that it becomes a self-fulfilling prophecy. People become reinforced in the paradigm that they are determined, and they produce evidence to support the belief. They feel increasingly victimized and out of control, not in charge of their life or their destiny. They blame outside forces—other people, circumstances, even the stars—for their own situation.

At one seminar where I was speaking on the concept of proactivity, a man came up and said, "Stephen, I like what you're saying. But every situation is so different. Look at my marriage. I'm really worried. My wife and I just don't have the same feelings for each other we used to have. I guess I just don't love her anymore and she doesn't love me. What can I do?"

"The feeling isn't there anymore?" I asked.

"That's right," he reaffirmed. "And we have three children we're really concerned about. What do you suggest?"

"Love her," I replied.

"I told you, the feeling just isn't there anymore."

"Love her."

"You don't understand. The feeling of love just isn't there."

"Then love her. If the feeling isn't there, that's a good reason to love her."

"But how do you love when you don't love?"

"My friend, love is a verb. Love—the feeling—is a fruit of love, the verb. So love her. Serve her. Sacrifice. Listen to her. Empathize. Appreciate. Affirm her. Are you willing to do that?"

In the great literature of all progressive societies, love is a verb. Reactive people make it a feeling. They're driven by feelings. Hollywood has generally scripted us to believe that we are not responsible, that we are a product of our feelings. But the Hollywood script does not describe the reality. If our feelings control our actions, it is because we have abdicated our responsibility and empowered them to do so.

Proactive people make love a verb. Love is something you do: the sacrifices you make, the giving of self, like a mother bringing a newborn into the world. If you want to study love, study those who sacrifice for others, even for people who offend or do not love in return. If you are a parent, look at the love you have for the children you sacrificed for. Love is a value that is actualized through loving actions. Proactive people subordinate feelings to values. Love, the feeling, can be recaptured.

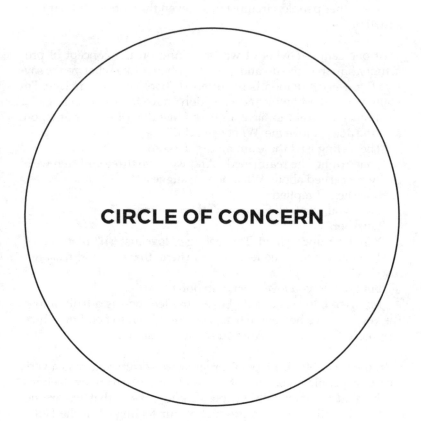

**NO CONCERN**

**CIRCLE OF CONCERN**

### CIRCLE OF CONCERN/CIRCLE OF INFLUENCE

Another excellent way to become more self-aware regarding our own degree of proactivity is to look at where we focus our time and energy. We each have a wide range of concerns—our health, our children, problems at work, the national debt, nuclear war. We could separate those from things in which we have no particular mental or emotional involvement by creating a "Circle of Concern."

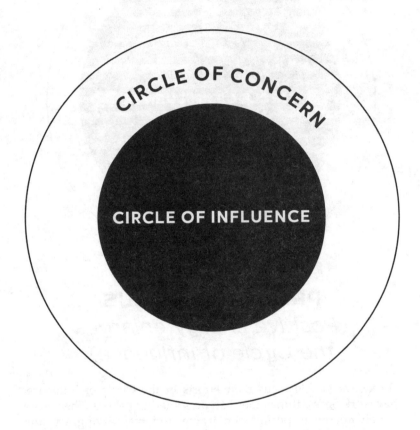

As we look at those things within our Circle of Concern, it becomes apparent that there are some things over which we have no real control and others that we can do something about. We could identify those concerns in the latter group by circumscribing them within a smaller Circle of Influence.

By determining which of these two circles is the focus of most of our time and energy, we can discover much about the degree of our proactivity.

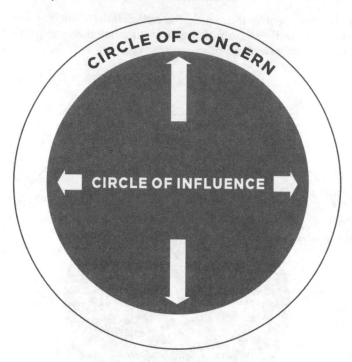

## PROACTIVE FOCUS
### (Positive energy enlarges the Circle of Influence)

Proactive people focus their efforts in the Circle of Influence. They work on the things they can do something about. The nature of their energy is positive, enlarging and magnifying, causing their Circle of Influence to increase.

Reactive people, on the other hand, focus their efforts in the Circle of Concern. They focus on the weakness of other people, the problems in the environment, and circumstances over which they have no control. Their focus results in blaming and accusing attitudes, reactive language, and increased feelings of victimization. The negative energy generated by that focus, combined with neglect in areas they could do something about, causes their Circle of Influence to shrink.

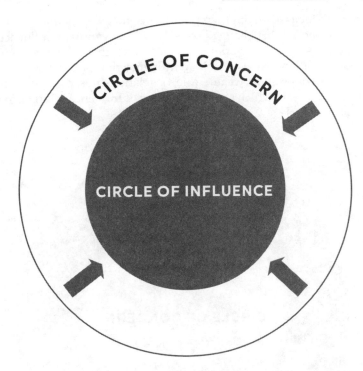

# REACTIVE FOCUS
## *(Negative energy reduces the Circle of Influence)*

As long as we are working in our Circle of Concern, we empower the things within it to control us. We aren't taking the proactive initiative necessary to effect positive change.

Earlier, I shared with you the story of my son who was having serious problems in school. Sandra and I were deeply concerned about his apparent weaknesses and about the way other people were treating him.

But those things were in our Circle of Concern. As long as we focused our efforts on those things, we accomplished nothing, except to increase our own feelings of inadequacy and helplessness and to reinforce our son's dependence.

It was only when we went to work in our Circle of Influence, when we focused on our own paradigms, that we began to create a positive energy that changed ourselves and eventually influenced our son as well. By working on ourselves instead of worrying about conditions, we were able to influence the conditions.

Because of position, wealth, role, or relationships, there are some circumstances in which a person's Circle of Influence is larger than his or her Circle of Concern.

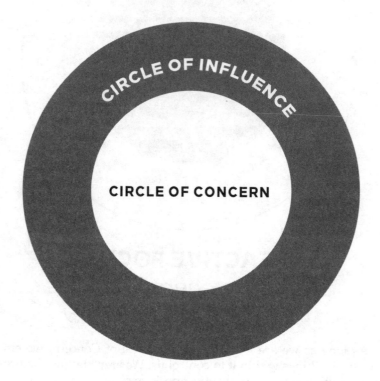

This situation reflects a self-inflicted emotional myopia—another reactive selfish life-style focused in the Circle of Concern.

Though they may have to prioritize the use of their influence, proactive people have a Circle of Concern that is at least as big as their Circle of Influence, accepting the responsibility to use their influence effectively.

## DIRECT, INDIRECT, AND NO CONTROL

The problems we face fall in one of three areas: direct control (problems involving our own behavior); indirect control (problems involving other people's behavior); or no control (problems we can do nothing about, such as our past or situational realities). The proactive approach puts the first step in the solution of all three kinds of problems within our present Circle of Influence.

*Direct control* problems are solved by working on our habits. They are obviously within our Circle of Influence. These are the "Private Victories" of Habits 1, 2, and 3.

*Indirect control* problems are solved by changing our methods of influence. These are the "Public Victories" of Habits 4, 5, and 6. I have personally identified over 30 separate methods of human influence—as separate as empathy is from confrontation, as separate as example is from persuasion. Most people have only three or four of these methods in their repertoire, starting usually with reasoning, and, if that doesn't work, moving to flight or fight. How liberating it is to accept the idea that I can learn new methods of human influence instead of constantly trying to use old ineffective methods to "shape up" someone else!

*No control* problems involve taking the responsibility to change the line on the bottom on our face—to smile, to genuinely and peacefully accept these problems and learn to live with them, even though we don't like them. In this way, we do not empower these problems to control us. We share in the spirit embodied in the Alcoholics Anonymous prayer, "Lord, give me the courage to change the things which can and ought to be changed, the serenity to accept the things which cannot be changed, and the wisdom to know the difference."

Whether a problem is direct, indirect, or no control, we have in our hands the first step to the solution. Changing our habits, changing our methods of influence and changing the way we see our no control problems are all within our Circle of Influence.

## EXPANDING THE CIRCLE OF INFLUENCE

It is inspiring to realize that in choosing our response to circumstance, we powerfully affect our circumstance. When we change one part of the chemical formula, we change the nature of the results.

\*    \*    \*

I worked with one organization for several years that was headed by a very dynamic person. He could read trends. He was creative, talented, capable, and brilliant—and everyone knew it. But he had a very dictatorial style of management. He tended to treat people like "gofers," as if they didn't have any judgment. His manner of speaking to those who worked in the organization was, "Go for this . . . go for that . . . now do this . . . now do that—I'll make the decisions."

The net effect was that he alienated almost the entire executive team surrounding him. They would gather in the corridors and complain to each other about him. Their discussion was all very sophisticated, very articulate, as if they were trying to help the situation. But they did it endlessly, absolving themselves of responsibility in the name of the president's weaknesses.

"You can't imagine what's happened this time," someone would say. "The other day he went into my department. I had everything all laid out. But he came in and gave totally different signals. Everything I'd done for months was shot, just like that. I don't know how I'm supposed to keep working for him. How long will it be until he retires?"

"He's only fifty-nine," someone else would respond. "Do you think you can survive for six more years?"

"I don't know. He's the kind of person they probably won't retire anyway."

But one of the executives was proactive. He was driven by values, not feelings. He took the initiative—he anticipated, he empathized, he read the situation. He was not blind to the president's weaknesses; but instead of criticizing them, he would compensate for them. Where the president was weak in his style, he'd try to buffer his own people and make such weaknesses irrelevant. And he'd work with the president's strengths—his vision, talent, creativity.

This man focused on his Circle of Influence. He was treated like a gofer, also. But he would do more than what was expected. He anticipated the president's need. He read with empathy the president's underlying concern, so when he presented information, he also gave his analysis and his recommendations based on that analysis.

As I sat one day with the president in an advisory capacity, he said, "Stephen, I just can't believe what this man has done. He's not only given me the information I requested, but he's provided additional information that's exactly what we needed. He even gave me his analysis of it in terms of my deepest concerns, and a list of his recommendations.

"The recommendations are consistent with the analysis, and the analysis is consistent with the data. He's remarkable! What a relief not to have to worry about this part of the business."

At the next meeting, it was "go for this" and "go for that" to all the executives . . . but one. To this man, it was "What's your opinion?" His Circle of Influence had grown.

This caused quite a stir in the organization. The reactive minds in the executive corridors began shooting their vindictive ammunition at this proactive man.

It's the nature of reactive people to absolve themselves of responsibility. It's so much safer to say, "I am not responsible." If I say "I am responsible," I might have to say, "I am irresponsible." It would be very hard for me to say that I have the power to choose my response and that the response I have chosen has resulted in my involvement in a negative, collusive environment, especially if for years I have absolved myself of responsibility for results in the name of someone else's weaknesses.

So these executives focused on finding more information, more ammunition, more evidence as to why they weren't responsible.

But this man was proactive toward them, too. Little by little, his Circle of Influence toward them grew also. It continued to expand to the extent that eventually no one made any significant moves in the organization without that man's involvement and approval, including the president. But the president did not feel threatened because this man's strength complemented his strength and compensated for his weaknesses. So he had the strength of two people, a complementary team.

This man's success was not dependent on his circumstances. Many others were in the same situation. It was his chosen response to those circumstances, his focus on his Circle of Influence, that made the difference.

There are some people who interpret "proactive" to mean pushy, aggressive, or insensitive; but that isn't the case at all. Proactive people aren't pushy. They're smart, they're value driven, they read reality, and they know what's needed.

Look at Gandhi. While his accusers were in the legislative

chambers criticizing him because he wouldn't join in their Circle of Concern rhetoric condemning the British Empire for their subjugation of the Indian people, Gandhi was out in the rice paddies, quietly, slowly, imperceptibly expanding his Circle of Influence with the field laborers. A ground swell of support, of trust, of confidence followed him through the countryside. Though he held no office or political position, through compassion, courage, fasting, and moral persuasion he eventually brought England to its knees, breaking political domination of three hundred million people with the power of his greatly expanded Circle of Influence.

## THE "HAVE'S" AND THE "BE'S"

One way to determine which circle our concern is in is to distinguish between the *have's* and the *be's*. The Circle of Concern is filled with the *have's*:

"I'll be happy *when I have* my house paid off."

"*If only I had* a boss who wasn't such a dictator . . ."

"*If only I had* a more patient husband . . ."

"*If I had* more obedient kids . . ."

"*If I had* my degree . . ."

"*If I could just have* more time to myself . . ."

The Circle of Influence is filled with the *be's*—I can *be* more patient, *be* wise, *be* loving. It's the character focus.

*Anytime we think the problem is "out there," that thought is the problem.* We empower what's out there to control us. The change paradigm is "outside-in"—what's out there has to change before we can change.

The proactive approach is to cha..ige from the inside-out: to *be* different, and by being different, to effect positive change in what's out there—I can *be* more resourceful, I can *be* more diligent, I can *be* more creative, I can *be* more cooperative.

One of my favorite stories is one in the Old Testament, part of the fundamental fabric of the Judeo-Christian tradition. It's the story of Joseph, who was sold into slavery in Egypt by his brothers at the age of seventeen. Can you imagine how easy it would have been for him to languish in self-pity as a servant of Potiphar, to focus on the weaknesses of his brothers and his captors and on all he didn't have? But Joseph was proactive. He worked on *be*. And within a short period of time, he was running Potiphar's household. He was in charge of all that Potiphar had because the trust was so high.

Then the day came when Joseph was caught in a difficult situation and refused to compromise his integrity. As a result, he was unjustly imprisoned for thirteen years. But again he was proactive. He worked on the inner circle, on *being* instead of *having*, and soon he was running the prison and eventually the entire nation of Egypt, second only to the Pharaoh.

I know this idea is a dramatic paradigm shift for many people. It is so much easier to blame other people, conditioning, or conditions for our own stagnant situation. But we are responsible—"response-able"—to control our lives and to powerfully influence our circumstances by working on *be*, on what we are.

If I have a problem in my marriage, what do I really gain by continually confessing my wife's sins? By saying I'm not responsible, I make myself a powerless victim; I immobilize myself in a negative situation. I also diminish my ability to influence her—my nagging, accusing, critical attitude only makes her feel validated in her own weakness. My criticism is worse than the conduct I want to correct. My ability to positively impact the situation withers and dies.

If I really want to improve my situation, I can work on the one thing over which I have control—myself. I can stop trying to shape up my wife and work on my own weaknesses. I can focus on being a great marriage partner, a source of unconditional love and support. Hopefully, my wife will feel the power of proactive example and respond in kind. But whether she does or doesn't, the most positive way I can influence my situation is to work on myself, on my *being*.

There are so many ways to work in the Circle of Influence—to *be* a better listener, to *be* a more loving marriage partner, to *be* a better student, to *be* a more cooperative and dedicated employee. Sometimes the most proactive thing we can do is to *be* happy, just to genuinely smile. Happiness, like unhappiness, is a proactive choice. There are things, like the weather, that our Circle of Influence will never include. But as proactive people, we can carry our own physical or social weather with us. We can be happy and accept those things that at present we can't control, while we focus our efforts on the things that we can.

## THE OTHER END OF THE STICK

Before we totally shift our life focus to our Circle of Influence, we need to consider two things in our Circle of Concern that merit deeper thought—*consequences* and *mistakes*.

While we are free to choose our actions, we are not free to choose the consequences of those actions. Consequences are governed by natural law. They are out in the Circle of Concern. We can decide to step in front of a fast-moving train, but we cannot decide what will happen when the train hits us.

We can decide to be dishonest in our business dealings. While the social consequences of that decision may vary depending on whether or not we are found out, the natural consequences to our basic character are a fixed result.

Our behavior is governed by principles. Living in harmony with them brings positive consequences; violating them brings negative consequences. We are free to choose our response in any situation, but in doing so, we choose the attendant consequence. "When we pick up one end of the stick, we pick up the other."

Undoubtedly, there have been times in each of our lives when we have picked up what we later felt was the wrong stick. Our choices have brought consequences we would rather have lived without. If we had the choice to make over again, we would make it differently. We call these choices mistakes, and they are the second thing that merits our deeper thought.

For those filled with regret, perhaps the most needful exercise of proactivity is to realize that past mistakes are also out there in the Circle of Concern. We can't recall them, we can't undo them, we can't control the consequences that came as a result.

As a college quarterback, one of my sons learned to snap his wristband between plays as a kind of mental checkoff whenever he or anyone made a "setting back" mistake, so the last mistake wouldn't affect the resolve and execution of the next play.

The proactive approach to a mistake is to acknowledge it instantly, correct and learn from it. This literally turns a failure into a success. "Success," said IBM founder T. J. Watson, "is on the far side of failure."

But not to acknowledge a mistake, not to correct it and learn from it, is a mistake of a different order. It usually puts a person on a self-deceiving, self-justifying path, often involving rationalization (rational lies) to self and to others. This second mistake, this

cover-up, empowers the first, giving it disproportionate importance, and causes far deeper injury to self.

It is not what others do or even our own mistakes that hurt us
the most; it is our response to those things. Chasing after the poi-
sonous snake that bites us will only drive the poison through our
entire system. It is far better to take measures immediately to get
the poison out.

Our response to any mistake affects the quality of the next moment. It is important to immediately admit and correct our mistakes so that they have no power over that next moment and we
are empowered again.

## MAKING AND KEEPING COMMITMENTS

At the very heart of our Circle of Influence is our ability to make
and keep commitments and promises. The commitments we make
to ourselves and to others, and our integrity to those commitments, is the essence and clearest manifestation of our proactivity.

It is also the essence of our growth. Through our human endowments of *self-awareness* and *conscience*, we become conscious
of areas of weakness, areas for improvement, areas of talent that
could be developed, areas that need to be changed or eliminated
from our lives. Then, as we recognize and use our *imagination*
and *independent will* to act on that awareness—making promises,
setting goals, and being true to them—we build the strength of
character, the being, that makes possible every other positive thing
in our lives.

It is here that we find two ways to put ourselves in control of our
lives immediately. We can *make a promise*—and keep it. Or we can
*set a goal*—and work to achieve it. As we make and keep commitments, even small commitments, we begin to establish an inner integrity that gives us the awareness of self-control and the courage
and strength to accept more of the responsibility for our own lives.
By making and keeping promises to ourselves and others, little by
little, our honor becomes greater than our moods.

The power to make and keep commitments to ourselves is the
essence of developing the basic habits of effectiveness. Knowledge,
skill, and desire are all within our control. We can work on any
one to improve the balance of the three. As the area of intersection
becomes larger, we more deeply internalize the principles upon
which the habits are based and create the strength of character to

move us in a balanced way toward increasing effectiveness in our lives.

## PROACTIVITY: THE THIRTY-DAY TEST

We don't have to go through the death camp experience of Frankl to recognize and develop our own proactivity. It is in the ordinary events of every day that we develop the proactive capacity to handle the extraordinary pressures of life. It's how we make and keep commitments, how we handle a traffic jam, how we respond to an irate customer or a disobedient child. It's how we view our problems and where we focus our energies. It's the language we use.

I would challenge you to test the principle of proactivity for thirty days. Simply try it and see what happens. For thirty days work only in your Circle of Influence. Make small commitments and keep them. Be a light, not a judge. Be a model, not a critic. Be part of the solution, not part of the problem.

Try it in your marriage, in your family, in your job. Don't argue for other people's weaknesses. Don't argue for your own. When you make a mistake, admit it, correct it, and learn from it—immediately. Don't get into a blaming, accusing mode. Work on things you have control over. Work on you. On *be.*

Look at the weaknesses of others with compassion, not accusation. It's not what they're not doing or should be doing that's the issue. The issue is your own chosen response to the situation and what you should be doing. If you start to think the problem is "out there," stop yourself. That thought is the problem.

People who exercise their embryonic freedom day after day will, little by little, expand that freedom. People who do not will find that it withers until they are literally "being lived." They are acting out the scripts written by parents, associates, and society.

We are responsible for our own effectiveness, for our own happiness, and ultimately, I would say, for most of our circumstances.

Samuel Johnson observed: "The fountain of content must spring up in the mind, and he who hath so little knowledge of human nature as to seek happiness by changing anything but his own disposition, will waste his life in fruitless efforts and multiply the grief he proposes to remove."

Knowing that we are responsible—"response-able"—is fundamental to effectiveness and to every other habit of effectiveness we will discuss.

## APPLICATION SUGGESTIONS

1. For a full day, listen to your language and to the language of the people around you. How often do you use and hear reactive phrases such as "If only," "I can't," or "I have to"?
2. Identify an experience you might encounter in the near future where, based on past experience, you would probably behave reactively. Review the situation in the context of your Circle of Influence. How could you respond proactively? Take several moments and create the experience vividly in your mind, picturing yourself responding in a proactive manner. Remind yourself of the gap between stimulus and response. Make a commitment to yourself to exercise your freedom to choose.
3. Select a problem from your work or personal life that is frustrating to you. Determine whether it is a direct, indirect, or no control problem. Identify the first step you can take in your Circle of Influence to solve it and then take that step.
4. Try the thirty-day test of proactivity. Be aware of the change in your Circle of Influence.

# Habit 2:
## Begin with the End in Mind

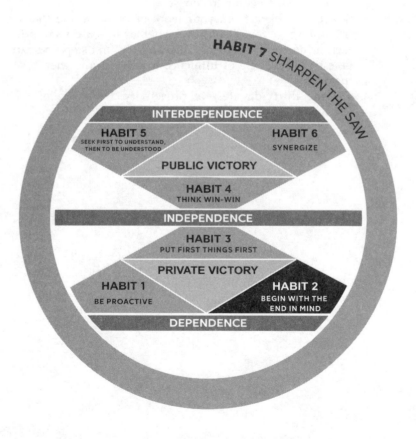

# Principles of Personal Leadership

*What lies behind us and what lies before us*
*are tiny matters*
*compared to what lies within us.*

OLIVER WENDELL HOLMES

PLEASE FIND A PLACE TO READ THESE NEXT FEW PAGES where you can be alone and uninterrupted. Clear your mind of everything except what you will read and what I will invite you to do. Don't worry about your schedule, your business, your family, or your friends. Just focus with me and really open your mind.

In your mind's eye, see yourself going to the funeral of a loved one. Picture yourself driving to the funeral parlor or chapel, parking the car, and getting out. As you walk inside the building, you notice the flowers, the soft organ music. You see the faces of friends and family you pass along the way. You feel the shared sorrow of losing, the joy of having known, that radiates from the hearts of the people there.

As you walk down to the front of the room and look inside the casket, you suddenly come face to face with yourself. This is your funeral, three years from today. All these people have come to honor you, to express feelings of love and appreciation for your life.

As you take a seat and wait for the services to begin, you look at the program in your hand. There are to be four speakers. The first is from your family, immediate and also extended—children, brothers, sisters, nephews, nieces, aunts, uncles, cousins, and grandparents who have come from all over the country to attend. The second speaker is one of your friends, someone who can give a sense of what you were as a person. The third speaker is from your work or profession. And the fourth is from your church or some community organization where you've been involved in service.

Now think deeply. What would you like each of these speakers to say about you and your life? What kind of husband, wife, father, or mother would you like their words to reflect? What kind of son or daughter or cousin? What kind of friend? What kind of working associate?

What character would you like them to have seen in you? What contributions, what achievements would you want them to remember? Look carefully at the people around you. What difference would you like to have made in their lives?

Before you read further, take a few minutes to jot down your impressions. It will greatly increase your personal understanding of Habit 2.

## What It Means to "Begin with the End in Mind"

If you participated seriously in this visualization experience, you touched for a moment some of your deep, fundamental values. You established brief contact with that inner guidance system at the heart of your Circle of Influence.

Consider the words of Joseph Addison:

> When I look upon the tombs of the great, every emotion of envy dies in me; when I read the epitaphs of the beautiful, every inordinate desire goes out; when I meet with the grief of parents upon a tombstone, my heart melts with compassion; when I see the tomb of the parents themselves, I consider the vanity of grieving for those whom we must quickly follow: when I see kings lying by those who deposed them, when I consider rival wits placed side by side, or the holy men that divided the world with their contests and disputes, I reflect with sorrow and astonishment on the little competitions, factions, and debates of mankind. When I read the several dates of the tombs, of some that died yesterday, and some six hundred years ago, I consider that great Day when we shall all of us be Contemporaries, and make our appearance together.

Although Habit 2 applies to many different circumstances and levels of life, the most fundamental application of "begin with the end in mind" is to begin today with the image, picture, or paradigm of the end of your life as your frame of reference or the criterion by which everything else is examined. Each part of your life—today's behavior, tomorrow's behavior, next week's behavior, next month's behavior—can be examined in the context of the whole, of what really matters most to you. By keeping that end clearly in mind, you can make certain that whatever you do on any particular day does not violate the criteria you have defined as supremely important, and that each day of your life contributes in a meaningful way to the vision you have of your life as a whole.

To begin with the end in mind means to start with a clear understanding of your destination. It means to know where you're going so that you better understand where you are now and so that the steps you take are always in the right direction.

It's incredibly easy to get caught up in an activity trap, in the busyness of life, to work harder and harder at climbing the ladder of success only to discover it's leaning against the wrong wall. It is possible to be busy—very busy—without being very effective.

People often find themselves achieving victories that are empty, successes that have come at the expense of things they suddenly realize were far more valuable to them. People from every walk of life—doctors, academicians, actors, politicians, business professionals, athletes, and plumbers—often struggle to achieve a higher income, more recognition of a certain degree of professional competence, only to find that their drive to achieve their goal blinded them to the things that really mattered most and now are gone.

How different our lives are when we really know what is deeply important to us, and, keeping that picture in mind, we manage ourselves each day to be and to do what really matters most. If the ladder is not leaning against the right wall, every step we take just gets us to the wrong place faster. We may be very busy, we may be very *efficient*, but we will also be truly *effective* only when we begin with the end in mind.

If you carefully consider what you wanted to be said of you in the funeral experience, you will find *your* definition of success. It may be very different from the definition you thought you had in mind. Perhaps fame, achievement, money, or some of the other things we strive for are not even part of the right wall.

When you begin with the end in mind, you gain a different perspective. One man asked another on the death of a mutual friend, "How much did he leave?" His friend responded, "He left it all."

## ALL THINGS ARE CREATED TWICE

"Begin with the end in mind" is based on the principle that *all things are created twice*. There's a mental or first creation, and a physical or second creation, to all things.

Take the construction of a home, for example. You create it in every detail before you ever hammer the first nail into place. You try to get a very clear sense of what kind of house you want. If you want a family-centered home, you plan to put a family room where it would be a natural gathering place. You plan sliding doors and a patio for children to play outside. You work with ideas. You work with your mind until you get a clear image of what you want to build.

Then you reduce it to blueprint and develop construction plans. All of this is done before the earth is touched. If not, then in the second creation, the physical creation, you will have to make expensive changes that may double the cost of your home.

The carpenter's rule is "measure twice, cut once." You have to make sure that the blueprint, the first creation, is really what you want, that you've thought everything through. Then you put it into bricks and mortar. Each day you go to the construction shed and pull out the blueprint to get marching orders for the day. You begin with the end in mind.

For another example, look at a business. If you want to have a successful enterprise, you clearly define what you're trying to accomplish. You carefully think through the product or service you want to provide in terms of your market target, then you organize all the elements—financial, research and development, operations, marketing, personnel, physical facilities, and so on—to meet that objective. The extent to which you begin with the end in mind often determines whether or not you are able to create a successful enterprise. Most business failures begin in the first creation, with problems such as undercapitalization, misunderstanding of the market, or lack of a business plan.

The same is true with parenting. If you want to raise responsible, self-disciplined children, you have to keep that end clearly in mind as you interact with your children on a daily basis. You can't behave toward them in ways that undermine their self-discipline or self esteem.

To varying degrees, people use this principle in many different areas of life. Before you go on a trip, you determine your destination and plan out the best route. Before you plant a garden, you plan it out in your mind, possibly on paper. You create speeches on paper before you give them, you envision the landscaping in your yard before you landscape it, you design the clothes you make before you thread the needle.

To the extent to which we understand the principle of two creations and accept the responsibility for both, we act within and enlarge the borders of our Circle of Influence. To the extent to which we do not operate in harmony with this principle and do not take charge of the first creation, we diminish it.

## By Design or Default

It's a principle that all things are created twice, but not all first creations are by conscious design. In our personal lives, if we do not develop our own self-awareness and do not become responsible for first creations, we empower other people and circumstances outside our Circle of Influence to shape much of our lives by default. We reactively live the scripts handed to us by family, associates, other people's agendas, the pressures of circumstance— scripts from our earlier years, from our training, our conditioning.

These scripts come from people, not principles. And they rise out of our deep vulnerabilities, our deep dependency on others and our needs for acceptance and love, for belonging, for a sense of importance and worth, for a feeling that we matter.

Whether we are aware of it or not, whether we are in control of it or not, there is a first creation to every part of our lives. We are either the second creation of our own proactive design, or we are the second creation of other people's agendas, of circumstances, or of past habits.

The unique human capacities of self-awareness, imagination, and conscience enable us to examine first creations and make it possible for us to take charge of our own first creation, to write our own script. Put another way, Habit 1 says, "You are the creator." Habit 2 is the first creation.

## LEADERSHIP AND MANAGEMENT—THE TWO CREATIONS

Habit 2 is based on principles of personal leadership, which means that leadership is the first creation. Leadership is not management. Management is the second creation, which we'll discuss in the chapter on Habit 3. But leadership has to come first.

Management is a bottom line focus: How can I best accomplish certain things? Leadership deals with the top line: What are the things I want to accomplish? In the words of both Peter Drucker and Warren Bennis, "Management is doing things right; leadership is doing the right things." Management is efficiency in climbing the ladder of success; leadership determines whether the ladder is leaning against the right wall.

You can quickly grasp the important difference between the two if you envision a group of producers cutting their way through the jungle with machetes. They're the producers, the problem solvers. They're cutting through the undergrowth, clearing it out.

The managers are behind them, sharpening their machetes, writing policy and procedure manuals, holding muscle development programs, bringing in improved technologies and setting up working schedules and compensation programs for machete wielders.

The leader is the one who climbs the tallest tree, surveys the entire situation, and yells, "Wrong jungle!"

But how do the busy, efficient producers and managers often respond? "Shut up! We're making progress."

As individuals, groups, and businesses, we're often so busy cutting through the undergrowth we don't even realize we're in the wrong jungle. And the rapidly changing environment in which we live makes effective leadership more critical than it has ever been—in every aspect of independent and interdependent life.

We are more in need of a vision or destination and a compass (a set of principles or directions) and less in need of a road map. We often don't know what the terrain ahead will be like or what we will need to go through it; much will depend on our judgment at the time. But an inner compass will always give us direction.

Effectiveness—often even survival—does not depend solely on how much effort we expend, but on whether or not the effort we expend is in the right jungle. And the metamorphosis taking place in most every industry and profession demands leadership first and management second.

In business, the market is changing so rapidly that many products and services that successfully met consumer tastes and needs a few years ago are obsolete today. Proactive powerful leadership must constantly monitor environmental change, particularly customer buying habits and motives, and provide the force necessary to organize resources in the right direction.

Such changes as deregulation of the airline industry, skyrocketing costs of health care, and the greater quality and quantity of imported cars impact the environment in significant ways. If industries do not monitor the environment, including their own work teams, and exercise the creative leadership to keep headed in the right direction, no amount of management expertise can keep them from failing.

Efficient management without effective leadership is, as one individual has phrased it, "like straightening deck chairs on the Titanic." No management success can compensate for failure in leadership. But leadership is hard because we're often caught in a management paradigm.

At the final session of a year-long executive development program in Seattle, the president of an oil company came up to me and said, "Stephen, when you pointed out the difference between leadership and management in the second month, I looked at my role as the president of this company and realized that I had never been into leadership. I was deep into management, buried by pressing challenges and the details of day-to-day logistics. So I decided to withdraw from management. I could get other people to do that. I wanted to really lead my organization.

"It was hard. I went through withdrawal pains because I stopped dealing with a lot of the pressing, urgent matters that were right in front of me and which gave me a sense of immediate accomplishment. I didn't receive much satisfaction as I started wrestling with the direction issues, the culture building issues, the deep analysis of problems, the seizing of new opportunities. Others also went through withdrawal pains from their working style comfort zones. They missed the easy accessibility I had given them before. They still wanted me to be available to them, to respond, to help solve their problems on a day-to-day basis.

"But I persisted. I was absolutely convinced that I needed to provide leadership. And I did. Today our whole business is different. We're more in line with our environment. We have doubled our revenues and quadrupled our profits. I'm into leadership."

I'm convinced that too often parents are also trapped in the management paradigm, thinking of control, efficiency, and rules instead of direction, purpose, and family feeling.

And leadership is even more lacking in our personal lives. We're into managing with efficiency, setting and achieving goals before we have even clarified our values.

## RESCRIPTING: BECOMING YOUR OWN FIRST CREATOR

As we previously observed, proactivity is based on the unique human endowment of self-awareness. The two additional unique human endowments that enable us to expand our proactivity and to exercise personal leadership in our lives are *imagination* and *conscience*.

Through imagination, we can visualize the uncreated worlds of potential that lie within us. Through conscience, we can come in contact with universal laws or principles with our own singular talents and avenues of contribution, and with the personal guidelines within which we can most effectively develop them. Combined with self-awareness, these two endowments empower us to write our own script.

Because we already live with many scripts that have been handed to us, the process of writing our own script is actually more a process of "rescripting," or paradigm shifting—of changing some of the basic paradigms that we already have. As we recognize the ineffective scripts, the incorrect or incomplete paradigms within us, we can proactively begin to rescript ourselves.

I think one of the most inspiring accounts of the rescripting process comes from the autobiography of Anwar Sadat, past president of Egypt. Sadat had been reared, nurtured, and deeply scripted in a hatred for Israel. He would make the statement on national television, "I will never shake the hand of an Israeli as long as they occupy one inch of Arab soil. Never, never, never!" And huge crowds all around the country would chant, "Never, never, never!"

He marshalled the energy and unified the will of the whole country in that script.

The script was very independent and nationalistic, and it aroused deep emotions in the people. But it was also very foolish, and Sadat knew it. It ignored the perilous, highly interdependent reality of the situation.

So he rescripted himself. It was a process he had learned when he was a young man imprisoned in Cell 54, a solitary cell in Cairo Central Prison, as a result of his involvement in a conspiracy plot against King Farouk. He learned to withdraw from his own mind and look at it to see if the scripts were appropriate and wise. He learned how to vacate his own mind and, through a deep personal process of meditation, to work with his own scriptures, his own form of prayer, and rescript himself.

He records that he was almost loath to leave his prison cell because it was there that he realized that real success is success with self. It's not in having things, but in having mastery, having victory over self.

For a period of time during Nasser's administration Sadat was relegated to a position of relative insignificance. Everyone felt that his spirit was broken, but it wasn't. They were projecting their own home movies onto him. They didn't understand him. He was biding his time.

And when that time came, when he became president of Egypt and confronted the political realities, he rescripted himself toward Israel. He visited the Knesset in Jerusalem and opened up one of the most precedent-breaking peace movements in the history of the world, a bold initiative that eventually brought about the Camp David Accord.

Sadat was able to use his self-awareness, his imagination and his conscience to exercise personal leadership, to change an essential paradigm, to change the way he saw the situation. He worked in the center of his Circle of Influence. And from that rescripting, that change in paradigm, flowed changes in behavior and attitude that affected millions of lives in the wider Circle of Concern.

In developing our own self-awareness many of us discover ineffective scripts, deeply embedded habits that are totally unworthy of us, totally incongruent with the things we really value in life. Habit 2 says we don't have to live with those scripts. We are response-able to use our imagination and creativity to write new ones that are more effective, more congruent with our deepest values and with the correct principles that give our values meaning.

Suppose, for example, that I am highly overreactive to my children. Suppose that whenever they begin to do something I feel is inappropriate, I sense an immediate tensing in the pit of my stomach. I feel defensive walls go up; I prepare for battle. My focus is not on the long-term growth and understanding but on the short-term behavior. I'm trying to win the battle, not the war.

I pull out my ammunition—my superior size, my position of authority—and I yell or intimidate or I threaten or punish. And I win. I stand there, victorious, in the middle of the debris of a shattered relationship while my children are outwardly submissive and inwardly rebellious, suppressing feelings that will come out later in uglier ways.

Now if I were sitting at that funeral we visualized earlier, and one of my children was about to speak, I would want his life to represent the victory of teaching, training, and disciplining with love over a period of years rather than the battle scars of quick fix skirmishes. I would want his heart and mind to be filled with the pleasant memories of deep, meaningful times together. I would want him to remember me as a loving father who shared the fun and the pain of growing up. I would want him to remember the times he came to me with his problems and concerns. I would want to have listened and loved and helped. I would want him to know I wasn't perfect, but that I had tried with everything I had. And that, perhaps more than anybody in the world, I loved him.

The reason I would want those things is because, deep down, I value my children. I love them, I want to help them. I value my role as their father.

But I don't always see those values. I get caught up in the "thick of thin things." What matters most gets buried under layers of pressing problems, immediate concerns, and outward behaviors. I become reactive. And the way I interact with my children every day often bears little resemblance to the way I deeply feel about them.

Because I am self-aware, because I have imagination and conscience, I can examine my deepest values. I can realize that the script I'm living is not in harmony with those values, that my life is not the product of my own proactive design, but the result of the first creation I have deferred to circumstances and other people. And I can change. I can live out of my imagination instead of my memory. I can tie myself to my limitless potential instead of my limiting past. I can become my own first creator.

To begin with the end in mind means to approach my role as a parent, as well as my other roles in life, with my values and directions clear. It means to be responsible for my own first creation, to rescript myself so that the paradigms from which my behavior and attitude flow are congruent with my deepest values and in harmony with correct principles.

It also means to begin each day with those values firmly in mind. Then as the vicissitudes, as the challenges come, I can make my decisions based on those values. I can act with integrity. I don't have to react to the emotion, the circumstance. I can be truly proactive, value driven, because my values are clear.

## A PERSONAL MISSION STATEMENT

The most effective way I know to begin with the end in mind is to develop a *personal mission statement* or philosophy or creed. It focuses on what you want to be (character) and to do (contributions and achievements) and on the values or principles upon which being and doing are based.

Because each individual is unique, a personal mission statement will reflect that uniqueness, both in content and form. My friend, Rolfe Kerr, has expressed his personal creed in this way:

Succeed at home first.
Seek and merit divine help.
Never compromise with honesty.
Remember the people involved.
Hear both sides before judging.
Obtain counsel of others.
Defend those who are absent.
Be sincere yet decisive.
Develop one new proficiency a year.
Plan tomorrow's work today.
Hustle while you wait.
Maintain a positive attitude.

Keep a sense of humor.

Be orderly in person and in work.

Do not fear mistakes—fear only the absence of creative, constructive, and corrective responses to those mistakes.

Facilitate the success of subordinates.

Listen twice as much as you speak.

Concentrate all abilities and efforts on the task at hand, not worrying about the next job or promotion.

A woman seeking to balance family and work values has expressed her sense of personal mission differently:

> I will seek to balance career and family as best I can since both are important to me.
>
> My home will be a place where I and my family, friends, and guests find joy, comfort, peace, and happiness. Still I will seek to create a clean and orderly environment, yet livable and comfortable. I will exercise wisdom in what we choose to eat, read, see, and do at home. I especially want to teach my children to love, to learn, and to laugh—and to work and develop their unique talents.
>
> I value the rights, freedoms, and responsibilities of our democratic society. I will be a concerned and informed citizen, involved in the political process to ensure my voice is heard and my vote is counted.
>
> I will be a self-starting individual who exercises initiative in accomplishing my life's goals. I will act on situations and opportunities, rather than to be acted upon.
>
> I will always try to keep myself free from addictive and destructive habits. I will develop habits that free me from old labels and limits and expand my capabilities and choices.
>
> My money will be my servant, not my master. I will seek financial independence over time. My wants will be subject to my needs and my means. Except for long-term home and car loans, I will seek to keep myself free from consumer debt. I will spend less than I earn and regularly save or invest part of my income.
>
> Moreover, I will use what money and talents I have to make life more enjoyable for others through service and charitable giving.

You could call a personal mission statement a personal constitution. Like the United States Constitution, it's fundamentally changeless. In over two hundred years, there have been only twenty-six amendments, ten of which were in the original Bill of Rights.

The United States Constitution is the standard by which every law in the country is evaluated. It is the document the president agrees to defend and support when he takes the Oath of Office. It is the criterion by which people are admitted into citizenship. It is the foundation and the center that enables people to ride through such major traumas as the Civil War, Vietnam, or Watergate. It is the written standard, the key criterion by which everything else is evaluated and directed.

The Constitution has endured and serves its vital function today because it is based on correct principles, on the self-evident truths contained in the Declaration of Independence. These principles empower the Constitution with a timeless strength, even in the midst of social ambiguity and change. "Our peculiar security," said Thomas Jefferson, "is in the possession of a written Constitution."

A personal mission statement based on correct principles becomes the same kind of standard for an individual. It becomes a personal constitution, the basis for making major, life-directing decisions, the basis for making daily decisions in the midst of the circumstances and emotions that affect our lives. It empowers individuals with the same timeless strength in the midst of change.

People can't live with change if there's not a changeless core inside them. The key to the ability to change is a changeless sense of who you are, what you are about and what you value.

With a mission statement, we can flow with changes. We don't need prejudgments or prejudices. We don't need to figure out everything else in life, to stereotype and categorize everything and everybody in order to accommodate reality.

Our personal environment is also changing at an ever-increasing pace. Such rapid change burns out a large number of people who feel they can hardly handle it, can hardly cope with life. They become reactive and essentially give up, hoping that the things that happen to them will be good.

But it doesn't have to be that way. In the Nazi death camps where Victor Frankl learned the principle of proactivity, he also learned the importance of purpose, of meaning in life. The essence of "logotherapy," the philosophy he later developed and taught, is that many so-called mental and emotional illnesses are really symptoms of an underlying sense of meaninglessness or emptiness. Logotherapy eliminates that emptiness by helping the individual to detect his unique meaning, his mission in life.

Once you have that sense of mission, you have the essence of your own proactivity. You have the vision and the values which direct your life. You have the basic direction from which you set your long- and short-term goals. You have the power of a written constitution based on correct principles, against which every decision concerning the most effective use of your time, your talents, and your energies can be effectively measured.

## AT THE CENTER

In order to write a personal mission statement, we must begin at the very center of our Circle of Influence, that center composed of our most basic paradigms, the lens through which we see the world.

It is here that we deal with our vision and our values. It is here that we use our endowment of self-awareness to examine our maps and, if we value correct principles, to make certain that our maps accurately describe the territory, that our paradigms are based on principles and reality. It is here that we use our endowment of conscience as a compass to help us detect our own unique talents and areas of contribution. It is here that we use our endowment of imagination to mentally create the end we desire, giving direction and purpose to our beginnings and providing the substance of a written personal constitution.

It is also here that our focused efforts achieve the greatest results. As we work within the very center of our Circle of Influence, we expand it. This is highest leverage PC work, significantly impacting the effectiveness of every aspect of our lives.

Whatever is at the center of our life will be the source of our security, guidance, wisdom, and power.

*Security* represents your sense of worth, your identity, your emotional anchorage, your self-esteem, your basic personal strength or lack of it.

*Guidance* means your source of direction in life. Encompassed by your map, your internal frame of reference that interprets for you what is happening out there, are standards or principles or

implicit criteria that govern moment by moment decision-making and doing.

*Wisdom* is your perspective on life, your sense of balance, your understanding of how the various parts and principles apply and relate to each other. It embraces judgment, discernment, comprehension. It is a gestalt or oneness, an integrated wholeness.

*Power* is the faculty or capacity to act, the strength and potency to accomplish something. It is the vital energy to make choices and decisions. It also includes the capacity to overcome deeply embedded habits and to cultivate higher, more effective ones.

These four factors—security, guidance, wisdom, and power—are interdependent. Security and clear guidance bring true wisdom, and wisdom becomes the spark or catalyst to release and direct power. When these four factors are present together, harmonized and enlivened by each other, they create the great force of a noble personality, a balanced character, a beautifully integrated individual.

These life-support factors also undergird every other dimension of life. And none of them is an all-or-nothing matter. The degree to which you have developed each one could be charted somewhere on a continuum, much like the maturity continuum described earlier. At the bottom end, the four factors are weak. You are basically dependent on circumstances or other people, things over which you have no direct control. At the top end you are in control. You have independent strength and the foundation for rich, interdependent relationships.

Your *security* lies somewhere on the continuum between extreme insecurity on one end, wherein your life is buffeted by all the fickle forces that play upon it, and a deep sense of high intrinsic worth and personal security on the other end. Your *guidance* ranges on the continuum from dependence on the social mirror or other unstable, fluctuating sources to strong inner direction. Your *wisdom* falls somewhere between a totally inaccurate map where everything is distorted and nothing seems to fit, and a complete and accurate map of life wherein all the parts and principles are properly related to each other. Your *power* lies somewhere between immobilization or being a puppet pulled by someone else's strings to high proactivity, the power to act according to your own values instead of being acted upon by other people and circumstances.

The location of these factors on the continuum, the resulting degree of their integration, harmony, and balance, and their positive impact on every aspect of your life is a function of your center, the basic paradigms at your very core.

## ALTERNATIVE CENTERS

Each of us has a center, though we usually don't recognize it as such. Neither do we recognize the all-encompassing effects of that center on every aspect of our lives.

Let's briefly examine several centers or core paradigms people typically have for a better understanding of how they affect these four fundamental dimensions and, ultimately, the sum of life that flows from them.

SPOUSE CENTEREDNESS.     Marriage can be the most intimate, the most satisfying, the most enduring, growth-producing of human relationships. It might seem natural and proper to be centered on one's husband or wife.

But experience and observation tell a different story. Over the years, I have been involved in working with many troubled marriages, and I have observed a certain thread weaving itself through almost every spouse-centered relationship I have encountered. That thread is strong emotional dependence.

If our sense of emotional worth comes primarily from our marriage, then we become highly dependent upon that relationship. We become vulnerable to the moods and feelings, the behavior and treatment of our spouse, or to any external event that may impinge on the relationship—a new child, in-laws, economic setbacks, social successes, and so forth.

When responsibilities increase and stresses come in the marriage, we tend to revert to the scripts we were given as we were growing up. But so does our spouse. And those scripts are usually different. Different ways of handling financial, child discipline, or in-law issues come to the surface. When these deep-seated tendencies combine with the emotional dependency in the marriage, the spouse-centered relationship reveals all its vulnerability.

When we are dependent on the person with whom we are in conflict, both need and conflict are compounded. Love-hate overreactions, fight-or-flight tendencies, withdrawal, aggressiveness, bitterness, resentment, and cold competition are some of the usual results. When these occur, we tend to fall even further back on background tendencies and habits in an effort to justify and defend our own behavior and we attack our spouse's.

Inevitably, anytime we are too vulnerable we feel the need to protect ourselves from further wounds. So we resort to sarcasm, cutting humor, criticism—anything that will keep from exposing the tenderness within. Each partner tends to wait on the initiative of the other for love, only to be disappointed but also confirmed as to the rightness of the accusations made.

There is only phantom security in such a relationship when all appears to be going well. Guidance is based on the emotion of the moment. Wisdom and power are lost in the counterdependent negative interactions.

FAMILY CENTEREDNESS.    Another common center is the family. This, too, may seem to be natural and proper. As an area of focus and deep investment, it provides great opportunities for deep relationships, for loving, for sharing, for much that makes life worthwhile. But as a center, it ironically destroys the very elements necessary to family success.

People who are family-centered get their sense of security or personal worth from the family tradition and culture or the family reputation. Thus, they become vulnerable to any changes in that tradition or culture and to any influences that would affect that reputation.

Family-centered parents do not have the emotional freedom, the power, to raise their children with their ultimate welfare truly in mind. If they derive their own security from the family, their need to be popular with their children may override the importance of a long-term investment in their children's growth and development. Or they may be focused on the proper and correct behavior of the moment. Any behavior that they consider improper threatens their security. They become upset, guided by the emotions of the moment, spontaneously reacting to the immediate concern rather than the long-term growth and development of the child. They may yell or scream. They may overreact and punish out of bad temper. They tend to love their children conditionally, making them emotionally dependent or counterdependent and rebellious.

MONEY CENTEREDNESS.    Another logical and extremely common center to people's lives is making money. Economic security is basic to one's opportunity to do much in any other dimension. In a hierarchy or continuum of needs, physical survival and financial security comes first. Other needs are not even activated until that basic need is satisfied, at least minimally.

Most of us face economic worries. Many forces in the wider culture can and do act upon our economic situation, causing or threatening such disruption that we often experience concern and worry that may not always rise to the conscious surface.

Sometimes there are apparently noble reasons given for making money, such as the desire to take care of one's family. And these things are important. But to focus on money-making as a center will bring about its own undoing.

Consider again the four life-support factors—security, guidance, wisdom, and power. Suppose I derive much of my security from my employment or from my income or net worth. Since many factors affect these economic foundations, I become anxious and uneasy, protective and defensive, about anything that may affect them. When my sense of personal worth comes from my net worth, I am vulnerable to anything that will affect that net worth. But work and money, per se, provide no wisdom, no guidance, and only a limited degree of power and security. All it takes to show the limitations of a money center is a crisis in my life or in the life of a loved one.

Money-centered people often put aside family or other priorities, assuming everyone will understand that economic demands come first. I know one father who was leaving with his children for a promised trip to the circus when a phone call came for him to come to work instead. He declined. When his wife suggested that perhaps he should have gone to work, he responded, "The work will come again, but childhood won't." For the rest of their lives his children remembered this little act of priority setting, not only as an object lesson in their minds but as an expression of love in their hearts.

WORK CENTEREDNESS.   Work-centered people may become "workaholics," driving themselves to produce at the sacrifice of health, relationships, and other important areas of their lives. Their fundamental identity comes from their work—"I'm a doctor," "I'm a writer," "I'm an actor."

Because their identity and sense of self-worth are wrapped up in their work, their security is vulnerable to anything that happens to prevent them from continuing in it. Their guidance is a function of the demands of the work. Their wisdom and power come in the limited areas of their work, rendering them ineffective in other areas of life.

POSSESSION CENTEREDNESS.   A driving force of many people is possessions—not only tangible, material possessions such as fashionable clothes, homes, cars, boats, and jewelry, but also the intangible possessions of fame, glory, or social prominence. Most of us are aware, through our own experience, how singularly flawed such a center is, simply because it can vanish rapidly and it is influenced by so many forces.

If my sense of security lies in my reputation or in the things I have, my life will be in a constant state of threat and jeopardy that these possessions may be lost or stolen or devalued. If I'm in the presence of someone of greater net worth or fame or status, I feel inferior. If I'm in the presence of someone of lesser net worth or fame or status, I feel superior. My sense of self-worth constantly fluctuates. I don't have any sense of constancy or anchorage or persistent selfhood. I am constantly trying to protect and insure my assets, properties, securities, position, or reputation. We have all heard stories of people committing suicide after losing their fortunes in a significant stock decline or their fame in a political reversal.

PLEASURE CENTEREDNESS. Another common center, closely allied with possessions, is that of fun and pleasure. We live in a world where instant gratification is available and encouraged. Television and movies are major influences in increasing people's expectations. They graphically portray what other people have and can do in living the life of ease and "fun."

But while the glitter of pleasure-centered life-styles is graphically portrayed, the natural result of such life-styles—the impact on the inner person, on productivity, on relationships—is seldom accurately seen.

Innocent pleasures in moderation can provide relaxation for the body and mind and can foster family and other relationships. But pleasure, per se, offers no deep, lasting satisfaction or sense of fulfillment. The pleasure-centered person, too soon bored with each succeeding level of "fun," constantly cries for more and more. So the next new pleasure has to be bigger and better, more exciting, with a bigger "high." A person in this state becomes almost entirely narcissistic, interpreting all of life in terms of the pleasure it provides to the self here and now.

Too many vacations that last too long, too many movies, too much TV, too much video game playing—too much undisciplined leisure time in which a person continually takes the course of least resistance gradually wastes a life. It ensures that a person's capacities stay dormant, that talents remain undeveloped, that the mind and spirit become lethargic and that the heart is unfulfilled. Where is the security, the guidance, the wisdom, and the power? At the low end of the continuum, in the pleasure of a fleeting moment.

Malcolm Muggeridge writes in "A Twentieth-Century Testimony":

> When I look back on my life nowadays, which I sometimes do, what strikes me most forcibly about it is that what seemed at the time most significant and seductive, seems now most futile and absurd. For instance, success in all of its various guises; being known and being praised; ostensible pleasures, like acquiring money or seducing women, or traveling, going to and fro in the world and up and down in it like Satan, explaining and experiencing whatever Vanity Fair has to offer.
>
> In retrospect, all these exercises in self-gratification seem pure fantasy, what Pascal called, "licking the earth."

FRIEND/ENEMY CENTEREDNESS. Young people are particularly, though certainly not exclusively, susceptible to becoming friend-centered. Acceptance and belonging to a peer group can become almost supremely important. The distorted and ever-changing social mirror becomes the source for the four life-support factors, creating a high degree of dependence on the fluctuating moods, feelings, attitudes, and behavior of others.

Friend centeredness can also focus exclusively on one person, taking on some of the dimensions of marriage. The emotional dependence on one individual, the escalating need/conflict spiral, and the resulting negative interactions can grow out of friend centeredness.

And what about putting an *enemy* at the center of one's life? Most people would never think of it, and probably no one would ever do it consciously. Nevertheless, enemy centering is very common, particularly when there is frequent interaction between people who are in real conflict. When someone feels he has been unjustly dealt with by an emotionally or socially significant person, it is very easy for him to become preoccupied with the injustice and make the other person the center of his life. Rather than proactively leading his own life, the enemy-centered person is counterdependently reacting to the behavior and attitudes of a perceived enemy.

One friend of mine who taught at a university became very distraught because of the weaknesses of a particular administrator with whom he had a negative relationship. He allowed himself to think about the man constantly until eventually it became an obsession. It so preoccupied him that it affected the quality of his relationships with his family, his church, and his working associates. He finally came to the conclusion that he had to leave the university and accept a teaching appointment somewhere else.

"Wouldn't you really prefer to teach at this university, if the man were not here?" I asked him.

"Yes, I would," he responded. "But as long as he is here, then my staying is too disruptive to everything in life. I have to go."

"Why have you made this administrator the center of your life?" I asked him.

He was shocked by the question. He denied it. But I pointed out to him that he was allowing one individual and his weaknesses to distort his entire map of life, to undermine his faith and the quality of his relationships with his loved ones.

He finally admitted that this individual had had such an impact on him, but he denied that he himself had made all these choices. He attributed the responsibility for the unhappy situation to the administrator. He, himself, he declared, was not responsible.

As we talked, little by little, he came to realize that he was indeed responsible, but that because he did not handle this responsibility well, he was being irresponsible.

Many divorced people fall into a similar pattern. They are still consumed with anger and bitterness and self-justification regarding an ex-spouse. In a negative sense, psychologically they are still married—they each need the weaknesses of the former partner to justify their accusations.

Many "older" children go through life either secretly or openly hating their parents. They blame them for past abuses, neglect, or favoritism and they center their adult life on that hatred, living out the reactive, justifying script that accompanies it.

The individual who is friend- or enemy-centered has no intrinsic security. Feelings of self-worth are volatile, a function of the emotional state or behavior of other people. Guidance comes from the person's perception of how others will respond, and wisdom is limited by the social lens or by an enemy-centered paranoia. The individual has no power. Other people are pulling the strings.

CHURCH CENTEREDNESS.  I believe that almost anyone who is seriously involved in any church will recognize that churchgoing is not synonymous with personal spirituality. There are some people who get so busy in church worship and projects that they become insensitive to the pressing human needs that surround them, contradicting the very precepts they profess to believe deeply. There are others who attend church less frequently or not at all but whose attitudes and behavior reflect a more genuine centering in the principles of the basic Judeo-Christian ethic.

Having participated throughout my life in organized church and community service groups, I have found that attending church does not necessarily mean living the principles taught in those meetings. You can be active in a church but inactive in its gospel.

In the church-centered life, image or appearance can become a person's dominant consideration, leading to hypocrisy that undermines personal security and intrinsic worth. Guidance comes from a social conscience, and the church-centered person tends to label others artificially in terms of "active," "inactive," "liberal," "orthodox," or "conservative."

Because the church is a formal organization made up of policies, programs, practices, and people, it cannot by itself give a person any deep, permanent security or sense of intrinsic worth. Living the principles taught by the church can do this, but the organization alone cannot.

Nor can the church give a person a constant sense of guidance. Church-centered people often tend to live in compartments, acting and thinking and feeling in certain ways on the Sabbath and in totally different ways on weekdays. Such a lack of wholeness or unity or integrity is a further threat to security, creating the need for increased labeling and self-justifying.

Seeing the church as an end rather than as a means to an end undermines a person's wisdom and sense of balance. Although the church claims to teach people about the source of power, it does not claim to be that power itself. It claims to be one vehicle through which divine power can be channeled into man's nature.

SELF-CENTEREDNESS. Perhaps the most common center today is the self. The most obvious form is *selfishness*, which violates the values of most people. But if we look closely at many of the popular approaches to growth and self-fulfillment, we often find self-centering at their core.

There is little security, guidance, wisdom, or power in the limited center of self. Like the Dead Sea in Palestine, it accepts but never gives. It becomes stagnant.

On the other hand, paying attention to the development of self in the greater perspective of improving one's ability to serve, to produce, to contribute in meaningful ways, gives context for dramatic increase in the four life-support factors.

These are some of the more common centers from which people approach life. It is often much easier to recognize the center in someone else's life than to see it in your own. You probably know someone who puts making money ahead of everything else. You probably know someone whose energy is devoted to justifying his or her position in an ongoing negative relationship. If you look, you can sometimes see beyond behavior into the center that creates it.

## IDENTIFYING YOUR CENTER

But where do you stand? What is at the center of your own life? Sometimes that isn't easy to see.

Perhaps the best way to identify your own center is to look closely at your life-support factors. If you can identify with one or more of the descriptions below, you can trace it back to the center from which it flows, a center which may be limiting your personal effectiveness.

More often than not, a person's center is some combination of these and/or other centers. Most people are very much a function of a variety of influences that play upon their lives. Depending on external or internal conditions, one particular center may be activated until the underlying needs are satisfied. Then another center becomes the compelling force.

As a person fluctuates from one center to another, the resulting relativism is like roller coasting through life. One moment you're high, the next moment you're low, making efforts to compensate for one weakness by borrowing strength from another weakness. There is no consistent sense of direction, no persistent wisdom, no steady power supply or sense of personal, intrinsic worth and identity.

The ideal, of course, is to create one clear center from which you consistently derive a high degree of security, guidance, wisdom,

| CENTER | SECURITY | GUIDANCE | WISDOM | POWER |
|---|---|---|---|---|
| If you are...<br>**Spouse-Centered** | • Your feelings of security are based on the way your spouse treats you.<br>• You are highly vulnerable to the moods and feelings of your spouse.<br>• There is deep disappointment resulting in withdrawal or conflict when your spouse disagrees with you or does not meet your expectations.<br>• Anything that may impinge on the relationship is perceived as a threat. | • Your direction comes from your own needs and wants and from those of your spouse.<br>• Your decision-making criterion is limited to what you think is best for your marriage or your mate, or to the preferences and opinions of your spouse. | • Your life perspective surrounds things that may positively or negatively influence your spouse or your relationship. | • Your power to act is limited by weaknesses in your spouse and in yourself. |
| If you are...<br>**Family-Centered** | • Your security is founded on family acceptance and fulfilling family expectations.<br>• Your sense of personal security is as volatile as the family.<br>• Your feelings of self-worth are based on the family reputation. | • Family scripting is your source of correct attitudes and behaviors.<br>• Your decision-making criterion is what is good for the family, or what family members want. | • You interpret all of life in terms of your family, creating a partial understanding and family narcissism. | • Your actions are limited by family models and traditions. |

*(continued on next page)*

| CENTER | SECURITY | GUIDANCE | WISDOM | POWER |
|---|---|---|---|---|
| If you are... **Money-Centered** | • Your personal worth is determined by your net worth.<br><br>• You are vulnerable to anything that threatens your economic security. | • Profit is your decision-making criterion. | • Moneymaking is the lens through which life is seen and understood, creating imbalanced judgment. | • You are restricted to what you can accomplish with your money and your limited vision. |
| If you are... **Work-Centered** | • You tend to define yourself by your occupational role.<br><br>• You are only comfortable when you are working. | • You make your decisions based on the needs and expectations of your work. | • You tend to be limited to your work role.<br><br>• You see your work as your life. | • Your actions are limited by work role models, occupational opportunities, organizational constraints, your boss's perceptions, and your possible inability at some point in your life to do that particular work. |
| If you are... **Posession-Centered** | • Your security is based on your reputation, your social status, or the tangible things you possess.<br><br>• You tend to compare what you have to what others have. | • You make your decisions based on what will protect, increase, or better display your possessions. | • You see the world in terms of comparative economic and social relationships. | • You function within the limits of what you can buy or the social prominence you can achieve. |
| If you are... **Pleasure-Centered** | • You feel secure only when you're on a pleasure "high."<br><br>• Your security is short-lived, anesthetizing, and dependent on your environment. | • You make your decisions based on what will give you the most pleasure. | • You see the world in terms of what's in it for you. | • Your power is almost negligible. |

| | | | |
|---|---|---|---|
| If you are... **Friend-Centered** | • Your security is a function of the social mirror.<br>• You are highly dependent on the opinions of others. | • Your decision-making criterion is "What will they think?"<br>• You are easily embarrassed. | • You see the world through a social lens. | • You are limited by your social comfort zone.<br>• Your actions are as fickle as opinion. |
| If you are... **Enemy-Centered** | • Your security is volatile, based on the movements of your enemy.<br>• You are always wondering what he is up to.<br>• You seek self-justification and validation from the like-minded. | • You are counter-dependently guided by your enemy's actions.<br>• You make your decisions based on what will thwart your enemy. | • Your judgment is narrow and distorted.<br>• You are defensive, over-reactive, and often paranoid. | • The little power you have comes from anger, envy, resentment, and vengeance—negative energy that shrivels and destroys, leaving energy for little else. |
| If you are... **Church-Centered** | • Your security is based on church activity and on the esteem in which you are held by those in authority or influence in the church.<br>• You find identity and security in religious labels and comparisons. | • You are guided by how others will evaluate your actions in the context of church teachings and expectations. | • You see the world in terms of "believers" and "nonbelievers," "belongers" and "nonbelongers." | • Perceived power comes from your church position or role. |
| If you are... **Self-Centered** | • Your security is constantly changing and shifting. | • Your judgment criteria are: "If it feels good..." "What I want." "What I need." "What's in it for me?" | • You view the world by how decisions, events, or circumstances will affect you. | • You ability to act is limited to your own resources, without the benefits of interdependency. |

and power, empowering your proactivity and giving congruency and harmony to every part of your life.

## A PRINCIPLE CENTER

By centering our lives on correct principles, we create a solid foundation for development of the four life-support factors.

Our *security* comes from knowing that, unlike other centers based on people or things which are subject to frequent and immediate change, correct principles do not change. We can depend on them.

Principles don't react to anything. They don't get mad and treat us differently. They won't divorce us or run away with our best friend. They aren't out to get us. They can't pave our way with shortcuts and quick fixes. They don't depend on the behavior of others, the environment, or the current fad for their validity. Principles don't die. They aren't here one day and gone the next. They can't be destroyed by fire, earthquake or theft.

Principles are deep, fundamental truths, classic truths, generic common denominators. They are tightly interwoven threads running with exactness, consistency, beauty, and strength through the fabric of life.

Even in the midst of people or circumstances that seem to ignore the principles, we can be secure in the knowledge that principles are bigger than people or circumstances, and that thousands of years of history have seen them triumph, time and time again. Even more important, we can be secure in the knowledge that we can validate them in our own lives, by our own experience.

Admittedly, we're not omniscient. Our knowledge and understanding of correct principles is limited by our own lack of awareness of our true nature and the world around us and by the flood of trendy philosophies and theories that are not in harmony with correct principles. These ideas will have their season of acceptance, but, like many before them, they won't endure because they're built on false foundations.

We are limited, but we can push back the borders of our limitations. An understanding of the principle of our own growth enables us to search out correct principles with the confidence that the more we learn, the more clearly we can focus the lens through which we see the world. The principles don't change; our understanding of them does.

The *wisdom* and *guidance* that accompany principle-centered living come from correct maps, from the way things really are, have been, and will be. Correct maps enable us to clearly see where we want to go and how to get there. We can make our decisions using the correct data that will make their implementation possible and meaningful.

The personal *power* that comes from principle-centered living is the power of a self-aware, knowledgeable, proactive individual, unrestricted by the attitudes, behaviors, and actions of others or by many of the circumstances and environmental influences that limit other people.

The only real limitation of power is the natural consequences of the principles themselves. We are free to choose our actions, based on our knowledge of correct principles, but we are not free to choose the consequences of those actions. Remember, "If you pick up one end of the stick, you pick up the other."

Principles always have natural consequences attached to them. There are positive consequences when we live in harmony with the principles. There are negative consequences when we ignore them. But because these principles apply to everyone, whether or not they are aware, this limitation is universal. And the more we know of correct principles, the greater is our personal freedom to act wisely.

By centering our lives on timeless, unchanging principles, we create a fundamental paradigm of effective living. It is the center that puts all other centers in perspective.

Remember that your paradigm is the source from which your attitudes and behaviors flow. A paradigm is like a pair of glasses; it affects the way you see everything in your life. If you look at things through the paradigm of correct principles, what you see in life is dramatically different from what you see through any other centered paradigm.

I have included in the Appendix section of this book a detailed chart which shows how each center we've discussed might possibly affect the way you see everything else.* But for a quick understanding of the difference your center makes, let's look at just one example of a specific problem as seen through the different para-

---

* Please refer to Appendix A:

| CENTER | SECURITY | GUIDANCE | WISDOM | POWER |
|---|---|---|---|---|
| If you are...<br>**Principle-<br>Centered** | • Your security is based on correct principles that do not change, regardless of external conditions or circumstances.<br>• You know that true principles can repeatedly be validated in your own life, through your own experiences.<br>• As a measurement of self-improvement, correct principles function with exactness, consistency, beauty, and strength.<br>• Correct principles help you understand your own development, endowing you with the confidence to learn more, thereby increasing your knowledge and understanding.<br>• Your source of security provides you with an immovable, unchanging, unfailing core enabling you to see change as an exciting adventure and opportunity to make significant contributions. | • You are guided by a compass, which enables you to see where you want to go and how you will get there.<br>• You use accurate data, which makes your decisions both implementable and meaningful.<br>• You stand apart from life's situations, emotions, and circumstances, and look at the balanced whole. Your decisions and actions reflect both short- and long-term considerations and implications.<br>• In every situation, you consciously, proactively determine the best alternative, basing decisions on conscience educated by principles. | • Your judgment encompasses a broad spectrum of long-term consequences and reflects a wise balance and quiet assurance.<br>• You see things differently and thus you think and act differently from the largely reactive world.<br>• You view the world through a fundamental paradigm for effective, provident living.<br>• You see the world in terms of what you can do for the world and its people.<br>• You adopt a proactive lifestyle, seeking to serve and build others.<br>• You interpret all of life's experiences in terms of opportunities for learning and contribution. | • Your power is limited only by your understanding and observance of natural law and correct principles and by the natural consequences of the principles themselves.<br>• You become a self-aware, knowledgeable, proactive individual, largely unrestricted by the attitudes, behaviors, or actions of others.<br>• Your ability to act reaches far beyond your own resources and encourages highly developed levels of interdependency.<br>• Your decisions and actions are not driven by your current financial or circumstantial limitations. You experience an interdependent freedom. |

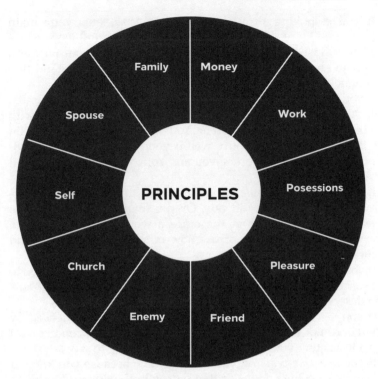

digms. As you read, try to put on each pair of glasses. Try to feel the response that flows from the different centers.

Suppose tonight you have invited your wife to go to a concert. You have the tickets; she's excited about going. It's four o'clock in the afternoon.

All of a sudden, your boss calls you into his office and says he needs your help through the evening to get ready for an important meeting at 9 A.M. tomorrow.

If you're looking through *spouse-centered* or *family-centered* glasses, your main concern will be your wife. You may tell the boss you can't stay and you take her to the concert in an effort to please her. You may feel you have to stay to protect your job, but you'll do so grudgingly, anxious about her response, trying to justify your decision and protect yourself from her disappointment or anger.

If you're looking through a *money-centered* lens, your main thought will be of the overtime you'll get or the influence working late will have on a potential raise. You may call your wife and simply tell her you have to stay, assuming she'll understand that economic demands come first.

If you're *work-centered*, you may be thinking of the opportunity. You can learn more about the job. You can make some points with the boss and further your career. You may give yourself a pat on the back for putting in hours well beyond what is required, evidence of what a hard worker you are. Your wife should be proud of you!

If you're *possession-centered*, you might be thinking of the things the overtime income could buy. Or you might consider what an asset to your reputation at the office it would be if you stayed. Everyone would hear tomorrow how noble, how sacrificing and dedicated you are.

If you're *pleasure-centered*, you'll probably can the work and go to the concert, even if your wife would be happy for you to work late. You deserve a night out!

If you're *friend-centered*, your decision would be influenced by whether or not you had invited friends to attend the concert with you. Or whether your friends at work were going to stay late, too.

If you're *enemy-centered*, you may stay late because you know it will give you a big edge over that person in the office who thinks he's the company's greatest asset. While he's off having fun, you'll be working and slaving, doing his work and yours, sacrificing your personal pleasure for the good of the company he can so blithely ignore.

If you're *church-centered*, you might be influenced by plans other church members have to attend the concert, by whether or not any church members work at your office, or by the nature of the concert—Handel's *Messiah* might rate higher priority than a rock concert. Your decision might also be affected by what you think a "good church member" would do and by whether you view the extra work as "service" or "seeking after material wealth."

If you're *self-centered*, you'll be focused on what will do you the most good. Would it be better for you to go out for the evening? Or would it be better for you to make a few points with the boss? How the different options affect *you* will be your main concern.

*    *    *

As we consider various ways of looking at a single event, is it any wonder that we have "young lady/old lady" perception problems in our interactions with each other? Can you see how fundamentally our centers affect us? Right down to our motivations, our daily decisions, our actions (or, in too many cases, our *reactions*), our interpretations of events? That's why understanding your own center is so important. And if that center does not empower you as a proactive person, it becomes fundamental to your effectiveness to make the necessary paradigm shifts to create a center that will.

As a *principle-centered* person, you try to stand apart from the emotion of the situation and from other factors that would act on you, and evaluate the options. Looking at the balanced whole—the work needs, the family needs, other needs that may be involved and the possible implications of the various alternative decisions— you'll try to come up with the best solution, taking all factors into consideration.

Whether you go to the concert or stay and work is really a small part of an effective decision. You might make the same choice with a number of other centers. But there are several important differences when you are coming from a principle-centered paradigm.

First, you are not being acted upon by other people or circumstances. You are proactively choosing what you determine to be the best alternative. You make your decision consciously and knowledgeably.

Second, you know your decision is most effective because it is based on principles with predictable long-term results.

Third, what you choose to do contributes to your ultimate values in life. Staying at work to get the edge on someone at the office is an entirely different evening in your life from staying because you value your boss's effectiveness and you genuinely want to contribute to the company's welfare. The experiences you have as you carry out your decisions take on quality and meaning in the context of your life as a whole.

Fourth, you can communicate to your wife and your boss within the strong networks you've created in your interdependent relationships. Because you are independent, you can be effectively interdependent. You might decide to delegate what is delegable and come in early the next morning to do the rest.

And finally, you'll feel comfortable about your decision. Whatever you choose to do, you can focus on it and enjoy it.

As a principle-centered person, you see things differently. And because you see things differently, you think differently, you act differently. Because you have a high degree of security, guidance, wisdom, and power that flows from a solid, unchanging core, you have the foundation of a highly proactive and highly effective life.

## WRITING AND USING A PERSONAL MISSION STATEMENT

As we go deeply within ourselves, as we understand and re-align our basic paradigms to bring them in harmony with correct principles, we create both an effective, empowering center and a clear lens through which we can see the world. We can then focus that lens on how we, as unique individuals, relate to that world.

Frankl says we *detect* rather than *invent* our missions in life. I like that choice of words. I think each of us has an internal monitor or sense, a *conscience*, that gives us an awareness of our own uniqueness and the singular contributions that we can make. In Frankl's words, "Everyone has his own specific vocation or mission in life. . . . Therein he cannot be replaced, nor can his life be repeated. Thus, everyone's task is as unique as is his specific opportunity to implement it."

In seeking to give verbal expression to that uniqueness, we are again reminded of the fundamental importance of proactivity and of working within our Circle of Influence. To seek some abstract meaning to our lives out in our Circle of Concern is to abdicate our proactive responsibility, to place our own first creation in the hands of circumstance and other people.

Our meaning comes from within. Again, in the words of Frankl, "Ultimately, man should not ask what the meaning of his life is, but rather must recognize that it is he who is asked. In a word, each man is questioned by life; and he can only answer to life by answering for his own life; to life he can only respond by being responsible."

Personal responsibility, or proactivity, is fundamental to the first creation. Returning to the computer metaphor, Habit 1 says "You are the programmer." Habit 2, then, says, "Write the program." Until you accept the idea that you are responsible, that you are the programmer, you won't really invest in writing the program.

As proactive people, we can begin to give expression to what we want to be and to do in our lives. We can write a personal mission statement, a personal constitution.

A mission statement is not something you write overnight. It takes deep introspection, careful analysis, thoughtful expression, and often many rewrites to produce it in final form. It may take you several weeks or even months before you feel really comfortable with it, before you feel it is a complete and concise expression of your innermost values and directions. Even then, you will want to review it regularly and make minor changes as the years bring additional insights or changing circumstances.

But fundamentally, your mission statement becomes your constitution, the solid expression of your vision and values. It becomes the criterion by which you measure everything else in your life.

I recently finished reviewing my own mission statement, which I do fairly regularly. Sitting on the edge of a beach, alone, at the end of a bicycle ride, I took out my organizer and hammered it out. It took several hours, but I felt a sense of clarity, a sense of organization and commitment, a sense of exhilaration and freedom.

I find the process is as important as the product. Writing or reviewing a mission statement changes you because it forces you to think through your priorities deeply, carefully, and to align your behavior with your beliefs. As you do, other people begin to sense that you're not being driven by everything that happens to you. You have a sense of mission about what you're trying to do and you are excited about it.*

## Using Your Whole Brain

Our self-awareness empowers us to examine our own thoughts. This is particularly helpful in creating a personal mission statement because the two unique human endowments that enable us to practice Habit 2—imagination and conscience—are primarily functions of the right side of the brain. Understanding how to tap into that right brain capacity greatly increases our first creation ability.

---

* If you would like to build your own mission statement or see additional examples of mission statements, go to www.franklincovey.com/MSB.

A great deal of research has been conducted for decades on what has come to be called brain dominance theory. The findings basically indicate that each hemisphere of the brain—left and right—tends to specialize in and preside over different functions, process different kinds of information, and deal with different kinds of problems.

Essentially, the left hemisphere is the more logical/verbal one and the right hemisphere the more intuitive, creative one. The left deals with words, the right with pictures; the left with parts and specifics, the right with wholes and the relationship between the parts. The left deals with analysis, which means to break apart; the right with synthesis, which means to put together. The left deals with sequential thinking; the right with simultaneous and holistic thinking. The left is time bound; the right is time free.

Although people use both sides of the brain, one side or the other generally tends to be dominant in each individual. Of course, the ideal would be to cultivate and develop the ability to have good crossover between both sides of the brain so that a person could first sense what the situation called for and then use the appropriate tool to deal with it. But people tend to stay in the "comfort zone" of their dominant hemisphere and process every situation according to either a right or left brain preference.

In the words of Abraham Maslow, "He that is good with a hammer tends to think everything is a nail." This is another factor that affects the "young lady/old lady" perception difference. Right brain and left brain people tend to look at things in different ways.

We live in a primarily left brain–dominant world, where words and measurement and logic are enthroned, and the more creative, intuitive, sensing, artistic aspect of our nature is often subordinated. Many of us find it more difficult to tap into our right brain capacity.

Admittedly this description is oversimplified and new studies will undoubtedly throw more light on brain functioning. But the point here is that we are capable of performing many different kinds of thought processes and we barely tap our potential. As we become aware of its different capacities, we can consciously use our minds to meet specific needs in more effective ways.

## Two Ways to Tap the Right Brain

If we use the brain dominance theory as a model, it becomes evident that the quality of our first creation is significantly impacted by our ability to use our creative right brain. The more we are able to draw upon our right brain capacity, the more fully we will be able to visualize, to synthesize, to transcend time and present circumstances, to project a holistic picture of what we want to do and to be in life.

### Expand Perspective

Sometimes we are knocked out of our left brain environment and thought patterns and into the right brain by an unplanned experience. The death of a loved one, a severe illness, a financial setback, or extreme adversity can cause us to stand back, look at our lives, and ask ourselves some hard questions: "What's really important? Why am I doing what I'm doing?"

But if you're proactive, you don't have to wait for circumstances or other people to create perspective-expanding experiences. You can consciously create your own.

There are a number of ways to do this. Through the powers of your imagination, you can visualize your own funeral, as we did at the beginning of this chapter. Write your own eulogy. Actually write it out. Be specific.

You can visualize your twenty-fifth and then your fiftieth wedding anniversary. Have your spouse visualize this with you. Try to capture the essence of the family relationship you want to have created through your day-by-day investment over a period of that many years.

You can visualize your retirement from your present occupation. What contributions, what achievements will you want to have made in your field? What plans will you have after retirement? Will you enter a second career?

Expand your mind. Visualize in rich detail. Involve as many emotions and feelings as possible. Involve as many of the senses as you can.

I have done similar visualization exercises with some of my university classes. "Assume you only have this one semester to live," I tell my students, "and that during this semester you are to stay in school as a good student. Visualize how you would spend your semester."

Things are suddenly placed in a different perspective. Values quickly surface that before weren't even recognized.

I have also asked students to live with that expanded perspective for a week and keep a diary of their experiences.

The results are very revealing. They start writing to parents to tell them how much they love and appreciate them. They reconcile with a brother, a sister, a friend where the relationship has deteriorated.

The dominant, central theme of their activities, the underlying principle, is love. The futility of bad-mouthing, bad thinking, put-downs, and accusation becomes very evident when they think in terms of having only a short time to live. Principles and values become more evident to everybody.

There are a number of techniques using your imagination that can put you in touch with your values. But the net effect of every one I have ever used is the same. When people seriously undertake to identify what really matters most to them in their lives, what they really want to be and to do, they become very reverent. They start to think in larger terms than today and tomorrow.

### Visualization and Affirmation

Personal leadership is not a singular experience. It doesn't begin and end with the writing of a personal mission statement. It is, rather, the ongoing process of keeping your vision and values before you and aligning your life to be congruent with those most important things. And in that effort, your powerful right brain capacity can be a great help to you on a daily basis as you work to integrate your personal mission statement into your life. It's another application of "begin with the end in mind."

Let's go back to an example we mentioned before. Suppose I am a parent who really deeply loves my children. Suppose I identify that as one of my fundamental values in my personal mission statement. But suppose, on a daily basis, I have trouble because I overreact.

I can use my right brain power of visualization to write an "affirmation" that will help me become more congruent with my deeper values in my daily life.

A good affirmation has five basic ingredients: it's *personal*, it's *positive*, it's *present tense*, it's *visual*, and it's *emotional*. So I might write something like this: "It is deeply satisfying (emotional) that

I (personal) respond (present tense) with wisdom, love, firmness, and self-control (positive) when my children misbehave."

Then I can visualize it. I can spend a few minutes each day and totally relax my mind and body. I can think about situations in which my children might misbehave. I can visualize them in rich detail. I can feel the texture of the chair I might be sitting on, the floor under my feet, the sweater I'm wearing. I can see the dress my daughter has on, the expression on her face. The more clearly and vividly I can imagine the detail, the more deeply I will experience it, the less I will see it as a spectator.

Then I can see her do something very specific which normally makes my heart pound and my temper start to flare. But instead of seeing my normal response, I can see myself handle the situation with all the love, the power, the self-control I have captured in my affirmation. I can write the program, write the script, in harmony with my values, with my personal mission statement.

And if I do this, day after day my behavior will change. Instead of living out of the scripts given to me by my own parents or by society or by genetics or my environment, I will be living out of the script I have written from my own self-selected value system.

I have helped and encouraged my son, Sean, to use this affirmation process extensively throughout his football career. We started when he played quarterback in high school, and eventually, I taught him how to do it on his own.

We would try to get him in a very relaxed state of mind through deep breathing and a progressive muscle relaxation technique so that he became very quiet inside. Then I would help him visualize himself right in the heat of the toughest situations imaginable.

He would imagine a big blitz coming at him fast. He had to read the blitz and respond. He would imagine giving audibles at the line after reading defenses. He would imagine quick reads with his first receiver, his second receiver, his third receiver. He would imagine options that he normally wouldn't do.

At one point in his football career, he told me he was constantly getting uptight. As we talked, I realized that he was visualizing uptightness. So we worked on visualizing relaxation in the middle of the big pressure circumstance. We discovered that the nature of the visualization is very important. If you visualize the wrong thing, you'll produce the wrong thing.

*   *   *

Dr. Charles Garfield has done extensive research on peak performers, both in athletics and in business. He became fascinated with peak performance in his work with the NASA program, watching the astronauts rehearse everything on earth, again and again in a simulated environment before they went to space. Although he had a doctorate in mathematics, he decided to go back and get another Ph.D. in the field of psychology and study the characteristics of peak performers.

One of the main things his research showed was that almost all of the world-class athletes and other peak performers are visualizers. They see it; they feel it; they experience it before they actually do it. They begin with the end in mind.

You can do it in every area of your life. Before a performance, a sales presentation, a difficult confrontation, or the daily challenge of meeting a goal, see it clearly, vividly, relentlessly, over and over again. Create an internal "comfort zone." Then, when you get into the situation, it isn't foreign. It doesn't scare you.

Your creative, visual right brain is one of your most important assets, both in creating your personal mission statement and in integrating it into your life.

There is an entire body of literature and audio and video tapes that deals with this process of visualization and affirmation. Some of the more recent developments in this field include such things as subliminal programming, neurolinguistic programming, and new forms of relaxation and self-talk processes. These all involve explanation, elaboration and different packaging of the fundamental principles of the first creation.

My review of the success literature brought me in contact with hundreds of books on this subject. Although some made extravagant claims and relied on anecdotal rather than scientific evidence, I think that most of the material is fundamentally sound. The majority of it appears to have originally come out of the study of the Bible by many individuals.

In effective personal leadership, visualization and affirmation techniques emerge naturally out of a foundation of well thought through purposes and principles that become the center of a person's life. They are extremely powerful in rescripting and reprogramming, in writing deeply committed-to purposes and principles into one's heart and mind. I believe that central to all enduring religions in society are the same principles and practices clothed in different language—meditation, prayer, covenants, ordinances, scripture study, empathy, compassion, and many different forms of the use of both conscience and imagination.

But if these techniques become part of the Personality Ethic and are severed from a base of character and principles, they can be misused and abused in serving other centers, primarily the center of self.

Affirmation and visualization are forms of programming, and we must be certain that we do not submit ourselves to any programming that is not in harmony with our basic center or that comes from sources centered on money-making, self interest, or anything other than correct principles.

The imagination can be used to achieve the fleeting success that comes when a person is focused on material gain or on "what's in it for me." But I believe the higher use of imagination is in harmony with the use of conscience to transcend self and create a life of contribution based on unique purpose and on the principles that govern interdependent reality.

## IDENTIFYING ROLES AND GOALS

Of course, the logical/verbal left brain becomes important also as you attempt to capture your right brain images, feelings, and pictures in the words of a written mission statement. Just as breathing exercises help integrate body and mind, writing is a kind of psycho-neural muscular activity which helps bridge and integrate the conscious and subconscious minds. Writing distills, crystallizes, and clarifies thought and helps break the whole into parts.

We each have a number of different roles in our lives—different areas or capacities in which we have responsibility. I may, for example, have a role as an individual, a husband, a father, a teacher, a church member, and a businessman. And each of these roles is important.

One of the major problems that arises when people work to become more effective in life is that they don't think broadly enough. They lose the sense of proportion, the balance, the natural ecology necessary to effective living. They may get consumed by work and neglect personal health. In the name of professional success, they may neglect the most precious relationships in their lives.

You may find that your mission statement will be much more

balanced, much easier to work with, if you break it down into the specific role areas of your life and the goals you want to accomplish in each area. Look at your professional role. You might be a salesperson, or a manager, or a product developer. What are you about in that area? What are the values that should guide you? Think of your personal roles—husband, wife, father, mother, neighbor, friend. What are you about in those roles? What's important to you? Think of community roles—the political area, public service, volunteer organizations.

One executive has used the idea of roles and goals to create the following mission statement:

**My mission is to live with integrity and to make a difference in the lives of others.**

*To fulfill this mission:*

**I have charity:** I seek out and love the one—each one—regardless of his situation.

**I sacrifice:** I devote my time, talents, and resources to my mission.

**I inspire:** I teach by example that we are all children of a loving Heavenly Father and that every Goliath can be overcome.

**I am impactful:** What I do makes a difference in the lives of others.

*These roles take priority in achieving my mission:*

**Husband**—my partner is the most important person in my life. Together we contribute the fruits of harmony, industry, charity, and thrift.

**Father**—I help my children experience progressively greater joy in their lives.

**Son/Brother**—I am frequently "there" for support and love.

**Christian**—God can count on me to keep my covenants and to serve his other children.

**Neighbor**—The love of Christ is visible through my actions toward others.

**Change Agent**—I am a catalyst for developing high performance in large organizations.

**Scholar**—I learn important new things every day.

Writing your mission in terms of the important roles in your life gives you balance and harmony. It keeps each role clearly before you. You can review your roles frequently to make sure that you don't get totally absorbed by one role to the exclusion of others that are equally or even more important in your life.

After you identify your various roles, then you can think about the long-term goals you want to accomplish in each of those roles. We're into the right brain again, using imagination, creativity, conscience, and inspiration. If these goals are the extension of a mission statement based on correct principles, they will be vitally different from the goals people normally set. They will be in harmony with correct principles, with natural laws, which gives you greater power to achieve them. They are not someone else's goals you have absorbed. They are your goals. They reflect your deepest values, your unique talent, your sense of mission. And they grow out of your chosen roles in life.

An effective goal focuses primarily on results rather than activity. It identifies where you want to be, and, in the process, helps you determine where you are. It gives you important information on how to get there, and it tells you when you have arrived. It unifies your efforts and energy. It gives meaning and purpose to all you do. And it can finally translate itself into daily activities so that you are proactive, you are in charge of your life, you are making happen each day the things that will enable you to fulfill your personal mission statement.

Roles and goals give structure and organized direction to your personal mission. If you don't yet have a personal mission statement, it's a good place to begin. Just identifying the various areas of your life and the two or three important results you feel you should accomplish in each area to move ahead gives you an overall perspective of your life and a sense of direction.

As we move into Habit 3, we'll go into greater depth in the area of short-term goals. The important application at this point is to identify roles and long-term goals as they relate to your personal mission statement. These roles and goals will provide the foundation for effective goal setting and achieving when we get to the Habit 3 day-to-day management of life and time.

## FAMILY MISSION STATEMENTS

Because Habit 2 is based on principle, it has broad application. In addition to individuals, families, service groups, and organizations of all kinds become significantly more effective as they begin with the end in mind.

Many families are managed on the basis of crises, moods, quick fixes, and instant gratification—not on sound principles. Symptoms surface whenever stress and pressure mount: people become cynical, critical, or silent or they start yelling and overreacting. Children who observe these kinds of behavior grow up thinking the only way to solve problems is flight or fight.

The core of any family is what is changeless, what is always going to be there—shared vision and values. By writing a family mission statement, you give expression to its true foundation.

This mission statement becomes its constitution, the standard, the criterion for evaluation and decision making. It gives continuity and unity to the family as well as direction. When individual values are harmonized with those of the family, members work together for common purposes that are deeply felt.

Again, the process is as important as the product. The very process of writing and refining a mission statement becomes a key way to improve the family. Working together to create a mission statement builds the PC capacity to live it.

By getting input from every family member, drafting a statement, getting feedback, revising it, and using wording from different family members, you get the family talking, communicating, on things that really matter deeply. The best mission statements are the result of family members coming together in a spirit of mutual respect, expressing their different views, and working together to create something greater than any one individual could do alone. Periodic review to expand perspective, shift emphasis or direction, amend or give new meaning to time-worn phrases can keep the family united in common values and purposes.

The mission statement becomes the framework for thinking, for governing the family. When the problems and crises come, the constitution is there to remind family members of the things that matter most and to provide direction for problem solving and decision making based on correct principles.

In our home, we put our mission statement up on a wall in the family room so that we can look at it and monitor ourselves daily.

When we read the phrases about the sounds of love in our home, order, responsible independence, cooperation, helpfulness, meeting needs, developing talents, showing interest in each other's talents, and giving service to others it gives us some criteria to know how we're doing in the things that matter most to us as a family.

When we plan our family goals and activities, we say, "In light of these principles, what are the goals we're going to work on? What are our action plans to accomplish our goals and actualize these values?"

We review the statement frequently and rework goals and jobs twice a year, in September and June—the beginning of school and the end of school—to reflect the situation as it is, to improve it, to strengthen it. It renews us, it recommits us to what we believe in, what we stand for.

## ORGANIZATIONAL MISSION STATEMENTS

Mission statements are also vital to successful organizations. One of the most important thrusts of my work with organizations is to assist them in developing effective mission statements. And to be effective, that statement has to come from within the bowels of the organization. Everyone should participate in a meaningful way—not just the top strategy planners, but everyone. Once again, the involvement process is as important as the written product and is the key to its use.

I am always intrigued whenever I go to IBM and watch the training process there. Time and time again, I see the leadership of the organization come into a group and say that IBM stands for three things: the dignity of the individual, excellence, and service.

These things represent the belief system of IBM. Everything else will change, but these three things will not change. Almost like osmosis, this belief system has spread throughout the entire organization, providing a tremendous base of shared values and personal security for everyone who works there.

Once I was training a group of people for IBM in New York. It was a small group, about twenty people, and one of them became ill. He called his wife in California, who expressed concern because his illness required special treatment. The IBM people responsible for the training session arranged to have him taken to an excellent hospital with medical specialists in the disease. But they could sense that his wife was uncertain and really wanted him home where their personal physician could handle the problem.

So they decided to get him home. Concerned about the time involved in driving him to the airport and waiting for a commercial plane, they brought in a helicopter, flew him to the airport, and hired a special plane just to take this man to California.

I don't know what costs that involved; my guess would be many thousands of dollars. But IBM believes in the dignity of the individual. That's what the company stands for. To those present, that experience represented its belief system and was no surprise. I was impressed.

At another time, I was scheduled to train 175 shopping center managers at a particular hotel. I was amazed at the level of service there. It wasn't a cosmetic thing. It was evident at all levels, spontaneously, without supervision.

I arrived quite late, checked in, and asked if room service were available. The man at the desk said, "No, Mr. Covey, but if you're interested, I could go back and get a sandwich or a salad or whatever you'd like that we have in the kitchen." His attitude was one of total concern about my comfort and welfare. "Would you like to see your convention room?" he continued. "Do you have everything you need? What can I do for you? I'm here to serve you."

There was no supervisor there checking up. This man was sincere.

The next day I was in the middle of a presentation when I discovered that I didn't have all the colored markers I needed. So I went out into the hall during the brief break and found a bellboy running to another convention. "I've got a problem," I said. "I'm here training a group of managers and I only have a short break. I need some more colored pens."

He whipped around and almost came to attention. He glanced at my name tag and said, "Mr. Covey, I will solve your problem."

He didn't say, "I don't know where to go" or "Well, go and check at the front desk." He just took care of it. And he made me feel like it was his privilege to do so.

Later, I was in the side lobby, looking at some of the art objects. Someone from the hotel came up to me and said, "Mr. Covey, would you like to see a book that describes the art objects in this hotel?" How anticipatory! How service-oriented!

I next observed one of the employees high up on a ladder cleaning windows in the lobby. From his vantage point he saw a woman having a little difficulty in the garden with a walker. She hadn't really fallen, and she was with other people. But he climbed down that ladder, went outside, helped the woman into the lobby and saw that she was properly taken care of. Then he went back and finished cleaning the windows.

I wanted to find out how this organization had created a culture where people bought so deeply into the value of customer service. I interviewed housekeepers, waitresses, bellboys in that hotel and found that this attitude had impregnated the minds, hearts, and attitudes of every employee there.

I went through the back door into the kitchen, where I saw the central value: "Uncompromising personalized service." I finally went to the manager and said, "My business is helping organizations develop a powerful team character, a team culture. I am amazed at what you have here."

"Do you want to know the real key?" he inquired. He pulled out the mission statement for the hotel chain.

After reading it, I acknowledged, "That's an impressive statement. But I know many companies that have impressive mission statements."

"Do you want to see the one for this hotel?" he asked.

"Do you mean you developed one just for this hotel?"

"Yes."

"Different from the one for the hotel chain?"

"Yes. It's in harmony with that statement, but this one pertains to our situation, our environment, our time." He handed me another paper.

"Who developed this mission statement?" I asked.

"Everybody," he replied.

"Everybody? Really, everybody?"

"Yes."

"Housekeepers?"

"Yes."

"Waitresses?"

"Yes."

"Desk clerks?"

"Yes. Do you want to see the mission statement written by the people who greeted you last night?" He pulled out a mission statement that they, themselves, had written that was interwoven with all the other mission statements. Everyone, at every level, was involved.

The mission statement for that hotel was the hub of a great wheel. It spawned the thoughtful, more specialized mission statements of particular groups of employees. It was used as the criterion for every decision that was made. It clarified what those people stood for—how they related to the customer, how they related to each other. It affected the style of the managers and the leaders. It affected the compensation system. It affected the kind of people they recruited and how they trained and developed them. Every aspect of that organization, essentially, was a function of that hub, that mission statement.

I later visited another hotel in the same chain, and the first thing I did when I checked in was to ask to see their mission statement, which they promptly gave me. At this hotel, I came to understand the motto "Uncompromising personalized service" a little more.

For a three-day period, I watched every conceivable situation where service was called for. I always found that service was delivered in a very impressive, excellent way. But it was always also very personalized. For instance, in the swimming area I asked the attendant where the drinking fountain was. He walked me to it.

But the thing that impressed me the very most was to see an employee, on his own, admit a mistake to his boss. We ordered room service, and were told when it would be delivered to the room. On the way to our room, the room service person spilled the hot chocolate, and it took a few extra minutes to go back and change the linen on the tray and replace the drink. So the room service was about fifteen minutes late, which was really not *that* important to us.

Nevertheless, the next morning the room service manager phoned us to apologize and invited us to have either the buffet breakfast or a room service breakfast, compliments of the hotel, to in some way compensate for the inconvenience.

What does it say about the culture of an organization when an employee admits his own mistake, unknown to anyone else, to the manager so that customer or guest is better taken care of!

As I told the manager of the first hotel I visited, I know a lot of companies with impressive mission statements. But there is a real difference, all the difference in the world, in the effectiveness of a mission statement created by everyone involved in the organization and one written by a few top executives behind a mahogany wall.

One of the fundamental problems in organizations, including families, is that people are not committed to the determinations of other people for their lives. They simply don't buy into them.

Many times as I work with organizations, I find people whose goals are totally different from the goals of the enterprise. I commonly find reward systems completely out of alignment with stated value systems.

When I begin work with companies that have already developed some kind of mission statement, I ask them, "How many of the people here know that you have a mission statement? How many of you know what it contains? How many were involved in creating it? How many really buy into it and *use* it as your frame of reference in making decisions?"

Without involvement, there is no commitment. Mark it down, asterisk it, circle it, underline it. *No involvement, no commitment.*

Now, in the early stages—when a person is new to an organization or when a child in the family is young—you can pretty well give them a goal and they'll buy it, particularly if the relationship, orientation, and training are good.

But when people become more mature and their own lives take on a separate meaning, they want involvement, significant involvement. And if they don't have that involvement, they don't buy it. Then you have a significant motivational problem which cannot be solved at the same level of thinking that created it.

That's why creating an organizational mission statement takes time, patience, involvement, skill, and empathy. Again, it's not a quick fix. It takes time and sincerity, correct principles, and the courage and integrity to align systems, structure, and management style to the shared vision and values. But it's based on correct principles and it works.

An organizational mission statement—one that truly reflects the deep shared vision and values of everyone within that organization—creates a great unity and tremendous commitment.

It creates in people's hearts and minds a frame of reference, a set of criteria or guidelines, by which they will govern themselves. They don't need someone else directing, controlling, criticizing, or taking cheap shots. They have bought into the changeless core of what the organization is about.

## Application Suggestions

1. Take the time to record the impressions you had in the funeral visualization at the beginning of this chapter. You may want to use the chart below to organize your thoughts.

| Area of Activity | Character | Contributions | Achievements |
|---|---|---|---|
| Family | | | |
| Friends | | | |
| Work | | | |
| Church/Community Service, etc. | | | |

2. Take a few moments and write down your roles as you now see them. Are you satisfied with that mirror image of your life?
3. Set up time to completely separate yourself from daily activities and to begin work on your personal mission statement.
4. Go through the chart in Appendix A showing different centers and circle all those you can identify with. Do they form a pattern for the behavior in your life? Are you comfortable with the implications of your analysis?
5. Start a collection of notes, quotes, and ideas you may want to use as resource material in writing your personal mission statement.

6. Identify a project you will be facing in the near future and apply the principle of mental creation. Write down the results you desire and what steps will lead to those results.
7. Share the principles of Habit 2 with your family or work group and suggest that together you begin the process of developing a family or group mission statement.

# HABIT 3:
## PUT FIRST THINGS FIRST

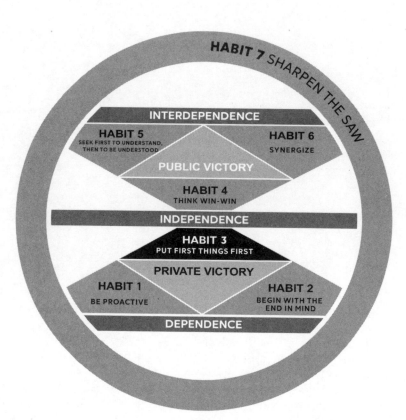

# PRINCIPLES OF PERSONAL MANAGEMENT

*Things which matter most*
*must never be at the mercy of things which matter least.*

GOETHE

WILL YOU TAKE JUST A MOMENT and write down a short answer to the following two questions? Your answers will be important to you as you begin work on Habit 3.

Question 1: What one thing could you do (something you aren't doing now) that, if you did it on a regular basis, would make a tremendous positive difference in your personal life?

Question 2: What one thing in your business or professional life would bring similar results?

We'll come back to these answers later. But first, let's put Habit 3 in perspective.

Habit 3 is the personal fruit, the practical fulfillment of Habits 1 and 2.

Habit 1 says, "You're the creator. You are in charge." It's based on the four unique human endowments of *imagination, conscience, independent will,* and, particularly, *self-awareness.* It empowers you to say, "That's an unhealthy program I've been given from my childhood, from my social mirror. I don't like that ineffective script. I can change."

Habit 2 is the first or mental creation. It's based on *imagination*—the ability to envision, to see the potential, to create with our minds what we cannot at present see with our eyes; and *conscience*—the ability to detect our own uniqueness and the personal, moral, and ethical guidelines within which we can most happily fulfill it. It's the deep contact with our basic paradigms and values and the vision of what we can become.

Habit 3, then, is the second creation, the physical creation. It's the fulfillment, the actualization, the natural emergence of Habits 1 and 2. It's the exercise of *independent will* toward becoming principle-centered. It's the day-in, day-out, moment-by-moment doing it.

Habits 1 and 2 are absolutely essential and prerequisite to Habit 3. You can't become principle-centered without first being aware of and developing your own proactive nature. You can't become principle-centered without first being aware of your paradigms and understanding how to shift them and align them with principles. You can't become principle-centered without a vision of and a focus on the unique contribution that is yours to make.

But with that foundation, you *can* become principle-centered, day-in and day-out, moment-by-moment, by living Habit 3—by practicing effective self-management.

Management, remember, is clearly different from leadership. Leadership is primarily a high-powered, right brain activity. It's more of an art; it's based on a philosophy. You have to ask the ultimate questions of life when you're dealing with personal leadership issues.

But once you have dealt with those issues, once you have resolved them, you then have to manage yourself effectively to create a life congruent with your answers. The ability to manage well doesn't make much difference if you're not even in the "right jungle." But if you are in the right jungle, it makes all the difference. In fact, the ability to manage well determines the quality and even the existence of the second creation. Management is the breaking down, the analysis, the sequencing, the specific application, the time-bound left-brain aspect of effective self-government. My own maxim of personal effectiveness is this: *Manage from the left; lead from the right.*

## THE POWER OF INDEPENDENT WILL

In addition to self-awareness, imagination, and conscience, it is the fourth human endowment—*independent will*—that really makes effective self-management possible. It is the ability to make decisions and choices and to act in accordance with them. It is the ability to act rather than to be acted upon, to proactively carry out the program we have developed through the other three endowments.

The human will is an amazing thing. Time after time, it has triumphed against unbelievable odds. The Helen Kellers of this world give dramatic evidence of the value, the power of the independent will.

But as we examine this endowment in the context of effective self-management, we realize it's usually not the dramatic, the visible, the once-in-a-lifetime, up-by-the-bootstraps effort that brings enduring success. Empowerment comes from learning how to use this great endowment in the decisions we make every day.

The degree to which we have developed our independent will in our everyday lives is measured by our personal integrity. Integrity is, fundamentally, the value we place on ourselves. It's our ability to make and keep commitments to ourselves, to "walk our talk." It's honor with self, a fundamental part of the Character Ethic, the essence of proactive growth.

Effective management is *putting first things first*. While leadership decides what "first things" are, it is management that puts them first, day-by-day, moment-by-moment. Management is discipline, carrying it out.

Discipline derives from *disciple*—disciple to a philosophy, disciple to a set of principles, disciple to a set of values, disciple to an overriding purpose, to a superordinate goal or a person who represents that goal.

In other words, if you are an effective manager of yourself, your discipline comes from within; it is a function of your independent will. You are a disciple, a follower, of your own deep values and their source. And you have the will, the integrity, to subordinate your feelings, your impulses, your moods to those values.

One of my favorite essays is "The Common Denominator of Success," written by E. M. Gray. He spent his life searching for the one denominator that all successful people share. He found it wasn't hard work, good luck, or astute human relations, though those were all important. The one factor that seemed to transcend all the rest embodies the essence of Habit 3—putting first things first.

"The successful person has the habit of doing the things failures don't like to do," he observed. "They don't like doing them either necessarily. But their disliking is subordinated to the strength of their purpose."

That subordination requires a purpose, a mission, a Habit 2 clear sense of direction and value, a burning "yes!" inside that makes it possible to say "no" to other things. It also requires independent will, the power to do something when you don't want to do it, to be a function of your values rather than a function of the impulse or desire of any given moment. It's the power to act with integrity to your proactive first creation.

## FOUR GENERATIONS OF TIME MANAGEMENT

In Habit 3 we are dealing with many of the questions addressed in the field of life and time management. As a longtime student of this fascinating field, I am personally persuaded that the essence of the best thinking in the area of time management can be captured in a single phrase: *Organize and execute around priorities.* That phrase represents the evolution of three generations of time management theory, and how to best do it is the focus of a wide variety of approaches and materials.

Personal management has evolved in a pattern similar to many other areas of human endeavor. Major developmental thrusts, or "waves" as Alvin Toffler calls them, follow each other in succession, each adding a vital new dimension. For example, in social development, the agricultural revolution was followed by the industrial revolution, which was followed by the informational revolution. Each succeeding wave created a surge of social and personal progress.

Likewise, in the area of time management, each generation builds on the one before it—each one moves us toward greater control of our lives. The first wave or generation could be characterized by notes and checklists, an effort to give some semblance of recognition and inclusiveness to the many demands placed on our time and energy.

The second generation could be characterized by calendars and appointment books. This wave reflects an attempt to look ahead, to schedule events and activities in the future.

The third generation reflects the current time management field. It adds to those preceding generations the important idea of prioritization, of clarifying values, and of comparing the relative worth of activities based on their relationship to those values. In addition, it focuses on setting goals—specific long-, intermediate-, and short-term targets toward which time and energy would be directed in harmony with values. It also includes the concept of daily planning, of making a specific plan to accomplish those goals and activities determined to be of greatest worth.

While the third generation has made a significant contribution, people have begun to realize that "efficient" scheduling and control of time are often counterproductive. The efficiency focus creates expectations that clash with the opportunities to develop rich relationships, to meet human needs, and to enjoy spontaneous moments on a daily basis.

As a result, many people have become turned off by time management programs and planners that make them feel too scheduled, too restricted, and they "throw the baby out with the bath water," reverting to first or second generation techniques to preserve relationships, spontaneity, and quality of life.

But there is an emerging fourth generation that is different in kind. It recognizes that "time management" is really a misnomer— the challenge is not to manage time, but to manage ourselves. Satisfaction is a function of expectation as well as realization. And expectation (and satisfaction) lie in our Circle of Influence.

Rather than focusing on *things* and *time*, fourth generation expectations focus on preserving and enhancing *relationships* and on accomplishing *results*—in short, on maintaining the P/PC Balance.

## Quadrant II

The essential focus of the fourth generation of management can be captured in the time management matrix diagrammed on the next page. Basically, we spend time in one of four ways.

As you can see, the two factors that define an activity are *urgent* and *important*. *Urgent* means it requires immediate attention. It's "Now!" Urgent things act on us. A ringing phone is urgent. Most people can't stand the thought of just allowing the phone to ring.

You could spend hours preparing materials, you could get all dressed up and travel to a person's office to discuss a particular issue, but if the phone were to ring while you were there, it would generally take precedence over your personal visit.

If you were to phone someone, there aren't many people who would say, "I'll get to you in 15 minutes; just hold." But most people would probably let you wait in an office for at least that long while they completed a telephone conversation with someone else.

Urgent matters are usually visible. They press on us; they insist on action. They're often popular with others. They're usually right in front of us. And often they are pleasant, easy, fun to do. But so often they are unimportant!

**TIME MANAGEMENT MATRIX**

|  | URGENT | NOT URGENY |
|---|---|---|
| **IMPORTANT** | **I**<br><br>ACTIVITIES:<br>Crises<br>Pressing problems<br>Deadline-driven projects | **II**<br><br>ACTIVITIES:<br>Prevention, PC activites<br>Relationship building<br>Recognizing new opportunities<br>Planning, recreation |
| **NOT IMPORTANT** | **III**<br><br>ACTIVITIES:<br>Interruptions, some calls<br>Some mail, some reports<br>Some meetings<br>Proximate, pressing matters<br>Popular activites | **IV**<br><br>ACTIVITIES:<br>Trivia, busywork<br>Some mail<br>Some phone calls<br>Time wasters<br>Pleasant activites |

*Importance*, on the other hand, has to do with results. If something is important, it contributes to your mission, your values, your high priority goals.

We *react* to urgent matters. Important matters that are not urgent require more initiative, more proactivity. We must *act* to seize opportunity, to make things happen. If we don't practice Habit 2, if we don't have a clear idea of what is important, of the results we desire in our lives, we are easily diverted into responding to the urgent.

Look for a moment at the four quadrants in the time management matrix. Quadrant I is both urgent and important. It deals with significant results that require immediate attention. We usually call the activities in Quadrant I "crises" or "problems." We all have some Quadrant I activities in our lives. But Quadrant I consumes many people. They are crisis managers, problem-minded people, deadline-driven producers.

As long as you focus on Quadrant I, it keeps getting bigger and bigger until it dominates you. It's like the pounding surf. A huge problem comes and knocks you down and you're wiped out. You struggle back up only to face another one that knocks you down and slams you to the ground.

Some people are literally beaten up by problems all day every day. The only relief they have is in escaping to the not important, not urgent activities of Quadrant IV. So when you look at their total matrix, 90 percent of their time is in Quadrant I and most of the remaining 10 percent is in Quadrant IV, with only negligible attention paid to Quadrants II and III. That's how people who manage their lives by crisis live.

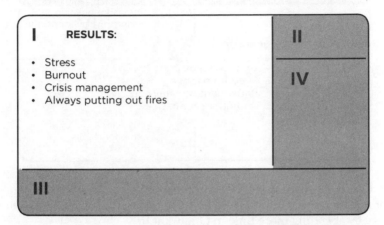

There are other people who spend a great deal of time in "urgent, but not important" Quadrant III, thinking they're in Quadrant I. They spend most of their time reacting to things that are urgent, assuming they are also important. But the reality is that the urgency of these matters is often based on the priorities and expectations of others.

| III **RESULTS:** |
| --- |
| • Short-term focus |
| • Crisis management |
| • Reputation-chameleon character |
| • See goals and plans as worthless |
| • Feel victimized, out of control |
| • Shallow or broken relationships |

People who spend time almost exclusively in Quadrants III and IV basically lead irresponsible lives.

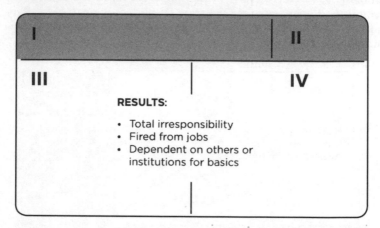

Effective people stay out of Quadrants III and IV because, urgent or not, they aren't important. They also shrink Quadrant I down to size by spending more time in Quadrant II.

Quadrant II is the heart of effective personal management. It deals with things that are not urgent, but are important. It deals with things like building relationships, writing a personal mission statement, long-range planning, exercising, preventive maintenance, preparation—all those things we know we need to do, but somehow seldom get around to doing, because they aren't urgent.

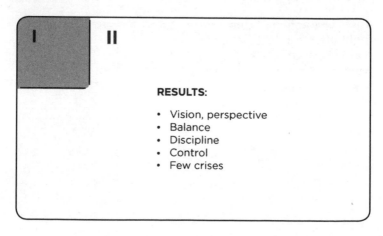

To paraphrase Peter Drucker, effective people are not problem-minded; they're opportunity-minded. They feed opportunities and starve problems. They think preventively. They have genuine Quadrant I crises and emergencies that require their immediate attention, but the number is comparatively small. They keep P and PC in balance by focusing on the important, but not urgent, high leverage capacity-building activities of Quadrant II.

With the time management matrix in mind, take a moment now and consider how you answered the questions at the beginning of this chapter. What quadrant do they fit in? Are they important? Are they urgent?

My guess is that they probably fit into Quadrant II. They are obviously important, deeply important, but not urgent. And because they aren't urgent, you don't do them.

Now look again at the nature of those questions: What one thing could you do in your personal and professional life that, if you did it on a regular basis, *would make a tremendous positive difference in your life?* Quadrant II activities have that kind of impact. Our effectiveness takes quantum leaps when we do them.

I asked a similar question of a group of shopping center managers. "If you were to do one thing in your professional work that you know would have enormously positive effects on the results, what would it be?" Their unanimous response was to build helpful personal relationships with the tenants, the owners of the stores inside the shopping center, which is a Quadrant II activity.

We did an analysis of the time they were spending on that activity. It was less than 5 percent. They had good reasons—problems, one right after another. They had reports to make out, meetings to go to, correspondence to answer, phone calls to make, constant interruptions. Quadrant I had consumed them.

They were spending very little time with the store managers, and the time they did spend was filled with negative energy. The only reason they visited the store managers at all was to enforce the contract—to collect the money or discuss advertising or other practices that were out of harmony with center guidelines, or some similar thing.

The store owners were struggling for survival, let alone prosperity. They had employment problems, cost problems, inventory problems, and a host of other problems. Most of them had no training in management at all. Some were fairly good merchandisers, but they needed help. The tenants didn't even want to see the shopping center owners; they were just one more problem to contend with.

So the owners decided to be proactive. They determined their purpose, their values, their priorities. In harmony with those priorities, they decided to spend about one-third of their time in helping relationships with the tenants.

In working with that organization for about a year and a half, I saw them climb to around 20 percent, which represented more than a fourfold increase. In addition, they changed their role. They became listeners, trainers, consultants to the tenants. Their interchanges were filled with positive energy.

The effect was dramatic, profound. By focusing on relationships and results rather than time and methods, the numbers went up, the tenants were thrilled with the results created by new ideas and skills, and the shopping center managers were more effective and satisfied and increased their list of potential tenants and lease revenue based on increased sales by the tenant stores. They were no longer policemen or hovering supervisors. They were problem solvers, helpers.

Whether you are a student at the university, a worker in an assembly line, a homemaker, fashion designer, or president of a company, I believe that if you were to ask what lies in Quadrant II and cultivate the proactivity to go after it, you would find the same results. Your effectiveness would increase dramatically. Your crises and problems would shrink to manageable proportions because you would be thinking ahead, working on the roots, doing the preventive things that keep situations from developing into crises in the first place. In time management jargon, this is called the Pareto Principle—80 percent of the results flow out of 20 percent of the activities.

## WHAT IT TAKES TO SAY "NO"

The only place to get time for Quadrant II in the beginning is from Quadrants III and IV. You can't ignore the urgent and important activities of Quadrant I, although it will shrink in size as you spend more time with prevention and preparation in Quadrant II. But the initial time for Quadrant II has to come out of III and IV.

You have to be proactive to work on Quadrant II because Quadrants I and III work on you. To say "yes" to important Quadrant II priorities, you have to learn to say "no" to other activities, sometimes apparently urgent things.

Some time ago, my wife was invited to serve as chairman of a committee in a community endeavor. She had a number of truly important things she was trying to work on, and she really didn't want to do it. But she felt pressured into it and finally agreed.

Then she called one of her dear friends to ask if she would serve on her committee. Her friend listened for a long time and then said, "Sandra, that sounds like a wonderful project, a really worthy undertaking. I appreciate so much your inviting me to be a part of it. I feel honored by it. For a number of reasons, I won't be participating myself, but I want you to know how much I appreciate your invitation."

Sandra was ready for anything but a pleasant "no." She turned to me and sighed, "I wish I'd said that."

I don't mean to imply that you shouldn't be involved in significant service projects. Those things are important. But you have to decide what your highest priorities are and have the courage—pleasantly, smilingly, nonapologetically—to say "no" to other things. And the way you do that is by having a bigger "yes" burning inside. The enemy of the "best" is often the "good."

Keep in mind that you are always saying "no" to something. If it isn't to the apparent, urgent things in your life, it is probably to the more fundamental, highly important things. Even when the urgent is good, the good can keep you from your best, keep you from your unique contribution, if you let it.

When I was Director of University Relations at a large university, I hired a very talented, proactive, creative writer. One day, after he had been on the job for a few months, I went into his office and asked him to work on some urgent matters that were pressing on me.

He said, "Stephen, I'll do whatever you want me to do. Just let me share with you my situation."

Then he took me over to his wallboard, where he had listed over two dozen projects he was working on, together with performance criteria and deadline dates that had been clearly negotiated before. He was highly disciplined, which is why I went to see him in the first place. "If you want to get something done, give it to a busy man."

Then he said, "Stephen, to do the jobs that you want done right would take several days. Which of these projects would you like me to delay or cancel to satisfy your request?"

Well, I didn't want to take the responsibility for that. I didn't want to put a cog in the wheel of one of the most productive people on the staff just because I happened to be managing by crisis at the time. The jobs I wanted done were urgent, but not important. So I went and found another crisis manager and gave the job to him.

We say "yes" or "no" to things daily, usually many times a day. A center of correct principles and a focus on our personal mission empowers us with wisdom to make those judgments effectively.

As I work with different groups, I tell them that the essence of effective time and life management is to organize and execute around balanced priorities. Then I ask this question: if you were to fault yourself in one of three areas, which would it be: (1) the inability to *prioritize;* (2) the inability or desire to *organize* around those priorities; or (3) the lack of *discipline* to execute around them, to stay with your priorities and organization?

Most people say their main fault is a lack of discipline. On deeper thought, I believe that is not the case. The basic problem is that their priorities have not become deeply planted in their hearts and minds. They haven't really internalized Habit 2.

There are many people who recognize the value of Quadrant II activities in their lives, whether they identify them as such or not. And they attempt to give priority to those activities and integrate them into their lives through self-discipline alone. But without a principle center and a personal mission statement, they don't have the necessary foundation to sustain their efforts. They're working on the leaves, on the attitudes and the behaviors of discipline, without even thinking to examine the roots, the basic paradigms from which their natural attitudes and behaviors flow.

A Quadrant II focus is a paradigm that grows out of a principle center. If you are centered on your spouse, your money, your friends, your pleasure, or any extrinsic factor, you will keep getting thrown back into Quadrants I and III, reacting to the outside forces your life is centered on. Even if you're centered on yourself, you'll end up in I and III reacting to the impulse of the moment. Your independent will alone cannot effectively discipline you against your center.

In the words of the architectural maxim, *form follows function.*

Likewise, management follows leadership. The way you spend your time is a result of the way you see your time and the way you really see your priorities. If your priorities grow out of a principle center and a personal mission, if they are deeply planted in your heart and in your mind, you will see Quadrant II as a natural, exciting place to invest your time.

It's almost impossible to say "no" to the popularity of Quadrant III or to the pleasure of escape to Quadrant IV if you don't have a bigger "yes" burning inside. Only when you have the self-awareness to examine your program—and the imagination and conscience to create a new, unique, principle-centered program to which you can say "yes"—only then will you have sufficient independent will power to say "no," with a genuine smile, to the unimportant.

## Moving into Quadrant II

If Quadrant II activities are clearly the heart of effective personal management—the "first things" we need to put first—then how do we organize and execute around those things?

The first generation of time management does not even recognize the concept of priority. It gives us notes and "to do" lists that we can cross off, and we feel a temporary sense of accomplishment every time we check something off, but no priority is attached to items on the list. In addition, there is no correlation between what's on the list and our ultimate values and purposes in life. We simply respond to whatever penetrates our awareness and apparently needs to be done.

Many people manage from this first-generation paradigm. It's the course of least resistance. There's no pain or strain; it's fun to "go with the flow." Externally imposed disciplines and schedules give people the feeling that they aren't responsible for results.

But first-generation managers, by definition, are not effective people. They produce very little, and their life-style does nothing to build their production capability. Buffeted by outside forces, they are often seen as undependable and irresponsible, and they have very little sense of control and self-esteem.

Second-generation managers assume a little more control. They plan and schedule in advance and generally are seen as more responsible because they "show up" when they're supposed to.

But again, the activities they schedule have no priority or recognized correlation to deeper values and goals. They have few significant achievements and tend to be schedule oriented.

Third-generation managers take a significant step forward. They clarify their values and set goals. They plan each day and prioritize their activities.

As I have said, this is where most of the time management field is today. But this third generation has some critical limitations. First, it limits vision—daily planning often misses important things that can only be seen from a larger perspective. The very language of "daily planning" focuses on the urgent—the "now." While third generation prioritization provides order to activity, it doesn't question the essential importance of the activity in the first place—it doesn't place the activity in the context of principles, personal mission, roles, and goals. The third-generation value-driven daily planning approach basically prioritizes the Quadrant I and III problems and crises of the day.

In addition, the third generation makes no provision for managing roles in a balanced way. It lacks realism, creating the tendency to over-schedule the day, resulting in frustration and the desire to occasionally throw away the plan and escape to Quadrant IV. And its efficiency, time management focus tends to strain relationships rather than build them.

While each of the three generations has recognized the value of some kind of management tool, none has produced a tool that empowers a person to live a principle-centered, Quadrant II life-style. The first-generation notepads and "to do" lists give us no more than a place to capture those things that penetrate our awareness so we won't forget them. The second-generation appointment books and calendars merely provide a place to record our future commitments so that we can be where we have agreed to be at the appropriate time.

Even the third generation, with its vast array of planners and materials, focuses primarily on helping people prioritize and plan their Quadrants I and III activities. Though many trainers and consultants recognize the value of Quadrant II activities, the actual planning tools of the third generation do not facilitate organizing and executing around them.

As each generation builds on those that have preceded it, the strengths and some of the tools of each of the first three generations provide elemental material for the fourth. But there is an added need for a new dimension, for the paradigm and the implementation that will empower us to move into Quadrant II, to become principle-centered and to manage ourselves to do what is truly most important.

## THE QUADRANT II TOOL

The objective of Quadrant II management is to manage our lives effectively—from a center of sound principles, from a knowledge of our personal mission, with a focus on the important as well as the urgent, and within the framework of maintaining a balance between increasing our production and increasing our production capability.

This is, admittedly, an ambitious objective for people caught in the thick of thin things in Quadrants III and IV. But striving to achieve it will have a phenomenal impact on personal effectiveness.

A Quadrant II organizer will need to meet six important criteria.

COHERENCE.    Coherence suggests that there is harmony, unity, and integrity between your vision and mission, your roles and goals, your priorities and plans, and your desires and discipline. In your planner, there should be a place for your personal mission statement so that you can constantly refer to it. There also needs to be a place for your roles and for both short- and long-term goals.

BALANCE.    Your tool should help you to keep balance in your life, to identify your various roles and keep them right in front of you, so that you don't neglect important areas such as your health, your family, professional preparation, or personal development.

Many people seem to think that success in one area can compensate for failure in other areas of life. But can it really? Perhaps it can for a limited time in some areas. But can success in your profession compensate for a broken marriage, ruined health, or weakness in personal character? True effectiveness requires balance, and your tool needs to help you create and maintain it.

QUADRANT II FOCUS.    You need a tool that encourages you, motivates you, actually helps you spend the time you need in Quadrant II, so that you're dealing with prevention rather than prioritizing crises. In my opinion, the best way to do this is to organize your life on a *weekly* basis. You can still adapt and prioritize on a daily basis, but the fundamental thrust is organizing the week.

Organizing on a weekly basis provides much greater balance and context than daily planning. There seems to be implicit cultural recognition of the week as a single, complete unit of time. Business, education, and many other facets of society operate within the framework of the week, designating certain days for focused investment and others for relaxation or inspiration. The basic Judeo-Christian ethic honors the Sabbath, the one day out of every seven set aside for uplifting purposes.

Most people think in terms of weeks. But most third-generation planning tools focus on daily planning. While they may help you prioritize your activities, they basically only help you organize crises and busywork. *The key is not to prioritize what's on your schedule, but to schedule your priorities.* And this can best be done in the context of the week.

A "PEOPLE" DIMENSION.   You also need a tool that deals with people, not just schedules. While you can think in terms of *efficiency* in dealing with time, a principle-centered person thinks in terms of *effectiveness* in dealing with people. There are times when principle-centered Quadrant II living requires the subordination of schedules to people. Your tool needs to reflect that value, to facilitate implementation rather than create guilt when a schedule is not followed.

FLEXIBILITY.   Your planning tool should be your servant, never your master. Since it has to work for you, it should be tailored to your style, your needs, your particular ways.

PORTABILITY.   Your tool should also be portable, so that you can carry it with you most of the time. You may want to review your personal mission statement while riding the bus. You may want to measure the value of a new opportunity against something you already have planned. If your organizer is portable, you will keep it with you so that important data is always within reach.

Since Quadrant II is the heart of effective self-management, you need a tool that moves you into Quadrant II. My work with the fourth-generation concept has led to the creation of a tool specifically designed according to the criteria listed above. But many good third-generation tools can easily be adapted. Because the principles are sound, the practices or specific applications can vary from one individual to the next.

## BECOMING A QUADRANT II SELF-MANAGER

Although my effort here is to teach principles, not practices, of effectiveness, I believe you can better understand the principles and the empowering nature of the fourth generation if you actually experience organizing a week from a principle-centered, Quadrant II base.

Quadrant II organizing involves four key activities.

IDENTIFYING ROLES.    The first task is to write down your key roles. If you haven't really given serious thought to the roles in your life, you can write down what immediately comes to mind. You have a role as an individual. You may want to list one or more roles as a family member—a husband or wife, mother or father, son or daughter, a member of the extended family of grandparents, aunts, uncles, and cousins. You may want to list a few roles in your work, indicating different areas in which you wish to invest time and energy on a regular basis. You may have roles in church or community affairs.

You don't need to worry about defining the roles in a way that you will live with for the rest of your life—just consider the week and write down the areas you see yourself spending time in during the next seven days.

Here are two examples of the way people might see their various roles.

| | |
|---|---|
| 1. Individual | 1. Personal Development |
| 2. Spouse/Parent | 2. Spouse |
| 3. Manager New Products | 3. Parent |
| 4. Manager Research | 4. Real Estate Salesperson |
| 5. Manager Staff Dev. | 5. Community Service |
| 6. Manager Administration | 6. Symphony Board Member |
| 7. Chairman United Way | |

SELECTING GOALS.    The next step is to think of one or two important results you feel you should accomplish in each role during the next seven days. These would be recorded as goals. (See next page.)

**INDIVIDUAL–PERSONAL DEVEL.**

- Rough draft mission statement
- Register seminar
- Visit Frank in hospital

**SPOUSE/PARENT**

- Confirm symphony tickets
- Tim's science project
- Sarah's bike

**MANAGER–NEW PRODUCTS**

- Test market parameters
- Interview ass't. candidates
- Study consumer survey

**MANAGER–RESEARCH**

- Study last test result
- Work on bonding problem
- Network with Ken and Peter

**MANAGER–STAFF DEVELOPMENT**

- Review responsibilities with Janie
- Visit with Samuels

**MANAGER–ADMINISTRATION**

- End of month reports
- Salary review report

**UNITED WAY CHAIRMAN**

- Prepare agenda
- P.R. visit with Conklin
- Start next year's plan

At least some of these goals should reflect Quadrant II activities. Ideally, these weekly goals would be tied to the longer-term goals you have identified in conjunction with your personal mission statement. But even if you haven't written your mission statement, you can get a feeling, a sense, of what is important as you consider each of your roles and one or two goals for each role.

SCHEDULING.    Now you can look at the week ahead with your goals in mind and schedule time to achieve them. For example, if your goal is to produce the first draft of your personal mission statement, you may want to set aside a two-hour block of time on Sunday to work on it. Sunday (or some other day of the week that is special to you, your faith, or your circumstances) is often the ideal time to plan your more personally uplifting activities, including weekly organizing. It's a good time to draw back, to seek inspiration, to look at your life in the context of principles and values.

If you set a goal to become physically fit through exercise, you may want to set aside an hour three or four days during the week, or possibly every day during the week, to accomplish that goal. There are some goals that you may only be able to accomplish during business hours, or some that you can only do on Saturday when your children are home. Can you begin to see some of the advantages of organizing the week instead of the day?

Having identified roles and set goals, you can translate each goal to a specific day of the week, either as a priority item or, even better, as a specific appointment. You can also check your annual or monthly calendar for any appointments you may have previously made and evaluate their importance in the context of your goals, transferring those you decide to keep to your schedule and making plans to reschedule or cancel others.

As you study the following weekly schedule, observe how each of the nineteen most important, often Quadrant II, goals has been scheduled or translated into a specific action plan. In addition, notice the box labeled "Sharpen the Saw" that provides a place to plan vital renewing Quadrant II activities in each of the four human dimensions that will be explained in Habit 7.

Even with time set aside to accomplish 19 important goals during the week, look at the amount of remaining unscheduled space on the schedule! As well as empowering you to put first things first, Quadrant II weekly organizing gives you the freedom and the flexibility to handle unanticipated events, to shift appoint-

## The WEEKLY SCHEDULE™

**Roles**        **Goals**

**INDIVIDUAL–PERSONAL DEVEL.**
- Rough draft mission statement ①
- Register seminar ②
- Visit Frank in hospital ③

**SPOUSE/PARENT**
- Confirm symphony tickets ④
- Tim's science project ⑤
- Sarah's bike ⑥

**MANAGER–NEW PRODUCTS**
- Test market parameters ⑦
- Interv. ass't candidates ⑧
- Study consumer survey ⑨

**MANAGER–RESEARCH**
- Study last test result ⑩
- Work on bonding prob ⑪
- Network with Ken and Peter ⑫

**MANAGER–STAFF DEVELOPMENT**
- Review responsibilities with Janie ⑬
- Visit with Samuels ⑭

**MANAGER–ADMINISTRATION**
- End of month reports ⑮
- Salary review report ⑯

**UNITED WAY CHAIRMAN**
- Prepare agenda ⑰
- P.R. visit with Conklin ⑱
- Start next year's plan ⑲

### SHARPEN THE SAW

Physical _____

Mental _____

Spiritual _____

Social / Emotional _____

| WEEK OF: | SUNDAY | MONDAY |
|---|---|---|
| **Weekly Priorities** | **Today's Priorities** | |
| | | ⑯ Salary review report |
| | | |
| | | |
| | | |
| | | |
| | | |
| | | |
| | | |
| | **Appointments/Commitments** | |
| | 8 ① Private time | 8 |
| | 9 Mission state-ment | 9 |
| | 10 | 10 |
| | 11 | 11 ⑧ Assistant job |
| | 12 | 12 interviews |
| | 1 | 1 |
| | 2 | 2 |
| | 3 | 3 |
| | 4 | 4 ③ Frank-hospital |
| | 5 | 5 |
| | 6 | 6 |
| | 7 | 7 ⑥ Sarah's bike |
| | 8 | 8 |
| | Evening | Evening |

| TUESDAY | WEDNESDAY | THURSDAY | FRIDAY | SATURDAY |
|---|---|---|---|---|
| Today's Priorities | | | | |
| ② Send in seminar<br>registration | ⑫ Ken<br>Peter | | ⑭ Visit Samuels | |
| | | | | |
| | | | | |
| | | | | |
| | | | | |
| | | | | |
| Appointments/Commitments | | | | |
| 8 | 8 | 8 | 8 | 8  Home mgmt.<br>④ Karla's class |
| 9 | 9  ⑦<br>Test market | 9  ⑪<br>Bonding | 9  ⑩<br>Test resuts | 9 |
| 10 | 10<br>parameters | 10<br>problem | 10<br>study | 10 |
| 11 | 11 | 11 | 11 | 11 |
| 12 | 12 | 12 | 12  ⑱<br>Conklin | 12 |
| 1  ⑨<br>Study consumer | 1 | 1 | 1 | 1 |
| 2<br>survey | 2 | 2 | 2 | 2 |
| 3 | 3 | 3  ⑬<br>Performance | 3  ⑮<br>EOM report | 3 |
| 4 | 4 | 4<br>review–Janie | 4 | 4 |
| 5 | 5 | 5 | 5 | 5 |
| 6  ⑤<br>Tim's project | 6 | 6  ⑰<br>United Way | 6 | 6 |
| 7 | 7 | 7<br>agenda | 7 | 7 |
| 8 | 8 | 8  ⑲<br>Next yrs. plans | 8 | 8 |
| Evening | Evening | Evening | Evening | Evening<br><br>7:00 Thearer–<br>Browns |

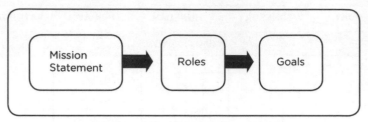

## LONG-TERM ORGANIZING

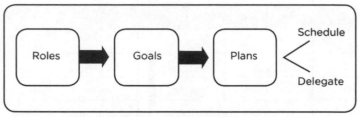

## WEEKLY ORGANIZING

ments if you need to, to savor relationships and interactions with others, to deeply enjoy spontaneous experiences, knowing that you have proactively organized your week to accomplish key goals in every area of your life.

DAILY ADAPTING.    With Quadrant II weekly organizing, daily planning becomes more a function of daily adapting, of prioritizing activities and responding to unanticipated events, relationships, and experiences in a meaningful way.

Taking a few minutes each morning to review your schedule can put you in touch with the value-based decisions you made as you organized the week as well as unanticipated factors that may have come up. As you overview the day, you can see that your roles and goals provide a natural prioritization that grows out of your innate sense of balance. It is a softer, more right-brain prioritization that ultimately comes out of your sense of personal mission.

You may still find that the third-generation A, B, C or 1, 2, 3 prioritization gives needed order to daily activities. It would be a false dichotomy to say that activities are either important or they aren't. They are obviously on a continuum, and some important activities are more important than others. In the context of weekly organizing, third-generation prioritization gives order to daily focus.

But trying to prioritize activities before you even know how they relate to your sense of personal mission and how they fit into the balance of your life is not effective. You may be prioritizing and accomplishing things you don't want or need to be doing at all.

Can you begin to see the difference between organizing your week as a principle-centered, Quadrant II manager and planning your days as an individual centered on something else? Can you begin to sense the tremendous difference the Quadrant II focus would make in your current level of effectiveness?

Having experienced the power of principle-centered Quadrant II organizing in my own life and having seen it transform the lives of hundreds of other people, I am persuaded it makes a difference—a quantum positive difference. And the more completely weekly goals are tied into a wider framework of correct principles and into a personal mission statement, the greater the increase in effectiveness will be.

## Living It

Returning once more to the computer metaphor, if Habit 1 says "You're the programmer" and Habit 2 says "Write the program," then Habit 3 says "Run the program," "Live the program." And living it is primarily a function of our independent will, our self-discipline, our integrity, and commitment—not to short-term goals and schedules or to the impulse of the moment, but to the correct principles and our own deepest values, which give meaning and context to our goals, our schedules, and our lives.

As you go through your week, there will undoubtedly be times when your integrity will be placed on the line. The popularity of reacting to the urgent but unimportant priorities of other people in Quadrant III or the pleasure of escaping to Quadrant IV will threaten to overpower the important Quadrant II activities you have planned. Your principle center, your self-awareness, and your conscience can provide a high degree of intrinsic security, guidance, and wisdom to empower you to use your independent will and maintain integrity to the truly important.

But because you aren't omniscient, you can't always know in advance what is truly important. As carefully as you organize the week, there will be times when, as a principle-centered person, you will need to subordinate your schedule to a higher value. Because you are principle-centered, you can do that with an inner sense of peace.

At one point, one of my sons was deeply into scheduling and efficiency. One day he had a very tight schedule, which included down-to-the-minute time allocations for every activity, including picking up some books, washing his car, and "dropping" Carol, his girlfriend, among other things.

Everything went according to schedule until it came to Carol. They had been dating for a long period of time, and he had finally come to the conclusion that a continued relationship would not work out. So, congruent with his efficiency model, he had scheduled a ten- to fifteen-minute telephone call to tell her.

But the news was very traumatic to her. One-and-a-half hours later, he was still deeply involved in a very intense conversation with her. Even then, the one visit was not enough. The situation was a very frustrating experience for them both.

Again, you simply can't think *efficiency* with people. You think *effectiveness* with *people* and *efficiency* with *things*. I've tried to be "efficient" with a disagreeing or disagreeable person and it simply doesn't work. I've tried to give ten minutes of "quality time" to a child or an employee to solve a problem, only to discover such "efficiency" creates new problems and seldom resolves the deepest concern.

I see many parents, particularly mothers with small children, often frustrated in their desire to accomplish a lot because all they seem to do is meet the needs of little children all day. Remember, frustration is a function of our expectations, and our expectations are often a reflection of the social mirror rather than our own values and priorities.

But if you have Habit 2 deep inside your heart and mind, you have those higher values driving you. You can subordinate your schedule to those values with integrity. You can adapt; you can be flexible. You don't feel guilty when you don't meet your schedule or when you have to change it.

## ADVANCES OF THE FOURTH GENERATION

One of the reasons why people resist using third-generation time management tools is because they lose spontaneity; they become rigid and inflexible. They subordinate people to schedules because the efficiency paradigm of the third generation of management is out of harmony with the principle that *people are more important than things*.

The fourth-generation tool recognizes that principle. It also recognizes that the first person you need to consider in terms of effectiveness rather than efficiency is yourself. It encourages you to spend time in Quadrant II, to understand and center your life on principles, to give clear expression to the purposes and values you want to direct your daily decisions. It helps you to create balance in your life. It helps you rise above the limitations of daily planning and organize and schedule in the context of the week. And when a higher value conflicts with what you have planned, it empowers you to use your self-awareness and your conscience to maintain integrity to the principles and purposes you have determined are most important. Instead of using a road map, you're using a compass.

The fourth generation of self-management is more advanced than the third in five important ways.

First, *it's principle-centered*. More than giving lip service to Quadrant II, it creates the central paradigm that empowers you to see your time in the context of what is really important and effective.

Second, *it's conscience-directed*. It gives you the opportunity to organize your life to the best of your ability in harmony with your deepest values. But it also gives you the freedom to peacefully subordinate your schedule to higher values.

Third, *it defines your unique mission, including values and long-term goals*. This gives direction and purpose to the way you spend each day.

Fourth, *it helps you balance your life by identifying roles*, and by setting goals and scheduling activities in each key role every week.

And fifth, *it gives greater context through weekly organizing* (with daily adaptation as needed), rising above the limiting perspective of a single day and putting you in touch with your deepest values through review of your key roles.

The practical thread running through all five of these advances is a primary focus on relationships and results and a secondary focus on time.

## DELEGATION: INCREASING P AND PC

We accomplish all that we do through delegation—either to time or to other people. If we delegate to time, we think *efficiency*. If we delegate to other people, we think *effectiveness*.

Many people refuse to delegate to other people because they feel it takes too much time and effort and they could do the job better themselves. But effectively delegating to others is perhaps the single most powerful high-leverage activity there is.

Transferring responsibility to other skilled and trained people enables you to give your energies to other high-leverage activities. Delegation means growth, both for individuals and for organizations. The late J. C. Penney was quoted as saying that the wisest decision he ever made was to "let go" after realizing that he couldn't do it all by himself any longer. That decision, made long ago, enabled the development and growth of hundreds of stores and thousands of people.

Because delegation involves other people, it is a Public Victory and could well be included in Habit 4. But because we are focusing here on principles of personal management, and the ability to delegate to others is the main difference between the roles of manager and independent producer, I am approaching delegation from the standpoint of your personal managerial skills.

A producer does whatever is necessary to accomplish desired results, to get the golden eggs. A parent who washes the dishes, an architect who draws up blueprints, or a secretary who types correspondence is a producer.

But when a person sets up and works with and through people and systems to produce golden eggs, that person becomes a manager in the interdependent sense. A parent who delegates washing the dishes to a child is a manager. An architect who heads a team of other architects is a manager. A secretary who supervises other secretaries and office personnel is an office manager.

A producer can invest one hour of effort and produce one unit of results, assuming no loss of efficiency.

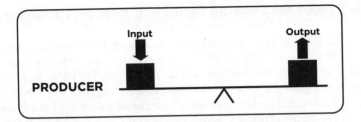

A manager, on the other hand, can invest one hour of effort and produce ten or fifty or a hundred units through effective delegation.

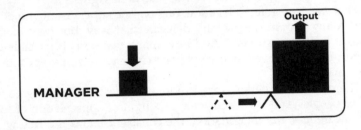

Management is essentially moving the fulcrum over, and the key to effective management is delegation.

## GOFER DELEGATION

There are basically two kinds of delegation: "gofer delegation" and "stewardship delegation." Gofer delegation means "Go for this, go for that, do this, do that, and tell me when it's done." Most people who are producers have a gofer delegation paradigm. Remember the machete wielders in the jungle? They are the producers. They roll up their sleeves and get the job done. If they are given a position of supervision or management, they still think like producers. They don't know how to set up a full delegation so that another person is committed to achieve results. Because they are focused on methods, they become responsible for the results.

I was involved in a gofer delegation once when our family went water skiing. My son, who is an excellent skier, was in the water being pulled and I was driving the boat. I handed the camera to Sandra and asked her to take some pictures.

At first, I told her to be selective in her picture taking because we didn't have much film left. Then I realized she was unfamiliar with the camera, so I became a little more specific. I told her to be sure to wait until the sun was ahead of the boat and until our son was jumping the wake or making a turn and touching his elbow.

But the more I thought about our limited footage and her inexperience with the camera, the more concerned I became. I finally said, "Look, Sandra, just push the button when I tell you. Okay?" And I spent the next few minutes yelling, "Take it!—Take it!— Don't take it!—Don't take it!" I was afraid that if I didn't direct her every move every second, it wouldn't be done right.

That was true gofer delegation, one-on-one supervision of methods. Many people consistently delegate that way. But how much does it really accomplish? And how many people is it possible to supervise or manage when you have to be involved in every move they make?

There's a much better way, a more effective way to delegate to other people. And it's based on a paradigm of appreciation of the self-awareness, the imagination, the conscience, and the free will of other people.

## STEWARDSHIP DELEGATION

Stewardship delegation is focused on results instead of methods. It gives people a choice of method and makes them responsible for results. It takes more time in the beginning, but it's time well invested. You can move the fulcrum over, you can increase your leverage, through stewardship delegation.

Stewardship delegation involves clear, up-front mutual understanding and commitment regarding expectations in five areas.

DESIRED RESULTS.    Create a clear, mutual understanding of what needs to be accomplished, focusing on *what*, not *how*; *results*, not *methods*. Spend time. Be patient. Visualize the desired result. Have the person see it, describe it, make out a quality statement of what the results will look like, and by when they will be accomplished.

GUIDELINES.    Identify the parameters within which the individual should operate. These should be as few as possible to avoid methods delegation, but should include any formidable restrictions. You wouldn't want a person to think he had considerable latitude as long as he accomplished the objectives, only to violate some long-standing traditional practice or value. That kills initiative and sends people back to the gofer's creed: "Just tell me what you want me to do, and I'll do it."

If you know the failure paths of the job, identify them. Be honest and open—tell a person where the quicksand is and where the wild animals are. You don't want to have to reinvent the wheel every day. Let people learn from your mistakes or the mistakes of others. Point out the potential failure paths, what *not* to do, but don't tell them what *to* do. Keep the responsibility for results with them—to do whatever is necessary within the guidelines.

RESOURCES.    Identify the human, financial, technical, or organizational resources the person can draw on to accomplish the desired results.

ACCOUNTABILITY.    Set up the standards of performance that will be used in evaluating the results and the specific times when reporting and evaluation will take place.

CONSEQUENCES.    Specify what will happen, both good and bad, as a result of the evaluation. This could include such things as financial rewards, psychic rewards, different job assignments, and natural consequences tied into the overall mission of an organization.

Some years ago, I had an interesting experience in delegation with one of my sons. We were having a family meeting, and we had our mission statement up on the wall to make sure our plans were in harmony with our values. Everybody was there.

I set up a big blackboard and we wrote down our goals—the key things we wanted to do—and the jobs that flowed out of those goals. Then I asked for volunteers to do the job.

"Who wants to pay the mortgage?" I asked. I noticed I was the only one with my hand up.

"Who wants to pay for the insurance? The food? The cars?" I seemed to have a real monopoly on the opportunities.

"Who wants to feed the new baby?" There was more interest here, but my wife was the only one with the right qualifications for the job.

As we went down the list, job by job, it was soon evident that Mom and Dad had more than sixty-hour work weeks. With that paradigm in mind, some of the other jobs took on a more proper perspective.

My seven-year-old son, Stephen, volunteered to take care of the yard. Before I actually gave him the job, I began a thorough training process. I wanted him to have a clear picture in his mind of what a well cared for yard was like, so I took him next door to our neighbor's.

"Look, Son," I said. "See how our neighbor's yard is green and clean? That's what we're after: *green and clean*. Now come look at our yard. See the mixed colors? That's not it; that's not green. Green and clean is what we want. Now how you get it green is up to you. You're free to do it any way you want, except paint it. But I'll tell you how I'd do it if it were up to me."

"How would you do it, Dad?"

"I'd turn on the sprinklers. But you may want to use buckets or a hose. It makes no difference to me. All we care about is that the color is green. Okay?"

"Okay."

"Now let's talk about 'clean,' Son. Clean means no messes around—no paper, strings, bones, sticks, or anything that messes up the place. I'll tell you what let's do. Let's just clean up half the yard right now and look at the difference."

So we got out two paper sacks and picked up one side of the yard. "Now look at this side. Look at the other side. See the difference? That's called clean."

"Wait!" he called. "I see some paper behind that bush!"

"Oh, good! I didn't notice that newspaper back there. You have good eyes, Son.

"Now before you decide whether or not you're going to take the job, let me tell you a few more things. Because when you take the job, I don't do it anymore. It's your job. It's called a stewardship. Stewardship means 'a job with a trust.' I trust you to do the job, to get it done. Now who's going to be your boss?"

"You, Dad?"

"No, not me. You're the boss. You boss yourself. How do you like Mom and Dad nagging you all the time?"

"I don't."

"We don't like doing it either. It sometimes causes a bad feeling, doesn't it? So you boss yourself. Now, guess who your helper is."

"Who?"

"I am," I said. "You boss me."

"I do?"

"That's right. But my time to help is limited. Sometimes I'm away. But when I'm here, you tell me how I can help. I'll do anything you want me to do."

"Okay!"

"Now guess who judges you."

"Who?"

"You judge yourself."

"I do?"

"That's right. Twice a week the two of us will walk around the yard, and you can show me how it's coming. How are you going to judge?"

"Green and clean."

"Right!"

I trained him with those two words for two weeks before I felt he was ready to take the job. Finally, the big day came.

"Is it a deal, Son?"

"It's a deal."

"What's the job?"

"Green and clean."

"What's green?"

He looked at our yard, which was beginning to look better. Then he pointed next door. "That's the color of his yard."

"What's clean?"

"No messes."

"Who's the boss?"

"I am."

"Who's your helper?"

"You are, when you have time."

"Who's the judge?"

"I am. We'll walk around two times a week and I can show you how it's coming."

"And what will we look for?"

"Green and clean."

At that time I didn't mention an allowance. But I wouldn't hesitate to attach an allowance to such a stewardship.

Two weeks and two words. I thought he was ready.

It was Saturday. And he did nothing. Sunday . . . nothing. Monday . . . nothing. As I pulled out of the driveway on my way to work on Tuesday, I looked at the yellow, cluttered yard and the hot July sun on its way up. "Surely he'll do it today," I thought. I could rationalize Saturday because that was the day we made the agreement. I could rationalize Sunday; Sunday was for other things. But I couldn't rationalize Monday. And now it was Tuesday. Certainly he'd do it today. It was summertime. What else did he have to do?

All day I could hardly wait to return home to see what happened. As I rounded the corner, I was met with the same picture I left that morning. And there was my son at the park across the street playing.

This was not acceptable. I was upset and disillusioned by his performance after two weeks of training and all those commitments. We had a lot of effort, pride, and money invested in the yard and I could see it going down the drain. Besides, my neighbor's yard was manicured and beautiful, and the situation was beginning to get embarrassing.

I was ready to go back to gofer delegation. *Son, you get over here and pick up this garbage right now or else!* I knew I could get the golden egg that way. But what about the goose? What would happen to his internal commitment?

So I faked a smile and yelled across the street, "Hi, Son. How's it going?"

"Fine!" he returned.

"How's the yard coming?" I knew the minute I said it I had broken our agreement. That's not the way we had set up an accounting. That's not what we had agreed.

So he felt justified in breaking it, too. "Fine, Dad."

I bit my tongue and waited until after dinner. Then I said, "Son, let's do as we agreed. Let's walk around the yard together and you can show me how it's going in your stewardship."

As we started out the door, his chin began to quiver. Tears welled up in his eyes and, by the time we got out to the middle of the yard, he was whimpering.

"It's so hard, Dad!"

*What's so hard?* I thought to myself. *You haven't done a single thing!* But I knew what was hard—self-management, self-supervision. So I said, "Is there anything I can do to help?"

"Would you, Dad?" he sniffed.

"What was our agreement?"

"You said you'd help me if you had time."

"I have time."

So he ran into the house and came back with two sacks. He handed me one. "Will you pick that stuff up?" He pointed to the garbage from Saturday night's barbecue. "It makes me sick!"

So I did. I did exactly what he asked me to do. And that was when he signed the agreement in his heart. It became his yard, his stewardship.

He only asked for help two or three more times that entire summer. He took care of that yard. He kept it greener and cleaner than it had ever been under my stewardship. He even reprimanded his brothers and sisters if they left so much as a gum wrapper on the lawn.

Trust is the highest form of human motivation. It brings out the very best in people. But it takes time and patience, and it doesn't preclude the necessity to train and develop people so that their competency can rise to the level of that trust.

I am convinced that if stewardship delegation is done correctly, both parties will benefit and ultimately much more work will get done in much less time. I believe that a family that is well organized, whose time has been spent effectively delegating on a one-on-one basis, can organize the work so that everyone can do everything in about an hour a day. But that takes the internal capacity to want to manage, not just to produce. The focus is on effectiveness, not efficiency.

Certainly you can pick up that room better than a child, but the key is that you want to empower the child to do it. It takes time. You have to get involved in the training and development. It takes time, but how valuable that time is downstream! It saves you so much in the long run.

This approach involves an entirely new paradigm of delegation. In effect, it changes the nature of the relationship. The steward becomes his own boss, governed by a conscience that contains the commitment to agreed upon desired results. But it also releases his creative energies toward doing whatever is necessary in harmony with correct principles to achieve those desired results.

The principles involved in stewardship delegation are correct and applicable to any kind of person or situation. With immature people, you specify fewer desired results and more guidelines, identify more resources, conduct more frequent accountability interviews, and apply more immediate consequences. With more mature people, you have more challenging desired results, fewer guidelines, less frequent accountability, and less measurable but more discernable criteria.

Effective delegation is perhaps the best indicator of effective management simply because it is so basic to both personal and organizational growth.

## THE QUADRANT II PARADIGM

The key to effective management of self, or of others through delegation, is not in any technique or tool or extrinsic factor. It is intrinsic—in the Quadrant II paradigm that empowers you to see through the lens of importance rather than urgency.

I have included in the Appendix an exercise called "A Quadrant II Day at the Office" which will enable you to see in a business setting how powerfully this paradigm can impact your effectiveness.*

As you work to develop a Quadrant II paradigm, you will increase your ability to organize and execute every week of your life around your deepest priorities, to walk your talk. You will not be dependent on any other person or thing for the effective management of your life.

Interestingly, every one of the Seven Habits is in Quadrant II. Every one deals with fundamentally important things that, if done on a regular basis, would make a tremendous positive difference in our lives.

## APPLICATION SUGGESTIONS:

1. Identify a Quadrant II activity you know has been neglected in your life—one that, if done well, would have a significant impact in your life, either personally or professionally. Write it down and commit to implement it.
2. Draw a time management matrix and try to estimate what percentage of your time you spend in each quadrant. Then log your time for three days in fifteen-minute intervals. How accurate was your estimate? Are you satisfied with the way you spend your time? What do you need to change?

---

* Please refer to Appendix B.

3. Make a list of responsibilities you could delegate and the people you could delegate to or train to be responsible in these areas. Determine what is needed to start the process of delegation or training.
4. Organize your next week. Start by writing down your roles and goals for the week, then transfer the goals to a specific action plan. At the end of the week, evaluate how well your plan translated your deep values and purposes into your daily life and the degree of integrity you were able to maintain to those values and purposes.
5. Commit yourself to start organizing on a weekly basis and set up a regular time to do it.
6. Either convert your current planning tool into a fourth generation tool or secure such a tool.
7. Go through "A Quadrant II Day at the Office" (Appendix B) for a more in-depth understanding of the impact of a Quadrant II paradigm.*

---

* To see how effective you are—where your strengths lie and how you can improve—take the Personal Effectiveness Quotient (PEQ) at www.7HabitsPEQ.com. .

| The WEEKLY SCHEDULE™ | | WEEK OF: | SUNDAY | MONDAY |
|---|---|---|---|---|
| Roles | Goals | Weekly Priorities | Today's Priorities | |
| | | | | |
| | | | | |
| | | | | |
| | | | | |
| | | | | |
| | | | Appointments/Commitments | |
| | | | 8 | 8 |
| | | | 9 | 9 |
| | | | 10 | 10 |
| | | | 11 | 11 |
| | | | 12 | 12 |
| | | | 1 | 1 |
| | | | 2 | 2 |
| | | | 3 | 3 |
| | | | 4 | 4 |
| | | | 5 | 5 |
| | | | 6 | 6 |
| | | | 7 | 7 |
| | | | 8 | 8 |
| | | | Evening | Evening |

**SHARPEN THE SAW**

Physical _____

Mental _____

Spiritual_____

Social/Emotional_____

| TUESDAY | WEDNESDAY | THURSDAY | FRIDAY | SATURDAY |
|---------|-----------|----------|--------|----------|
| Today's Priorities | | | | |
| | | | | |
| | | | | |
| | | | | |
| | | | | |
| | | | | |
| | | | | |
| | | | | |
| Appointments/Commitments | | | | |
| 8 | 8 | 8 | 8 | 8 |
| 9 | 9 | 9 | 9 | 9 |
| 10 | 10 | 10 | 10 | 10 |
| 11 | 11 | 11 | 11 | 11 |
| 12 | 12 | 12 | 12 | 12 |
| 1 | 1 | 1 | 1 | 1 |
| 2 | 2 | 2 | 2 | 2 |
| 3 | 3 | 3 | 3 | 3 |
| 4 | 4 | 4 | 4 | 4 |
| 5 | 5 | 5 | 5 | 5 |
| 6 | 6 | 6 | 6 | 6 |
| 7 | 7 | 7 | 7 | 7 |
| 8 | 8 | 8 | 8 | 8 |
| Evening | Evening | Evening | Evening | Evening |

*Part Three*

# PUBLIC VICTORY

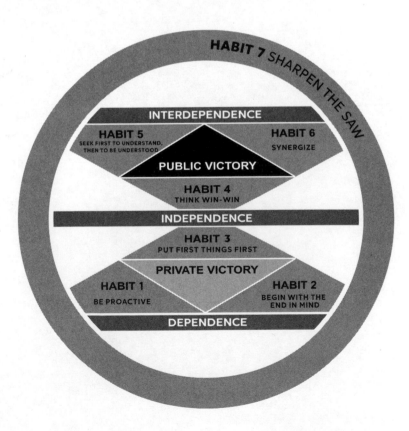

# PARADIGMS OF INTERDEPENDENCE

*There can be no friendship without confidence,*
*and no confidence without integrity.*

SAMUEL JOHNSON

B EFORE MOVING INTO THE AREA OF PUBLIC VICTORY, we should remember that effective interdependence can only be built on a foundation of true independence. Private Victory precedes Public Victory. Algebra comes before calculus.

As we look back and survey the terrain to determine where we've been and where we are in relationship to where we're going, we clearly see that we could not have gotten where we are without coming the way we came. There aren't any other roads; there aren't any shortcuts. There's no way to parachute into this terrain. The landscape ahead is covered with the fragments of broken relationships of people who have tried. They've tried to jump into effective relationships without the maturity, the strength of character, to maintain them.

But you just can't do it; you simply have to travel the road. You can't be successful with other people if you haven't paid the price of success with yourself.

A few years ago when I was giving a seminar on the Oregon coast, a man came up to me and said, "You know, Stephen, I really don't enjoy coming to these seminars." He had my attention.

"Look at everyone else here," he continued. "Look at this beautiful coastline and the sea out there and all that's happening. And all I can do is sit and worry about the grilling I'm going to get from my wife tonight on the phone.

"She gives me the third degree every time I'm away. Where did

I eat breakfast? Who else was there? Was I in meetings all morning? When did we stop for lunch? What did I do during lunch? How did I spend the afternoon? What did I do for entertainment in the evening? Who was with me? What did we talk about?

"And what she really wants to know, but never quite asks, is who she can call to verify everything I tell her. She just nags me and questions everything I do whenever I'm away. It's taken the bloom out of this whole experience. I really don't enjoy it at all."

He did look pretty miserable. We talked for a while, and then he made a very interesting comment. "I guess she knows all the questions to ask," he said a little sheepishly. "It was at a seminar like this that I met her . . . when I was married to someone else!"

I considered the implications of his comment and then said, "You're kind of into 'quick fix,' aren't you?"

"What do you mean?" he replied.

"Well, you'd like to take a screwdriver and just open up your wife's head and rewire that attitude of hers really fast, wouldn't you?"

"Sure, I'd like her to change," he exclaimed. "I don't think it's right for her to constantly grill me like she does."

"My friend," I said, "you can't talk your way out of problems you behave yourself into."

We're dealing with a very dramatic and very fundamental paradigm shift here. You may try to lubricate your social interactions with personality techniques and skills, but in the process, you may truncate the vital character base. You can't have the fruits without the roots. It's the principle of sequencing: Private Victory precedes Public Victory. Self-mastery and self-discipline are the foundation of good relationships with others.

Some people say that you have to like yourself before you can like others. I think that idea has merit, but if you don't know yourself, if you don't control yourself, if you don't have mastery over yourself, it's very hard to like yourself, except in some short-term, psych-up, superficial way.

Real self-respect comes from dominion over self, from true independence. And that's the focus of Habits 1, 2, and 3. Independence is an achievement. Interdependence is a choice only independent people can make. Unless we are willing to achieve real independence, it's foolish to try to develop human relations skills. We might try. We might even have some degree of success when the sun is shining. But when the difficult times come—and they will—we won't have the foundation to keep things together.

The most important ingredient we put into any relationship is not what we say or what we do, but what we are. And if our words and our actions come from superficial human relations techniques (the Personality Ethic) rather than from our own inner core (the Character Ethic), others will sense that duplicity. We simply won't be able to create and sustain the foundation necessary for effective interdependence.

The techniques and skills that really make a difference in human interaction are the ones that almost naturally flow from a truly independent character. So the place to begin building any relationship is inside ourselves, inside our Circle of Influence, our own character. As we become independent—proactive, centered in correct principles, value driven and able to organize and execute around the priorities in our life with integrity—we then can choose to become interdependent—capable of building rich, enduring, highly productive relationships with other people.

As we look at the terrain ahead, we see that we're entering a whole new dimension. Interdependence opens up worlds of possibilities for deep, rich, meaningful associations, for geometrically increased productivity, for serving, for contributing, for learning, for growing. But it is also where we feel the greatest pain, the greatest frustration, the greatest roadblocks to happiness and success. And we're very aware of that pain because it is acute.

We can often live for years with the chronic pain of our lack of vision, leadership or management in our personal lives. We feel vaguely uneasy and uncomfortable and occasionally take steps to ease the pain, at least for a time. Because the pain is chronic, we get used to it, we learn to live with it.

But when we have problems in our interactions with other people, we're very aware of acute pain—it's often intense, and we want it to go away.

That's when we try to treat the symptoms with quick fixes and techniques—the Band-Aids of the Personality Ethic. We don't understand that the acute pain is an outgrowth of the deeper, chronic problem. And until we stop treating the symptoms and start treating the problem, our efforts will only bring counterproductive results. We will only be successful at obscuring the chronic pain even more.

Now, as we think of effective interaction with others, let's go back to our earlier definition of effectiveness. We've said it's the P/PC balance, the fundamental concept in the story of the goose and the golden egg.

In an interdependent situation, the golden eggs are the effectiveness, the wonderful synergy, the results created by open communication and positive interaction with others. And to get those eggs on a regular basis, we need to take care of the goose. We need to create and care for the relationships that make those results realities.

So before we descend from our point of reconnaissance and get into Habits 4, 5, and 6, I would like to introduce what I believe to be a very powerful metaphor in describing relationships and in defining the P/PC balance in an interdependent reality.

## THE EMOTIONAL BANK ACCOUNT

We all know what a financial bank account is. We make deposits into it and build up a reserve from which we can make withdrawals when we need to. An Emotional Bank Account is a metaphor that describes the amount of trust that's been built up in a relationship. It's the feeling of safeness you have with another human being.

If I make deposits into an Emotional Bank Account with you through courtesy, kindness, honesty, and keeping my commitments to you, I build up a reserve. Your trust toward me becomes higher, and I can call upon that trust many times if I need to. I can even make mistakes and that trust level, that emotional reserve, will compensate for it. My communication may not be clear, but you'll get my meaning anyway. You won't make me "an offender for a word." When the trust account is high, communication is easy, instant, and effective.

But if I have a habit of showing discourtesy, disrespect, cutting you off, overreacting, ignoring you, becoming arbitrary, betraying your trust, threatening you, or playing little tin god in your life, eventually my Emotional Bank Account is overdrawn. The trust level gets very low. Then what flexibility do I have?

None. I'm walking on mine fields. I have to be very careful of everything I say. I measure every word. It's tension city, memo haven. It's protecting my backside, politicking. And many organizations are filled with it. Many families are filled with it. Many marriages are filled with it.

If a large reserve of trust is not sustained by continuing deposits, a marriage will deteriorate. Instead of rich, spontaneous understanding and communication, the situation becomes one of accommodation, where two people simply attempt to live independent life-styles in a fairly respectful and tolerant way. The relationship may further deteriorate to one of hostility and defensiveness. The "fight or flight" response creates verbal battles, slammed doors, refusal to talk, emotional withdrawal and self-pity. It may end up in a cold war at home, sustained only by children, sex, social pressure, or image protection. Or it may end up in open warfare in the courts, where bitter ego-destroying legal battles can be carried on for years as people endlessly confess the sins of a former spouse.

And this is in the most intimate, the most potentially rich, joyful, satisfying and productive relationship possible between two people on this earth. The P/PC lighthouse is there; we can either break ourselves against it or we can use it as a guiding light.

Our most constant relationships, like marriage, require our most constant deposits. With continuing expectations, old deposits evaporate. If you suddenly run into an old high school friend you haven't seen for years, you can pick up right where you left off because the earlier deposits are still there. But your accounts with the people you interact with on a regular basis require more constant investment. There are sometimes automatic withdrawals in your daily interactions or in their perception of you that you don't even know about. This is especially true with teenagers in the home.

Suppose you have a teenage son and your normal conversation is something like, "Clean your room. Button your shirt. Turn down the radio. Go get a haircut. And don't forget to take out the garbage!" Over a period of time, the withdrawals far exceed the deposits.

Now, suppose this son is in the process of making some important decisions that will affect the rest of his life. But the trust level is so low and the communication process so closed, mechanical, and unsatisfying that he simply will not be open to your counsel. You may have the wisdom and the knowledge to help him, but because your account is so overdrawn, he will end up making his decisions from a short-range emotional perspective, which may well result in many negative long-range consequences.

You need a positive balance to communicate on these tender issues. What do you do?

What would happen if you started making deposits into the relationship? Maybe the opportunity comes up to do him a little kindness—to bring home a magazine on skateboarding, if that's his interest, or just to walk up to him when he's working on a project and offer to help. Perhaps you could invite him to go to a movie with you or take him out for some ice cream. Probably the most important deposit you could make would be just to listen, without judging or preaching or reading your own autobiography into what he says. Just listen and seek to understand. Let him feel your concern for him, your acceptance of him as a person.

He may not respond at first. He may even be suspicious. "What's Dad up to now? What technique is Mom trying on me this time?" But as those genuine deposits keep coming, they begin to add up. That overdrawn balance is shrinking.

Remember that quick fix is a mirage. Building and repairing relationships takes time. If you become impatient with his apparent lack of response or his seeming ingratitude, you may make huge withdrawals and undo all the good you've done. "After all we've done for you, the sacrifices we've made, how can you be so ungrateful? We try to be nice and you act like this. I can't believe it!"

It's hard not to get impatient. It takes character to be proactive, to focus on your Circle of Influence, to nurture growing things, and not to "pull up the flowers to see how the roots are coming."

But there really is no quick fix. Building and repairing relationships are long-term investments.

## Six Major Deposits

Let me suggest six major deposits that build the Emotional Bank Account.

### Understanding the Individual

Really seeking to understand another person is probably one of the most important deposits you can make, and it is the key to every other deposit. You simply don't know what constitutes a deposit to another person until you understand that individual. What might be a deposit for you—going for a walk to talk things over, going out for ice cream together, working on a common project—might not be perceived by someone else as a deposit at all. It might even be perceived as a withdrawal, if it doesn't touch the person's deep interests or needs.

One person's mission is another person's minutiae. To make a deposit, what is important to another person must be as important to you as the other person is to you. You may be working on a high priority project when your six-year-old child interrupts with something that seems trivial to you, but it may be very important from his point of view. It takes Habit 2 to recognize and recommit yourself to the value of that person and Habit 3 to subordinate your schedule to that human priority. By accepting the value he places on what he has to say, you show an understanding of him that makes a great deposit.

I have a friend whose son developed an avid interest in baseball. My friend wasn't interested in baseball at all. But one summer, he took his son to see every major league team play one game. The trip took over six weeks and cost a great deal of money, but it became a powerful bonding experience in their relationship.

My friend was asked on his return, "Do you like baseball that much?"

"No," he replied, "but I like my son that much."

I have another friend, a college professor, who had a terrible relationship with his teenage son. This man's entire life was essentially academic, and he felt his son was totally wasting his life by working with his hands instead of working to develop his mind. As a result, he was almost constantly on the boy's back, and, in moments of regret, he would try to make deposits that just didn't work. The boy perceived the gestures as new forms of rejection, comparison, and judgment, and they precipitated huge withdrawals. The relationship was turning sour, and it was breaking the father's heart.

One day I shared with him this principle of making what is important to the other person as important to you as the other person is to you. He took it deeply to heart. He engaged his son in a project to build a miniature Wall of China around their home. It was a consuming project, and they worked side by side on it for over a year and a half.

Through that bonding experience, the son moved through that phase in his life and into an increased desire to develop his mind. But the real benefit was what happened to the relationship. Instead of a sore spot, it became a source of joy and strength to both father and son.

Our tendency is to project out of our own autobiographies what we think other people want or need. We project our intentions on the behavior of others. We interpret what constitutes a deposit based on our own needs and desires, either now or when we were at a similar age or stage in life. If they don't interpret our effort as a deposit, our tendency is to take it as a rejection of our well intentioned effort and to give up.

The Golden Rule says to "Do unto others as you would have others do unto you." While on the surface that could mean to do for them what you would like to have done for you, I think the more essential meaning is to understand them deeply as individuals, the way you would want to be understood, and then to treat them in terms of that understanding. As one successful parent said about raising children, "Treat them all the same by treating them differently."

## Attending to the Little Things

The little kindnesses and courtesies are so important. Small discourtesies, little unkindnesses, little forms of disrespect make large withdrawals. In relationships, the little things are the big things.

I remember an evening I spent with two of my sons some years ago. It was an organized father and son outing, complete with gymnastics, wrestling matches, hotdogs, orangeade, and a movie—the works.

In the middle of the movie, Sean, who was then four years old, fell asleep in his seat. His older brother, Stephen, who was six, stayed awake, and we watched the rest of the movie together. When it was over, I picked Sean up in my arms, carried him out to the car and laid him in the back seat. It was very cold that night, so I took off my coat and gently arranged it over and around him.

When we arrived home, I quickly carried Sean in and tucked him into bed. After Stephen put on his "jammies" and brushed his teeth, I lay down next to him to talk about the night out together.

"How'd you like it, Stephen?"

"Fine," he answered.

"Did you have fun?"

"Yes."

"What did you like most?"

"I don't know. The trampoline, I guess."

"That was quite a thing, wasn't it—doing those somersaults and tricks in the air like that?"

There wasn't much response on his part. I found myself making conversation. I wondered why Stephen wouldn't open up more. He usually did when exciting things happened. I was a little disappointed. I sensed something was wrong; he had been so quiet on the way home and getting ready for bed.

Suddenly Stephen turned over on his side, facing the wall. I wondered why and lifted myself up just enough to see his eyes welling up with tears.

"What's wrong, honey? What is it?"

He turned back, and I could sense he was feeling some embarrassment for the tears and his quivering lips and chin.

"Daddy, if I were cold, would you put your coat around me, too?"

Of all the events of that special night out together, the most important was a little act of kindness—a momentary, unconscious showing of love to his little brother.

What a powerful, personal lesson that experience was to me then and is even now. People are very tender, very sensitive inside. I don't believe age or experience makes much difference. Inside, even within the most toughened and calloused exteriors, are the tender feelings and emotions of the heart.

### Keeping Commitments

Keeping a commitment or a promise is a major deposit; breaking one is a major withdrawal. In fact, there's probably not a more massive withdrawal than to make a promise that's important to someone and then not to come through. The next time a promise is made, they won't believe it. People tend to build their hopes around promises, particularly promises about their basic livelihood.

I've tried to adopt a philosophy as a parent never to make a promise I don't keep. I therefore try to make them very carefully, very sparingly, and to be aware of as many variables and contingencies as possible so that something doesn't suddenly come up to keep me from fulfilling it.

Occasionally, despite all my effort, the unexpected does come up, creating a situation where it would be unwise or impossible to keep a promise I've made. But I value that promise. I either keep it anyway, or explain the situation thoroughly to the person involved and ask to be released from the promise.

I believe that if you cultivate the habit of always keeping the promises you make, you build bridges of trust that span the gaps of understanding between you and your child. Then, when your child wants to do something you don't want him to do, and out of your maturity you can see consequences that the child cannot see, you can say, "Son, if you do this, I promise you that this will be the result." If that child has cultivated trust in your word, in your promises, he will act on your counsel.

### Clarifying Expectations

Imagine the difficulty you might encounter if you and your boss had different assumptions regarding whose *role* it was to create your job description.

"When am I going to get my job description?" you might ask.

"I've been waiting for you to bring one to me so that we could discuss it," your boss might reply.

"I thought defining my job was your role."

"That's not my role at all. Don't you remember? Right from the first, I said that how you do in the job largely depends on you."

"I thought you meant that the quality of my job depended on me. But I don't even know what my job really is."

Unclear expectations in the area of *goals* also undermine communication and trust.

"I did exactly what you asked me to do and here is the report."

"I don't want a report. The goal was to solve the problem—not to analyze it and report on it."

"I thought the goal was to get a handle on the problem so we could delegate it to someone else."

How many times have we had these kinds of conversations?

"You said . . ."

"No, you're wrong! I said . . ."

"You did not! You never said I was supposed to . . ."

"Oh, yes I did! I clearly said . . ."

"You never even mentioned . . ."

"But that was our agreement . . ."

The cause of almost all relationship difficulties is rooted in conflicting or ambiguous expectations around roles and goals.

Whether we are dealing with the question of who does what at work, how you communicate with your daughter when you tell her to clean her room, or who feeds the fish and takes out the garbage, we can be certain that unclear expectations will lead to misunderstanding, disappointment, and withdrawals of trust.

Many expectations are implicit. They haven't been explicitly stated or announced, but people nevertheless bring them to a particular situation. In marriage, for example, a man and a woman have implicit expectations of each other in their marriage roles. Although these expectations have not been discussed, or sometimes even recognized by the person who has them, fulfilling them makes great deposits in the relationship and violating them makes withdrawals.

That's why it's so important whenever you come into a new situation to get all the expectations out on the table. People will begin to judge each other through those expectations. And if they feel like their basic expectations have been violated, the reserve of trust is diminished. We create many negative situations by simply assuming that our expectations are self-evident and that they are clearly understood and shared by other people.

The deposit is to make the expectations clear and explicit in the beginning. This takes a real investment of time and effort up front, but it saves great amounts of time and effort down the road. When expectations are not clear and shared, people begin to become emotionally involved and simple misunderstandings become compounded, turning into personality clashes and communication breakdowns.

Clarifying expectations sometimes takes a great deal of courage. It seems easier to act as though differences don't exist and to hope things will work out than it is to face the differences and work together to arrive at a mutually agreeable set of expectations.

## Showing Personal Integrity

Personal Integrity generates trust and is the basis of many different kinds of deposits.

Lack of integrity can undermine almost any other effort to create high trust accounts. People can seek to understand, remember the little things, keep their promises, clarify and fulfill expectations, and still fail to build reserves of trust if they are inwardly duplicitous.

Integrity includes but goes beyond honesty. Honesty is telling the truth—in other words, *conforming our words to reality*. Integrity is *conforming reality to our words*—in other words, keeping promises and fulfilling expectations. This requires an integrated character, a oneness, primarily with self but also with life.

One of the most important ways to manifest integrity is to *be loyal to those who are not present*. In doing so, we build the trust of those who are present. When you defend those who are absent, you retain the trust of those present.

Suppose you and I were talking alone, and we were criticizing our supervisor in a way that we would not dare to do if he were present. Now what will happen when you and I have a falling out? You know I'm going to be discussing your weaknesses with someone else. That's what you and I did behind our supervisor's back. You know my nature. I'll sweet-talk you to your face and bad-mouth you behind your back. You've seen me do it.

That's the essence of duplicity. Does that build a reserve of trust in my account with you?

On the other hand, suppose you were to start criticizing our supervisor and I basically told you I agree with the content of some of the criticism and suggest that the two of us go directly to him and make an effective presentation on how things might be improved. Then what would you know I would do if someone were to criticize you to me behind your back?

For another example, suppose in my effort to build a relationship with you, I told you something someone else had shared with me in confidence. "I really shouldn't tell you this," I might say, "but since you're my friend. . . ." Would my betraying another person build my trust account with you? Or would you wonder if the things you had told me in confidence were being shared with others?

Such duplicity might appear to be making a deposit with the person you're with, but it is actually a withdrawal because you communicate your own lack of integrity. You may get the golden egg of temporary pleasure from putting someone down or sharing privileged information, but you're strangling the goose, weakening the relationship that provides enduring pleasure in association.

Integrity in an interdependent reality is simply this: you treat everyone by the same set of principles. As you do, people will come to trust you. They may not at first appreciate the honest confrontational experiences such integrity might generate. Confrontation takes considerable courage, and many people would prefer to take the course of least resistance, belittling and criticizing, betraying confidences, or participating in gossip about others behind their backs. But in the long run, people will trust and respect you if you are honest and open and kind with them. You care enough to confront. And to be trusted, it is said, is greater than to be loved. In the long run, I am convinced, to be trusted will be also to be loved.

When my son Joshua was quite young, he would frequently ask me a soul-searching question. Whenever I overreacted to someone else or was the least bit impatient or unkind, he was so vulnerable and so honest and our relationship was so good that he would simply look me in the eye and say, "Dad, do you love me?" If he thought I was breaking a basic principle of life toward someone else, he wondered if I wouldn't break it with him.

As a teacher, as well as a parent, I have found that the key to the ninety-nine is the one—particularly the one that is testing the patience and the good humor of the many. It is the love and the discipline of the one student, the one child, that communicates love for the others. It's how you treat the one that reveals how you regard the ninety-nine, because everyone is ultimately a one.

Integrity also means avoiding any communication that is deceptive, full of guile, or beneath the dignity of people. "A lie is any communication with intent to deceive," according to one definition of the word. Whether we communicate with words or behavior, if we have integrity, our intent cannot be to deceive.

## Apologizing Sincerely When You Make a Withdrawal

When we make withdrawals from the Emotional Bank Account, we need to apologize and we need to do it sincerely. Great deposits come in the sincere words:

"I was wrong."

"That was unkind of me."

"I showed you no respect."

"I gave you no dignity, and I'm deeply sorry."

"I embarrassed you in front of your friends and I had no call to do that. Even though I wanted to make a point, I never should have done it. I apologize."

It takes a great deal of character strength to apologize quickly out of one's heart rather than out of pity. A person must possess himself and have a deep sense of security in fundamental principles and values in order to genuinely apologize.

People with little internal security can't do it. It makes them too vulnerable. They feel it makes them appear soft and weak, and they fear that others will take advantage of their weakness. Their security is based on the opinions of other people, and they worry about what others might think. In addition, they usually feel justified in what they did. They rationalize their own wrong in the name of the other person's wrong, and if they apologize at all, it's superficial.

"If you're going to bow, bow low," says Eastern wisdom. "Pay the uttermost farthing," says the Christian ethic. To be a deposit, an apology must be sincere. And it must be perceived as sincere.

Leo Roskin taught, "It is the weak who are cruel. Gentleness can only be expected from the strong."

I was in my office at home one afternoon writing, of all things, on the subject of patience. I could hear the boys running up and down the hall making loud banging noises, and I could feel my own patience beginning to wane.

Suddenly, my son David started pounding on the bathroom door, yelling at the top of his lungs. "Let me in! Let me in!"

I rushed out of the office and spoke to him with great intensity. "David, do you have any idea how disturbing that is to me? Do you know how hard it is to try to concentrate and write creatively? Now, you go into your room and stay in there until you can behave yourself." So in he went, dejected, and shut the door.

As I turned around, I became aware of another problem. The boys had been playing tackle football in the four-foot-wide hallway, and one of them had been elbowed in the mouth. He was lying there in the hall, bleeding from the mouth. David, I discovered, had gone to the bathroom to get a wet towel for him. But his sister, Maria, who was taking a shower, wouldn't open the door.

When I realized that I had completely misinterpreted the situation and had overreacted, I immediately went in to apologize to David.

As I opened the door, the first thing he said to me was, "I won't forgive you."

"Well, why not, honey?" I replied. "Honestly, I didn't realize you were trying to help your brother. Why won't you forgive me?"

"Because you did the same thing last week," he replied. In other words, he was saying, "Dad, you're overdrawn, and you're not going to talk your way out of a problem you behaved yourself into."

Sincere apologies make deposits; repeated apologies interpreted as insincere make withdrawals. And the quality of the relationship reflects it.

It is one thing to make a mistake, and quite another thing not to admit it. People will forgive mistakes, because mistakes are usually of the mind, mistakes of judgment. But people will not easily forgive the mistakes of the heart, the ill intention, the bad motives, the prideful justifying cover-up of the first mistake.

### The Laws of Love and the Laws of Life

When we make deposits of unconditional love, when we live the primary laws of love, we encourage others to live the primary laws of life. In other words, when we truly love others without condition, without strings, we help them feel secure and safe and validated and affirmed in their essential worth, identity, and integrity. Their natural growth process is encouraged. We make it easier for them to live the laws of life—cooperation, contribution, self-discipline, integrity—and to discover and live true to the highest and best within them. We give them the freedom to act on their own inner imperatives rather than react to our conditions and limitations. This does not mean we become permissive or soft. That itself is a massive withdrawal. We counsel, we plead, we set limits and consequences. But we love, regardless.

When we violate the primary laws of love—when we attach strings and conditions to that gift—we actually encourage others to violate the primary laws of life. We put them in a reactive, defensive position where they feel they have to prove "I matter as a person, independent of you."

In reality, they aren't independent. They are counter-dependent, which is another form of dependency and is at the lowest end of the Maturity Continuum. They become reactive, almost enemy-centered, more concerned about defending their "rights" and producing evidence of their individuality than they are about proactively listening to and honoring their own inner imperatives.

Rebellion is a knot of the heart, not of the mind. The key is to make deposits—constant deposits of unconditional love.

*    *    *

I once had a friend who was dean of a very prestigious school.* He planned and saved for years to provide his son the opportunity to attend that institution, but when the time came, the boy refused to go.

This deeply concerned his father. Graduating from that particular school would have been a great asset to the boy. Besides, it was a family tradition. Three generations of attendance preceded the boy. The father pleaded and urged and talked. He also tried to listen to the boy to understand him, all the while hoping that the son would change his mind.

The subtle message being communicated was one of conditional love. The son felt that in a sense the father's desire for him to attend the school outweighed the value he placed on him as a person and as a son, which was terribly threatening. Consequently, he fought for and with his own identity and integrity, and he increased in his resolve and his efforts to rationalize his decision not to go.

After some intense soul-searching, the father decided to make a sacrifice—to renounce conditional love. He knew that his son might choose differently than he had wished; nevertheless, he and his wife resolved to love their son unconditionally, regardless of his choice. It was an extremely difficult thing to do because the value of his educational experience was so close to their hearts and because it was something they had planned and worked for since his birth.

The father and mother went through a very difficult rescripting process, struggling to really understand the nature of unconditional love. They communicated to the boy what they were doing and why, and told him that they had come to the point at which they could say in all honesty that his decision would not affect their complete feeling of unconditional love toward him. They didn't do this to manipulate him, to try to get him to "shape up." They did it as the logical extension of their growth and character.

The boy didn't give much of a response at the time, but his par-

---

* Some of the details of this story have been changed to protect the privacy of those involved.

ents had such a paradigm of unconditional love at that point that it would have made no difference in their feelings for him. About a week later, he told his parents that he had decided not to go. They were perfectly prepared for this response and continued to show unconditional love for him. Everything was settled and life went along normally.

A short time later, an interesting thing happened. Now that the boy no longer felt he had to defend his position, he searched within himself more deeply and found that he really did want to have this educational experience. He applied for admission, and then he told his father, who again showed unconditional love by fully accepting his son's decision. My friend was happy, but not excessively so, because he had truly learned to love without condition.

Dag Hammarskjöld, past Secretary-General of the United Nations, once made a profound, far-reaching statement: "It is more noble to give yourself completely to one individual than to labor diligently for the salvation of the masses."

I take that to mean that I could devote eight, ten, or twelve hours a day, five, six, or seven days a week to the thousands of people and projects "out there" and still not have a deep, meaningful relationship with my own spouse, with my own teenage son, with my closest working associate. And it would take more nobility of character—more humility, courage, and strength—to rebuild that one relationship than it would to continue putting in all those hours for all those people and causes.

In twenty-five years of consulting with organizations, I have been impressed over and over again by the power of that statement. Many of the problems in organizations stem from relationship difficulties at the very top—between two partners in a professional firm, between the owner and the president of a company, between the president and an executive vice-president. It truly takes more nobility of character to confront and resolve those issues than it does to continue to diligently work for the many projects and people "out there."

When I first came across Hammarskjold's statement, I was working in an organization where there were unclear expectations between the individual who was my right-hand man and myself.

I simply did not have the courage to confront our differences regarding role and goal expectations and values, particularly in our methods of administration. So I worked for a number of months in a compromise mode to avoid what might turn out to be an ugly confrontation. All the while, bad feelings were developing inside both of us.

After reading that it is more noble to give yourself completely to *one individual* than to labor diligently for the salvation of the masses, I was deeply affected by the idea of rebuilding that relationship.

I had to steel myself for what lay ahead, because I knew it would be hard to really get the issues out and to achieve a deep, common understanding and commitment. I remember actually shaking in anticipation of the visit. He seemed like such a hard man, so set in his own ways and so right in his own eyes; yet I needed his strengths and abilities. I was afraid a confrontation might jeopardize the relationship and result in my losing those strengths.

I went through a mental dress rehearsal of the anticipated visit, and I finally became settled within myself around the principles rather than the practices of what I was going to do and say. At last I felt peace of mind and the courage to have the communication.

When we met together, to my total surprise, I discovered that this man had been going through the very same process and had been longing for such a conversation. He was anything but hard and defensive.

Nevertheless, our administrative styles were considerably different, and the entire organization was responding to these differences. We both acknowledged the problems that our disunity had created. Over several visits, we were able to confront the deeper issues, to get them all out on the table, and to resolve them, one by one, with a spirit of high mutual respect. We were able to develop a powerful complementary team and and a deep personal affection which added tremendously to our ability to work effectively together.

Creating the unity necessary to run an effective business or a family or a marriage requires great personal strength and courage. No amount of technical administrative skill in laboring for the masses can make up for lack of nobility of personal character in developing relationships. It is at a very essential, one-on-one level that we live the primary laws of love and life.

# P Problems Are PC Opportunities

This experience also taught me another powerful paradigm of interdependence. It deals with the way in which we see problems. I had lived for months trying to avoid the problem, seeing it as a source of irritation, a stumbling block, and wishing it would somehow go away. But, as it turned out, the very problem created the opportunity to build a deep relationship that empowered us to work together as a strong complementary team.

I suggest that in an interdependent situation, *every P problem is a PC opportunity*—a chance to build the Emotional Bank Accounts that significantly affect interdependent production.

When parents see their children's problems as opportunities to build the relationship instead of as negative, burdensome irritations, it totally changes the nature of parent-child interaction. Parents become more willing, even excited, about deeply understanding and helping their children. When a child comes to them with a problem, instead of thinking, "Oh, no! Not another problem!" their paradigm is, "Here is a great opportunity for me to really help my child and to invest in our relationship." Many interactions change from transactional to transformational, and strong bonds of love and trust are created as children sense the value parents give to their problems and to them as individuals.

This paradigm is powerful in business as well. One department store chain that operates from this paradigm has created a great loyalty among its customers. Any time a customer comes into the store with a problem, no matter how small, the clerks immediately see it as an opportunity to build the relationship with the customer. They respond with a cheerful, positive desire to solve the problem in a way that will make the customer happy. They treat the customer with such grace and respect, giving such second-mile service, that many of the customers don't even think of going anywhere else.

By recognizing that the P/PC balance is necessary to effectiveness in an interdependent reality, we can value our problems as opportunities to increase PC.

# The Habits of Interdependence

With the paradigm of the Emotional Bank Account in mind, we're ready to move into the habits of Public Victory, of success in working with other people. As we do, we can see how these habits work together to create effective interdependence. We can also see how powerfully scripted we are in other patterns of thought and behavior.

In addition, we can see on an even deeper level that effective interdependence can only be achieved by truly independent people. It is impossible to achieve Public Victory with popular "Win/Win negotiation" techniques or "reflective listening" techniques or "creative problem-solving" techniques that focus on personality and truncate the vital character base.

Let's now focus on each of the Public Victory habits in depth.

# HABIT 4:
## THINK WIN/WIN

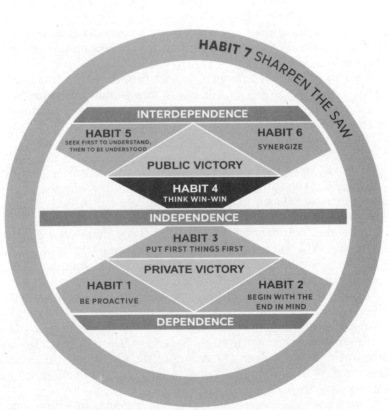

# Principles of Interpersonal Leadership

*We have committed the Golden Rule to memory;*
*let us now commit it to life.*

EDWIN MARKHAM

ONE TIME I WAS ASKED TO WORK WITH A COMPANY whose president was very concerned about the lack of cooperation among his people.

"Our basic problem, Stephen, is that they're selfish," he said. "They just won't cooperate. I know if they would cooperate, we could produce so much more. Can you help us develop a human relations program that will solve the problem?"

"Is your problem the people or the paradigm?" I asked.

"Look for yourself," he replied.

So I did. And I found that there was a real selfishness, an unwillingness to cooperate, a resistance to authority, defensive communication. I could see that overdrawn Emotional Bank Accounts had created a culture of low trust. But I pressed the question.

"Let's look at it deeper," I suggested. "Why don't your people cooperate? What is the reward for not cooperating?"

"There's no reward for not cooperating," he assured me. "The rewards are much greater if they do cooperate."

"Are they?" I asked. Behind a curtain on one wall of this man's office was a chart. On the chart were a number of racehorses all lined up on a track. Superimposed on the face of each horse was the face of one of his managers. At the end of the track was a beautiful travel poster of Bermuda, an idyllic picture of blue skies and fleecy clouds and a romantic couple walking hand in hand down a white sandy beach.

Once a week, this man would bring all his people into this office and talk cooperation. "Let's all work together. We'll all make more money if we do." Then he would pull the curtain and show them the chart. "Now which of you is going to win the trip to Bermuda?"

It was like telling one flower to grow and watering another, like saying "firings will continue until morale improves." He wanted cooperation. He wanted his people to work together, to share ideas, to all benefit from the effort. But he was setting them up in competition with each other. One manager's success meant failure for the other managers.

As with many, many problems between people in business, family, and other relationships, the problem in this company was the result of a flawed paradigm. The president was trying to get the fruits of cooperation from a paradigm of competition. And when it didn't work, he wanted a technique, a program, a quick fix antidote to make his people cooperate.

But you can't change the fruit without changing the root. Working on the attitudes and behaviors would have been hacking at the leaves. So we focused instead on producing personal and organizational excellence in an entirely different way by developing information and reward systems which reinforced the value of cooperation.

Whether you are the president of a company or the janitor, the moment you step from independence into interdependence in any capacity, you step into a leadership role. You are in a position of influencing other people. And the habit of effective interpersonal leadership is Think Win/Win.

## SIX PARADIGMS OF HUMAN INTERACTION

Win/Win is not a technique; it's a total philosophy of human interaction. In fact, it is one of six paradigms of interaction. The alternative paradigms are Win/Lose, Lose/Win, Lose/Lose, Win, and Win/Win or No Deal.

- Win/Win
- Win/Lose
- Lose/Win
- Lose/Lose
- Win
- Win/Win or No Deal

### Win/Win

Win/Win is a frame of mind and heart that constantly seeks mutual benefit in all human interactions. Win/Win means that

agreements or solutions are mutually beneficial, mutually satisfying. With a Win/Win solution, all parties feel good about the
decision and feel committed to the action plan. Win/Win sees
life as a cooperative, not a competitive arena. Most people tend to
think in terms of dichotomies: strong or weak, hardball or softball,
win or lose. But that kind of thinking is fundamentally flawed. It's
based on power and position rather than on principle. Win/Win is
based on the paradigm that there is plenty for everybody, that one
person's success is not achieved at the expense or exclusion of the
success of others.

Win/Win is a belief in the Third Alternative. It's not your way or
my way; it's a *better* way, a higher way.

## Win/Lose

One alternative to Win/Win is Win/Lose, the paradigm of the
race to Bermuda. It says "If I win, you lose."

In leadership style, Win/Lose is the authoritarian approach:
"I get my way; you don't get yours." Win/Lose people are prone to
use position, power, credentials, possessions, or personality to get
their way.

Most people have been deeply scripted in the Win/Lose mentality since birth. First and most important of the powerful forces
at work is the family. When one child is compared with another—
when patience, understanding or love is given or withdrawn on
the basis of such comparisons—people are into Win/Lose thinking. Whenever love is given on a conditional basis, when someone
has to earn love, what's being communicated to them is that they
are not intrinsically valuable or lovable. Value does not lie inside
them, it lies outside. It's in comparison with somebody else or
against some expectation.

And what happens to a young mind and heart, highly vulnerable, highly dependent upon the support and emotional affirmation
of the parents, in the face of conditional love? The child is molded,
shaped, and programmed in the Win/Lose mentality.

"If I'm better than my brother, my parents will love me more."

"My parents don't love me as much as they love my sister. I must
not be as valuable."

Another powerful scripting agency is the peer group. A child
first wants acceptance from his parents and then from his peers,
whether they be siblings or friends. And we all know how cruel
peers sometimes can be. They often accept or reject totally on the

basis of conformity to their expectations and norms, providing additional scripting toward Win/Lose.

The academic world reinforces Win/Lose scripting. The "normal distribution curve" basically says that you got an "A" because someone else got a "C." It interprets an individual's value by comparing him or her to everyone else. No recognition is given to intrinsic value; everyone is extrinsically defined.

"Oh, how nice to see you here at our PTA meeting. You ought to be really proud of your daughter, Caroline. She's in the upper 10 percent."

"That makes me feel good."

"But your son, Johnny, is in trouble. He's in the lower quartile."

"Really? Oh, that's terrible! What can we do about it?"

What this kind of comparative information doesn't tell you is that perhaps Johnny is going on all eight cylinders while Caroline is coasting on four of her eight. But people are not graded against their potential or against the full use of their present capacity. They are graded in relation to other people. And grades are carriers of social value; they open doors of opportunity or they close them. Competition, not cooperation, lies at the core of the educational process. Cooperation, in fact, is usually associated with cheating.

Another powerful programming agent is athletics, particularly for young men in their high school or college years. Often they develop the basic paradigm that life is a big game, a zero sum game where some win and some lose. "Winning" is "beating" in the athletic arena.

Another agent is law. We live in a litigious society. The first thing many people think about when they get into trouble is suing someone, taking them to court, "winning" at someone else's expense. But defensive minds are neither creative nor cooperative.

Certainly we need law or else society will deteriorate. It provides survival, but it doesn't create synergy. At best it results in compromise. Law is based on an adversarial concept. The recent trend of encouraging lawyers and law schools to focus on peaceable negotiation, the techniques of Win/Win, and the use of private courts, may not provide the ultimate solution, but it does reflect a growing awareness of the problem.

Certainly there is a place for Win/Lose thinking in truly competitive and low-trust situations. But most of life is not a competition. We don't have to live each day competing with our spouse, our children, our coworkers, our neighbors, and our friends. "Who's winning in your marriage?' " is a ridiculous question. If both people aren't winning, both are losing.

Most of life is an interdependent, not an independent, reality. Most results you want depend on cooperation between you and others. And the Win/Lose mentality is dysfunctional to that cooperation.

## Lose/Win

Some people are programmed the other way—Lose/Win.

"I lose, you win."

"Go ahead. Have your way with me."

"Step on me again. Everyone does."

"I'm a loser. I've always been a loser."

"I'm a peacemaker. I'll do anything to keep peace."

Lose/Win is worse than Win/Lose because it has no standards— no demands, no expectations, no vision. People who think Lose/ Win are usually quick to please or appease. They seek strength from popularity or acceptance. They have little courage to express their own feelings and convictions and are easily intimidated by the ego strength of others.

In negotiation, Lose/Win is seen as capitulation—giving in or giving up. In leadership style, it's permissiveness or indulgence. Lose/Win means being a nice guy, even if "nice guys finish last."

Win/Lose people love Lose/Win people because they can feed on them. They love their weaknesses—they take advantage of them. Such weaknesses complement their strengths.

But the problem is that Lose/Win people bury a lot of feelings. And unexpressed feelings never die: they're buried alive and come forth later in uglier ways. Psychosomatic illnesses, particularly of the respiratory, nervous, and circulatory systems, often are the reincarnation of cumulative resentment, deep disappointment and disillusionment repressed by the Lose/Win mentality. Disproportionate rage or anger, overreaction to minor provocation, and cynicism are other embodiments of suppressed emotion.

People who are constantly repressing, not transcending feelings toward a higher meaning find that it affects the quality of their self-esteem and eventually the quality of their relationships with others.

Both Win/Lose and Lose/Win are weak positions, based in personal insecurities. In the short run, Win/Lose will produce more results because it draws on the often considerable strengths and talents of the people at the top. Lose/Win is weak and chaotic from the outset.

Many executives, managers, and parents swing back and forth, as if on a pendulum, from Win/Lose inconsideration to Lose/Win indulgence. When they can't stand confusion and lack of structure, direction, expectation, and discipline any longer, they swing back to Win/Lose—until guilt undermines their resolve and drives them back to Lose/Win—until anger and frustration drive them back to Win/Lose again.

### Lose/Lose

When two Win/Lose people get together—that is, when two determined, stubborn, ego-invested individuals interact—the result will be Lose/Lose. Both will lose. Both will become vindictive and want to "get back" or "get even," blind to the fact that murder is suicide, that revenge is a two-edged sword.

I know of a divorce in which the husband was directed by the judge to sell the assets and turn over half the proceeds to his ex-wife. In compliance, he sold a car worth over $10,000 for $50 and gave $25 to the wife. When the wife protested, the court clerk checked on the situation and discovered that the husband was proceeding in the same manner systematically through all of the assets.

Some people become so centered on an enemy, so totally obsessed with the behavior of another person that they become blind to everything except their desire for that person to lose, even if it means losing themselves. Lose/Lose is the philosophy of adversarial conflict, the philosophy of war.

Lose/Lose is also the philosophy of the highly dependent person without inner direction who is miserable and thinks everyone else should be, too. "If nobody ever wins, perhaps being a loser isn't so bad."

### Win

Another common alternative is simply to think Win. People with the Win mentality don't necessarily want someone else to lose. That's irrelevant. What matters is that they get what they want.

When there is no sense of contest or competition, Win is probably the most common approach in everyday negotiation. A person with the Win mentality thinks in terms of securing his own ends—and leaving it to others to secure theirs.

## Which Option Is Best?

Of these five philosophies discussed so far—Win/Win, Win/Lose, Lose/Win, Lose/Lose, and Win—which is the most effective? The answer is, "It depends." If you win a football game, that means the other team loses. If you work in a regional office that is miles away from another regional office, and you don't have any functional relationship between the offices, you may want to compete in a Win/Lose situation to stimulate business. However, you would not want to set up a Win/Lose situation like the "Race to Bermuda" contest within a company or in a situation where you need cooperation among people or groups of people to achieve maximum success.

If you value a relationship and the issue isn't really that important, you may want to go for Lose/Win in some circumstances to genuinely affirm the other person. "What I want isn't as important to me as my relationship with you. Let's do it your way this time." You might also go for Lose/Win if you feel the expense of time and effort to achieve a win of any kind would violate other higher values. Maybe it just isn't worth it.

There are circumstances in which you would want to Win, and you wouldn't be highly concerned with the relationship of that win to others. If your child's life were in danger, for example, you might be peripherally concerned about other people and circumstances. But saving that life would be supremely important.

The best choice, then, depends on reality. The challenge is to read that reality accurately and not to translate Win/Lose or other scripting into every situation.

Most situations, in fact, are part of an interdependent reality, and then Win/Win is really the only viable alternative of the five.

Win/Lose is not viable because, although I appear to win in a confrontation with you, your feelings, your attitudes toward me and our relationship have been affected. If I am a supplier to your company, for example, and I win on my terms in a particular negotiation, I may get what I want now. But will you come to me again? My short-term Win will really be a long-term Lose if I don't get your repeat business. So an interdependent Win/Lose is really Lose/Lose in the long run.

If we come up with a Lose/Win, you may appear to get what

you want for the moment. But how will that affect my attitude about working with you, about fulfilling the contract? I may not feel as anxious to please you. I may carry battle scars with me into any future negotiations. My attitude about you and your company may be spread as I associate with others in the industry. So we're into Lose/Lose again. Lose/Lose obviously isn't viable in any context.

And if I focus on my own Win and don't even consider your point of view, there's no basis for any kind of productive relationship.

In the long run, if it isn't a win for both of us, we both lose. That's why Win/Win is the only real alternative in interdependent realities.

I worked with a client once, the president of a large chain of retail stores, who said, "Stephen, this Win/Win idea sounds good, but it is so idealistic. The tough, realistic business world isn't like that. There's Win/Lose everywhere, and if you're not out there playing the game, you just can't make it."

"All right," I said, "try going for Win/Lose with your customers. Is that realistic?"

"Well, no," he replied.

"Why not?"

"I'd lose my customers."

"Then, go for Lose/Win—give the store away. Is that realistic?"

"No. No margin, no mission."

As we considered the various alternatives, Win/Win appeared to be the only truly realistic approach.

"I guess that's true with customers," he admitted, "but not with suppliers."

"You are the customer of the supplier," I said. "Why doesn't the same principle apply?"

"Well, we recently renegotiated our lease agreements with the mall operators and owners," he said. "We went in with a Win/Win attitude. We were open, reasonable, conciliatory. But they saw that position as being soft and weak, and they took us to the cleaners."

"Well, why did you go for Lose/Win?" I asked.

"We didn't. We went for Win/Win."

"I thought you said they took you to the cleaners."

"They did."

"In other words, you lost."

"That's right."

"And they won."

"That's right."

"So what's that called?"

When he realized that what he had called Win/Win was really Lose/Win, he was shocked. And as we examined the long-term impact of that Lose/Win, the suppressed feelings, the trampled values, the resentment that seethed under the surface of the relationship, we agreed that it was really a loss for both parties in the end.

If this man had had a real Win/Win attitude, he would have stayed longer in the communication process, listened to the mall owner more, then expressed his point of view with more courage. He would have continued in the Win/Win spirit until a solution was reached they both felt good about. And that solution, that Third Alternative, would have been synergistic—probably something neither of them had thought of on his own.

## Win/Win or No Deal

If these individuals had not come up with a synergistic solution—one that was agreeable to both—they could have gone for an even higher expression of Win/Win—Win/Win or No Deal.

*No Deal* basically means that if we can't find a solution that would benefit us both, we agree to disagree agreeably—No Deal. No expectations have been created, no performance contracts established. I don't hire you or we don't take on a particular assignment together because it's obvious that our values or our goals are going in opposite directions. It is so much better to realize this up front instead of downstream when expectations have been created and both parties have been disillusioned.

When you have No Deal as an option in your mind, you feel liberated because you have no need to manipulate people, to push your own agenda, to drive for what you want. You can be open. You can really try to understand the deeper issues underlying the positions.

With No Deal as an option, you can honestly say, "I only want to go for Win/Win. I want to win, and I want you to win. I wouldn't want to get my way and have you not feel good about it, because downstream it would eventually surface and create a withdrawal. On the other hand, I don't think you would feel good if you got your way and I gave in. So let's work for a Win/Win. Let's really hammer it out. And if we can't find it, then let's agree that we

won't make a deal at all. It would be better not to deal than to live
with a decision that wasn't right for us both. Then maybe another
time we might be able to get together."

Some time after learning the concept of Win/Win or No Deal,
the president of a small computer software company shared with
me the following experience.

"We had developed new software which we sold on a five-year
contract to a particular bank. The bank president was excited
about it, but his people weren't really behind the decision.

"About a month later, that bank changed presidents. The new
president came to me and said, 'I am uncomfortable with these
software conversions. I have a mess on my hands. My people are
all saying that they can't go through this and I really feel I just
can't push it at this point in time.'

"My own company was in deep financial trouble. I knew I had
every legal right to enforce the contract. But I had become convinced of the value of the principle of Win/Win.

"So I told him 'We have a contract. Your bank has secured our
products and our services to convert you to this program. But we
understand that you're not happy about it. So what we'd like to
do is give you back the contract, give you back your deposit, and
if you are ever looking for a software solution in the future, come
back and see us.'

"I literally walked away from an $84,000 contract. It was close
to financial suicide. But I felt that, in the long run, if the principle
were true, it would come back and pay dividends.

"Three months later, the new president called me. "I'm now going to make changes in my data processing,' he said, 'and I want to
do business with you.' He signed a contract for $240,000."

Anything less than Win/Win in an interdependent reality is a
poor second best that will have impact in the long-term relationship. The cost of that impact needs to be carefully considered. If
you can't reach a true Win/Win, you're very often better off to go
for No Deal.

Win/Win or No Deal provides tremendous emotional freedom
in the family relationship. If family members can't agree on a
video that everyone will enjoy, they can simply decide to do something else—No Deal—rather than having some enjoy the evening
at the expense of others.

\*    \*    \*

I have a friend whose family has been involved in singing to-gether for several years. When they were young, she arranged the music, made the costumes, accompanied them on the piano and directed the performances.

As the children grew older, their taste in music began to change and they wanted to have more say in what they performed and what they wore. They became less responsive to direction.

Because she had years of experience in performing herself and felt closer to the needs of the older people at the rest homes where they planned to perform, she didn't feel that many of the ideas they were suggesting would be appropriate. At the same time, however, she recognized their need to express themselves and to be part of the decision-making process.

So she set up a Win/Win or No Deal. She told them she wanted to arrive at an agreement that everyone felt good about—or they would simply find other ways to enjoy their talents. As a result, everyone felt free to express his or her feelings and ideas as they worked to set up a Win/Win agreement, knowing that whether or not they could agree, there would be no emotional strings.

The Win/Win or No Deal approach is most realistic at the *beginning* of a business relationship or enterprise. In a continuing business relationship, No Deal may not be a viable option, which can create serious problems, especially for family businesses or businesses that are begun initially on the basis of friendship.

In an effort to preserve the relationship, people sometimes go on for years making one compromise after another, thinking Win/Lose or Lose/Win even while talking Win/Win. This creates serious problems for the people and for the business, particularly if the competition operates on Win/Win and synergy.

Without No Deal, many such businesses simply deteriorate and either fail or have to be turned over to professional managers. Experience shows that it is often better in setting up a family business or a business between friends to acknowledge the possibility of No Deal downstream and to establish some kind of buy/sell agreement so that the business can prosper without permanently damaging the relationship.

Of course there are some relationships where No Deal is not viable. I wouldn't abandon my child or my spouse and go for No Deal (it would be better, if necessary, to go for compromise—a low form of Win/Win). But in many cases, it is possible to go into negotiation with a full Win/Win or No Deal attitude. And the freedom in that attitude is incredible.

## FIVE DIMENSIONS OF WIN/WIN

Think Win/Win is the habit of interpersonal leadership. It involves the exercise of each of the unique human endowments—self-awareness, imagination, conscience, and independent will—in our relationships with others. It involves mutual learning, mutual influence, mutual benefits.

It takes great courage as well as consideration to create these mutual benefits, particularly if we're interacting with others who are deeply scripted in Win/Lose.

That is why this habit involves principles of interpersonal leadership. Effective interpersonal leadership requires the vision, the proactive initiative and the security, guidance, wisdom, and power that come from principle-centered personal leadership.

The principle of Win/Win is fundamental to success in all our interactions, and it embraces five interdependent dimensions of life. It begins with *character* and moves toward *relationships*, out of which flow *agreements*. It is nurtured in an environment where *structure and systems* are based on Win/Win. And it involves *process*; we cannot achieve Win/Win ends with Win/Lose or Lose/Win means.

The following diagram shows how these five dimensions relate to each other.

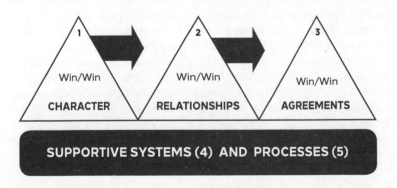

Now let's consider each of the five dimensions in turn.

## Character

Character is the foundation of Win/Win, and everything else builds on that foundation. There are three character traits essential to the Win/Win paradigm.

INTEGRITY. We've already defined integrity as the value we place on ourselves. Habits 1, 2, and 3 help us develop and maintain integrity. As we clearly identify our values and proactively organize and execute around those values on a daily basis, we develop self-awareness and independent will by making and keeping meaningful promises and commitments.

There's no way to go for a Win in our own lives if we don't even know, in a deep sense, what constitutes a Win—what is, in fact, harmonious with our innermost values. And if we can't make and keep commitments to ourselves as well as to others, our commitments become meaningless. We know it; others know it. They sense duplicity and become guarded. There's no foundation of trust and Win/Win becomes an ineffective superficial technique. Integrity is the cornerstone in the foundation.

MATURITY. Maturity is *the balance between courage and consideration*. I first learned this definition of maturity in the fall of 1955 from a marvelous professor, Hrand Saxenian, who instructed my Control class at the Harvard Business School. He taught the finest, simplest, most practical, yet profound, definition of emotional maturity I've ever come across—"the ability to express one's own feelings and convictions balanced with consideration for the thoughts and feelings of others." As a part of his doctoral research, Hrand Saxenian had developed this criterion over years of historical and direct field research. He later wrote up his original research format in its completeness with supportive reasoning and application suggestions in a *Harvard Business Review* article (January–February 1958). Even though it is complementary and also developmental, Hrand's use of the word "maturity" is different from its use in the 7 Habits "Maturity Continuum," which focuses on a growth and development process from dependency through independency to interdependency.

If you examine many of the psychological tests used for hiring, promoting, and training purposes, you will find that they are designed to evaluate this kind of maturity. Whether it's called the ego strength/empathy balance, the self confidence/respect for others balance, the concern for people/concern for tasks balance, "I'm okay, you're okay" in transactional analysis language, or 9.1, 1.9, 5.5, 9.9, in management grid language—the quality sought for is the balance of what I call courage and consideration.

Respect for this quality is deeply ingrained in the theory of human interaction, management, and leadership. It is a deep embodiment of the P/PC balance. While courage may focus on getting the golden egg, consideration deals with the long-term welfare of the other stakeholders. The basic task of leadership is to increase the standard of living and the quality of life for all stakeholders.

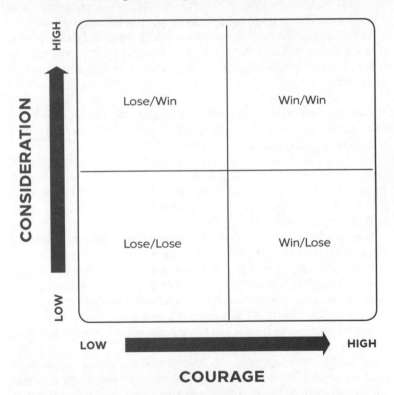

Many people think in dichotomies, in either/or terms. They think if you're nice, you're not tough. But Win/Win is nice . . . and tough. It's twice as tough as Win/Lose. To go for Win/Win, you not only have to be nice, you have to be courageous. You not only have to be empathic, you have to be confident. You not only have to be considerate and sensitive, you have to be brave. To do that, to achieve that balance between courage and consideration, is the essence of real maturity and is fundamental to Win/Win.

If I'm high on courage and low on consideration, how will I think? Win/Lose. I'll be strong and ego bound. I'll have the courage of my convictions, but I won't be very considerate of yours.

To compensate for my lack of internal maturity and emotional strength, I might borrow strength from my position and power, or from my credentials, my seniority, my affiliations.

If I'm high on consideration and low on courage, I'll think Lose/Win. I'll be so considerate of your convictions and desires that I won't have the courage to express and actualize my own.

High courage and consideration are both essential to Win/Win. It is the balance that is the mark of real maturity. If I have it, I can listen, I can empathically understand, but I can also courageously confront.

ABUNDANCE MENTALITY.   The third character trait essential to Win/Win is the Abundance Mentality, the paradigm that there is plenty out there for everybody.

Most people are deeply scripted in what I call the Scarcity Mentality. They see life as having only so much, as though there were only one pie out there. And if someone were to get a big piece of the pie, it would mean less for everybody else. The Scarcity Mentality is the zero-sum paradigm of life.

People with a Scarcity Mentality have a very difficult time sharing recognition and credit, power or profit—even with those who help in the production. They also have a very hard time being genuinely happy for the successes of other people—even, and sometimes especially, members of their own family or close friends and associates. It's almost as if something is being taken from them when someone else receives special recognition or windfall gain or has remarkable success or achievement.

Although they might verbally express happiness for others' success, inwardly they are eating their hearts out. Their sense of worth comes from being compared, and someone else's success, to some degree, means their failure. Only so many people can be "A" students; only one person can be "number one." To "win" simply means to "beat."

Often, people with a Scarcity Mentality harbor secret hopes that others might suffer misfortune—not terrible misfortune, but acceptable misfortune that would keep them "in their place." They're always comparing, always competing. They give their energies to possessing things or other people in order to increase their sense of worth.

They want other people to be the way they want them to be. They often want to clone them, and they surround themselves with "yes" people—people who won't challenge them, people who are weaker than they.

It's difficult for people with a Scarcity Mentality to be members of a complementary team. They look on differences as signs of insubordination and disloyalty.

The Abundance Mentality, on the other hand, flows out of a deep inner sense of personal worth and security. It is the paradigm that there is plenty out there and enough to spare for everybody. It results in sharing of prestige, of recognition, of profits, of decision making. It opens possibilities, options, alternatives, and creativity.

The Abundance Mentality takes the personal joy, satisfaction, and fulfillment of Habits 1, 2, and 3 and turns it outward, appreciating the uniqueness, the inner direction, the proactive nature of others. It recognizes the unlimited possibilities for positive interactive growth and development, creating new Third Alternatives.

Public Victory does not mean victory over other people. It means success in effective interaction that brings mutually beneficial results to everyone involved. Public Victory means working together, communicating together, making things happen together that even the same people couldn't make happen by working independently. And Public Victory is an outgrowth of the Abundance Mentality paradigm.

A character rich in integrity, maturity, and the Abundance Mentality has a genuineness that goes far beyond technique, or lack of it, in human interaction.

One thing I have found particularly helpful to Win/Lose people in developing a Win/Win character is to associate with some model or mentor who really thinks Win/Win. When people are deeply scripted in Win/Lose or other philosophies and regularly associate with others who are likewise scripted, they don't have much opportunity to see and experience the Win/Win philosophy in action. So I recommend reading literature, such as the inspiring biography of Anwar Sadat, *In Search of Identity*, and seeing movies like *Chariots of Fire* or plays like *Les Misérables* that expose you to models of Win/Win.

But remember: If we search deeply enough within ourselves—beyond the scripting, beyond the learned attitudes and behaviors—the real validation of Win/Win, as well as every other correct principle, is in our own lives.

### Relationships

From the foundation of character, we build and maintain Win/Win relationships. The trust, the Emotional Bank Account, is the essence of Win/Win. Without trust, the best we can do is compromise; without trust, we lack the credibility for open, mutual learning and communication and real creativity.

But if our Emotional Bank Account is high, credibility is no longer an issue. Enough deposits have been made so that you know and I know that we deeply respect each other. We're focused on the issues, not on personalities or positions.

Because we trust each other, we're open. We put our cards on the table. Even though we see things differently, I know that you're willing to listen with respect while I describe the young woman to you, and you know that I'll treat your description of the old woman with the same respect. We're both committed to try to understand each other's point of view deeply and to work together for the Third Alternative, the synergistic solution, that will be a better answer for both of us.

A relationship where bank accounts are high and both parties are deeply committed to Win/Win is the ideal springboard for tremendous synergy (Habit 6). That relationship neither makes the issues any less real or important, nor eliminates the differences in perspective. But it does eliminate the negative energy normally focused on differences in personality and position and creates a positive, cooperative energy focused on thoroughly understanding the issues and resolving them in a mutually beneficial way.

But what if that kind of relationship isn't there? What if you have to work out an agreement with someone who hasn't even heard of Win/Win and is deeply scripted in Win/Lose or some other philosophy?

Dealing with Win/Lose is the real test of Win/Win. Rarely is Win/Win easily achieved in any circumstance. Deep issues and fundamental differences have to be dealt with. But it is much easier when both parties are aware of and committed to it and where there is a high Emotional Bank Account in the relationship.

When you're dealing with a person who is coming from a paradigm of Win/Lose, the relationship is still the key. The place to focus is on your Circle of Influence. You make deposits into the Emotional Bank Account through genuine courtesy, respect, and appreciation for that person and for the other point of view. You stay longer in the communication process. You listen more, you listen in greater depth. You express yourself with greater courage. You aren't reactive. You go deeper inside yourself for strength of character to be proactive. You keep hammering it out until the other person begins to realize that you genuinely want the resolution to be a real win for both of you. That very process is a tremendous deposit in the Emotional Bank Account.

And the stronger you are—the more genuine your character, the higher your level of proactivity, the more committed you really are to Win/Win—the more powerful your influence will be with that other person. This is the real test of interpersonal leadership. It goes beyond *transactional* leadership into *transformational* leadership, transforming the individuals involved as well as the relationship.

Because Win/Win is a principle people can validate in their own lives, you will be able to bring most people to a realization that they will win more of what they want by going for what you both want. But there will be a few who are so deeply embedded in the Win/Lose mentality that they just won't think Win/Win. So remember that No Deal is always an option. Or you may occasionally choose to go for the low form of Win/Win—compromise.

It's important to realize that not all decisions need to be Win/Win, even when the Emotional Bank Account is high. Again, the key is the relationship. If you and I worked together, for example, and you were to come to me and say, "Stephen, I know you won't like this decision. I don't have time to explain it to you, let alone get you involved. There's a good possibility you'll think it's wrong. But will you support it?"

If you had a positive Emotional Bank Account with me, of course I'd support it. I'd hope you were right and I was wrong. I'd work to make your decision work.

But if the Emotional Bank Account weren't there, and if I were reactive, I wouldn't really support it. I might say I would to your face, but behind your back I wouldn't be very enthusiastic.

I wouldn't make the investment necessary to make it succeed. "It didn't work," I'd say. "So what do you want me to do now?"

If I were overreactive, I might even torpedo your decision and do what I could to make sure others did too. Or I might become "maliciously obedient" and do exactly and only what you tell me to do, accepting no responsibility for results.

During the five years I lived in Great Britain, I saw that country brought twice to its knees because the train conductors were maliciously obedient in following all the rules and procedures written on paper.

An agreement means very little in letter without the character and relationship base to sustain it in spirit. So we need to approach Win/Win from a genuine desire to invest in the relationships that make it possible.

## Agreements

From relationships flow the agreements that give definition and direction to Win/Win. They are sometimes called *performance agreements* or *partnership agreements*, shifting the paradigm of productive interaction from vertical to horizontal, from hovering supervision to self-supervision, from positioning to being partners in success.

Win/Win agreements cover a wide scope of interdependent interaction. We discussed one important application when we talked about delegation in the "Green and Clean" story in Habit 3. The same five elements we listed there provide the structure for Win/ Win agreements between employers and employees, between independent people working together on projects, between groups of people cooperatively focused on a common objective, between companies and suppliers—between any people who need to interact to accomplish. They create an effective way to clarify and manage expectations between people involved in any interdependent endeavor.

In the Win/Win agreement, the following five elements are made very explicit:

> *Desired results* (not methods) identify what is to be done and when.
> *Guidelines* specify the parameters (principles, policies, etc.) within which results are to be accomplished.
> *Resources* identify the human, financial, technical, or organizational support available to help accomplish the results.

*Accountability* sets up the standards of performance and the time of evaluation.

*Consequences* specify—good and bad, natural and logical—what does and will happen as a result of the evaluation.

These five elements give Win/Win agreements a life of their own. A clear mutual understanding and agreement up front in these areas creates a standard against which people can measure their own success.

Traditional authoritarian supervision is a Win/Lose paradigm. It's also the result of an overdrawn Emotional Bank Account. If you don't have trust or a common vision of desired results, you tend to hover over, check up on, and direct. Trust isn't there, so you feel as though you have to control people.

But if the trust account is high, what is your method? Get out of their way. As long as you have an up-front Win/Win agreement and they know exactly what is expected, your role is to be a source of help and to receive their accountability reports.

It is much more ennobling to the human spirit to let people judge themselves than to judge them. And in a high trust culture, it's much more accurate. In many cases people know in their hearts how things are going much better than the records show. Discernment is often far more accurate than either observation or measurement.

### Win/Win Management Training

Several years ago, I was indirectly involved in a consulting project with a very large banking institution that had scores of branches. They wanted us to evaluate and improve their management training program, which was supported by an annual budget of $750,000. The program involved selecting college graduates and putting them through twelve two-week assignments in various departments over a six-month period of time so that they could get a general sense of the industry. They spent two weeks in commercial loans, two weeks in industrial loans, two weeks in marketing, two weeks in operations, and so forth. At the end of the six-month period, they were assigned as assistant managers in the various branch banks.

Our assignment was to evaluate the six-month formal training period. As we began, we discovered that the most difficult part of the assignment was to get a clear picture of the desired results.

We asked the top executives the key hard question: "What should these people be able to do when they finish the program?" And the answers we got were vague and often contradictory.

The training program dealt with methods, not results; so we suggested that they set up a pilot training program based on a different paradigm called "learner-controlled instruction." This was a Win/Win agreement that involved identifying specific objectives and criteria that would demonstrate their accomplishment and identifying the guidelines, resources, accountability, and consequences that would result when the objectives were met. The consequences in this case were promotion to assistant manager, where they would receive the on-the-job part of their training, and a significant increase in salary.

We had to really press to get the objectives hammered out. "What is it you want them to understand about accounting? What about marketing? What about real estate loans?" And we went down the list. They finally came up with over one hundred objectives, which we simplified, reduced, and consolidated until we came down to 39 specific behavioral objectives with criteria attached to them.

The trainees were highly motivated by both the opportunity and the increased salary to meet the criteria as soon as possible. There was a big win in it for them, and there was also a big win for the company because they would have assistant branch managers who met results-oriented criteria instead of just showing up for twelve different activity traps.

So we explained the difference between learner-controlled instruction and system-controlled instruction to the trainees. We basically said, "Here are the objectives and the criteria. Here are the resources, including learning from each other. So go to it. As soon as you meet the criteria, you will be promoted to assistant managers."

They were finished in three-and-a-half weeks. Shifting the training paradigm had released unbelievable motivation and creativity.

As with many paradigm shifts, there was resistance. Almost all of the top executives simply wouldn't believe it. When they were shown the evidence that the criteria had been met, they basically said, "These trainees don't have the experience. They lack the seasoning necessary to give them the kind of judgment we want them to have as assistant branch managers."

In talking with them later, we found that what many of them were really saying was, "We went through goat week; how come these guys don't have to?" But of course they couldn't put it that way. "They lack seasoning" was a much more acceptable expression.

In addition, for obvious reasons (including the $750,000 budget for a six-month program), the personnel department was upset.

So we responded, "Fair enough. Let's develop some more objectives and attach criteria to them. But let's stay with the paradigm of learner-controlled instruction." We hammered out eight more objectives with very tough criteria in order to give the executives the assurance that the people were adequately prepared to be assistant branch managers and continue the on-the-job part of the training program. After participating in some of the sessions where these criteria were developed, several of the executives remarked that if the trainees could meet these tough criteria, they would be better prepared than almost any who had gone through the six-month program.

We had prepared the trainees to expect resistance. We took the additional objectives and criteria back to them and said, "Just as we expected, management wants you to accomplish some additional objectives with even tougher criteria than before. They have assured us this time that if you meet these criteria, they will make you assistant managers."

They went to work in unbelievable ways. They went to the executives in departments such as accounting and basically said, "Sir, I am a member of this new pilot program called learner-controlled instruction, and it is my understanding that you participated in developing the objectives and the criteria.

"I have six criteria to meet in this particular department. I was able to pass three of them off with skills I gained in college; I was able to get another one out of a book; I learned the fifth one from Tom, the fellow you trained last week. I only have one criterion left to meet, and I wonder if you or someone else in the department might be able to spend a few hours with me to show me how." So they spend half a day in a department instead of two weeks.

These trainees cooperated with each other, brainstormed with each other, and they accomplished the additional objectives in a week and a half. The six-month program was reduced to five weeks, and the results were significantly increased.

This kind of thinking can similarly affect every area of organizational life if people have the courage to explore their paradigms and to concentrate on Win/Win. I am always amazed at the results that happen, both to individuals and to organizations, when responsible, proactive, self-directing individuals are turned loose on a task.

## Win/Win Performance Agreements

Creating Win/Win performance agreements requires vital paradigm shifts. The focus is on results, not methods. Most of us tend to supervise methods. We use the gofer delegation discussed in Habit 3, the methods management I used with Sandra when I asked her to take pictures of our son as he was water skiing. But Win/Win agreements focus on results, releasing tremendous individual human potential and creating greater synergy, building PC in the process instead of focusing exclusively on P.

With Win/Win accountability, people evaluate themselves. The traditional evaluation games people play are awkward and emotionally exhausting. In Win/Win, people evaluate themselves, using the criteria that they themselves helped to create up front. And if you set it up correctly, people can do that. With a Win/Win delegation agreement, even a seven-year-old boy can tell for himself how well he's keeping the yard "green and clean."

My best experiences in teaching university classes have come when I have created a Win/Win shared understanding of the goal up front. "This is what we're trying to accomplish. Here are the basic requirements for an A, B, or C grade. My goal is to help every one of you get an A. Now you take what we've talked about and analyze it and come up with your own understanding of what you want to accomplish that is unique to you. Then let's get together and agree on the grade you want and what you plan to do to get it."

Management philosopher and consultant Peter Drucker recommends the use of a "manager's letter" to capture the essence of performance agreements between managers and their employees. Following a deep and thorough discussion of expectations, guidelines and resources to make sure they are in harmony with organizational goals, the employee writes a letter to the manager that summarizes the discussion and indicates when the next performance plan or review discussion will take place.

Developing such a Win/Win performance agreement is the central activity of management. With an agreement in place, employees can manage themselves within the framework of that agreement. The manager then can serve like a pace car in a race. He can get things going and then get out of the way. His job from then on is to remove the oil spills.

When a boss becomes the first assistant to each of his subordinates, he can greatly increase his span of control. Entire levels of administration and overhead can be eliminated. Instead of supervising six or eight, such a manager can supervise twenty, thirty, fifty, or more.

In Win/Win performance agreements, consequences become the natural or logical result of performance rather than a reward or punishment arbitrarily handed out by the person in charge.

There are basically four kinds of consequences (rewards and penalties) that management or parents can control—financial, psychic, opportunity, and responsibility. *Financial* consequences include such things as income, stock options, allowances, or penalties. *Psychic* or psychological consequences include recognition, approval, respect, credibility, or the loss of them. Unless people are in a survival mode, psychic compensation is often more motivating than financial compensation. *Opportunity* includes training, development, perks, and other benefits. *Responsibility* has to do with scope and authority, either of which can be enlarged or diminished. Win/Win agreements specify consequences in one or more of those areas and the people involved know it up front. So you don't play games. Everything is clear from the beginning.

In addition to these logical, personal consequences, it is also important to clearly identify what the natural organizational consequences are. For example, what will happen if I'm late to work, if I refuse to cooperate with others, if I don't develop good Win/Win performance agreements with my subordinates, if I don't hold them accountable for desired results, or if I don't promote their professional growth and career development?

When my daughter turned 16, we set up a Win/Win agreement regarding use of the family car. We agreed that she would obey the laws of the land and that she would keep the car clean and properly maintained. We agreed that she would use the car only for responsible purposes and would serve as a cab driver for her mother and me within reason. And we also agreed that she would do all her other jobs cheerfully without being reminded. These were our wins.

We also agreed that I would provide some resources—the car, gas, and insurance. And we agreed that she would meet weekly with me, usually on Sunday afternoon, to evaluate how she was doing based on our agreement. The consequences were clear. As long as she kept her part of the agreement, she could use the car. If she didn't keep it, she would lose the privilege until she decided to.

This Win/Win agreement set up clear expectations from the beginning on both our parts. It was a win for her—she got to use the car—and it was certainly a win for Sandra and me. Now she could handle her own transportation needs and even some of ours. We didn't have to worry about maintaining the car or keeping it clean. And we had a built-in accountability, which meant I didn't have to hover over her or manage her methods. Her integrity, her conscience, her power of discernment and our high Emotional Bank Account managed her infinitely better. We didn't have to get emotionally strung out, trying to supervise her every move and coming up with punishments or rewards on the spot if she didn't do things the way we thought she should. We had a Win/Win agreement, and it liberated us all.

Win/Win agreements are tremendously liberating. But as the product of isolated techniques, they won't hold up. Even if you set them up in the beginning, there is no way to maintain them without personal integrity and a relationship of trust.

A true Win/Win agreement is the product of the paradigm, the character, and the relationships out of which it grows. In that context, it defines and directs the interdependent interaction for which it was created.

### Systems

Win/Win can only survive in an organization when the systems support it. If you talk Win/Win but reward Win/Lose, you've got a losing program on your hands.

You basically get what you reward. If you want to achieve the goals and reflect the values in your mission statement, then you need to align the reward system with these goals and values. If it isn't aligned systematically, you won't be walking your talk. You'll be in the situation of the manager I mentioned earlier who talked cooperation but practiced competition by creating a "Race to Bermuda" contest.

*    *    *

I worked for several years with a very large real estate organization in the Middle West. My first experience with this organization was at a large sales rally where over 800 sales associates gathered for the annual reward program. It was a psych-up cheerleading session, complete with high school bands and a great deal of frenzied screaming.

Out of the 800 people there, around forty received awards for top performance, such as "Most Sales," "Greatest Volume," "Highest Earned Commissions," and "Most Listings." There was a lot of hoopla—excitement, cheering, applause—around the presentation of these awards. There was no doubt that those forty people had *won;* but there was also the underlying awareness that 760 people had *lost.*

We immediately began educational and organizational development work to align the systems and structures of the organization toward the Win/Win paradigm. We involved people at a grass roots level to develop the kinds of systems that would motivate them. We also encouraged them to cooperate and synergize with each other so that as many as possible could achieve the desired results of their individually tailored performance agreements.

At the next rally one year later, there were over 1,000 sales associates present, and about 800 of them received awards. There were a few individual winners based on comparisons, but the program primarily focused on people achieving self-selected performance objectives and on groups achieving team objectives. There was no need to bring in the high school bands to artificially contrive the fanfare, the cheerleading, and the psych up. There was tremendous natural interest and excitement because people could share in each other's happiness, and teams of sales associates could experience rewards together, including a vacation trip for the entire office.

The remarkable thing was that almost all of the 800 who received the awards that year had produced as much per person in terms of volume and profit as the previous year's forty. The spirit of Win/Win had significantly increased the number of golden eggs and had fed the goose as well, releasing enormous human energy and talent. The resulting synergy was astounding to almost everyone involved.

*    *    *

Competition has its place in the marketplace or against last year's performance—perhaps even against another office or individual where there is no particular interdependence, no need to cooperate. But cooperation in the workplace is as important to free enterprise as competition in the marketplace. The spirit of Win/Win cannot survive in an environment of competition and contests.

For Win/Win to work, the systems have to support it. The training system, the planning system, the communication system, the budgeting system, the information system, the compensation system—all have to be based on the principle of Win/Win.

I did some consulting for another company that wanted training for their people in human relations. The underlying assumption was that the problem was the people.

The president said, "Go into any store you want and see how they treat you. They're just order takers. They don't understand how to get close to the customers. They don't know the product, and they don't have the knowledge and the skill in the sales process necessary to create a marriage between the product and the need."

So I went to the various stores. And he was right. But that still didn't answer the question in my mind: What caused the attitude?

"Look, we're on top of the problem," the president said. "We have department heads out there setting a great example. We've told them their job is two-thirds selling and one-third management, and they're outselling everybody. We just want you to provide some training for the salespeople."

Those words raised a red flag. "Let's get some more data," I said.

He didn't like that. He "knew" what the problem was, and he wanted to get on with training. But I persisted, and within two days we uncovered the real problem. Because of the job definition and the compensation system, the managers were "creaming." They'd stand behind the cash register and cream all the business during the slow times. Half the time in retail is slow and the other half is frantic. So the managers would give all the dirty jobs—inventory control, stock work, and cleaning—to the salespeople. And they would stand behind the registers and cream. That's why the department heads were tops in sales.

So we changed one system—the compensation system—and the problem was corrected overnight. We set up a system whereby the managers only made money when their salespeople made money. We overlapped the needs and goals of the managers with the needs and goals of the salespeople. And the need for human relations training suddenly disappeared. The key was developing a true Win/Win reward system.

In another instance, I worked with a manager in a company that required formal performance evaluations. He was frustrated over the evaluation rating he had given a particular manager. "He deserved a three," he said, "but I had to give him a one" (which meant superior, promotable).

"What did you give him a one for?" I asked.

"He gets the numbers," was his reply.

"So why do you think he deserves a three?"

"It's the way he gets them. He neglects people; he runs over them. He's a troublemaker."

"It sounds like he's totally focused on P—on production. And that's what he's being rewarded for. But what would happen if you talked with him about the problem, if you helped him understand the importance of PC?"

He said he had done so, with no effect.

"Then what if you set up a Win/Win contract with him where you both agreed that two-thirds of his compensation would come from P—from the numbers—and the other one-third would come from PC—how other people perceive him, what kind of leader, people builder, team builder he is?"

"Now that would get his attention," he replied.

So often the problem is in the system, not in the people. If you put good people in bad systems, you get bad results. You have to water the flowers you want to grow.

As people really learn to think Win/Win, they can set up the systems to create and reinforce it. They can transform unnecessarily competitive situations to cooperative ones and can powerfully impact their effectiveness by building both P and PC.

In business, executives can align their systems to create teams of highly productive people working together to compete against external standards of performance. In education, teachers can set up grading systems based on an individual's performance in the context of agreed upon criteria and can encourage students to cooperate in productive ways to help each other learn and achieve.

In families, parents can shift the focus from competition with each other to cooperation. In activities such as bowling, for example, they can keep a family score and try to beat a previous one. They can set up home responsibilities with Win/Win agreements that eliminate constant nagging and enable parents to do the things only they can do.

A friend once shared with me a cartoon he'd seen of two children talking to each other. "If mommy doesn't get us up soon," one was saying, "we're going to be late for school." These words brought forcibly to his attention the nature of the problems created when families are not organized on a responsible Win/Win basis.

Win/Win puts the responsibility on the individual for accomplishing specified results within clear guidelines and available resources. It makes a person accountable to perform and evaluate the results and provides consequences as a natural result of performance. And Win/Win systems create the environment which supports and reinforces the Win/Win performance agreements.

**Processes**

There's no way to achieve Win/Win ends with Win/Lose or Lose/Win means. You can't say, "You're going to think Win/Win, whether you like it or not." So the question becomes how to arrive at a Win/Win solution.

Roger Fisher and William Ury, two Harvard law professors, have done some outstanding work in what they call the "principled" approach versus the "positional" approach to bargaining in their tremendously useful and insightful book, *Getting to Yes*. Although the words Win/Win are not used, the spirit and underlying philosophy of the book are in harmony with the Win/Win approach.

They suggest that the essence of principled negotiation is to separate the person from the problem, to focus on interests and not on positions, to invent options for mutual gain, and to insist on objective criteria—some external standard or principle that both parties can buy into.

In my own work with various people and organizations seeking Win/Win solutions, I suggest that they become involved in the following four-step process:

First, see the problem from the other point of view. Really seek to understand and to give expression to the needs and concerns of the other party as well as or better than they can themselves.

Second, identify the key issues and concerns (not positions) involved.

Third, determine what results would constitute a fully acceptable solution.

And fourth, identify possible new options to achieve those results.

Habits 5 and 6 deal directly with two of the elements of this process, and we will go into those in depth in the next two chapters.

But at this juncture, let me point out the highly interrelated nature of the process of Win/Win with the essence of Win/Win itself. You can only achieve Win/Win solutions with Win/Win processes—the end and the means are the same.

Win/Win is not a personality technique. It's a total paradigm of human interaction. It comes from a character of integrity, maturity, and the Abundance Mentality. It grows out of high-trust relationships. It is embodied in agreements that effectively clarify and manage expectations as well as accomplishment. It thrives in supportive systems. And it is achieved through the process we are now prepared to more fully examine in Habits 5 and 6.

### APPLICATION SUGGESTIONS:

1. Think about an upcoming interaction wherein you will be attempting to reach an agreement or negotiate a solution. Commit to maintain a balance between courage and consideration.

2. Make a list of obstacles that keep you from applying the Win/Win paradigm more frequently. Determine what could be done within your Circle of Influence to eliminate some of those obstacles.

3. Select a specific relationship where you would like to develop a Win/Win agreement. Try to put yourself in the other person's place, and write down explicitly how you think that person sees the solution. Then list, from your own perspective, what results would constitute a Win for you. Approach the other person and ask if he or she would

be willing to communicate until you reach a point of agreement and mutually beneficial solution.

4. Identify three key relationships in your life. Give some indication of what you feel the balance is in each of the Emotional Bank Accounts. Write down some specific ways you could make deposits in each account.

5. Deeply consider your own scripting. Is it Win/Lose? How does that scripting affect your interactions with other people? Can you identify the main source of that script? Determine whether or not those scripts serve well in your current reality.

6. Try to identify a model of Win/Win thinking who, even in hard situations, really seeks mutual benefit. Determine now to more closely watch and learn from this person's example.

# HABIT 5:
## SEEK FIRST TO UNDERSTAND, THEN TO BE UNDERSTOOD

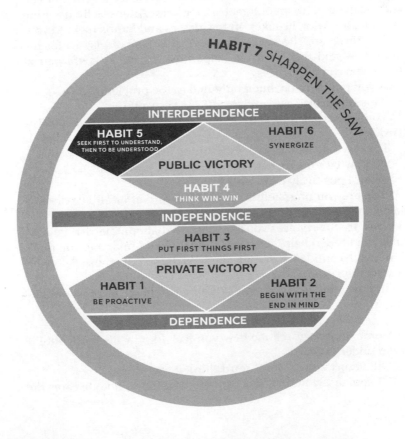

# Principles of Empathic Communication

*The heart has its reasons which reason knows not of.*

PASCAL

SUPPOSE YOU'VE BEEN HAVING TROUBLE WITH YOUR EYES and you decide to go to an optometrist for help. After briefly listening to your complaint, he takes off his glasses and hands them to you.

"Put these on," he says. "I've worn this pair of glasses for ten years now and they've really helped me. I have an extra pair at home; you can wear these."

So you put them on, but it only makes the problem worse.

"This is terrible!" you exclaim. "I can't see a thing!"

"Well, what's wrong?" he asks. "They work great for me. Try harder."

"I am trying," you insist. "Everything is a blur."

"Well, what's the matter with you? Think positively."

"Okay. I positively can't see a thing."

"Boy, are you ungrateful!" he chides. "And after all I've done to help you!"

What are the chances you'd go back to that optometrist the next time you needed help? Not very good, I would imagine. You don't have much confidence in someone who doesn't diagnose before he or she prescribes.

But how often do we diagnose before we prescribe in communication?

"Come on, honey, tell me how you feel. I know it's hard, but I'll try to understand."

"Oh, I don't know, Mom. You'd think it was stupid."

"Of course I wouldn't! You can tell me. Honey, no one cares for you as much as I do. I'm only interested in your welfare. What's making you so unhappy?"

"Oh, I don't know."

"Come on, honey. What is it?"

"Well, to tell you the truth, I just don't like school anymore."

"What?" you respond incredulously. "What do you mean you don't like school? And after all the sacrifices we've made for your education! Education is the foundation of your future. If you'd apply yourself like your older sister does, you'd do better and then you'd like school. Time and time again, we've told you to settle down. You've got the ability, but you just don't apply yourself. Try harder. Get a positive attitude about it."

Pause.

"Now go ahead. Tell me how you feel."

We have such a tendency to rush in, to fix things up with good advice. But we often fail to take the time to diagnose, to really, deeply understand the problem first.

If I were to summarize in one sentence the single most important principle I have learned in the field of interpersonal relations, it would be this: *Seek first to understand, then to be understood.* This principle is the key to effective interpersonal communication.

## CHARACTER AND COMMUNICATION

Right now, you're reading a book I've written. Reading and writing are both forms of communication. So are speaking and listening. In fact, those are the four basic types of communication. And think of all the hours you spend doing at least one of those four things. The ability to do them well is absolutely critical to your effectiveness.

Communication is the most important skill in life. We spend most of our waking hours communicating. But consider this: You've spent years learning how to read and write, years learning how to speak. But what about listening? What training or education have you had that enables you to listen so that you really, deeply understand another human being from that individual's own frame of reference?

Comparatively few people have had any training in listening at all. And, for the most part, their training has been in the Personality Ethic of technique, truncated from the character base and the relationship base absolutely vital to authentic understanding of another person.

If you want to interact effectively with me, to influence me— your spouse, your child, your neighbor, your boss, your coworker, your friend—you first need to understand me. And you can't do that with technique alone. If I sense you're using some technique, I sense duplicity, manipulation. I wonder why you're doing it, what your motives are. And I don't feel safe enough to open myself up to you.

The real key to your influence with me is your example, your actual conduct. Your example flows naturally out of your character, or the kind of person you truly are—not what others say you are or what you may want me to think you are. It is evident in how I actually experience you.

Your character is constantly radiating, communicating. From it, in the long run, I come to instinctively trust or distrust you and your efforts with me.

If your life runs hot and cold, if you're both caustic and kind, and, above all, if your private performance doesn't square with your public performance, it's very hard for me to open up with you. Then, as much as I may want and even need to receive your love and influence, I don't feel safe enough to expose my opinions and experiences and my tender feelings. Who knows what will happen?

But unless I open up with you, unless you understand me and my unique situation and feelings, you won't know how to advise or counsel me. What you say is good and fine, but it doesn't quite pertain to me.

You may say you care about and appreciate me. I desperately want to believe that. But how can you appreciate me when you don't even understand me? All I have are your words, and I can't trust words.

I'm too angry and defensive—perhaps too guilty and afraid—to be influenced, even though inside I know I need what you could tell me.

Unless you're influenced by my uniqueness, I'm not going to be influenced by your advice. So if you want to be really effective in the habit of interpersonal communication, you cannot do it with technique alone. You have to build the skills of empathic listening on a base of character that inspires openness and trust. And you have to build the Emotional Bank Accounts that create a commerce between hearts.

## EMPATHIC LISTENING

"Seek first to understand" involves a very deep shift in paradigm. We typically seek first to be understood. Most people do not listen with the intent to understand; they listen with the intent to reply. They're either speaking or preparing to speak. They're filtering everything through their own paradigms, reading their autobiography into other people's lives.

"Oh, I know exactly how you feel!"

"I went through the very same thing. Let me tell you about my experience."

They're constantly projecting their own home movies onto other people's behavior. They prescribe their own glasses for everyone with whom they interact.

If they have a problem with someone—a son, a daughter, a spouse, an employee—their attitude is, "That person just doesn't understand."

A father once told me, "I can't understand my kid. He just won't listen to me at all."

"Let me restate what you just said," I replied. "You don't understand your son because he won't listen to you?"

"That's right," he replied.

"Let me try again," I said. "You don't understand your son because *he* won't listen to *you*?"

"That's what I said," he impatiently replied.

"I thought that to understand another person, *you* needed to listen to *him*," I suggested.

"Oh!" he said. There was a long pause. "Oh!" he said again, as the light began to dawn. "Oh, yeah! But I do understand him. I know what he's going through. I went through the same thing myself. I guess what I don't understand is why he won't listen to me."

This man didn't have the vaguest idea of what was really going on inside his boy's head. He looked into his own head and thought he saw the world, including his boy.

That's the case with so many of us. We're filled with our own rightness, our own autobiography. We want to be understood. Our conversations become collective monologues, and we never really understand what's going on inside another human being.

When another person speaks, we're usually "listening" at one of four levels. We may be *ignoring* another person, not really listening at all. We may practice *pretending*. "Yeah. Uh-huh. Right." We may practice *selective listening*, hearing only certain parts of the conversation. We often do this when we're listening to the constant chatter of a preschool child. Or we may even practice *attentive listening*, paying attention and focusing energy on the words that are being said. But very few of us ever practice the fifth level, the highest form of listening, *empathic listening*.

When I say empathic listening, I am not referring to the techniques of "active" listening or "reflective" listening, which basically involve mimicking what another person says. That kind of listening is skill-based, truncated from character and relationships, and often insults those "listened" to in such a way. It is also essentially autobiographical. If you practice those techniques, you may not project your autobiography in the actual interaction, but your motive in listening is autobiographical. You listen with reflective skills, but you listen with intent to reply, to control, to manipulate.

When I say empathic listening, I mean listening with intent to *understand*. I mean *seeking first* to understand, to really understand. It's an entirely different paradigm.

Empathic (from *empathy*) listening gets inside another person's frame of reference. You look out through it, you see the world the way they see the world, you understand their paradigm, you understand how they feel.

Empathy is not sympathy. Sympathy is a form of agreement, a form of judgment. And it is sometimes the more appropriate emotion and response. But people often feed on sympathy. It makes them dependent. The essence of empathic listening is not that you agree with someone; it's that you fully, deeply, understand that person, emotionally as well as intellectually.

Empathic listening involves much more than registering, reflecting, or even understanding the words that are said. Communications experts estimate, in fact, that only 10 percent of our communication is represented by the words we say. Another 30 percent is represented by our sounds, and 60 percent by our body language. In empathic listening, you listen with your ears, but you also, and more importantly, listen with your eyes and with your heart. You listen for feeling, for meaning. You listen for behavior. You use your right brain as well as your left. You sense, you intuit, you feel.

Empathic listening is so powerful because it gives you accurate data to work with. Instead of projecting your own autobiography and assuming thoughts, feelings, motives and interpretation, you're dealing with the reality inside another person's head and heart. You're listening to understand. You're focused on receiving the deep communication of another human soul.

In addition, empathic listening is the key to making deposits in Emotional Bank Accounts, because nothing you do is a deposit unless the other person perceives it as such. You can work your fingers to the bone to make a deposit, only to have it turn into a withdrawal when a person regards your efforts as manipulative, self-serving, intimidating, or condescending because you don't understand what really matters to him.

Empathic listening is, in and of itself, a tremendous deposit in the Emotional Bank Account. It's deeply therapeutic and healing because it gives a person "psychological air."

If all the air were suddenly sucked out of the room you're in right now, what would happen to your interest in this book? You wouldn't care about the book; you wouldn't care about anything except getting air. Survival would be your only motivation.

But now that you have air, it doesn't motivate you. This is one of the greatest insights in the field of human motivation: *Satisfied needs do not motivate*. It's only the unsatisfied need that motivates. Next to physical survival, the greatest need of a human being is psychological survival—to be understood, to be affirmed, to be validated, to be appreciated.

When you listen with empathy to another person, you give that person psychological air. And after that vital need is met, you can then focus on influencing or problem solving.

This need for psychological air impacts communication in every area of life.

I taught this concept at a seminar in Chicago one time, and I instructed the participants to practice empathic listening during the evening. The next morning, a man came up to me almost bursting with news.

"Let me tell you what happened last night," he said. "I was trying to close a big commercial real estate deal while I was here in Chicago. I met with the principals, their attorneys, and another real estate agent who had just been brought in with an alternative proposal.

"It looked as if I were going to lose the deal. I had been working on this deal for over six months and, in a very real sense, all my eggs were in this one basket. All of them. I panicked. I did everything I could—I pulled out all the stops—I used every sales technique I could. The final stop was to say, 'Could we delay this decision just a little longer?' But the momentum was so strong and they were so disgusted by having this thing go on so long, it was obvious they were going to close.

"So I said to myself, 'Well, why not try it? Why not practice what I learned today and seek first to understand, then to be understood? I've got nothing to lose.'

"I just said to the man, 'Let me see if I really understand what your position is and what your concerns about my recommendations really are. When you feel I understand them, then we'll see whether my proposal has any relevance or not.'

"I really tried to put myself in his shoes. I tried to verbalize his needs and concerns, and he began to open up.

"The more I sensed and expressed the things he was worried about, the results he anticipated, the more he opened up.

"Finally, in the middle of our conversation, he stood up, walked over to the phone, and dialed his wife. Putting his hand over the mouthpiece, he said, 'You've got the deal.'

"I was totally dumbfounded," he told me. "I still am this morning."

He had made a huge deposit in the Emotional Bank Account by giving the man psychological air. When it comes right down to it, other things being relatively equal, the human dynamic is more important than the technical dimensions of the deal.

Seeking first to understand, diagnosing before you prescribe, is hard. It's so much easier in the short run to hand someone a pair of glasses that have fit you so well these many years.

But in the long run, it severely depletes both P and PC. You can't achieve maximum interdependent production from an inaccurate understanding of where other people are coming from. And you can't have interpersonal PC—high Emotional Bank Accounts—if the people you relate with don't really feel understood.

Empathic listening is also risky. It takes a great deal of security to go into a deep listening experience because you open yourself up to be influenced. You become vulnerable. It's a paradox, in a sense, because in order to have influence, you have to be influenced. That means you have to really understand.

That's why Habits 1, 2, and 3 are so foundational. They give you the changeless inner core, the principle center, from which you can handle the more outward vulnerability with peace and strength.

## DIAGNOSE BEFORE YOU PRESCRIBE

Although it's risky and hard, seek first to understand, or diagnose before you prescribe, is a correct principle manifest in many areas of life. It's the mark of all true professionals. It's critical for the optometrist, it's critical for the physician. You wouldn't have any confidence in a doctor's prescription unless you had confidence in the diagnosis.

When our daughter Jenny was only two months old, she was sick one Saturday, the day of a football game in our community that dominated the consciousness of almost everyone. It was an important game—some 60,000 people were there. Sandra and I would like to have gone, but we didn't want to leave little Jenny. Her vomiting and diarrhea had us concerned.

The doctor was at that game. He wasn't our personal physician, but he was the one on call. When Jenny's situation got worse, we decided we needed some medical advice.

Sandra dialed the stadium and had him paged. It was right at a critical time in the game, and she could sense an officious tone in his voice. "Yes?" he said briskly. "What is it?"

"This is Mrs. Covey, Doctor, and we're concerned about our daughter, Jenny."

"What's the situation?" he asked.

Sandra described the symptoms, and he said, "Okay. I'll call in a prescription. Which is your pharmacy?"

When she hung up, Sandra felt that in her rush she hadn't really given him full data, but that what she had told him was adequate.

"Do you think he realizes that Jenny is just a newborn?" I asked her.

"I'm sure he does," Sandra replied.

"But he's not our doctor. He's never even treated her."

"Well, I'm pretty sure he knows."

"Are you willing to give her the medicine unless you're absolutely sure he knows?"

Sandra was silent. "What are we going to do?" she finally said.

"Call him back," I said.

"You call him back," Sandra replied.

So I did. He was paged out of the game once again. "Doctor," I said, "when you called in that prescription, did you realize that Jenny is just two months old?"

"No!" he exclaimed. "I didn't realize that. It's good you called me back. I'll change the prescription immediately."

If you don't have confidence in the diagnosis, you won't have confidence in the prescription.

This principle is also true in sales. An effective sales person first seeks to understand the needs, the concerns, the situation of the customer. The amateur salesman sells products; the professional sells solutions to needs and problems. It's a totally different approach. The professional learns how to diagnose, how to understand. He also learns how to relate people's needs to his products and services. And he has to have the integrity to say, "My product or service will not meet that need" if it will not.

Diagnosing before you prescribe is also fundamental to law. The professional lawyer first gathers the facts to understand the situation, to understand the laws and precedents, before preparing a case. A good lawyer almost writes the opposing attorney's case before he writes his own.

It's also true in product design. Can you imagine someone in a company saying, "This consumer research stuff is for the birds. Let's design products." In other words, forget understanding the consumer's buying habits and motives—just design products. It would never work.

A good engineer will understand the forces, the stresses at work, before designing the bridge. A good teacher will assess the class before teaching. A good student will understand before he applies. A good parent will understand before evaluating or judging. The key to good judgment is understanding. By judging first, a person will never fully understand.

Seek first to understand is a correct principle evident in all areas of life. It's a generic, common denominator principle, but it has its greatest power in the area of interpersonal relations.

## FOUR AUTOBIOGRAPHICAL RESPONSES

Because we listen autobiographically, we tend to respond in one of four ways. We *evaluate*—we either agree or disagree; we *probe*—

we ask questions from our own frame of reference; we *advise*—we give counsel based on our own experience; or we *interpret*—we try to figure people out, to explain their motives, their behavior, based on our own motives and behavior.

These responses come naturally to us. We are deeply scripted in them; we live around models of them all the time. But how do they affect our ability to really understand?

If I'm trying to communicate with my son, can he feel free to open himself up to me when I evaluate everything he says before he really explains it? Am I giving him psychological air?

And how does he feel when I probe? Probing is playing twenty questions. It's autobiographical, it controls, and it invades. It's also logical, and the language of logic is different from the language of sentiment and emotion. You can play twenty questions all day and not find out what's important to someone. Constant probing is one of the main reasons parents do not get close to their children.

"How's it going, Son?"

"Fine."

"Well, what's been happening lately?"

"Nothing."

"So what's exciting in school?"

"Not much."

"And what are your plans for the weekend?"

"I don't know."

You can't get him off the phone talking with his friends, but all he gives you is one- and two-word answers. Your house is a motel where he eats and sleeps, but he never shares, never opens up.

And when you think about it, honestly, why should he, if every time he does open up his soft underbelly, you elephant stomp it with autobiographical advice and "I told you so's."

We are so deeply scripted in these responses that we don't even realize when we use them. I have taught this concept to thousands of people in seminars across the country, and it never fails to shock them deeply as we role-play empathic listening situations and they finally begin to listen to their own typical responses. But as they begin to see how they normally respond and learn how to listen with empathy, they can see the dramatic results in communication. To many, *seek first to understand* becomes the most exciting, the most immediately applicable, of all the Seven Habits.

Let's take a look at what well might be a typical communication between a father and his teenage son. Look at the father's words in terms of the four different responses we have just described.

"Boy, Dad, I've had it! School is for the birds!"

"What's the matter, Son?" (probing).

"It's totally impractical. I don't get a thing out of it."

"Well, you just can't see the benefits yet, Son. I felt the same way when I was your age. I remember thinking what a waste some of the classes were. But those classes turned out to be the most helpful to me later on. Just hang in there. Give it some time" (advising).

"I've given it ten years of my life! Can you tell me what good 'x plus y' is going to be to me as an auto mechanic?"

"An auto mechanic? You've got to be kidding" (evaluating).

"No, I'm not. Look at Joe. He's quit school. He's working on cars. And he's making lots of money. Now that's practical."

"It may look that way now. But several years down the road, Joe's going to wish he'd stayed in school. You don't want to be an auto mechanic. You need an education to prepare you for something better than that" (advising).

"I don't know. Joe's got a pretty good set up."

"Look, Son, have you really tried?" (probing, evaluating).

"I've been in high school two years now. Sure I've tried. It's just a waste."

"That's a highly respected school, Son. Give them a little credit" (advising, evaluating).

"Well, the other guys feel the same way I do."

"Do you realize how many sacrifices your mother and I have made to get you where you are? You can't quit when you've come this far" (evaluating).

"I know you've sacrificed, Dad. But it's just not worth it."

"Look, maybe if you spent more time doing your homework and less time in front of TV . . ." (advising, evaluating).

"Look, Dad. It's just no good. Oh . . . never mind! I don't want to talk about this anyway."

Obviously, his father was well intended. Obviously, he wanted to help. But did he even begin to really understand?

Let's look more carefully at the son—not just his words, but his thoughts and feelings (expressed parenthetically below) and the possible effect of some of his dad's autobiographical responses.

*    *    *

"Boy, Dad, I've had it! School is for the birds!" (*I want to talk with you, to get your attention.*)

"What's the matter, Son?" (*You're interested! Good!*)

"It's totally impractical. I don't get a thing out of it." (*I've got a problem with school, and I feel just terrible.*)

"Well, you just can't see the benefits yet, Son. I felt the same way when I was your age." (*Oh, no! Here comes Chapter three of Dad's autobiography. This isn't what I want to talk about. I don't really care how many miles he had to trudge through the snow to school without any boots. I want to get to the problem.*) "I remember thinking what a waste some of the classes were. But those classes turned out to be the most helpful to me later on. Just hang in there. Give it some time." (*Time won't solve my problem. I wish I could tell you. I wish I could just spit it out.*)

"I've given it ten years of my life! Can you tell me what good 'x plus y' is going to do me as an auto mechanic?"

"An auto mechanic? You've got to be kidding." (*He wouldn't like me if I were an auto mechanic. He wouldn't like me if I didn't finish school. I have to justify what I said.*)

"No, I'm not. Look at Joe. He's quit school. He's working on cars. And he's making lots of money. Now that's practical."

"It may look that way now. But several years down the road, Joe's going to wish he'd stayed in school." (*Oh, boy! Here comes lecture number sixteen on the value of an education.*) "You don't want to be an auto mechanic." (*How do you know that, Dad? Do you really have any idea what I want?*) "You need an education to prepare you for something better than that."

"I don't know. Joe's got a pretty good set up." (*He's not a failure. He didn't finish school and he's not a failure.*)

"Look, Son, have you really tried?" (*We're beating around the bush, Dad. If you'd just listen, I really need to talk to you about something important.*)

"I've been in high school two years now. Sure I've tried. It's just a waste."

"That's a highly respected school, Son. Give them a little credit." (*Oh, great. Now we're talking credibility. I wish I could talk about what I want to talk about.*)

"Well, the other guys feel the same way I do." (*I have some credibility, too. I'm not a moron.*)

"Do you realize how many sacrifices your mother and I have made to get you where you are?" (*Uh-oh, here comes the guilt trip.*

*Maybe I am a moron. The school's great, Mom and Dad are great, and I'm a moron.*) "You can't quit when you've come this far."

"I know you've sacrificed, Dad. But it's just not worth it." (*You just don't understand.*)

"Look, maybe if you spent more time doing your homework and less time in front of the TV . . ." (*That's not the problem, Dad! That's not it at all! I'll never be able to tell you. I was dumb to try.*)

"Look, Dad. It's just no good. Oh . . . never mind! I don't want to talk about this anyway."

Can you see how limited we are when we try to understand another person on the basis of words alone, especially when we're looking at that person through our own glasses? Can you see how limiting our autobiographical responses are to a person who is genuinely trying to get us to understand his autobiography?

You will never be able to truly step inside another person, to see the world as he sees it, until you develop the pure desire, the strength of personal character, and the positive Emotional Bank Account, as well as the empathic listening skills to do it.

The skills, the tip of the iceberg of empathic listening, involve four developmental stages.

The first and least effective is to *mimic content*. This is the skill taught in "active" or "reflective" listening. Without the character and relationship base, it is often insulting to people and causes them to close up. It is, however, a first stage skill because it at least causes you to listen to what's being said.

Mimicking content is easy. You just listen to the words that come out of someone's mouth and you repeat them. You're hardly even using your brain at all.

"Boy, Dad, I've had it! School is for the birds!"

"You've had it. You think school is for the birds."

You have essentially repeated back the content of what was being said. You haven't evaluated or probed or advised or interpreted. You've at least showed you're paying attention to his words. But to understand, you want to do more.

The second stage of empathic listening is to *rephrase the content*. It's a little more effective, but it's still limited to the verbal communication.

"Boy, Dad, I've had it! School is for the birds!"

"You don't want to go to school anymore."

This time, you've put his meaning into your own words. Now

you're thinking about what he said, mostly with the left side, the reasoning, logical side of the brain.

The third stage brings your right brain into operation. You *reflect feeling.*

"Boy, Dad, I've had it! School is for the birds!"

"You're feeling really frustrated."

Now you're not paying as much attention to what he's saying as you are to the way he feels about what he's saying. The fourth stage includes both the second and the third. You *rephrase the content and reflect the feeling.*

"Boy, Dad, I've had it! School is for the birds!"

"You're really frustrated about school."

Frustration is the feeling; school is the content. You're using both sides of your brain to understand both sides of his communication.

Now, what happens when you use fourth stage empathic listening skills is really incredible. As you authentically seek to understand, as you rephrase content and reflect feeling, you give him psychological air. You also help him work through his own thoughts and feelings. As he grows in his confidence of your sincere desire to really listen and understand, the barrier between what's going on inside him and what's actually being communicated to you disappears. It opens a soul-to-soul flow. He's not thinking and feeling one thing and communicating another. He begins to trust you with his innermost tender feelings and thoughts.

"Boy, Dad, I've had it! School is for the birds!" (*I want to talk with you, to get your attention.*)

"You're really frustrated about school." (*That's right! That's how I feel.*)

"I sure am. It's totally impractical. I'm not getting a thing out of it."

"You feel like school's not doing you any good." (*Let me think—is that what I mean?*)

"Well, yeah. I'm just not learning anything that's going to help me. I mean, look at Joe. He's dropped out of school and he's working on cars. He's making money. Now that's practical."

"You feel that Joe really has the right idea." (*Well. . . .*)

"Well, I guess he does in a way. He's really making money now. But in a few years, I bet he'll probably be ticked off at himself."

"You think Joe's going to feel he made the wrong decision."

"He's got to. Just look at what he's giving up. I mean, if you don't have an education, you just can't make it in this world."

"Education is really important."

"Oh, yeah! I mean, if you don't have a diploma, if you can't get jobs or go to college, what are you going to do? You've just got to get an education."

"It's important to your future."

"It is. And . . . you know what? I'm really worried. Listen, you won't tell Mom, will you?"

"You don't want your mother to find out."

"Well, not really. Oh, I guess you can tell her. She'll probably find out anyway. Look, I took this test today, this reading test. And, Dad, they said I'm reading on a fourth-grade level. Fourth grade! And I'm a junior in high school!"

What a difference real understanding can make! All the well-meaning advice in the world won't amount to a hill of beans if we're not even addressing the real problem. And we'll never get to the problem if we're so caught up in our own autobiography, our own paradigms, that we don't take off our glasses long enough to see the world from another point of view.

"I'm going to flunk, Dad. I guess I figure if I'm going to flunk, I might as well quit. But I don't want to quit."

"You feel torn. You're in the middle of a dilemma."

"What do you think I should do, Dad?"

By seeking first to understand, this father has just turned a transactional opportunity into a transformational opportunity. Instead of interacting on a surface, get-the-job-done level of communication, he has created a situation in which he can now have transforming impact, not only on his son but also on the relationship. By setting aside his own autobiography and really seeking to understand, he has made a tremendous deposit in the Emotional Bank Account and has empowered his son to open, layer upon layer, and to get to the real issue.

Now father and son are on the same side of the table looking at the problem, instead of on opposite sides looking across at each other. The son is opening his father's autobiography and asking for advice.

Even as the father begins to counsel, however, he needs to be sensitive to his son's communication. As long as the response is *logical*, the father can effectively ask questions and give counsel. But the moment the response becomes *emotional*, he needs to go back to empathic listening.

"Well, I can see some things you might want to consider."

"Like what, Dad?"

"Like getting some special help with your reading. Maybe they have some kind of tutoring program over at the tech school."

"I've already checked into that. It takes two nights and all day Saturday. That would take so much time!"

Sensing *emotion* in that reply, the father moves back to *empathy*.

"That's too much of a price to pay."

"Besides, Dad, I told the sixth graders I'd be their coach."

"You don't want to let them down."

"But I'll tell you this, Dad. If I really thought that tutoring course would help, I'd be down there every night. I'd get someone else to coach those kids."

"You really want the help, but you doubt if the course will make a difference."

"Do you think it would, Dad?"

The son is once more open and *logical*. He's opening his father's autobiography again. Now the father has another opportunity to influence and transform.

There are times when transformation requires no outside counsel. Often when people are really given the chance to open up, they unravel their own problems and the solutions become clear to them in the process.

At other times, they really need additional perspective and help. The key is to genuinely seek the welfare of the individual, to listen with empathy, to let the person get to the problem and the solution at his own pace and time. Layer upon layer—it's like peeling an onion until you get to the soft inner core.

When people are really hurting and you really listen with a pure desire to understand, you'll be amazed how fast they will open up. They want to open up. Children desperately want to open up, even more to their parents than to their peers. And they will, if they feel their parents will love them unconditionally and will be faithful to them afterwards and not judge or ridicule them.

If you really seek to understand, without hypocrisy and without guile, there will be times when you will be literally stunned with the pure knowledge and understanding that will flow to you from another human being. It isn't even always necessary to talk in order to empathize. In fact, sometimes words may just get in your way. That's one very important reason why technique alone will not work. That kind of understanding transcends technique. Isolated technique only gets in the way.

I have gone through the skills of empathic listening because skill is an important part of any habit. We need to have the skills. But let me reiterate that the skills will not be effective unless they come from a *sincere desire* to understand. People resent any attempt to manipulate them. In fact, if you're dealing with people you're close to, it's helpful to tell them what you're doing.

"I read this book about listening and empathy and I thought about my relationship with you. I realized I haven't listened to you like I should. But I want to. It's hard for me. I may blow it at times, but I'm going to work at it. I really care about you and I want to understand. I hope you'll help me." Affirming your motive is a huge deposit.

But if you're not sincere, I wouldn't even try it. It may create an openness and a vulnerability that will later turn to your harm when a person discovers that you really didn't care, you really didn't want to listen, and he's left open, exposed, and hurt. The technique, the tip of the iceberg, has to come out of the massive base of character underneath.

Now there are people who protest that empathic listening takes too much time. It may take a little more time initially but it saves so much time downstream. The most efficient thing you can do if you're a doctor and want to prescribe a wise treatment is to make an accurate diagnosis. You can't say, "I'm in too much of a hurry. I don't have time to make a diagnosis. Just take this treatment."

I remember writing one time in a room on the north shore of Oahu, Hawaii. There was a soft breeze blowing, and so I had opened two windows—one at the front and one at the side—to keep the room cool. I had a number of papers laid out, chapter by chapter, on a large table.

Suddenly, the breeze started picking up and blowing my papers about. I remember the frantic sense of loss I felt because things were no longer in order, including unnumbered pages, and I began rushing around the room trying desperately to put them back.

Finally, I realized it would be better to take ten seconds and close one of the windows.

Empathic listening takes time, but it doesn't take anywhere near as much time as it takes to back up and correct misunderstandings when you're already miles down the road, to redo, to live with unexpressed and unsolved problems, to deal with the results of not giving people psychological air.

A discerning empathic listener can read what's happening down deep fast, and can show such acceptance, such understanding, that other people feel safe to open up layer after layer until they get to that soft inner core where the problem really lies.

People want to be understood. And whatever investment of time it takes to do that will bring much greater returns of time as you work from an accurate understanding of the problems and issues and from the high Emotional Bank Account that results when a person feels deeply understood.

## UNDERSTANDING AND PERCEPTION

As you learn to listen deeply to other people, you will discover tremendous differences in perception. You will also begin to appreciate the impact that these differences can have as people try to work together in interdependent situations.

You see the young woman; I see the old lady. And both of us can be right.

You may look at the world through spouse-centered glasses; I see it through the money-centered lens of economic concern.

You may be scripted in the abundance mentality; I may be scripted in the scarcity mentality.

You may approach problems from a highly visual, intuitive, holistic right brain paradigm; I may be very left brain, very sequential, analytical, and verbal in my approach.

Our perceptions can be vastly different. And yet we both have lived with our paradigms for years, thinking they are "facts," and questioning the character or the mental competence of anyone who can't "see the facts."

Now, with all our differences, we're trying to work together—in a marriage, in a job, in a community service project—to manage resources and accomplish results. So how do we do it? How do we transcend the limits of our individual perceptions so that we can deeply communicate, so that we can cooperatively deal with the issues and come up with Win/Win solutions?

The answer is Habit 5. It's the first step in the process of Win/Win. Even if (and especially when) the other person is not coming from that paradigm, seek first to understand.

This principle worked powerfully for one executive who shared with me the following experience:

"I was working with a small company that was in the process of negotiating a contract with a large national banking institution. This institution flew in their lawyers from San Francisco, their negotiator from Ohio, and presidents of two of their large banks to create an eight-person negotiating team. The company I worked with had decided to go for Win/Win or No Deal. They wanted to significantly increase the level of service and the cost, but they had been almost overwhelmed with the demands of this large financial institution.

"The president of our company sat across the negotiating table and told them, 'We would like for you to write the contract the way you want it so that we can make sure we understand your needs and your concerns. We will respond to those needs and concerns. Then we can talk about pricing.'

"The members of the negotiating team were overwhelmed. They were astounded that they were going to have the opportunity to write the contract. They took three days to come up with the deal.

"When they presented it, the president said, 'Now let's make sure we understand what you want.' And he went down the contract, rephrasing the content, reflecting the feeling, until he was sure and they were sure he understood what was important to them. 'Yes. That's right. No, that's not exactly what we meant here . . . yes, you've got it now.'

"When he thoroughly understood their perspective, he proceeded to explain some concerns from his perspective . . . and they listened. They were ready to listen. They weren't fighting for air. What had started out as a very formal, low-trust, almost hostile atmosphere had turned into a fertile environment for synergy.

"At the conclusion of the discussions, the members of the negotiating team basically said, 'We want to work with you. We want to do this deal. Just let us know what the price is and we'll sign.' "

## THEN SEEK TO BE UNDERSTOOD

Seek first to understand . . . *then to be understood*. Knowing how to be understood is the other half of Habit 5, and is equally critical in reaching Win/Win solutions.

Earlier we defined maturity as the balance between courage and consideration. Seeking to understand requires consideration; seeking to be understood takes courage. Win/Win requires a high degree of both. So it becomes important in interdependent situations for us to be understood.

The early Greeks had a magnificient philosophy which is embodied in three sequentially arranged words: *ethos, pathos*, and *logos*. I suggest these three words contain the essence of seeking first to understand and making effective presentations.

*Ethos* is your personal credibility, the faith people have in your integrity and competency. It's the trust that you inspire, your Emotional Bank Account. *Pathos* is the empathic side—it's the feeling. It means that you are in alignment with the emotional thrust of another person's communication. *Logos* is the logic, the reasoning part of the presentation.

Notice the sequence: ethos, pathos, logos—your character, and your relationships, and then the logic of your presentation. This represents another major paradigm shift. Most people, in making presentations, go straight to the logos, the left brain logic, of their ideas. They try to convince other people of the validity of that logic without first taking ethos and pathos into consideration.

I had an acquaintance who was very frustrated because his boss was locked into what he felt was an unproductive leadership style.

"Why doesn't he do anything?" he asked me. "I've talked to him about it, he's aware of it, but he does nothing."

"Well, why don't you make an effective presentation?" I asked.

"I did," was the reply.

"How do you define 'effective'? Who do they send back to school when the salesman doesn't sell—the buyer? Effective means it works; it means P/PC. Did you create the change you wanted? Did you build the relationship in the process? What were the results of your presentation?"

"I told you, he didn't do anything. He wouldn't listen."

"Then make an *effective* presentation. You've got to empathize with his head. You've got to get into his frame of mind. You've got to make your point simply and visually and describe the alternative he is in favor of better than he can himself. That will take some homework. Are you willing to do that?"

"Why do I have to go through all that?" he asked.

"In other words, you want him to change his whole leadership style and you're not willing to change your method of presentation?"

"I guess so," he replied.

"Well, then," I said, "just smile about it and learn to live with it."

"I can't live with it," he said. "It compromises my integrity."

"Okay, then get to work on an effective presentation. That's in your Circle of Influence."

In the end, he wouldn't do it. The investment seemed too great.

Another acquaintance, a university professor, was willing to pay the price. He approached me one day and said, "Stephen, I can't get to first base in getting the funding I need for my research because my research is really not in the mainstream of this department's interests."

After discussing his situation at some length, I suggested that he develop an effective presentation using ethos, pathos, and logos. "I know you're sincere and the research you want to do would bring great benefits. Describe the alternative they are in favor of better than they can themselves. Show that you understand them in depth. Then carefully explain the logic behind your request."

"Well, I'll try," he said.

"Do you want to practice with me?" I asked. He was willing, and so we dress rehearsed his approach.

When he went in to make his presentation, he started by saying, "Now let me see if I first understand what your objectives are, and what your concerns are about this presentation and my recommendation."

He took the time to do it slowly, gradually. In the middle of his presentation, demonstrating his depth of understanding and respect for their point of view, a senior professor turned to another professor, nodded, turned back to him, and said, "You've got your money."

When you can present your own ideas clearly, specifically, visually, and most important, contextually—in the context of a deep understanding of other people's paradigms and concerns—you significantly increase the credibility of your ideas.

You're not wrapped up in your "own thing," delivering grandiose rhetoric from a soapbox. You really understand. What you're presenting may even be different from what you had originally thought because in your effort to understand, you learned.

Habit 5 lifts you to greater accuracy, greater integrity, in your presentations. And people know that. They know you're presenting the ideas that you genuinely believe, taking all known facts and perceptions into consideration, which will benefit everyone.

## ONE ON ONE

Habit 5 is powerful because it is right in the middle of your Circle of Influence. Many factors in interdependent situations are in your Circle of Concern—problems, disagreements, circumstances, other people's behavior. And if you focus your energies out there, you deplete them with little positive results.

But you can always seek first to understand. That's something that's within your control. And as you do that, as you focus on your Circle of Influence, you really, deeply understand other people. You have accurate information to work with, you get to the heart of matters quickly, you build Emotional Bank Accounts, and you give people the psychological air they need so you can work together effectively.

It's the inside-out approach. And as you do it, watch what happens to your Circle of Influence. Because you really listen, you become influenceable. And being influenceable is the key to influencing others. Your circle begins to expand. You increase your ability to influence many of the things in your Circle of Concern.

And watch what happens to you. The more deeply you understand other people, the more you will appreciate them, the more reverent you will feel about them. To touch the soul of another human being is to walk on holy ground.

Habit 5 is something you can practice right now. The next time you communicate with anyone, you can put aside your own autobiography and genuinely seek to understand. Even when people don't want to open up about their problems, you can be empathic. You can sense their hearts, you can sense the hurt, and you can respond, "You seem down today." They may say nothing. That's all right. You've shown understanding and respect.

Don't push; be patient; be respectful. People don't have to open up verbally before you can empathize. You can empathize all the time with their behavior. You can be discerning, sensitive, and aware and you can live outside your autobiography when that is needed.

And if you're highly proactive, you can create opportunities to do preventive work. You don't have to wait until your son or daughter has a problem with school or you have your next business negotiation to seek first to understand.

Spend time with your children now, one on one. Listen to them; understand them. Look at your home, at school life, at the challenges and the problems they're facing, through their eyes. Build the Emotional Bank Account. Give them air.

Go out with your spouse on a regular basis. Have dinner or do something together you both enjoy. Listen to each other; seek to understand. See life through each other's eyes.

My daily time with Sandra is something I wouldn't trade for anything. As well as seeking to understand each other, we often take time to actually practice empathic listening skills to help us in communicating with our children.

We often share our different perceptions of the situation, and we role-play more effective approaches to difficult interpersonal family problems.

I may act as if I am a son or daughter requesting a special privilege even though I haven't fulfilled a basic family responsibility, and Sandra plays herself.

We interact back and forth and try to visualize the situation in a very real way so that we can train ourselves to be consistent in modeling and teaching correct principles to our children. Some of our most helpful role-plays come from redoing a past difficult or stressful scene in which one of us "blew it."

The time you invest to deeply understand the people you love brings tremendous dividends in open communication. Many of the problems that plague families and marriages simply don't have time to fester and develop. The communication becomes so open that potential problems can be nipped in the bud. And there are great reserves of trust in the Emotional Bank Account to handle the problems that do arise.

In business, you can set up one-on-one time with your employees. Listen to them, understand them. Set up human resource accounting or stakeholder information systems in your business to get honest, accurate feedback at every level: from customers, suppliers, and employees. Make the human element as important as the financial or the technical element. You save tremendous amounts of time, energy, and money when you tap into the human resources of a business at every level. When you listen, you learn. And you also give the people who work for you and with you psychological air. You inspire loyalty that goes well beyond the eight-to-five physical demands of the job.

Seek first to understand. Before the problems come up, before you try to evaluate and prescribe, before you try to present your own ideas—seek to understand. It's a powerful habit of effective interdependence.

When we really, deeply understand each other, we open the door to creative solutions and third alternatives. Our differences are no longer stumbling blocks to communication and progress. Instead, they become the stepping stones to synergy.

## APPLICATION SUGGESTIONS:

1. Select a relationship in which you sense the Emotional Bank Account is in the red. Try to understand and write down the situation from the other person's point of view. In your next interaction, listen for understanding, comparing what you are hearing with what you wrote down. How valid were your assumptions? Did you really understand that individual's perspective?

2. Share the concept of empathy with someone close to you. Tell him or her you want to work on really listening to others and ask for feedback in a week. How did you do? How did it make that person feel?

3. The next time you have an opportunity to watch people communicate, cover your ears for a few minutes and just watch. What emotions are being communicated that may not come across in words alone?

4. Next time you catch yourself inappropriately using one of the autobiographical responses—probing, evaluating, advising, or interpreting—try to turn the situation into a

deposit by acknowledgment and apology. (*"I'm sorry, I just realized I'm not really trying to understand. Could we start again?"*)

5. Base your next presentation on empathy. Describe the other point of view as well as or better than its proponents; then seek to have your point understood from their frame of reference.

# HABIT 6:
## SYNERGIZE

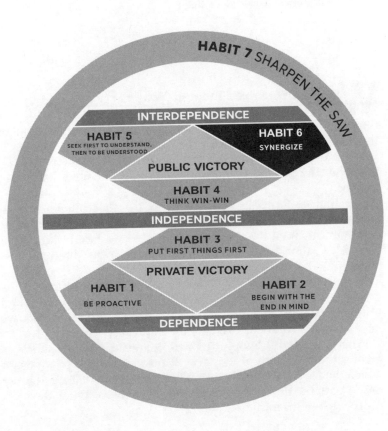

# PRINCIPLES OF CREATIVE COOPERATION

*I take as my guide the hope of a saint:*
*in crucial things, unity—*
*in important things, diversity—*
*in all things, generosity.*

INAUGURAL ADDRESS OF
PRESIDENT GEORGE H. W. BUSH

WHEN SIR WINSTON CHURCHILL WAS CALLED to head up the war effort for Great Britain, he remarked that all his life had prepared him for this hour. In a similar sense, the exercise of all of the other habits prepares us for the habit of synergy.

When properly understood, synergy is the highest activity in all life—the true test and manifestation of all of the other habits put together.

The highest forms of synergy focus the four unique human endowments, the motive of Win/Win, and the skills of empathic communication on the toughest challenges we face in life. What results is almost miraculous. We create new alternatives—something that wasn't there before.

Synergy is the essence of principle-centered leadership. It is the essence of principle-centered parenting. It catalyzes, unifies, and unleashes the greatest powers within people. All the habits we have covered prepare us to create the miracle of synergy.

What is synergy? Simply defined, it means that the whole is greater than the sum of its parts. It means that the relationship which the parts have to each other is a part in and of itself. It is not only a part, but the most catalytic, the most empowering, the most unifying, and the most exciting part.

The creative process is also the most terrifying part because you don't know exactly what's going to happen or where it is going to lead. You don't know what new dangers and challenges you'll find. It takes an enormous amount of internal security to begin with the spirit of adventure, the spirit of discovery, the spirit of creativity. Without doubt, you have to leave the comfort zone of base camp and confront an entirely new and unknown wilderness. You become a trailblazer, a pathfinder. You open new possibilities, new territories, new continents, so that others can follow.

Synergy is everywhere in nature. If you plant two plants close together, the roots comingle and improve the quality of the soil so that both plants will grow better than if they were separated. If you put two pieces of wood together, they will hold much more than the total of the weight held by each separately. The whole is greater than the sum of its parts. One plus one equals three or more.

The challenge is to apply the principles of creative cooperation, which we learn from nature, in our social interactions. Family life provides many opportunities to observe synergy and to practice it.

The very way that a man and a woman bring a child into the world is synergistic. The essence of synergy is to value differences—to respect them, to build on strengths, to compensate for weaknesses.

We obviously value the physical differences between men and women, husbands and wives. But what about the social, mental, and emotional differences? Could these differences not also be sources of creating new, exciting forms of life—creating an environment that is truly fulfilling for each person, that nurtures the self-esteem and self-worth of each, that creates opportunities for each to mature into independence and then gradually into interdependence? Could synergy not create a new script for the next generation—one that is more geared to service and contribution, and is less protective, less adversarial, less selfish; one that is more open, more trusting, more giving, and is less defensive, protective, and political; one that is more loving, more caring, and is less possessive and judgmental?

## SYNERGISTIC COMMUNICATION

When you communicate synergistically, you are simply opening your mind and heart and expressions to new possibilities, new alternatives, new options. It may seem as if you are casting aside Habit 2 (to begin with the end in mind); but, in fact, you're doing the opposite—you're fulfilling it. You're not sure when you engage in synergistic communication how things will work out or what the end will look like, but you do have an inward sense of excitement and security and adventure, believing that it will be significantly better than it was before. And that is the end that you have in mind.

You begin with the belief that parties involved will gain more insight, and that the excitement of that mutual learning and insight will create a momentum toward more and more insights, learnings, and growth.

Many people have not really experienced even a moderate degree of synergy in their family life or in other interactions. They've been trained and scripted into defensive and protective communications or into believing that life or other people can't be trusted. As a result, they are never really open to Habit 6 and to these principles.

This represents one of the great tragedies and wastes in life, because so much potential remains untapped—completely undeveloped and unused. Ineffective people live day after day with unused potential. They experience synergy only in small, peripheral ways in their lives.

They may have memories of some unusual creative experiences, perhaps in athletics, where they were involved in a real team spirit for a period of time. Or perhaps they were in an emergency situation where people cooperated to an unusually high degree and submerged ego and pride in an effort to save someone's life or to produce a solution to a crisis.

To many, such events may seem unusual, almost out of character with life, even miraculous. But this is not so. These things can be produced regularly, consistently, almost daily in people's lives. But it requires enormous personal security and openness and a spirit of adventure.

Most all creative endeavors are somewhat unpredictable. They often seem ambiguous, hit-or-miss, trial and error. And unless people have a high tolerance for ambiguity and get their security from integrity to principles and inner values they find it unnerving and unpleasant to be involved in highly creative enterprises. Their need for structure, certainty, and predictability is too high.

## SYNERGY IN THE CLASSROOM

As a teacher, I have come to believe that many truly great classes teeter on the very edge of chaos. Synergy tests whether teachers and students are really open to the principle of the whole being greater than the sum of its parts.

There are times when neither the teacher nor the student knows for sure what's going to happen. In the beginning, there's a safe environment that enables people to be really open and to learn and to listen to each other's ideas. Then comes brainstorming, where the spirit of evaluation is subordinated to the spirit of creativity, imagining, and intellectual networking. Then an absolutely unusual phenomenon begins to take place. The entire class is transformed with the excitement of a new thrust, a new idea, a new direction that's hard to define, yet it's almost palpable to the people involved.

Synergy is almost as if a group collectively agrees to subordinate old scripts and to write a new one.

I'll never forget a university class I taught in leadership philosophy and style. We were about three weeks into a semester when, in the middle of a presentation, one person started to relate some very powerful personal experiences which were both emotional and insightful. A spirit of humility and reverence fell upon the class—reverence toward this individual and appreciation for his courage.

This spirit became fertile soil for a synergistic and creative endeavor. Others began to pick up on it, sharing some of their experiences and insights and even some of their self-doubts. The spirit of trust and safety prompted many to become extremely open. Rather than present what they prepared, they fed on each other's insights and ideas and started to create a whole new scenario as to what that class could mean.

I was deeply involved in the process. In fact, I was almost mesmerized by it because it seemed so magical and creative. And I found myself gradually loosening up my commitment to the structure of the class and sensing entirely new possibilities. It wasn't just a flight of fancy; there was a sense of maturity and stability and substance which transcended by far the old structure and plan.

We abandoned the old syllabus, the purchased textbooks and all the presentation plans, and we set up new purposes and projects and assignments. We became so excited about what was happening that in about three more weeks, we all sensed an overwhelming desire to share what was happening with others.

We decided to write a book containing our learnings and insights on the subject of our study—principles of leadership. Assignments were changed, new projects undertaken, new teams formed. People worked much harder than they ever would have in the original class structure, and for an entirely different set of reasons.

Out of this experience emerged a unique, extremely cohesive, and synergistic culture that did not end with the semester. For years, alumni meetings were held among members of that class. Even today, many years later, when we see each other, we talk about it and often attempt to describe what happened and why.

One of the interesting things to me was how little time had elapsed before there was sufficient trust to create such synergy. I think it was largely because the people were relatively mature. They were in the final semester of their senior year, and I think they wanted more than just another good classroom experience. They were hungry for something new and exciting, something that they could create that was truly meaningful. It was "an idea whose time had come" for them.

In addition, the chemistry was right. I felt that experiencing synergy was more powerful than talking about it, that producing something new was more meaningful than simply reading something old.

I've also experienced, as I believe most people have, times that were almost synergistic, times that hung on the edge of chaos and for some reason descended into it. Sadly, people who are burned by such experiences often begin their next new experience with that failure in mind. They defend themselves against it and cut themselves off from synergy.

It's like administrators who set up new rules and regulations based on the abuses of a few people inside an organization, thus limiting the freedom and creative possibilities for many—or business partners who imagine the worst scenarios possible and write them up in legal language, killing the whole spirit of creativity, enterprise, and synergistic possibility.

As I think back on many consulting and executive education

experiences, I can say that the highlights were almost always synergistic. There was usually an early moment that required considerable courage, perhaps in becoming extremely authentic, in confronting some inside truth about the individual or the organization or the family which really needed to be said, but took a combination of considerable courage and genuine love to say. Then others became more authentic, open, and honest, and the synergistic communication process began. It usually became more and more creative, and ended up in insights and plans that no one had anticipated initially.

As Carl Rogers taught, "That which is most personal is most general." The more authentic you become, the more genuine in your expression, particularly regarding personal experiences and even self-doubts, the more people can relate to your expression and the safer it makes them feel to express themselves. That expression in turn feeds back on the other person's spirit, and genuine creative empathy takes place, producing new insights and learnings and a sense of excitement and adventure that keeps the process going.

People then begin to interact with each other almost in half sentences, sometimes incoherent, but they get each other's meanings very rapidly. Then whole new worlds of insights, new perspectives, new paradigms that ensure options, new alternatives are opened up and thought about. Though occasionally these new ideas are left up in the air, they usually come to some kind of closure that is practical and useful.

## SYNERGY IN BUSINESS

I enjoyed one particularly meaningful synergistic experience as I worked with my associates to create the corporate mission statement for our business. Almost all members of the company went high up into the mountains where, surrounded by the magnificence of nature, we began with a first draft of what some of us considered to be an excellent mission statement.

At first the communication was respectful, careful and predictable. But as we began to talk about the various alternatives, possibilities and opportunities ahead, people became very open and authentic and simply started to think out loud. The mission statement agenda gave way to a collective free association, a spontaneous piggybacking of ideas. People were genuinely empathic as well as courageous, and we moved from mutual respect and understanding to creative synergistic communication.

Everyone could sense it. It was exciting. As it matured, we returned to the task of putting the evolved collective vision into words, each of which contains specific and committed-to meaning for each participant.

The resulting corporate mission statement reads:

> Our mission is to empower people and organizations to significantly increase their performance capability in order to achieve worthwhile purposes through understanding and living principle-centered leadership.

The synergistic process that led to the creation of our mission statement engraved it in the hearts and minds of everyone there, and it has served us well as a frame of reference of what we are about, as well as what we are not about.

Another high level synergy experience took place when I accepted an invitation to serve as the resource and discussion catalyst at the annual planning meeting of a large insurance company. Several months ahead, I met with the committee responsible to prepare for and stage the two-day meeting which was to involve all the top executives. They informed me that the traditional pattern was to identify four or five major issues through questionnaires and interviews, and to have alternative proposals presented by the executives. Past meetings had been generally respectful exchanges, occasionally deteriorating into defensive Win/Lose ego battles. They were usually predictable, uncreative, and boring.

As I talked with the committee members about the power of synergy, they could sense its potential. With considerable trepidation, they agreed to change the pattern. They requested various executives to prepare anonymous "white papers" on each of the high priority issues, and then asked all the executives to immerse themselves in these papers ahead of time in order to understand the issues and the differing points of view. They were to come to the meeting prepared to listen rather than to present, prepared to create and synergize rather than to defend and protect.

We spent the first half-day in the meeting teaching the principles and practicing the skills of Habits 4, 5, and 6. The rest of the time was spent in creative synergy.

The release of creative energy was incredible. Excitement replaced boredom. People became very open to each other's influence and generated new insights and options. By the end of the meeting an entirely new understanding of the nature of the central company challenge evolved. The white paper proposals became obsolete. Differences were valued and transcended. A new common vision began to form.

Once people have experienced real synergy, they are never quite the same again. They know the possibility of having other such mind-expanding adventures in the future.

Often attempts are made to recreate a particular synergistic experience, but this seldom can be done. However, the essential purpose behind creative work *can* be recaptured. Like the Far Eastern philosophy, "We seek not to imitate the masters, rather we seek what they sought," we seek not to imitate past creative synergistic experiences, rather we seek new ones around new and different and sometimes higher purposes.

## SYNERGY AND COMMUNICATION

Synergy is exciting. Creativity is exciting. It's phenomenal what openness and communication can produce. The possibilities of truly significant gain, of significant improvement are so real that it's worth the risk such openness entails.

After World War II, the United States commissioned David Lilienthal to head the new Atomic Energy Commission. Lilienthal brought together a group of people who were highly influential—celebrities in their own right—disciples, as it were, of their own frames of reference.

This very diverse group of individuals had an extremely heavy agenda, and they were impatient to get at it. In addition, the press was pushing them.

But Lilienthal took several weeks to create a high Emotional Bank Account. He had these people get to know each other—their interests, their hopes, their goals, their concerns, their backgrounds, their frames of reference, their paradigms. He facilitated the kind of human interaction that creates a great bonding between people, and he was heavily criticized for taking the time to do it because it wasn't "efficient."

But the net result was that this group became closely knit together, very open with each other, very creative, and synergistic.
The respect among the members of the commission was so high
that if there was disagreement, instead of opposition and defense,
there was a genuine effort to understand. The attitude was "If
a person of your intelligence and competence and commitment
disagrees with me, then there must be something to your disagreement that I don't understand, and I need to understand it.
You have a perspective, a frame of reference I need to look at."
Nonprotective interaction developed, and an unusual culture was
born.

The following diagram illustrates how closely trust is related to
different levels of communication.

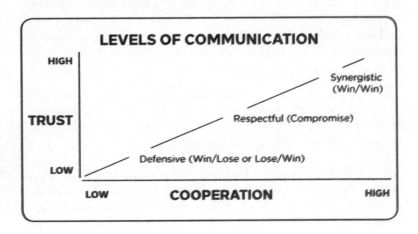

The lowest level of communication coming out of low-trust situations would be characterized by defensiveness, protectiveness,
and often legalistic language, which covers all the bases and spells
out qualifiers and the escape clauses in the event things go sour.
Such communication produces only Win/Lose or Lose/Lose. It
isn't effective—there's no P/PC balance—and it creates further reasons to defend and protect.

The middle position is respectful communication. This is the
level where fairly mature people interact. They have respect for
each other, but they want to avoid the possibility of ugly confron-

tations, so they communicate politely but not empathically. They might understand each other intellectually, but they really don't deeply look at the paradigms and assumptions underlying their own positions and become open to new possibilities.

Respectful communication works in independent situations and even in interdependent situations, but the creative possibilities are not opened up. In interdependent situations compromise is the position usually taken. Compromise means that 1 + 1 = 1½. Both give and take. The communication isn't defensive or protective or angry or manipulative; it is honest and genuine and respectful. But it isn't creative or synergistic. It produces a low form of Win/Win.

Synergy means that 1 + 1 may equal 8, 16, or even 1,600. The synergistic position of high trust produces solutions better than any originally proposed, and all parties know it. Furthermore, they genuinely enjoy the creative enterprise. A miniculture is formed to satisfy in and of itself. Even if it is short lived, the P/PC balance is there.

There are some circumstances in which synergy may not be achievable and No Deal isn't viable. But even in these circumstances, the spirit of sincere trying will usually result in a more effective compromise.

## FISHING FOR THE THIRD ALTERNATIVE

To get a better idea of how our level of communication affects our interdependent effectiveness, envision the following scenario:

It's vacation time, and a husband wants to take his family out to the lake country to enjoy camping and fishing. This is important to him; he's been planning it all year. He's made reservations at a cottage on the lake and arranged to rent a boat, and his sons are really excited about going.

His wife, however, wants to use the vacation time to visit her ailing mother some 250 miles away. She doesn't have the opportunity to see her very often, and this is important to her.

Their differences could be the cause of a major negative experience.

"The plans are set. The boys are excited. We should go on the fishing trip," he says.

"But we don't know how much longer my mother will be around, and I want to be by her," she replies. "This is our only opportunity to have enough time to do that."

"All year long we've looked forward to this one-week vacation. The boys would be miserable sitting around grandmother's house for a week. They'd drive everybody crazy. Besides, your mother's not that sick. And she has your sister less than a mile away to take care of her."

"She's my mother, too. I want to be with her."

"You could phone her every night. And we're planning to spend time with her at the Christmas family reunion. Remember?"

"That's not for five more months. We don't even know if she'll still be here by then. Besides, she needs me, and she wants me."

"She's being well taken care of. Besides, the boys and I need you, too."

"My mother is more important than fishing."

"Your husband and sons are more important than your mother."

As they disagree, back and forth, they finally may come up with some kind of compromise. They may decide to split up—he takes the boys fishing at the lake while she visits her mother. And they both feel guilty and unhappy. The boys sense it, and it affects their enjoyment of the vacation.

The husband may give in to his wife, but he does it grudgingly. And consciously or unconsciously, he produces evidence to fulfill his prophecy of how miserable the week will be for everyone.

The wife may give in to her husband, but she's withdrawn and overreactive to any new developments in her mother's health situation. If her mother were to become seriously ill and die, the husband could never forgive himself, and she couldn't forgive him either.

Whatever compromise they finally agree on, it could be re- hearsed over the years as evidence of insensitivity, neglect, or a bad priority decision on either part. It could be a source of conten- tion for years and could even polarize the family. Many marriages that once were beautiful and soft and spontaneous and loving have deteriorated to the level of a hostility through a series of inci- dents just like this.

The husband and wife see the situation differently. And that difference can polarize them, separate them, create wedges in the relationship. Or it can bring them closer together on a higher level. If they have cultivated the habits of effective interdependence, they approach their differences from an entirely different paradigm. Their communication is on a higher level.

Because they have a high Emotional Bank Account, they have trust and open communication in their marriage. Because they think Win/Win, they believe in a third alternative, a solution that is mutually beneficial and is better than what either of them originally proposed. Because they listen empathically and seek first to understand, they create within themselves and between them a comprehensive picture of the values and the concerns that need to be taken into account in making a decision.

And the combination of those ingredients—the high Emotional Bank Account, thinking Win/Win, and seeking first to understand—creates the ideal environment for synergy.

Buddhism calls this "the middle way." *Middle* in this sense does not mean compromise; it means higher, like the apex of the triangle.

In searching for the "middle" or higher way, this husband and wife realize that their love, their relationship, is part of their synergy.

As they communicate, the husband really, deeply feels his wife's desire, her need to be with her mother. He understands how she wants to relieve her sister, who has had the primary responsibility for their mother's care. He understands that they really don't know how long she will be with them, and that she certainly is more important than fishing.

And the wife deeply understands her husband's desire to have the family together and to provide a great experience for the boys. She realizes the investment that has been made in lessons and equipment to prepare for this fishing vacation, and she feels the importance of creating good memories with them.

So they pool those desires. And they're not on opposite sides of the problem. They're together on one side, looking at the problem, understanding the needs, and working to create a third alternative that will meet them.

"Maybe we could arrange another time within the month for you to visit with your mother," he suggests. "I could take over the home responsibilities for the weekend and arrange for some help at the first of the week so that you could go. I know it's important to you to have that time.

"Or maybe we could locate a place to camp and fish that would be close to your mother. The area wouldn't be as nice, but we could still be outdoors and meet other needs as well. And the boys wouldn't be climbing the walls. We could even plan some recreational activities with the cousins, aunts, and uncles, which would be an added benefit."

They synergize. They communicate back and forth until they come up with a solution they both feel good about. It's better than the solutions either of them originally proposed. It's better than compromise. It's a synergistic solution that builds P and PC.

Instead of a transaction, it's a transformation. They get what they both really want and build their relationship in the process.

## NEGATIVE SYNERGY

Seeking the third alternative is a major paradigm shift from the dichotomous, either/or mentality. But look at the difference in results!

How much negative energy is typically expended when people try to solve problems or make decisions in an interdependent reality? How much time is spent in confessing other people's sins, politicking, rivalry, interpersonal conflict, protecting one's backside, masterminding, and second guessing? It's like trying to drive down the road with one foot on the gas and the other foot on the brake!

And instead of getting a foot off the brake, most people give it more gas. They try to apply more pressure, more eloquence, more logical information to strengthen their position.

The problem is that highly dependent people are trying to succeed in an interdependent reality. They're either dependent on borrowing strength from position power and they go for Win/ Lose, or they're dependent on being popular with others and they go for Lose/Win. They may talk Win/Win technique, but they don't really want to listen; they want to manipulate. And synergy can't thrive in that environment.

Insecure people think that all reality should be amenable to their paradigms. They have a high need to clone others, to mold them over into their own thinking. They don't realize that the very strength of the relationship is in having another point of view. Sameness is not oneness; uniformity is not unity. Unity, or oneness, is complementariness, not sameness. Sameness is uncreative . . . and boring. The essence of synergy is to value the differences.

I've come to believe that the key to interpersonal synergy is intrapersonal synergy, that is synergy within ourselves. The heart of intrapersonal synergy is embodied in the principles in the first three habits, which give the internal security sufficient to handle the risks of being open and vulnerable. By internalizing those principles, we develop the abundance mentality of Win/Win and the authenticity of Habit 5.

One of the very practical results of being principle-centered is that it makes us whole—truly integrated. People who are scripted deeply in logical, verbal, left-brain thinking will discover how totally inadequate that thinking is in solving problems which require a great deal of creativity. They become aware and begin to open up a new script inside their right brain. It's not that the right brain wasn't there; it just lay dormant. The muscles had not been developed, or perhaps they had atrophied after early childhood because of the heavy left-brain emphasis of formal education or social scripting.

When a person has access to both the intuitive, creative, and visual right brain, and the analytical, logical, verbal left brain, then the whole brain is working. In other words, there is psychic synergy taking place in our own head. And this tool is best suited to the reality of what life is, because life is not just logical—it is also emotional.

One day I was presenting a seminar which I titled, "Manage from the Left, Lead from the Right" to a company in Orlando, Florida. During the break, the president of the company came up to me and said, "Stephen, this is intriguing. But I have been thinking about this material more in terms of its application to my marriage than to my business. My wife and I have a real communication problem. I wonder if you would have lunch with the two of us and just kind of watch how we talk to each other?"

"Let's do it," I replied.

As we sat down together, we exchanged a few pleasantries. Then this man turned to his wife and said, "Now, honey, I've invited Stephen to have lunch with us to see if he could help us in our communication with each other. I know you feel I should be a more sensitive, considerate husband. Could you give me something specific you think I ought to do?" His dominant left brain wanted facts, figures, specifics, parts.

"Well, as I've told you before, it's nothing specific. It's more of a general sense I have about priorities." Her dominant right brain was dealing with sensing and with the gestalt, the whole, the relationship between the parts.

"What do you mean, 'a general feeling about priorities'? What is it you want me to do? Give me something specific I can get a handle on."

"Well, it's just a feeling." Her right brain was dealing in images, intuitive feelings. "I just don't think our marriage is as important to you as you tell me it is."

"Well, what can I do to make it more important? Give me something concrete and specific to go on."

"It's hard to put into words."

At that point, he just rolled his eyes and looked at me as if to say, "Stephen, could you endure this kind of dumbness in your marriage?"

"It's just a feeling," she said, "a very strong feeling."

"Honey," he said to her, "that's your problem. And that's the problem with your mother. In fact, it's the problem with every woman I know."

Then he began to interrogate her as though it were some kind of legal deposition.

"Do you live where you want to live?"

"That's not it," she sighed. "That's not it at all."

"I know," he replied with a forced patience. "But since you won't tell me exactly what it is, I figure the best way to find out what it is is to find out what it is not. Do you live where you want to live?"

"I guess."

"Honey, Stephen's here for just a few minutes to try to help us. Just give a quick 'yes' or 'no' answer. Do you live where you want to live?"

"Yes."

"Okay. That's settled. Do you have the things you want to have?"

"Yes."

"All right. Do you do the things you want to do?"

This went on for a little while, and I could see I wasn't helping at all. So I intervened and said, "Is this kind of how it goes in your relationship?"

"Every day, Stephen," he replied.

"It's the story of our marriage," she sighed.

I looked at the two of them and the thought crossed my mind that they were two half-brained people living together. "Do you have any children?" I asked.

"Yes, two."

"Really?" I asked incredulously. "How did you do it?"

"What do you mean how did we do it?"

"You were synergistic!" I said. "One plus one usually equals two. But you made one plus one equal four. Now that's synergy. The whole is greater than the sum of the parts. So how did you do it?"

"You know how we did it," he replied.

"You must have valued the differences!" I exclaimed.

## VALUING THE DIFFERENCES

Valuing the differences is the essence of synergy—the mental, the emotional, the psychological differences between people. And the key to valuing those differences is to realize that all people see the world, not as it is, but as they are.

If I think I see the world as it is, why would I want to value the differences? Why would I even want to bother with someone who's "off track"? My paradigm is that I am objective; I see the world as it is. Everyone else is buried by the minutiae, but I see the larger picture. That's why they call me a supervisor—I have super vision.

If that's my paradigm, then I will never be effectively interdependent, or even effectively independent, for that matter. I will be limited by the paradigms of my own conditioning.

The person who is truly effective has the humility and reverence to recognize his own perceptual limitations and to appreciate the rich resources available through interaction with the hearts and minds of other human beings. That person values the differences because those differences add to his knowledge, to his understanding of reality. When we're left to our own experiences, we constantly suffer from a shortage of data.

Is it logical that two people can disagree and that both can be right? It's not logical: it's *psychological*. And it's very real. You see the young lady; I see the old woman. We're both looking at the same picture, and both of us are right. We see the same black lines, the same white spaces. But we interpret them differently because we've been conditioned to interpret them differently.

And unless we value the differences in our perceptions, unless we value each other and give credence to the possibility that we're both right, that life is not always a dichotomous either/or, that there are almost always third alternatives, we will never be able to transcend the limits of that conditioning.

All I may see is the old woman. But I realize that you see something else. And I value you. I value your perception. I want to understand.

So when I become aware of the difference in our perceptions, I say, "Good! You see it differently! Help me see what you see."

If two people have the same opinion, one is unnecessary. It's not going to do me any good at all to communicate with someone else who sees only the old woman also. I don't want to talk, to communicate, with someone who agrees with me; I want to communicate with you because you see it differently. I value that difference.

By doing that, I not only increase my own awareness; I also affirm you. I give you psychological air. I take my foot off the brake and release the negative energy you may have invested in defending a particular position. I create an environment for synergy.

The importance of valuing the difference is captured in an often quoted fable called "The Animal School," written by educator Dr. R. H. Reeves:

> Once upon a time, the animals decided they must do something heroic to meet the problems of a "New World," so they organized a school. They adopted an activity curriculum consisting of running, climbing, swimming and flying. To make it easier to administer, all animals took all the subjects.
>
> The duck was excellent in swimming, better in fact than his instructor, and made excellent grades in flying, but he was very poor in running. Since he was low in running he had to stay after school and also drop swimming to practice running. This was kept up until his web feet were badly worn and he was only average in swimming. But average was acceptable in school, so nobody worried about that except the duck.
>
> The rabbit started at the top of the class in running, but had a nervous breakdown because of so much makeup in swimming.
>
> The squirrel was excellent in climbing until he developed frustrations in the flying class where his teacher made him start from the ground up instead of from the tree-top down. He also developed charley horses from over-exertion and he got a C in climbing and a D in running.
>
> The eagle was a problem child and had to be disciplined severely. In climbing class he beat all the others to the top of the tree, but insisted on using his own way of getting there.

At the end of the year, an abnormal eel that could swim exceedingly well and also could run, climb and fly a little had the highest average and was valedictorian.

The prairie dogs stayed out of school and fought the tax levy because the administration would not add digging and burrowing to the curriculum. They apprenticed their children to the badger and later joined the groundhogs and gophers to start a successful private school.

### FORCE FIELD ANALYSIS

In an interdependent situation, synergy is particularly powerful in dealing with negative forces that work against growth and change.

Sociologist Kurt Lewin developed a "Force Field Analysis" model in which he described any current level of performance or being as a state of equilibrium between the driving forces that encourage upward movement and the restraining forces that discourage it.

Driving forces generally are positive, reasonable, logical, conscious, and economic. In juxtaposition, restraining forces are often negative, emotional, illogical, unconscious, and social/psychological. Both sets of forces are very real and must be taken into account in dealing with change.

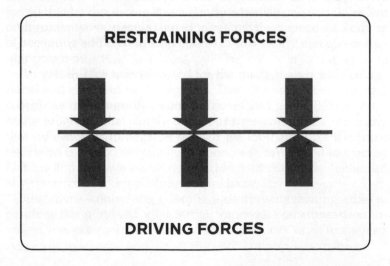

In a family, for example, you have a certain "climate" in the home—a certain level of positive or negatiye interaction, of feeling safe or unsafe in expressing feelings or talking about concerns, of respect or disrespect in communication among family members. You may really want to change that level. You may want to create a climate that is more positive, more respectful, more open and trusting. Your logical reasons for doing that are the driving forces that act to raise the level.

But increasing those driving forces is not enough. Your efforts are opposed by restraining forces—by the competitive spirit between children in the family, by the different scripting of home life you and your spouse have brought to the relationship, by habits that have developed in the family, by work or other demands on your time and energies.

Increasing the driving forces may bring results—for a while. But as long as the restraining forces are there, it becomes increasingly harder. It's like pushing against a spring: the harder you push, the harder it is to push until the force of the spring suddenly thrusts the level back down.

The resulting up and down, yo-yo effect causes you to feel, after several attempts, that people are "just the way they are" and that "it's too difficult to change."

But when you introduce synergy, you use the motive of Habit 4, the skill of Habit 5, and the interaction of Habit 6 to work directly on the restraining forces. You create an atmosphere in which it is safe to talk about these forces. You unfreeze them, loosen them up, and create new insights that actually transform those restraining forces into driving ones. You involve people in the problem, immerse them in it, so that they soak it in and feel it is their problem and they tend to become an important part of the solution.

As a result, new goals, shared goals, are created, and the whole enterprise moves upward, often in ways that no one could have anticipated. And the excitement contained within that movement creates a new culture. The people involved in it are enmeshed in each other's humanity and empowered by new, fresh thinking, by new creative alternatives and opportunities.

I've been involved several times in negotiations between people who were angry at each other and hired lawyers to defend their positions. And all that did was to exacerbate the problem because the interpersonal communication deteriorated as it went through the legal process. But the trust level was so low that the parties felt they had no other alternative than to take the issues to court.

"Would you be interested in going for a Win/Win solution that both parties feel really good about?" I would ask.

The response was usually affirmative, but most people didn't really think it was possible.

"If I can get the other party to agree, would you be willing to start the process of really communicating with each other?"

Again, the answer was usually "yes."

The results in almost every case have been astounding. Problems that had been legally and psychologically wrangled about for months have been settled in a matter of a few hours or days. Most of the solutions weren't the courthouse compromise solutions, either; they were synergistic, better than the solutions proposed independently by either party. And, in most cases, the relationships continued even though it had appeared in the beginning that the trust level was so low and the rupture in the relationship so large as to be almost irreparable.

At one of our development programs, an executive reported a situation where a manufacturer was being sued by a longtime industrial customer for lack of performance. Both parties felt totally justified by the rightness of their position and each perceived the other as unethical and completely untrustworthy.

As they began to practice Habit 5, two things became clear. First, early communication problems resulted in a misunderstanding which was later exacerbated by accusations and counteraccusations. Second, both were initially acting in good faith and didn't like the cost and hassle of a legal fight, but saw no other way out.

Once these two things became clear, the spirit of Habits 4, 5, and 6 took over, the problem was rapidly resolved, and the relationship continues to prosper.

In another circumstance, I received an early morning phone call from a land developer desperately searching for help. The bank wanted to foreclose because he was not complying with the principal and interest payment schedule, and he was suing the bank to avoid the foreclosure. He needed additional funding to finish and market the land so that he could repay the bank, but the bank refused to provide additional funds until scheduled payments were met. It was a chicken and egg problem with undercapitalization.

In the meantime, the project was languishing. The streets were beginning to look like weed fields, and the owners of the few homes that had been built were up in arms as they saw their property values drop. The city was also upset over the "prime land" project falling behind schedule and becoming an eyesore. Tens of thousands of dollars in legal costs had already been spent by the bank and the developer and the case wasn't scheduled to come to court for several months.

In desperation, this developer reluctantly agreed to try the principles of Habits 4, 5, and 6. He arranged a meeting with even more reluctant bank officials.

The meeting started at 8 A.M. in one of the bank conference rooms. The tension and mistrust were palpable. The attorney for the bank had committed the bank officials to say nothing. They were only to listen and he alone would speak. He wanted nothing to happen that would compromise the bank's position in court.

For the first hour and a half, I taught Habits 4, 5, and 6. At 9:30 I went to the blackboard and wrote down the bank's concerns based on our prior understanding. Initially the bank officials said nothing, but the more we communicated Win/Win intentions and ·sought first to understand, the more they opened up to explain and clarify.

As they began to feel understood, the whole atmosphere changed and a sense of momentum, of excitement over the prospect of peacefully settling the problem was clearly evident. Over the attorney's objections the bank officials opened up even more, even about personal concerns. "When we walk out of here the first thing the bank president will say is, 'Did we get our money?' What are we going to say?"

By 11:00, the bank officers were still convinced of their rightness, but they felt understood and were no longer defensive and officious. At that point, they were sufficiently open to listen to the developer's concerns, which we wrote down on the other side of the blackboard. This resulted in deeper mutual understanding and a collective awareness of how poor early communication had resulted in misunderstanding and unrealistic expectations, and how continuous communication in a Win/Win spirit could have prevented the subsequent major problems from developing.

The shared sense of both chronic and acute pain combined with a sense of genuine progress kept everyone communicating. By noon, when the meeting was scheduled to end, the people were positive, creative, and synergistic and wanted to keep talking. The very first recommendation made by the developer was seen as a beginning Win/Win approach by all. It was synergized on and improved, and at 12:45 P.M. the developer and the two bank officers left with a plan to present together to the Home Owners Association and the city. Despite subsequent complicating developments, the legal fight was aborted and the building project continued to a successful conclusion.

I am not suggesting that people should not use legal processes. Some situations absolutely require it. But I see it as a court of last, not first, resort. If it is used too early, even in a preventive sense, sometimes fear and the legal paradigm create subsequent thought and action processes that are not synergistic.

## ALL NATURE IS SYNERGISTIC

Ecology is a word which basically describes the synergism in nature—everything is related to everything else. It's in the relationship that creative powers are maximized, just as the real power in these Seven Habits is in their relationship to each other, not just in the individual habits themselves.

The relationship of the parts is also the power in creating a synergistic culture inside a family or an organization. The more genuine the involvement, the more sincere and sustained the participation in analyzing and solving problems, the greater the release of everyone's creativity, and of their commitment to what they create. This, I'm convinced, is the essence of the power in the Japanese approach to business, which has changed the world marketplace.

Synergy works; it's a correct principle. It is the crowning achievement of all the previous habits. It is effectiveness in an interdependent reality—it is teamwork, team building, the development of unity and creativity with other human beings.

Although you cannot control the paradigms of others in an interdependent interaction or the synergistic process itself, a great deal of synergy is within your Circle of Influence.

Your own internal synergy is completely within the circle. You can respect both sides of your own nature—the analytical side and the creative side. You can value the difference between them and use that difference to catalyze creativity.

You can be synergistic within yourself even in the midst of a very adversarial environment. You don't have to take insults personally. You can sidestep negative energy; you can look for the good in others and utilize that good, as different as it may be, to improve your point of view and to enlarge your perspective.

You can exercise the courage in interdependent situations to be open, to express your ideas, your feelings, and your experiences in a way that will encourage other people to be open also.

You can value the difference in other people. When someone disagrees with you, you can say, "Good! You see it differently." You don't have to agree with them; you can simply affirm them. And you can seek to understand.

When you see only two alternatives—yours and the "wrong" one—you can look for a synergistic third alternative. There's almost always a third alternative, and if you work with a Win/Win philosophy and really seek to understand, you usually can find a solution that will be better for everyone concerned.

## APPLICATION SUGGESTIONS:

1. Think about a person who typically sees things differently than you do. Consider ways in which those differences might be used as stepping-stones to third alternative solutions. Perhaps you could seek out his or her views on a current project or problem, valuing the different views you are likely to hear.

2. Make a list of people who irritate you. Do they represent different views that could lead to synergy if you had greater intrinsic security and valued the difference?

3. Identify a situation in which you desire greater teamwork and synergy. What conditions would need to exist to support synergy? What can you do to create those conditions?

4. The next time you have a disagreement or confrontation with someone, attempt to understand the concerns underlying that person's position. Address those concerns in a creative and mutually beneficial way.*

---

* To see how effective you are—where your strengths lie and how you can improve—take the Personal Effectiveness Quotient (PEQ) at www.7HabitsPEQ.com.

*Part Four*

# RENEWAL

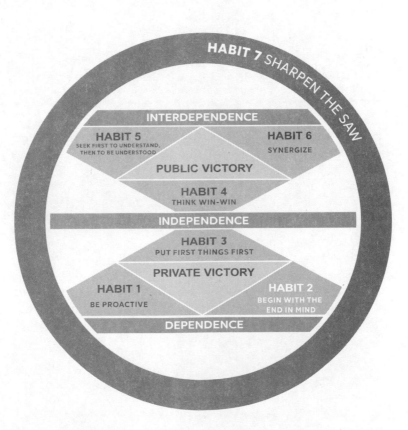

# HABIT 7:
## SHARPEN THE SAW

## PRINCIPLES OF BALANCED
## SELF-RENEWAL

*Sometimes when I consider what tremendous*
*consequences come from little things . . .*
*I am tempted to think . . .*
*there are no little things.*

BRUCE BARTON

SUPPOSE YOU WERE TO COME UPON SOMEONE in the woods working feverishly to saw down a tree.

"What are you doing?" you ask.

"Can't you see?" comes the impatient reply. "I'm sawing down this tree."

"You look exhausted!" you exclaim. "How long have you been at it?"

"Over five hours," he returns, "and I'm beat! This is hard work."

"Well, why don't you take a break for a few minutes and sharpen that saw?" you inquire. "I'm sure it would go a lot faster."

"I don't have time to sharpen the saw," the man says emphatically. "I'm too busy sawing!"

Habit 7 is taking time to sharpen the saw. It surrounds the other habits on the Seven Habits paradigm because it is the habit that makes all the others possible.

## FOUR DIMENSIONS OF RENEWAL

Habit 7 is personal PC. It's preserving and enhancing the greatest asset you have—you. It's renewing the four dimensions of your nature—physical, spiritual, mental, and social/emotional.

**PHYSICAL**
Exercise, Nutrition,
Stress Management

**MENTAL**
Reading, Visualizing,
Planning, Writing

**SOCIAL/EMOTIONAL**
Service, Empathy,
Synergy, Intrinsic Security

**SPIRITUAL**
Value Clarification
& Commitment, Study
& Meditation

Although different words are used, most philosophies of life deal either explicitly or implicitly with these four dimensions. Philosopher Herb Shepherd describes the healthy balanced life around four values: *perspective* (spiritual), *autonomy* (mental), *connectedness* (social), and *tone* (physical). George Sheehan, the running guru, describes four roles: being a good animal (physical), a good craftsman (mental), a good friend (social), and a saint (spiritual). Sound motivation and organization theory embrace these four dimensions or motivations—the economic (physical); how people are treated (social); how people are developed and used (mental); and the service, the job, the contribution the organization gives (spiritual).

"Sharpen the saw" basically means expressing all four motivations. It means exercising all four dimensions of our nature, regularly and consistently in wise and balanced ways.

To do this, we must be proactive. Taking time to sharpen the saw is a definite Quadrant II activity, and Quadrant II must be acted on. Quadrant I, because of its urgency, acts on us; it presses upon us constantly. Personal P/C must be pressed upon until it becomes second nature, until it becomes a kind of healthy addiction. Because it's at the center of our Circle of Influence, no one else can do it for us. We must do it for ourselves.

This is the single most powerful investment we can ever make in life—investment in ourselves, in the only instrument we have with which to deal with life and to contribute. We are the instruments of our own performance, and to be effective, we need to recognize the importance of taking time regularly to sharpen the saw in all four ways.

### The Physical Dimension

The physical dimension involves caring effectively for our physical body—eating the right kinds of foods, getting sufficient rest and relaxation, and exercising on a regular basis.

Exercise is one of those Quadrant II, high-leverage activities that most of us don't do consistently because it isn't urgent. And because we don't do it, sooner or later we find ourselves in Quadrant I, dealing with the health problems and crises that come as a natural result of our neglect.

Most of us think we don't have enough time to exercise. What a distorted paradigm! We don't have time not to. We're talking about three to six hours a week—or a minimum of thirty minutes a day, every other day. That hardly seems an inordinate amount of time considering the tremendous benefits in terms of the impact on the other 162–165 hours of the week.

And you don't need any special equipment to do it. If you want to go to a gym or a spa to use the equipment or enjoy some skill sports such as tennis or racquetball, that's an added opportunity. But it isn't necessary to sharpen the saw.

A good exercise program is one that you can do in your own home and one that will build your body in three areas: endurance, flexibility, and strength.

*Endurance* comes from aerobic exercise, from cardiovascular efficiency—the ability of your heart to pump blood through your body.

Although the heart is a muscle, it cannot be exercised directly.

It can only be exercised through the large muscle groups, particularly the leg muscles. That's why exercises like rapid walking, running, biking, swimming, cross-country skiing, and jogging are so beneficial.

You are considered minimally fit if you can increase your heart rate to at least one hundred beats per minute and keep it at that level for thirty minutes.

Ideally you should try to raise your heart rate to at least sixty percent of your maximum pulse rate, the top speed your heart can beat and still pump blood through your body. Your maximum heart rate is generally accepted to be 220 less your age. So, if you are 40, you should aim for an exercise heart rate of 108 (220 – 40 = 180 × 0.6 = 108). The "training effect" is generally considered to be between 72 and 87 percent of your personal maximum rate.

*Flexibility* comes through stretching. Most experts recommend warming up before and cooling down/stretching after aerobic exercise. Before, it helps loosen and warm the muscles to prepare for more vigorous exercise. After, it helps to dissipate the lactic acid so that you don't feel sore and stiff.

*Strength* comes from muscle resistance exercises—like simple calisthenics, push-ups, pull-ups, and sit-ups, and from working with weights. How much emphasis you put on developing strength depends on your situation. If you're involved in physical labor or athletic activities, increased strength will improve your skill. If you have a basically sedentary job and success in your life-style does not require a lot of strength, a little toning through calisthenics in addition to your aerobic and stretching exercises might be sufficient.

I was in a gym one time with a friend of mine who has a Ph.D. in exercise physiology. He was focusing on building strength. He asked me to "spot" him while he did some bench presses and told me at a certain point he'd ask me to take the weight. "But don't take it until I tell you," he said firmly.

So I watched and waited and prepared to take the weight. The weight went up and down, up and down. And I could see it begin to get harder. But he kept going. He would start to push it up and I'd think, "There's no way he's going to make it." But he'd make it.

Then he'd slowly bring it back down and start back up again. Up and down, up and down.

Finally, as I looked at his face, straining with the effort, his blood vessels practically jumping out of his skin, I thought, "This is going to fall and collapse his chest. Maybe I should take the weight. Maybe he's lost control and he doesn't even know what he's doing." But he'd get it safely down. Then he'd start back up again. I couldn't believe it.

When he finally told me to take the weight, I said, "Why did you wait so long?"

"Almost all the benefit of the exercise comes at the very end, Stephen," he replied. "I'm trying to build strength. And that doesn't happen until the muscle fiber ruptures and the nerve fiber registers the pain. Then nature overcompensates and within 48 hours, the fiber is made stronger."

I could see his point. It's the same principle that works with emotional muscles as well, such as patience. When you exercise your patience beyond your past limits, the emotional fiber is broken, nature overcompensates, and next time the fiber is stronger.

Now my friend wanted to build muscular strength. And he knew how to do it. But not all of us need to develop that kind of strength to be effective. "No pain, no gain" has validity in some circumstances, but it is not the essence of an effective exercise program.

The essence of renewing the physical dimension is to sharpen the saw, to exercise our bodies on a regular basis in a way that will preserve and enhance our capacity to work and adapt and enjoy.

And we need to be wise in developing an exercise program. There's a tendency, especially if you haven't been exercising at all, to overdo. And that can create unnecessary pain, injury, and even permanent damage. It's best to start slowly. Any exercise program should be in harmony with the latest research findings, with your doctor's recommendations and with your own self-awareness.

If you haven't been exercising, your body will undoubtedly protest this change in its comfortable downhill direction. You won't like it at first. You may even hate it. But be proactive. Do it anyway. Even if it's raining on the morning you've scheduled to jog, do it anyway. "Oh good! It's raining! I get to develop my willpower as well as my body!"

You're not dealing with quick fix; you're dealing with a Quadrant II activity that will bring phenomenal long-term results. Ask anyone who has done it consistently. Little by little, your resting pulse rate will go down as your heart and oxygen processing system becomes more efficient. As you increase your body's ability to do more demanding things, you'll find your normal activities much more comfortable and pleasant. You'll have more afternoon energy, and the fatigue you've felt that's made you "too tired" to exercise in the past will be replaced by an energy that will invigorate everything you do.

Probably the greatest benefit you will experience from exercising will be the development of your Habit 1 muscles of proactivity. As you act based on the value of physical well-being instead of reacting to all the forces that keep you from exercising, your paradigm of yourself, your self-esteem, your self-confidence, and your integrity will be profoundly affected.

### The Spiritual Dimension

Renewing the spiritual dimension provides leadership to your life. It's highly related to Habit 2.

The spiritual dimension is your core, your center, your commitment to your value system. It's a very private area of life and a supremely important one. It draws upon the sources that inspire and uplift you and tie you to the timeless truths of all humanity. And people do it very, very differently.

I find renewal in daily prayerful meditation on the scriptures because they represent my value system. As I read and meditate, I feel renewed, strengthened, centered and recommitted to serve.

Immersion in great literature or great music can provide a similar renewal of the spirit for some. There are others who find it in the way they communicate with nature. Nature bequeaths its own blessing on those who immerse themselves in it. When you're able to leave the noise and the discord of the city and give yourself up to the harmony and rhythm of nature, you come back renewed. For a time, you're undisturbable, almost unflappable, until gradually the noise and the discord from outside start to invade that sense of inner peace.

Arthur Gordon shares a wonderful, intimate story of his own spiritual renewal in a little story called "The Turn of the Tide." It tells of a time in his life when he began to feel that everything was stale and flat. His enthusiasm waned; his writing efforts were fruitless. And the situation was growing worse day by day.

Finally, he determined to get help from a medical doctor. Observing nothing physically wrong, the doctor asked him if he would be able to follow his instructions for one day.

When Gordon replied that he could, the doctor told him to spend the following day in the place where he was happiest as a child. He could take food, but he was not to talk to anyone or to read or write or listen to the radio. He then wrote out four prescriptions and told him to open one at nine, twelve, three, and six o'clock.

"Are you serious?" Gordon asked him.

"You won't think I'm joking when you get my bill!" was the reply.

So the next morning, Gordon went to the beach. As he opened the first prescription, he read "Listen carefully." He thought the doctor was insane. How could he listen for three hours? But he had agreed to follow the doctor's orders, so he listened. He heard the usual sounds of the sea and the birds. After a while, he could hear the other sounds that weren't so apparent at first. As he listened, he began to think of lessons the sea had taught him as a child—patience, respect, an awareness of the interdependence of things. He began to listen to the sounds—and the silence—and to feel a growing peace.

At noon, he opened the second slip of paper and read "Try reaching back." "Reaching back to what?" he wondered. Perhaps to childhood, perhaps to memories of happy times. He thought about his past, about the many little moments of joy. He tried to remember them with exactness. And in remembering, he found a growing warmth inside.

At three o'clock, he opened the third piece of paper. Until now, the prescriptions had been easy to take. But this one was different; it said "Examine your motives." At first he was defensive. He thought about what he wanted—success, recognition, security—and he justified them all. But then the thought occurred to him that those motives weren't good enough, and that perhaps therein was the answer to his stagnant situation.

He considered his motives deeply. He thought about past happiness. And at last, the answer came to him.

"In a flash of certainty," he wrote, "I saw that if one's motives are wrong, nothing can be right. It makes no difference whether you are a mailman, a hairdresser, an insurance salesman, a housewife—whatever. As long as you feel you are serving others, you do the job well. When you are concerned only with helping yourself, you do it less well—a law as inexorable as gravity."

When six o'clock came, the final prescription didn't take long to fill. "Write your worries on the sand," it said. He knelt and wrote several words with a piece of broken shell; then he turned and walked away. He didn't look back; he knew the tide would come in.

Spiritual renewal takes an investment of time. But it's a Quadrant II activity we don't really have time to neglect.

The great reformer Martin Luther is quoted as saying, "I have so much to do today, I'll need to spend another hour on my knees." To him, prayer was not a mechanical duty but rather a source of power in releasing and multiplying his energies.

Someone once inquired of a Far Eastern Zen master, who had a great serenity and peace about him no matter what pressures he faced, "How do you maintain that serenity and peace?" He replied, "I never leave my place of meditation." He meditated early in the morning and for the rest of the day, he carried the peace of those moments with him in his mind and heart.

The idea is that when we take time to draw on the leadership center of our lives, what life is ultimately all about, it spreads like an umbrella over everything else. It renews us, it refreshes us, particularly if we recommit to it.

This is why I believe a personal mission statement is so important. If we have a deep understanding of our center and our purpose, we can review and recommit to it frequently. In our daily spiritual renewal, we can visualize and "live out" the events of the day in harmony with those values.

Religious leader David O. McKay taught, "The greatest battles of life are fought out daily in the silent chambers of the soul." If you win the battles there, if you settle the issues that inwardly conflict, you feel a sense of peace, a sense of knowing what you're about. And you'll find that the public victories—where you tend to think cooperatively, to promote the welfare and good of other people, and to be genuinely happy for other people's successes—will follow naturally.

## The Mental Dimension

Most of our mental development and study discipline comes through formal education. But as soon as we leave the external discipline of school, many of us let our minds atrophy. We don't do any more serious reading, we don't explore new subjects in any real depth outside our action fields, we don't think analytically, we don't write—at least not critically or in a way that tests our ability to express ourselves in distilled, clear, and concise language. Instead, we spend our time watching TV.

Continuing surveys indicate that television is on in most homes some thirty-five to forty-five hours a week. That's as much time as many people put into their jobs, more than most put into school. It's the most powerful socializing influence there is. And when we watch, we're subject to all the values that are being taught through it. That can powerfully influence us in very subtle and imperceptible ways.

Wisdom in watching television requires the effective self-management of Habit 3, which enables you to discriminate and to select the informing, inspiring, and entertaining programs which best serve and express your purpose and values.

In our family, we limit television watching to around seven hours a week, an average of about an hour a day. We had a family council at which we talked about it and looked at some of the data regarding what's happening in homes because of television. We found that by discussing it as a family when no one was defensive or argumentative, people started to realize the dependent sickness of becoming addicted to soap operas or to a steady diet of a particular program.

I'm grateful for television and for the many high quality educational and entertainment programs. They can enrich our lives and contribute meaningfully to our purposes and goals. But there are many programs that simply waste our time and minds and many that influence us in negative ways if we let them. Like the body, television is a good servant but a poor master. We need to practice Habit 3 and manage ourselves effectively to maximize the use of any resource in accomplishing our missions.

Education—continuing education, continually honing and expanding the mind—is vital mental renewal. Sometimes that involves the external discipline of the classroom or systematized study programs; more often it does not. Proactive people can figure out many, many ways to educate themselves.

It is extremely valuable to train the mind to stand apart and examine its own program. That, to me, is the definition of a liberal education—the ability to examine the programs of life against larger questions and purposes and other paradigms. Training, without such education, narrows and closes the mind so that the assumptions underlying the training are never examined. That's why it is so valuable to read broadly and to expose yourself to great minds.

There's no better way to inform and expand your mind on a regular basis than to get into the habit of reading good literature. That's another high leverage Quadrant II activity. You can get into the best minds that are now or that have ever been in the world. I highly recommend starting with a goal of a book a month, then a book every two weeks, then a book a week. "The person who doesn't read is no better off than the person who can't read."

Quality literature, such as the Great Books, the Harvard Classics, autobiographies, *National Geographic* and other publications that expand our cultural awareness, and current literature in various fields can expand our paradigms and sharpen our mental saw, particularly if we practice Habit 5 as we read and seek first to understand. If we use our own autobiography to make early judgments before we really understand what an author has to say, we limit the benefits of the reading experience.

Writing is another powerful way to sharpen the mental saw. Keeping a journal of our thoughts, experiences, insights, and learnings promotes mental clarity, exactness, and context. Writing good letters—communicating on the deeper level of thoughts, feelings, and ideas rather than on the shallow, superficial level of events—also affects our ability to think clearly, to reason accurately, and to be understood effectively.

Organizing and planning represent other forms of mental renewal associated with Habits 2 and 3. It's beginning with the end in mind and being able mentally to organize to accomplish that end. It's exercising the visualizing, imagining power of your mind to see the end from the beginning and to see the entire journey, at least in principles, if not in steps.

It is said that wars are won in the general's tent. Sharpening the saw in the first three dimensions—the physical, the spiritual, and the mental—is a practice I call the "Daily Private Victory." And

I commend to you the simple practice of spending one hour a day every day doing it—one hour a day for the rest of your life. There's no other way you could spend an hour that would begin to compare with the Daily Private Victory in terms of value and results. It will affect every decision, every relationship. It will greatly improve the quality, the effectiveness, of every other hour of the day, including the depth and restfulness of your sleep. It will build the long-term physical, spiritual, and mental strength to enable you to handle difficult challenges in life.

In the words of Phillips Brooks:

> Some day, in the years to come, you will be wrestling with the great temptation, or trembling under the great sorrow of your life. But the real struggle is here, now . . . *Now* it is being decided whether, in the day of your supreme sorrow or temptation, you shall miserably fail or gloriously conquer. Character cannot be made except by a steady, long continued process.

### The Social/Emotional Dimension

While the physical, spiritual, and mental dimensions are closely related to Habits 1, 2, and 3—centered on the principles of personal vision, leadership, and management—the social/emotional dimension focuses on Habits 4, 5, and 6—centered on the principles of interpersonal leadership, empathic communication, and creative cooperation.

The social and the emotional dimensions of our lives are tied together because our emotional life is primarily, but not exclusively, developed out of and manifested in our relationships with others.

Renewing our social/emotional dimension does not take time in the same sense that renewing the other dimensions does. We can do it in our normal everyday interactions with other people. But it definitely requires exercise. We may have to push ourselves because many of us have not achieved the level of Private Victory and the skills of Public Victory necessary for Habits 4, 5, and 6 to come naturally to us in all our interactions.

Suppose that you are a key person in my life. You might be my boss, my subordinate, my coworker, my friend, my neighbor, my spouse, my child, a member of my extended family—anyone with whom I want or need to interact. Suppose we need to communicate together, to work together, to discuss a jugular issue, to accomplish a purpose or solve a problem. But we see things differently; we're looking through different glasses. You see the young lady, and I see the old woman.

So I practice Habit 4. I come to you and I say, "I can see that we're approaching this situation differently. Why don't we agree to communicate until we can find a solution we both feel good about. Would you be willing to do that?" Most people would be willing to say "yes" to that.

Then I move to Habit 5. "Let me listen to you first." Instead of listening with intent to reply, I listen empathically in order to deeply, thoroughly understand your paradigm. When I can explain your point of view as well as you can, then I focus on communicating my point of view to you so that you can understand it as well.

Based on the commitment to search for a solution that we both feel good about and a deep understanding of each other's points of view, we move to Habit 6. We work together to produce third alternative solutions to our differences that we both recognize are better than the ones either you or I proposed initially.

Success in Habits 4, 5, and 6 is not primarily a matter of intellect; it's primarily a matter of emotion. It's highly related to our sense of personal security.

If our personal security comes from sources within ourselves, then we have the strength to practice the habits of Public Victory. If we are emotionally insecure, even though we may be intellectually very advanced, practicing Habits 4, 5, and 6 with people who think differently on jugular issues of life can be terribly threatening.

Where does intrinsic security come from? It doesn't come from what other people think of us or how they treat us. It doesn't come from the scripts they've handed us. It doesn't come from our circumstances or our position.

It comes from within. It comes from accurate paradigms and correct principles deep in our own mind and heart. It comes from inside-out congruence, from living a life of integrity in which our daily habits reflect our deepest values.

I believe that a life of integrity is the most fundamental source of personal worth. I do not agree with the popular success literature that says that self-esteem is primarily a matter of mind set, of attitude—that you can psych yourself into peace of mind.

Peace of mind comes when your life is in harmony with true principles and values and in no other way.

There is also the intrinsic security that comes as a result of effective interdependent living. There is security in knowing that Win/

Win solutions do exist, that life is not always "either/or," that there are almost always mutually beneficial Third Alternatives. There is security in knowing that you can step out of your own frame of reference without giving it up, that you can really, deeply understand another human being. There is security that comes when you authentically, creatively and cooperatively interact with other people and really experience these interdependent habits.

There is intrinsic security that comes from service, from helping other people in a meaningful way. One important source is your work, when you see yourself in a contributive and creative mode, really making a difference. Another source is anonymous service—no one knows it and no one necessarily ever will. And that's not the concern; the concern is blessing the lives of other people. Influence, not recognition, becomes the motive.

Victor Frankl focused on the need for meaning and purpose in our lives, something that transcends our own lives and taps the best energies within us. The late Dr. Hans Selye, in his monumental research on stress, basically says that a long, healthy, and happy life is the result of making contributions, of having meaningful projects that are personally exciting and contribute to and bless the lives of others. His ethic was "earn thy neighbor's love."

In the words of George Bernard Shaw,

> This is the true joy in life—that being used for a purpose recognized by yourself as a mighty one. That being a force of nature, instead of a feverish, selfish little clod of ailments and grievances complaining that the world will not devote itself to making you happy. I am of the opinion that my life belongs to the whole community and as long as I live it is my privilege to do for it whatever I can. I want to be thoroughly used up when I die. For the harder I work the more I live. I rejoice in life for its own sake. Life is no brief candle to me. It's a sort of splendid torch which I've got to hold up for the moment and I want to make it burn as brightly as possible before handing it on to future generations.

N. Eldon Tanner has said, "Service is the rent we pay for the privilege of living on this earth." And there are so many ways to serve. Whether or not we belong to a church or service organization or have a job that provides meaningful service opportunities, not a day goes by that we can't at least serve one other human being by making deposits of unconditional love.

## SCRIPTING OTHERS

Most people are a function of the social mirror, scripted by the opinions, the perceptions, the paradigms of the people around them. As interdependent people, you and I come from a paradigm which includes the realization that we are a part of that social mirror.

We can choose to reflect back to others a clear, undistorted vision of themselves. We can affirm their proactive nature and treat them as responsible people. We can help script them as principle-centered, value-based, independent, worthwhile individuals. And, with the Abundance Mentality, we realize that giving a positive reflection to others in no way diminishes us. It increases us because it increases the opportunities for effective interaction with other proactive people.

At some time in your life, you probably had someone believe in you when you didn't believe in yourself. They scripted you. Did that make a difference in your life?

What if you were a positive scripter, an affirmer, of other people? When they're being directed by the social mirror to take the lower path, you inspire them toward a higher path because you believe in them. You listen to them and empathize with them. You don't absolve them of responsibility; you encourage them to be proactive.

Perhaps you are familiar with the musical *Man of La Mancha*. It's a beautiful story about a medieval knight who meets a woman of the street, a prostitute. She's being validated in her life-style by all of the people in her life.

But this poet knight sees something else in her, something beautiful and lovely. He also sees her virtue, and he affirms it, over and over again. He gives her a new name—Dulcinea—a new name associated with a new paradigm.

At first, she utterly denies it; her old scripts are overpowering. She writes him off as a wild-eyed fantasizer. But he is persistent. He makes continual deposits of unconditional love and gradually it penetrates her scripting. It goes down into her true nature, her potential, and she starts to respond. Little by little, she begins to change her life-style. She believes it and she acts from her new paradigm, to the initial dismay of everyone else in her life.

Later, when she begins to revert to her old paradigm, he calls her to his deathbed and sings that beautiful song, "The Impossible Dream," looks her in the eyes, and whispers, "Never forget, you're Dulcinea."

One of the classic stories in the field of self-fulfilling prophecies is of a computer in England that was accidently programmed incorrectly. In academic terms, it labeled a class of "bright" kids "dumb" kids and a class of supposedly "dumb" kids "bright." And that computer report was the primary criterion that created the teachers' paradigms about their students at the beginning of the year.

When the administration finally discovered the mistake five and a half months later, they decided to test the kids again without telling anyone what had happened. And the results were amazing. The "bright" kids had gone down significantly in IQ test points. They had been seen and treated as mentally limited, uncooperative, and difficult to teach. The teachers' paradigms had become a self-fulfilling prophecy.

But scores in the supposedly "dumb" group had gone up. The teachers had treated them as though they were bright, and their energy, their hope, their optimism, their excitement had reflected high individual expectations and worth for those kids.

These teachers were asked what it was like during the first few weeks of the term. "For some reason, our methods weren't working," they replied. "So we had to change our methods." The information showed that the kids were bright. If things weren't working well, they figured it had to be the teaching methods. So they worked on methods. They were proactive; they worked in their Circle of Influence. Apparent learner disability was nothing more or less than teacher inflexibility.

What do we reflect to others about themselves? And how much does that reflection influence their lives? We have so much we can invest in the Emotional Bank Accounts of other people. The more we can see people in terms of their unseen potential, the more we can use our imagination rather than our memory, with our spouse, our children, our coworkers or employees. We can refuse to label them—we can "see" them in new fresh ways each time we're with them. We can help them become independent, fulfilled people capable of deeply satisfying, enriching, and productive relationships with others.

Goethe taught, "Treat a man as he is and he will remain as he is.

Treat a man as he can and should be and he will become as he can and should be."

## BALANCE IN RENEWAL

The self-renewal process must include balanced renewal in all four dimensions of our nature: the physical, the spiritual, the mental, and the social/emotional.

Although renewal in each dimension is important, it only becomes optimally effective as we deal with all four dimensions in a wise and balanced way. To neglect any one area negatively impacts the rest.

I have found this to be true in organizations as well as in individual lives. In an organization, the physical dimension is expressed in economic terms. The mental or psychological dimension deals with the recognition, development, and use of talent. The social/emotional dimension has to do with human relations, with how people are treated. And the spiritual dimension deals with finding meaning through purpose or contribution and through organizational integrity.

When an organization neglects any one or more of these areas, it negatively impacts the entire organization. The creative energies that could result in tremendous, positive synergy are instead used to fight against the organization and become restraining forces to growth and productivity.

I have found organizations whose only thrust is economic—to make money. They usually don't publicize that purpose. They sometimes even publicize something else. But in their hearts, their only desire is to make money.

Whenever I find this, I also find a great deal of negative synergy in the culture, generating such things as interdepartmental rivalries, defensive and protective communication, politicking, and masterminding. We can't effectively thrive without making money, but that's not sufficient reason for organizational existence. We can't live without eating, but we don't live to eat.

At the other end of the spectrum, I've seen organizations that focused almost exclusively on the social/emotional dimension. They are, in a sense, some kind of social experiment and they have no economic criteria in their value system. They have no measure or gauge of their effectiveness, and as a result, they lose all kinds of efficiencies and eventually their viability in the marketplace.

I have found many organizations that develop as many as three of the dimensions—they may have good service criteria, good economic criteria, and good human relations criteria, but they are not really committed to identifying, developing, utilizing, and recognizing the talent of people. And if these psychological forces are missing, the style will be a benevolent autocracy and the resulting culture will reflect different forms of collective resistance, adversarialism, excessive turnover, and other deep, chronic, cultural problems.

Organizational as well as individual effectiveness requires development and renewal of all four dimensions in a wise and balanced way. Any dimension that is neglected will create negative force field resistance that pushes against effectiveness and growth. Organizations and individuals that give recognition to each of these four dimensions in their mission statement provide a powerful framework for balanced renewal.

This process of continuous improvement is the hallmark of the Total Quality Movement and a key to Japan's economic ascendency.

## SYNERGY IN RENEWAL

Balanced renewal is optimally synergetic. The things you do to sharpen the saw in any one dimension have positive impact in other dimensions because they are so highly interrelated. Your physical health affects your mental health; your spiritual strength affects your social/emotional strength. As you improve in one dimension, you increase your ability in other dimensions as well.

The Seven Habits of Highly Effective People create optimum synergy among these dimensions. Renewal in any dimension increases your ability to live at least one of the Seven Habits. And although the habits are sequential, improvement in one habit synergetically increases your ability to live the rest.

The more proactive you are (Habit 1), the more effectively you can exercise personal leadership (Habit 2) and management (Habit 3) in your life. The more effectively you manage your life (Habit 3), the more Quadrant II renewing activities you can do (Habit 7). The more you seek first to understand (Habit 5), the more effectively you can go for synergetic Win/Win solutions (Habits 4 and 6). The more you improve in any of the habits that lead to independence (Habits 1, 2, and 3), the more effective you will be in interdependent situations (Habits 4, 5, and 6). And renewal (Habit 7) is the process of renewing all the habits.

As you renew your physical dimension, you reinforce your personal vision (Habit 1), the paradigm of your own self-awareness and free will, of proactivity, of knowing that you are free to act instead of being acted upon, to choose your own response to any stimulus. This is probably the greatest benefit of physical exercise. Each Daily Private Victory makes a deposit in your personal intrinsic security account.

As you renew your spiritual dimension, you reinforce your personal leadership (Habit 2). You increase your ability to live out of your imagination and conscience instead of only your memory, to deeply understand your innermost paradigms and values, to create within yourself a center of correct principles, to define your own unique mission in life, to rescript yourself to live your life in harmony with correct principles and to draw upon your personal sources of strength. The rich private life you create in spiritual renewal makes tremendous deposits in your personal security account.

As you renew your mental dimension, you reinforce your personal management (Habit 3). As you plan, you force your mind to recognize high leverage Quadrant II activities, priority goals, and activities to maximize the use of your time and energy, and you organize and execute your activities around your priorities. As you become involved in continuing education, you increase your knowledge base and you increase your options. Your economic security does not lie in your job; it lies in your own power to produce—to think, to learn, to create, to adapt. That's true financial independence. It's not having wealth; it's having the power to produce wealth. It's intrinsic.

The Daily Private Victory—a minimum of one hour a day in renewal of the physical, spiritual, and mental dimensions—is the key to the development of the Seven Habits and it's completely within your Circle of Influence. It is the Quadrant II focus time necessary to integrate these habits into your life, to become principle-centered.

It's also the foundation for the Daily Public Victory. It's the source of intrinsic security you need to sharpen the saw in the social/emotional dimension. It gives you the personal strength to focus on your Circle of Influence in interdependent situations—to look at others through the Abundance Mentality paradigm, to genuinely value their differences and to be happy for their success. It gives you the foundation to work for genuine understanding and for synergetic Win/Win solutions, to practice Habits 4, 5, and 6 in an interdependent reality.

## The Upward Spiral

Renewal is the principle—and the process—that empowers us to move on an upward spiral of growth and change, of continuous improvement.

To make meaningful and consistent progress along that spiral, we need to consider one other aspect of renewal as it applies to the unique human endowment that directs this upward movement— our *conscience*. In the words of Madame de Staël, "The voice of conscience is so delicate that it is easy to stifle it: but it is also so clear that it is impossible to mistake it."

Conscience is the endowment that senses our congruence or disparity with correct principles and lifts us toward them—when it's in shape.

Just as the education of nerve and sinew is vital to the excellent athlete and education of the mind is vital to the scholar, education of the conscience is vital to the truly proactive, highly effective person. Training and educating the conscience, however, requires even greater concentration, more balanced discipline, more consistently honest living. It requires regular feasting on inspiring literature, thinking noble thoughts and, above all, living in harmony with its still small voice.

Just as junk food and lack of exercise can ruin an athlete's condition, those things that are obscene, crude, or pornographic can breed an inner darkness that numbs our higher sensibilities and substitutes the social conscience of "Will I be found out?" for the natural or divine conscience of "What is right and wrong?"

In the words of Dag Hammarskjöld,

> You cannot play with the animal in you without becoming wholly animal, play with falsehood without forfeiting your right to truth, play with cruelty without losing your sensitivity of mind. He who wants to keep his garden tidy doesn't reserve a plot for weeds.

Once we are self-aware, we must choose purposes and principles to live by; otherwise the vacuum will be filled, and we will lose our self-awareness and become like groveling animals who live primarily for survival and propagation. People who exist on that level aren't living; they are "being lived." They are reacting, unaware of the unique endowments that lie dormant and undeveloped within.

And there is no shortcut in developing them. The law of the harvest governs; we will always reap what we sow—no more, no less. The law of justice is immutable, and the closer we align ourselves with correct principles, the better our judgment will be about how the world operates and the more accurate our paradigms—our maps of the territory—will be.

I believe that as we grow and develop on this upward spiral, we must show diligence in the process of renewal by educating and obeying our conscience. An increasingly educated conscience will propel us along the path of personal freedom, security, wisdom, and power.

Moving along the upward spiral requires us to *learn, commit,* and *do* on increasingly higher planes. We deceive ourselves if we think that any one of these is sufficient. To keep progressing, we must learn, commit, and do—learn, commit, and do—and learn, commit, and do again.

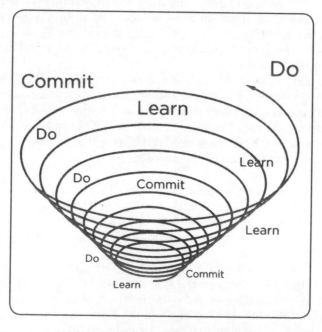

# THE UPWARD SPIRAL

APPLICATION SUGGESTIONS:

1. Make a list of activities that would help you keep in good physical shape, that would fit your life-style and that you could enjoy over time.
2. Select one of the activities and list it as a goal in your personal role area for the coming week. At the end of the week evaluate your performance. If you didn't make your goal, was it because you subordinated it to a genuinely higher value? Or did you fail to act with integrity to your values?
3. Make a similar list of renewing activities in your spiritual and mental dimensions. In your social-emotional area, list relationships you would like to improve or specific circumstances in which Public Victory would bring greater effectiveness. Select one item in each area to list as a goal for the week. Implement and evaluate.
4. Commit to write down specific "sharpen the saw" activities in all four dimensions every week, to do them, and to evaluate your performance and results.

# INSIDE-OUT AGAIN

*The Lord works from the inside out. The world works from the outside in. The world would take people out of the slums. Christ takes the slums out of people, and then they take themselves out of the slums. The world would mold men by changing their environment. Christ changes men, who then change their environment. The world would shape human behavior, but Christ can change human nature.*

EZRA TAFT BENSON
FORMER SECRETARY OF AGRICULTURE

I WOULD LIKE TO SHARE WITH YOU a personal story which I feel contains the essence of this book. In doing so, it is my hope that you will relate to the underlying principles it contains.

Some years ago, our family took a sabbatical leave from the university where I taught so that I could write. We lived for a full year in Laie on the north shore of Oahu, Hawaii.

Shortly after getting settled, we developed a living and working routine which was not only very productive but extremely pleasant.

After an early morning run on the beach, we would send two of our children, barefoot and in shorts, to school. I went to an isolated building next to the canefields where I had an office to do my writing. It was very quiet, very beautiful, very serene—no phone, no meetings, no pressing engagements.

My office was on the outside edge of a college, and one day as I was wandering between stacks of books in the back of the college library, I came across a book that drew my interest. As I opened it, my eyes fell upon a single paragraph that powerfully influenced the rest of my life.

I read the paragraph over and over again. It basically contained the simple idea that there is a gap or a space between stimulus and response, and that the key to both our growth and happiness is how we use that space.

I can hardly describe the effect that idea had on my mind. Though I had been nurtured in the philosophy of self-determinism, the way the idea was phrased—"a gap between stimulus and response"—hit me with fresh, almost unbelievable force. It was almost like "knowing it for the first time," like an inward revolution, "an idea whose time had come."

I reflected on it again and again, and it began to have a powerful effect on my paradigm of life. It was as if I had become an observer of my own participation. I began to stand in that gap and to look outside at the stimuli. I reveled in the inward sense of freedom to choose my response—even to become the stimulus, or at least to influence it—even to reverse it.

Shortly thereafter, and partly as a result of this "revolutionary" idea, Sandra and I began a practice of deep communication. I would pick her up a little before noon on an old red Honda 90 trail cycle, and we would take our two preschool children with us—one between us and the other on my left knee—as we rode out in the canefields by my office. We rode slowly along for about an hour, just talking.

The children looked forward to the ride and hardly ever made any noise. We seldom saw another vehicle, and the cycle was so quiet we could easily hear each other. We usually ended up on an isolated beach where we parked the Honda and walked about 200 yards to a secluded spot where we ate a picnic lunch.

The sandy beach and a freshwater river coming off the island totally absorbed the interest of the children, so Sandra and I were able to continue our talks uninterrupted. Perhaps it doesn't take too much imagination to envision the level of understanding and trust we were able to reach by spending at least two hours a day, every day, for a full year in deep communication.

At the very first of the year, we talked about all kinds of interesting topics—people, ideas, events, the children, my writing, our family at home, future plans, and so forth. But little by little, our communication deepened and we began to talk more and more about our internal worlds—about our upbringing, our scripting, our feelings and self-doubts. As we were deeply immersed in these communications, we also observed them and observed ourselves in them. We began to use that space between stimulus and response in some new and interesting ways which caused us to think about how we were programmed and how those programs shaped how we saw the world.

We began an exciting adventure into our interior worlds and found it to be more exciting, more fascinating, more absorbing, more compelling, more filled with discovery and insight than anything we'd ever known in the outside world.

It wasn't all "sweetness and light." We occasionally hit some raw nerves and had some painful experiences, embarrassing experiences, self-revealing experiences—experiences that made us extremely open and vulnerable to each other. And yet we found we had been wanting to go into those things for years. When we did go into the deeper, more tender issues and then came out of them, we felt in some way healed.

We were so initially supportive and helpful, so encouraging and empathic to each other, that we nurtured and facilitated these internal discoveries in each other.

We gradually evolved two unspoken ground rules. The first was "no probing." As soon as we unfolded the inner layers of vulnerability, we were not to question each other, only to empathize. Probing was simply too invasive. It was also too controlling and too logical. We were covering new, difficult terrain that was scary and uncertain, and it stirred up fears and doubts. We wanted to cover more and more of it, but we grew to respect the need to let each other open up in our own time.

The second ground rule was that when it hurt too much, when it was painful, we would simply quit for the day. Then we would either begin the next day where we left off or wait until the person who was sharing felt ready to continue. We carried around the loose ends, knowing that we wanted to deal with them. But because we had the time and the environment conducive to it, and because we were so excited to observe our own involvement and to grow within our marriage, we simply knew that sooner or later we would deal with all those loose ends and bring them to some kind of closure.

The most difficult and eventually the most fruitful part of this kind of communication came when my vulnerability and Sandra's vulnerability touched. Then, because of our subjective involvement, we found that the space between stimulus and response was no longer there. A few bad feelings surfaced. But our deep desire and our implicit agreement was to prepare ourselves to start where we left off and deal with those feelings until we resolved them.

One of those difficult times had to do with a basic tendency in my personality. My father was a very private individual—very controlled and very careful. My mother was and is very public, very open, very spontaneous. I find both sets of tendencies in me, and when I feel insecure, I tend to become private, like my father. I live inside myself and safely observe.

Sandra is more like my mother—social, authentic, and spontaneous. We had gone through many experiences over the years in which I felt her openness was inappropriate, and she felt my constraint was dysfunctional, both socially and to me as an individual because I would become insensitive to the feelings of others. All of this and much more came out during those deep visits. I came to value Sandra's insight and wisdom and the way she helped me to be a more open, giving, sensitive, social person.

Another of those difficult times had to do with what I perceived to be a "hang up" Sandra had which had bothered me for years. She seemed to have an obsession about Frigidaire appliances which I was at an absolute loss to understand. She would not even consider buying another brand of appliance. Even when we were just starting out and on a very tight budget, she insisted that we drive the fifty miles to the "big city" where Frigidaire appliances were sold, simply because no dealer in our small university town carried them at that time.

This was a matter of considerable agitation to me. Fortunately, the situation came up only when we purchased an appliance. But when it did come up, it was like a stimulus that triggered off a hot button response. This single issue seemed to be symbolic of all irrational thinking, and it generated a whole range of negative feelings within me.

I usually resorted to my dysfunctional private behavior. I suppose I figured that the only way I could deal with it was not to deal with it; otherwise, I felt I would lose control and say things I shouldn't say. There were times when I did slip and say something negative, and I had to go back and apologize.

What bothered me the most was not that she liked Frigidaire, but that she persisted in making what I considered utterly illogical and indefensible statements to defend Frigidaire which had no basis in fact whatsoever. If she had only agreed that her response was irrational and purely emotional, I think I could have handled it. But her justification was upsetting.

It was sometime in early spring when the Frigidaire issue came up. All our prior communication had prepared us. The ground rules had been deeply established—not to probe and to leave it alone if it got to be too painful for either or both.

I will never forget the day we talked it through. We didn't end up on the beach that day; we just continued to ride through the canefields, perhaps because we didn't want to look each other in the eye. There had been so much psychic history and so many bad feelings associated with the issue, and it had been submerged for so long. It had never been so critical as to rupture the relationship, but when you're trying to cultivate a beautiful unified relationship, any divisive issue is important.

Sandra and I were amazed at what we learned through the interaction. It was truly synergistic. It was as if Sandra were learning, almost for the first time herself, the reason for her so-called hang-up. She started to talk about her father, about how he had worked as a high school history teacher and coach for years, and how, to help make ends meet, he had gone into the appliance business. During an economic downturn, he had experienced serious financial difficulties, and the only thing that enabled him to stay in business during that time was the fact that Frigidaire would finance his inventory.

Sandra had an unusually deep and sweet relationship with her father. When he returned home at the end of a very tiring day, he would lie on the couch, and Sandra would rub his feet and sing to him. It was a beautiful time they enjoyed together almost daily for years. He would also open up and talk through his worries and concerns about the business, and he shared with Sandra his deep appreciation for Frigidaire financing his inventory so that he could make it through the difficult times.

This communication between father and daughter had taken place in a spontaneous way during very natural times, when the most powerful kind of scripting takes place. During those relaxed times guards are down and all kinds of images and thoughts are planted deep in the subconscious mind. Perhaps Sandra had forgotten about all of this until the safety of that year of communication when it could come out also in very natural and spontaneous ways.

Sandra gained tremendous insight into herself and into the emotional root of her feelings about Frigidaire. I also gained insight and a whole new level of respect. I came to realize that Sandra wasn't talking about appliances; she was talking about her father, and about loyalty—about loyalty to his needs.

I remember both of us becoming tearful on that day, not so much because of the insights, but because of the increased sense of reverence we had for each other. We discovered that even seemingly trivial things often have roots in deep emotional experiences. To deal only with the superficial trivia without seeing the deeper, more tender issues is to trample on the sacred ground of another's heart.

There were many rich fruits of those months. Our communication became so powerful that we could almost instantly connect with each other's thoughts. When we left Hawaii, we resolved to continue the practice. During the many years since, we have continued to go regularly on our Honda trail cycle, or in the car if the weather's bad, just to talk. We feel the key to staying in love is to talk, particularly about feelings. We try to communicate with each other several times every day, even when I'm traveling. It's like coming into home base, which accesses all the happiness, security, and values it represents.

Thomas Wolfe was wrong. You *can* go home again—if your home is a treasured relationship, a precious companionship.

## INTERGENERATIONAL LIVING

As Sandra and I discovered that wonderful year, the ability to use wisely the gap between stimulus and response, to exercise the four unique endowments of our human nature, empowered us from the inside out.

We had tried the outside-in approach. We loved each other, and we had attempted to work through our differences by controlling our attitudes and our behaviors, by practicing useful techniques of human interaction. But our Band-Aids and aspirin only lasted so long. Until we worked and communicated on the level of our essential paradigms, the chronic underlying problems were still there.

When we began to work from the inside out, we were able to build a relationship of trust and openness and to resolve dysfunctional differences in a deep and lasting way that never could have come by working from the outside in. The delicious fruits—a rich Win/Win relationship, a deep understanding of each other, and a marvelous synergy—grew out of the roots we nurtured as we examined our programs, rescripted ourselves, and managed our lives so that we could create time for the important Quadrant II activity of communicating deeply with each other.

And there were other fruits. We were able to see on a much deeper level that, just as powerfully as our own lives had been affected by our parents, the lives of our children were being influenced and shaped by us, often in ways we didn't even begin to realize. Understanding the power of scripting in our own lives, we felt a renewed desire to do everything we could to make certain that what we passed on to future generations, by both precept and example, was based on correct principles.

I have drawn particular attention in this book to those scripts we have been given which we proactively want to change. But as we examine our scripting carefully, many of us will also begin to see beautiful scripts, positive scripts that have been passed down to us which we have blindly taken for granted. Real self-awareness helps us to appreciate those scripts and to appreciate those who have gone before us and nurtured us in principle-based living, mirroring back to us not only what we are, but what we can become.

There is transcendant power in a strong intergenerational family. An effectively interdependent family of children, parents, grandparents, aunts, uncles, and cousins can be a powerful force in helping people have a sense of who they are and where they came from and what they stand for.

It's great for children to be able to identify themselves with the "tribe," to feel that many people know them and care about them, even though they're spread all over the country. And that can be a tremendous benefit as you nurture your family. If one of your children is having difficulty and doesn't really relate with you at a particular time in his life, maybe he can relate to your brother or sister who can become a surrogate father or mother, a mentor or a hero for a period of time.

Grandparents who show a great interest in their grandchildren are among the most precious people on this earth. What a marvelous positive social mirror they can be! My mother is like that. Even now, in her late 80's, she takes a deep personal interest in every one of her descendants. She writes us love letters. I was reading one the other day on a plane with tears streaming down my cheeks. I could call her up tonight and I know she'd say, "Stephen, I want you to know how much I love you and how wonderful I think you are." She's constantly reaffirming.

A strong intergenerational family is potentially one of the most fruitful, rewarding, and satisfying interdependent relationships. And many people feel the importance of that relationship. Look at the fascination we all had with *Roots* some years ago. Each of us has roots and the ability to trace those roots, to identify our ancestors.

The highest and most powerful motivation in doing that is not for ourselves only, but for our *posterity*, for the posterity of all mankind. As someone once observed, "There are only two lasting bequests we can give our children—one is roots, the other wings."

## Becoming a Transition Person

Among other things, I believe that giving "wings" to our children and to others means empowering them with the freedom to rise above negative scripting that had been passed down to us. I believe it means becoming what my friend and associate, Dr. Terry Warner, calls a "transition" person. Instead of transferring those scripts to the next generation, we can change them. And we can do it in a way that will build relationships in the process.

If your parents abused you as a child, that does not mean that you have to abuse your own children. Yet there's plenty of evidence to indicate that you will tend to live out that script. But because you're proactive, you can rewrite the script. You can choose not only not to abuse your children, but to affirm them, to script them in positive ways.

You can write it in your personal mission statement and into your mind and heart. You can visualize yourself living in harmony with that mission statement in your Daily Private Victory. You can take steps to love and forgive your own parents, and if they are still living, to build a positive relationship with them by seeking to understand.

A tendency that's run through your family for generations can stop with you. You're a transition person—a link between the past and the future. And your own change can affect many, many lives downstream.

One powerful transition person of the twentieth century, Anwar Sadat, left us as part of his legacy a profound understanding of the nature of change. Sadat stood between a past that had created a "huge wall of suspicion, fear, hate and misunderstanding" between Arabs and Israelis, and a future in which increased conflict and isolation seemed inevitable. Efforts at negotiation had been met with objections on every scale—even to formalities and procedural points, to an insignificant comma or period in the text of proposed agreements.

While others attempted to resolve the tense situation by hacking at the leaves, Sadat drew upon his earlier centering experience in a lonely prison cell and went to work on the root. And in doing so, he changed the course of history for millions of people.

He records in his autobiography:

> It was then that I drew, almost unconsciously, on the inner strength I had developed in Cell 54 of Cairo Central Prison— a strength, call it a talent or capacity, for change. I found that I faced a highly complex situation, and that I couldn't hope to change it until I had armed myself with the necessary psychological and intellectual capacity. My contemplation of life and human nature in that secluded place had taught me that he who cannot change the very fabric of his thought will never be able to change reality, and will never, therefore, make any progress.

Change—real change—comes from the inside out. It doesn't come from hacking at the leaves of attitude and behavior with quick fix personality ethic techniques. It comes from striking at the root—the fabric of our thought, the fundamental, essential paradigms, which give definition to our character and create the lens through which we see the world. In the words of Amiel,

> Moral truth can be conceived in thought. One can have feelings about it. One can will to live it. But moral truth may have been penetrated and possessed in all these ways, and escape us still. Deeper even than consciousness there is our being itself—our very substance, our nature. Only those truths which have entered into this last region, which have become ourselves, become spontaneous and involuntary as well as voluntary, unconscious as well as conscious,

are really our life—that is to say, something more than property. So long as we are able to distinguish any space whatever between Truth and us we remain outside it. The thought, the feeling, the desire or the consciousness of life may not be quite life. To become divine is then the aim of life. Then only can truth be said to be ours beyond the possibility of loss. It is no longer outside us, nor in a sense even in us, but we are it, and it is we.

Achieving *unity*—oneness—with ourselves, with our loved ones, with our friends and working associates, is the highest and best and most delicious fruit of the Seven Habits. Most of us have tasted this fruit of true unity from time to time in the past, as we have also tasted the bitter, lonely fruit of disunity—and we know how precious and fragile unity is.

Obviously building a character of total integrity and living the life of love and service that creates such unity isn't easy. It isn't quick fix.

But it's possible. It begins with the desire to center our lives on correct principles, to break out of the paradigms created by other centers and the comfort zones of unworthy habits.

Sometimes we make mistakes, we feel awkward. But if we start with the Daily Private Victory and work from the inside out, the results will surely come. As we plant the seed and patiently weed and nourish it, we begin to feel the excitement of real growth and eventually taste the incomparably delicious fruits of a congruent, effective life.

Again, I quote Emerson: "That which we persist in doing becomes easier—not that the nature of the task has changed, but our ability to do has increased."

By centering our lives on correct principles and creating a balanced focus between doing and increasing our ability to do, we become empowered in the task of creating effective, useful, and peaceful lives . . . for ourselves, and for our posterity.

## A Personal Note

As I conclude this book, I would like to share my own personal conviction concerning what I believe to be the source of correct principles. I believe that correct principles are natural laws, and that God, the Creator and Father of us all, is the source of them, and also the source of our conscience. I believe that to the degree people live by this inspired conscience, they will grow to fulfill their natures; to the degree that they do not, they will not rise above the animal plane.

I believe that there are parts to human nature that cannot be reached by either legislation or education, but require the power of God to deal with. I believe that as human beings, we cannot perfect ourselves. To the degree to which we align ourselves with correct principles, divine endowments will be released within our nature in enabling us to fulfill the measure of our creation. In the words of Teilhard de Chardin, "We are not human beings having a spiritual experience. We are spiritual beings having a human experience."

I personally struggle with much of what I have shared in this book. But the struggle is worthwhile and fulfilling. It gives meaning to my life and enables me to love, to serve, and to try again.

Again, T. S. Eliot expresses so beautifully my own personal discovery and conviction: "We must not cease from exploration. And the end of all our exploring will be to arrive where we began and to know the place for the first time."

# Afterword:
# Questions I am Often Asked

Frankly, I've always been embarrassed by personal questions like some in this afterword. But I am asked them so often and with such interest that I've gone ahead and included them here. Many of these questions and answers were also included in *Living the 7 Habits*.

*The 7 Habits* **was published in 1989. Given your experiences in the many years that have followed, what would you change, add, or subtract?**

I'm not responding lightly, but frankly I wouldn't change anything. I might go deeper and apply wider but I have had the opportunity to do that in some of the books released since then.

For example, over 250,000 individuals were profiled showing Habit 3, Put First Things First, as the habit most neglected. So, the *First Things First* book (published 1996) went deeper into Habits 2 and 3 but also added more substance and illustrations for all the other habits.

*The 7 Habits of Highly Effective Families* applied the 7 Habits framework of thinking into building strong, happy, highly effective families.

Also, my son, Sean, applied the framework to the unique needs, interests and challenges of teens in a very visually attractive, entertaining, and edifying way in *The 7 Habits of Highly Effective Teens*.

We have also had tens of thousands of people tell us of the significant impact of becoming the creative force of their own lives through internalizing the 7 Habits. Seventy-six of them shared the details of their fascinating stories of courage and inspiration in *Living the 7 Habits*—showing the transforming power of the principles in all kinds of personal, family, and organizational settings regardless of their circumstances, organizational position, or prior life experiences.

## What have you learned about the 7 Habits since the book's release?

I have learned or had reinforced many things. I'll briefly mention ten learnings.

1. The importance of understanding the difference between principles and values. Principles are natural laws that are external to us and that ultimately control the consequences of our actions. Values are internal and subjective and represent that which we feel strongest about in guiding our behavior. Hopefully we will come to *value principles,* so that we get the results we want now in a way that enables us to get even greater results in the future, which is how I define effectiveness. Everyone has values; even criminal gangs have values. Values govern people's behavior but principles govern the consequences of those behaviors. Principles are independent of us. They operate regardless of our awareness of them, acceptance of them, liking of them, belief in them, or obeying of them. I have come to believe that humility is the mother of all virtues. Humility says we are not in control, principles are in control, therefore we submit ourselves to principles. Pride says that we are in control, and since our values govern our behavior, we can simply do life our way. We may do so but the consequences of our behavior flow from principles not our values. Therefore we should *value principles.*

2. From experiences all over the world with this material I have come to see the *universal* nature of the principles undergirding this material. Illustrations and practices may vary and are culturally specific, but the principles are the same. I have found the principles contained in the 7 Habits in all six major world religions and have actually drawn upon quotations from sacred writings of those religions when teaching in those cultures.

I have done this in the Middle East, India, Asia, Australia and the South Pacific, South America, Europe, North America, Africa, and among Native Americans and other indigenous peoples. All of us, men and women alike, face similar problems, have similar needs, and internally resonate with the underlying principles. There is an internal sense of the principle of justice or win/win. There is an internal moral sense of the principle of responsibility, of the principle of purpose, of integrity, of respect, of cooperation, of communication, of renewal. These are universal. But practices are not. They are situationally specific. Every culture interprets universal principles in unique ways.

3. I have come to see the organizational implications of the 7 Habits, although, in the strict technical sense, an organization does not have habits. Its culture has norms or mores or social codes, which represent habits. An organization also has established systems, processes, and procedures. These represent habits. In fact, in the last analysis, all behavior is personal. It is individual even though it often is part of collective behavior in the form of decisions made by management regarding structure and systems, processes and practices. We have worked with thousands of organizations in most every industry and profession and have found that the same basic principles contained in the 7 Habits apply and define effectiveness.

4. You can teach all 7 Habits by starting with any one habit. And you can also teach one habit in a way that leads to the teaching of the other six. It's like a hologram where the whole is contained in the part and the part is contained in the whole.

5. Even though the 7 Habits represents an inside-out approach, it works most successfully when you start with the outside challenge and then take the inside-out approach. In other words, if you are having a relationship challenge, say a breakdown of communication and trust, this will define the nature of the needed inside-out approach in winning the kind of private victory that enables the public victory meeting that challenge. This is the reason I often teach Habits 4, 5, and 6 before I teach Habits 1, 2, and 3.

6. Interdependence is ten times more difficult than independence. It demands so much more mental and emotional independence to think win/win when another person is into win/lose, to seek to understand first when everything inside you cries out for understanding, and to search for a better third alternative when compromise is so much easier. In other words, to work successfully with others in creative cooperative ways requires an enormous amount of independence, internal security, and self-mastery. Otherwise, what we call interdependency is really counter-dependency where people do the opposite to assert their independence, or codependency where they literally need the other person's weakness to fulfill their need and to justify their own weakness.

7. You can pretty well summarize the first three habits with the expression "make and keep a promise." And you can pretty well summarize the next three habits with the expression "involve others in the problem and work out the solution together."

8. The 7 Habits represents a new language even though there are fewer than a dozen unique words or phrases. This new language becomes a code, a shorthand way of saying a great deal. When you say to another "Was that a deposit or a withdrawal?" "Is that reactive or proactive?" "Is that synergistic or a compromise?" "Is that win/win or win/lose or lose/win?" "Is that putting first things first or second things first?" "Is that beginning with the means in mind or the end in mind?" I've seen entire cultures transformed by a wide understanding of and commitment to the principles and concepts symbolized by these very special code words.

9. Integrity is a higher value than loyalty. Or better put, integrity is the highest form of loyalty. Integrity means being integrated or centered on principles not on people, organizations, or even family. You will find that the root of most issues that people are dealing with is "is it popular (acceptable, political), or is it right?" When we prioritize being loyal to a person or group over doing what we feel to be right, we lose integrity. We may temporarily gain popularity or build loyalty, but, downstream, this loss of integrity will undermine even those relationships. It's like bad-

mouthing someone behind their back. The person you are temporarily united with through badmouthing someone else knows you would bad mouth them under different pressures and circumstances. In a sense, the first three habits represent integrity and the next three loyalty; but they are totally interwoven. Over time, integrity produces loyalty. If you attempt to reverse them and go for loyalty first, you will find yourself temporizing and compromising integrity. It's better to be trusted than to be liked. Ultimately, trust and respect will generally produce love.

10. Living the 7 Habits is a constant struggle for everyone. Everyone falters from time to time on each of the seven and sometimes all seven simultaneously. They really are simple to understand but difficult to consistently practice. They are common sense but what is common sense is not always common practice.

## Which habit do you personally have the greatest difficulty with?

Habit 5. When I am really tired and already convinced I'm right, I really don't want to listen. I may even pretend to listen. Basically I am guilty of the same thing I talk about, listening with the intent to reply, not to understand. In fact, in some sense, I struggle almost daily with all 7 Habits. I have conquered none of them. I see them more as life principles that we never really master and that the closer we come to their mastery, the more aware we become of how far we really have yet to go. It's like the more you know the more you know you don't know.

This is why I often gave my university students 50 percent of the grade for the quality of their questions and the other 50 percent for the quality of their answer to their questions. Their true level of knowledge is better revealed that way.

Similarly, the 7 Habits represents an upward cycle.

Habit 1 at a high level is vastly different from Habit 1 at a lower level. To be proactive at the beginning level may only be awareness of the space between stimulus and response. At the next level it may involve a choice, such as not to get back at or to get even. At the next level, to give feedback. At the next level, to ask forgiveness. At the next level, to forgive. At the next, to forgive parents. At the next level, to forgive dead parents. And the next level, to simply not take offense.

1-7
AN UPWARD SPIRAL

**You're the vice-chairman of FranklinCovey Company. Does FranklinCovey live the 7 Habits?**

We try to. Continually trying to live what we teach is one of our most fundamental values. But we don't do it perfectly. Like any other business, we're challenged by changing market realities and by integrating the two cultures of the former Covey Leadership Center and Franklin Quest. The merger took place in the summer of 1997. It takes time, patience, and persistence in applying the principles and the true test of our success will be in the long run. No snapshot will give an accurate picture.

Any airplane is off track much of the time but just keeps coming back to the flight plan. Eventually, it arrives at its destination. This is true with all of us as individuals, families, or organizations. The key is to have an "End in Mind" and a shared commitment to constant feedback and constant course correction.

**Why seven? Why not six or eight or ten or fifteen? What is so sacred about seven?**

Nothing is sacred about seven, it just so happens that the three private victory habits (freedom to choose, choice, action) precede the three public victory habits (respect, understanding, creation) and then there is one to renew the rest and that equals seven.

When asked this question, I've always said if there were some other desirable characteristic you would like make into a habit, you would simply put that under Habit 2 as one of the values you are trying to live by. In other words, if punctuality is a desirable trait you want to make a habit, that would be one of the values of Habit 2. So no matter what else you came up with you would put it under Habit 2, your value system. Habit 1 is the idea that you can have a value system, that you can choose your own value system. Habit 2 is what those choices or values are and Habit 3 is to live by them. So they are very basic, generic, and interconnected.

It so happens that at the writing of this afterword for this new edition of *The 7 Habits,* I have just completed a new book entitled *The 8th Habit: From Effectiveness to Greatness.* To some, calling it the 8th Habit may appear to be a departure from my standard answer. But you see, as I say in the opening chapter of this new book, the world has profoundly changed since *The 7 Habits of Highly Effective People* was published in 1989. The challenges and complexity we face in our personal lives and relationships, in our families, in our professional lives, and in our organizations are of a different order of magnitude. In fact, many mark 1989—the year we witnessed the fall of the Berlin Wall—as the beginning of the Information Age, the birth of a new reality, a sea change of incredible significance . . . truly a new era.

Being *highly effective* as individuals and organizations is no longer optional in today's world—it's the price of entry to the playing field. But surviving, thriving, innovating, excelling and leading in this new reality will require us to build on and reach beyond effectiveness. The call and need of a new era is for *fulfillment.* It's for *passionate optimization,* for *significant contribution* and *greatness.* These are on a different plane or *dimension.* They are different in kind—just as *significance* is different in *kind,* not in *degree,* from success. Tapping into the higher reaches of human genius and motivation—what we could call *voice*— requires a new mindset, a new skill-set, a new tool-set . . . a new habit.

The 8th Habit, then, is not about adding one more habit to the

7th—one that somehow got forgotten. It's about seeing and harnessing the power of *a third dimension* to the 7 Habits that meets *the* central challenge of the new Knowledge Worker Age.

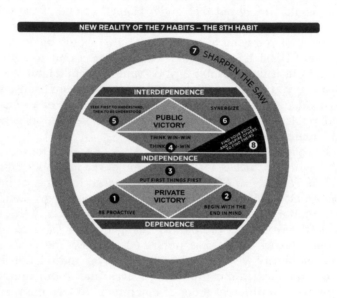

### How does fame affect you?

It affects me in different ways. From an ego standpoint, it's flattering. From a teaching standpoint it is humbling, but I must strongly acknowledge that I am not the author of any of these principles and deserve absolutely no recognition. I am not saying this because of a desire to be modest and humble. I am saying this because I believe it—that I, myself, believe it. I see myself like most of you—as a seeker of truth, of understanding. I am not a guru; I disdain being called a guru. I want no disciples. I am only trying to promote a discipleship toward principles that are already in people's hearts, that people will live true to their conscience.

**If you had it to do over again, what is the one thing you would do differently as a businessperson?**

I would do more strategic, proactive recruiting and selecting. When you are buried by the urgent and have a thousand balls in the air, it is so easy to put people that appear to have solutions into key positions. The tendency is not to look deeply into their backgrounds and patterns, not to do "due diligence," nor is it to carefully develop the criteria that need to be met in the particular roles or assignments. I am convinced that when recruiting and selecting is done strategically, that is, thinking long-term and proactively, not based upon the pressures of the moment, it pays enormous long-term dividends. Someone once said, "That which we desire most earnestly we believe most easily." You really have to look deeply into both character and competence because eventually, downstream, flaws in either area will manifest themselves in both areas. I am convinced that although training and development is important, recruiting and selection are much more important.

**If you had it to do over again, what is the one thing you would do differently as a parent?**

As a parent, I wish I had spent more time in carefully developing soft, informal win/win agreements with each of my children in the different phases of their lives. Because of business and travels I often indulged my children and went for lose/win too much instead of paying the price in relationship building sufficient to really develop thorough, sound win/win agreements more consistently.

**How is technology going to change business in the future?**

I believe in Stan Davis's statement that "When the infrastructure changes, everything rumbles," and I think the technical infrastructure is central to everything. It will accelerate all good *and* bad trends. I'm also convinced that it is for these very reasons that the human element becomes even more important. High tech without high touch does not work, and the more influential technology becomes, the more important the human factor which controls that technology becomes, particularly in developing a cultural commitment to the criteria in the use of that technology.

**Are you surprised or astounded at the universal popularity of the 7 Habits (with other countries/cultures/ages/gender)?**

Yes and no. Yes, in that I had no idea it would become a worldwide phenomenon and that a few of the words would become part of Americana. No, in the sense that the material had been tested for over twenty-five years and I knew that it would work primarily because it is based upon principles I did not invent and therefore take no credit for.

**How would you begin to teach the 7 Habits to very young children?**

I think I would live by Albert Schweitzer's three basic rules for raising children: First, example; second, example; third, example. But I wouldn't go quite that far. I would say, first, example; second, build a caring and affirming relationship; and third, teach some of the simple ideas underlying the habits in the language of children—help them gain a basic understanding and vocabulary of the 7 Habits and show them how to process their own experiences through the principles; let them identify what particular principles and habits are being illustrated in their lives.

**My boss (spouse, child, friend, etc.) really needs the 7 Habits. How would you recommend I get them to read it?**

People don't care how much you know until they know how much you care. Build a relationship of trust and openness based upon a character example of trustworthiness and then share how the 7 Habits have helped you. Simply let them see the 7 Habits in action through your life. Then, at the appropriate time, you might invite them to participate in a training program or share your book as a gift or teach some of the basic ideas when the occasion calls for it.

## What is your background and how did you come to write *The 7 Habits*?

It was implicitly understood that I would follow in my father's footsteps and go into the family business. However, I found that I enjoyed teaching and training leaders even more than business. I became deeply interested and involved in the human side of organizations when I was at Harvard Business School. Later I taught business subjects at Brigham Young University and did consulting, advising, and training on the side for several years. During that time, I became interested in creating integrated leadership and management development programs around a sequential and balanced set of principles. These eventually evolved into the 7 Habits and then while applying it to organizations it evolved into the concept of principle-centered leadership. I decided to leave the university and go full-time into training executives from all different kinds of organizations. After a year of following a very carefully developed curriculum came the development of a business that has enabled us to take the material to people throughout the world.

## What is your response to the people who claim to have the true formula for success?

I would say two things. First, if what they are saying is based on principles or natural laws, I want to learn from them and I commend them. Second, I would say we are probably using different words to describe the same basic principles or natural laws.

**Are you really bald or do you shave your head for efficiency's sake?**

Hey, listen, while you're busy blow-drying your hair, I'm out serving the customers. In fact, the first time I heard the expression, "Bald is beautiful," I kicked the slats out of my crib!

*Appendix*
*A*

# POSSIBLE PERCEPTIONS FLOWING out of VARIOUS CENTERS

These are alternative ways you may tend to perceive other areas of your life:

| IF YOUR CENTER IS: | SPOUSE | FAMILY | MONEY | WORK | POSSESSIONS |
|---|---|---|---|---|---|
| SPOUSE | • The main source of need satisfaction | • Good in its place<br>• Less important<br>• A common project | • Necessary to properly take care of spouse | • Necessary to earn money to care for spouse | • Means to bless, impress, or manipulate |
| FAMILY | • Part of the family | • The highest priority | • Family economic support | • A means to an end | • Family comfort and opportunities |
| MONEY | • Asset or liability in acquiring money | • Economic drain | • Source of security and fulfillment | • Necessary to the acquisition of money | • Evidence of economic success |
| WORK | • Help or hindrance in work | • Help or interruption to work<br>• People to instruct in work ethic | • Of secondary importance<br>• Evidence of hard work | • Main source of fulfillment and satisfaction<br>• Highest ethic | • Tools to increase work effectiveness<br>• Fruits, badge of work |

| | | | | | |
|---|---|---|---|---|---|
| **POSSESSIONS** | • Main possession<br>• Assistant in acquiring posessions | • Possession to use, exploit, dominate, smother, control<br>• Showcase | • Key to increasing possessions<br>• Another possession to control | • Opportunity to possess status, authority, recognition | • Status symbols |
| **PLEASURE** | • Companion in fun and pleasure or obstacle to it | • Vehicle or interference | • Means to increase opportunities for pleasure | • Means to an end<br>• "Fun" work OK | • Objects of fun<br>• Means to move fun |
| **A FRIEND OR FRIENDS** | • Possible friend or possible competitor<br>• Social status symbol | • Friends or obstacle to developing friendships<br>• Social status symbol | • Source of economic and social good | • Social opportunity | • Means of buying friendship<br>• Means to entertaining or providing social pleasure |

These are alternative ways you may tend to perceive other areas of your life:

| IF YOUR CENTER IS: | PLEASURE | A FRIEND OR FRIENDS | ENEMY OR ENEMIES | CHURCH | SELF | PRINCIPLES |
|---|---|---|---|---|---|---|
| SPOUSE | • Mutual, unifying activity or unimportant | • Spouse is best or only friend<br>• Only friends are "our" friends | • Spouse is my defender, or common enemy provides source of marriage definition | • Activity to enjoy together<br>• Subordinate to relationship | • Self-worth is spouse-based<br>• Highly vulnerable to spouse attitudes and behaviors | • Ideas that create and maintain relationship with spouse |
| FAMILY | • Family activities or relatively unimportant | • Friends of the family, or competition<br>• Threat to strong family life | • Defined by family<br>• Source of family strength and unity<br>• Possible threat to family strength | • Source of help | • Vital part of but subordinate to family | • Rules that keep family unified and strong<br>• Subordinate to family |
| MONEY | • Economic drain or evidence of economic stress | • Chosen because of economic status or influence | • Economic competitors<br>• Threat to economic security | • Tax write-off<br>• Hand in your pocket | • Self-worth is determined by net worth | • Ways that work in making and managing money |
| WORK | • Waste of time<br>• Interferes with work | • Developed from work setting or shared interest<br>• Basically unnecessary | • Obstacles to work productivity | • Important to corporate image<br>• Imposition on your time<br>• Opportunity to network in profession | • Defined by job role | • Ideas that make you successful in your work<br>• Need to adapt to work conditions |

| | | | | | |
|---|---|---|---|---|---|
| **POSSESSIONS** | • Buying, shopping, joining clubs | • Personal objects<br>• Usable | • Takers, thieves<br>• Others with more possessions or recognition | • "My" church, a status symbol<br>• Source of unfair criticism or good things in life | • Defined by the things I own<br>• Defined by social status, recognition | • Concepts that enable you to acquire and enhance possessions |
| **PLEASURE** | • Supreme end in life<br>• Main source of satisfaction | • Companions in fun | • Take life too seriously<br>• Guilt trippers, destroyers | • Inconvenient, obstacle to recreation<br>• Guilt trip | • Instrument for pleasure | • Natural drives and instincts that need to be satisfied |
| **A FRIEND OR FRIENDS** | • Enjoyed always with friends<br>• Primarily social events | • Critical to personal happiness<br>• Belonging, acceptance, popularity is crucial | • Outside the social circle<br>• Common enemies provide unity or definition for friendship | • Place for social gathering | • Socially defined<br>• Afraid of embarrassment or rejection | • Basic laws that enable you to get along with others |

This is the way you may tend to perceive other areas of your life:

| IF YOUR CENTER IS: | SPOUSE | FAMILY | MONEY | WORK | POSSESSIONS |
|---|---|---|---|---|---|
| AN ENEMY OR ENEMIES | • Sympathizer or scapegoat | • Refuge (emotional support) or scapegoat | • Means to fight with or prove superiority | • Escape or opportunity to vent feelings | • Fighting tools<br>• Means to secure allies<br>• Escape, refuge |
| CHURCH | • A companion in or facilitator for church service, or a trial of faith | • Models to exemplify adherence to church teachings, or trials of faith | • Means to support church and family<br>• Evil, if greater in priority than church service or teachings | • Necessary for temporal support | • Temporal possessions of minimal importance<br>• Reputation and image of great worth |
| SELF | • Possession<br>• Satisfier and pleaser | • Possession<br>• Need satisfier | • Source of needs satisfaction | • Opportunity to "do my own thing" | • Source of self-definition, protection, enhancement |

**PRINCIPLES**

- Equal partner in a mutually beneficial interdependent relationship

- Friends
- Opportunity for service, contribution, and fulfillment
- Opportunity for intergenerational rescripting and change

- Enabling resource in the accomplishment of important priorities and goals

- Opportunity to use talents and abilites in a meaningful way
- Means to provide economic resource
- Time investment to be kept in balance with other time investments and in harmony with priorities and values in life

- Enabling resources
- Responsibilities to be properly cared for
- Secondary to people in importance

This is the way you may tend to perceive other areas of your life:

| IF YOUR CENTER IS: | PLEASURE | A FRIEND OR FRIENDS | ENEMY OR ENEMIES | CHURCH | SELF | PRINCIPLES |
|---|---|---|---|---|---|---|
| AN ENEMY OR ENEMIES | • Rest and relaxation time before the next battle | • Emotional supporters and sympathizers<br>• Possibly defined by common enemy | • Objects of hate<br>• Source of personal problems<br>• Stimuli to self-protection and self-justification | • Source of self-justification | • Victimized<br>• Immobilized by enemy | • Justification for labeling enemies<br>• Source of your enemy's wrongness |
| CHURCH | • "Innocent" pleasures as an opportunity to gather with other church members<br>• Others as sinful or time wasters, to be self-righteously denied | • Other members of the church | • Nonbelievers; those who disagree with church teachings or whose lives are in blatant opposition to them | • Highest-priority source of guidance | • Self-worth is determined by activity in the church, contributions to the church, or performance of deeds that reflect the church ethic | • Doctrines taught by the church<br>• Subordinate to the church |
| SELF | • Deserved sensate satisfactions<br>• "My rights"<br>• "My needs" | • Supporter, provider for "me" | • Source of self-definition, self-justification | • Vehicle to serve self-interests | • Better, smarter, more right<br>• Justified in focusing all resources on personal gratification | • Source of justification<br>• Those ideas that serve my best interests; can be adapted to need |

| PRINCIPLES | | | | |
|---|---|---|---|---|
| • Joy that comes from almost any activity in a focused life<br>• True re-creation as an important part of a balanced, integrated life-style | • Companions in interdependent living<br>• Confidants—those to share with, serve, and support | • No real perceived "enemies"; just people with different paradigms and agendas to be understood and cared about | • Vehicle for true principles<br>• Opportunity for service and contribution | • One unique, talented, creative individual in the midst of many unique, talented, creative individuals who, working independently and interdependently, can accomplish great things | • Immutable natural laws, which cannot be violated with impunity<br>• When honored, preserve integrity and thus lead to true growth and happiness |

# A QUADRANT II DAY at the OFFICE

THE FOLLOWING EXERCISE AND ANALYSIS is designed to help you see the impact of a Quadrant II paradigm in a business setting on a very practical level.

Suppose that you are the director of marketing for a major pharmaceutical firm. You are about to begin an average day at the office, and as you look over the items to attend to that day, you estimate the amount of time each one will take.

Your unprioritized list includes the following:

1. You'd like to have lunch with the general manager (1–1½ hours).
2. You were instructed the day before to prepare your media budget for the following year (2 or 3 days).
3. Your "IN" basket is overflowing into your "OUT" basket (1–1½ hours).
4. You need to talk to the sales manager about last month's sales; his office is down the hall (4 hours).
5. You have several items of correspondence that your secretary says are urgent (1 hour).
6. You'd like to catch up on the medical journals piled upon your desk (½ hour).
7. You need to prepare a presentation for a sales meeting slated for next month (2 hours).
8. There's a rumor that the last batch of product X didn't pass quality control.
9. Someone from the FDA wants you to return his call about product "X" (½ hour).
10. There is a meeting at two P.M. for the executive board, but you don't know what it is about (1 hour).

Take a few minutes now and use what you have learned from Habits 1, 2, and 3 that might help you to effectively schedule your day.

## 8-to-5 SCHEDULE

```
 8 _____
 9 _____
10 _____
11 _____
12 _____
 1 _____
 2 _____
 3 _____
 4 _____
 5 _____
```

By asking you to plan only one day, I have automatically elimi-nated the wider context of the week so fundamental to fourth generation time management. But you will be able to see the power of a Quadrant II, principle-centered paradigm even in the context of one nine-hour period of time.

It is fairly obvious that most of the items on the list are Quadrant I activities. With the exception of item number six—catching up on medical journals—everything else is seemingly both important and urgent.

If you were a third generation time manager, using prioritized values and goals, you would have a framework for making such scheduling decisions and would perhaps assign a letter such as A, B, or C next to each item and then number 1, 2, 3 under each A, B, and C. You would also consider the circumstances, such as the availability of other people involved, and the logical amount of time required to eat lunch. Finally, based on all of these factors, you would schedule the day.

Many third generation time managers who have done this exercise do exactly what I have described. They schedule when they will do what, and based on various assumptions which are made and explicitly identified, they would accomplish or at least begin most of the items in that day and push the remainder onto the next day or to some other time.

For instance, most people indicate that they would use the time between eight and nine A.M. to find out exactly what was on the agenda for the executive board meeting so that they could prepare for it, to set up lunch with the general manager around noon, and to return the call from the FDA. They usually plan to spend the next hour or two talking to the sales manager, handling those correspondence items which are most important and urgent, and checking out the rumor regarding the last batch of product "X" which apparently didn't pass quality control. The rest of that morning is spent in preparing for the luncheon visit with the general manager and/or for the two P.M. executive board meeting, or dealing with whatever problems were uncovered regarding product "X" and last month's sales.

After lunch, the afternoon is usually spent attending to the unfinished matters just mentioned and/or attempting to finish the other most important and urgent correspondence, making some headway into the overflowing "IN" basket, and handling other important and urgent items that may have come up during the course of the day.

Most people feel the media budget preparations for the following year and the preparation for the next month's sales meeting could probably be put off until another day, which may not have as many Quadrant I items in it. Both of those are obviously more Quadrant II activities, having to do with long-term thinking and planning. The medical journals continue to be set aside because they are clearly Quadrant II and are probably less important than the other two Quadrant II matters just mentioned.

This is the kind of thinking which third generation time managers generally go through, even though they may vary as to when they will do what.

What approach did you take as you scheduled those items? Was it similar to the third generation approach? Or did you take a Quadrant II, fourth generation approach? (Refer to the Time Management Matrix on page 160.)

### The Quadrant II Approach

Let's go through the items on the list using a Quadrant II approach. This is only one possible scenario; others could be created, which may also be consistent with the Quadrant II paradigm, but this is illustrative of the kind of thinking it embodies.

As a Quadrant II manager, you would recognize that most P activities are in Quadrant I and most PC activities are in Quadrant II. You would know that the only way to make Quadrant I manageable is to give considerable attention to Quadrant II, primarily by working on prevention and opportunity and by having the courage to say "no" to Quadrants III and IV.

THE TWO P.M. BOARD MEETING.    We will assume the two P.M. executive board meeting did not have an agenda for the attending executives, or perhaps you would not see the agenda until you arrived at the meeting. This is not uncommon. As a result, people tend to come unprepared and to "shoot from the hip." Such meetings are usually disorganized and focus primarily on Quadrant I issues, which are both important and urgent, and around which there is often a great deal of sharing of ignorance. These meetings generally result in wasted time and inferior results and are often little more than an ego trip for the executive in charge.

In most meetings, Quadrant II items are usually categorized as "other business." Because "work expands to fill the time allotted for its completion" in accordance with Parkinson's Law, there usually isn't time to discuss them. If there is, people have been so beaten and smashed by Quadrant I, they have little or no energy left to address them.

So you might move into Quadrant II by first attempting to get yourself on the agenda so that you can make a presentation regarding how to optimize the value of executive board meetings. You might also spend an hour or two in the morning preparing for that presentation, even if you are only allowed a few minutes to stimulate everyone's interest in hearing a more extended preparation at the next board meeting. This presentation would focus on the importance of always having a clearly specified purpose for each meeting and a well thought out agenda to which each person at the meeting has had the opportunity to contribute. The final agenda would be developed by the chairman of the executive board and would focus first on Quadrant II issues that usually require more creative thinking rather than Quadrant I issues that generally involve more mechanical thinking.

The presentation would also stress the importance of having minutes sent out immediately following the meeting, specifying assignments given and dates of accountability. These items would then be placed on appropriate future agendas which would be sent out in plenty of time for others to prepare to discuss them.

Now this is what might be done by looking at one item on the schedule—the two P.M. executive board meeting—through a Quadrant II frame of reference. This requires a high level of proactivity, including the courage to challenge the assumption that you even need to schedule the items in the first place. It also requires consideration in order to avoid the kind of crisis atmosphere that often surrounds a board meeting.

Almost every other item on the list can be approached with the same Quadrant II thinking, with perhaps the exception of the FDA call.

RETURNING THE FDA CALL.   Based on the background of the quality of the relationship with the FDA, you make that call in the morning so that whatever it reveals can be dealt with appropriately. This might be difficult to delegate, since another organization is involved that may have a Quadrant I culture and an individual who wants you, and not some delegatee, to respond.

While you may attempt to directly influence the culture of your own organization as a member of the executive board, your Circle of Influence is probably not large enough to really influence the culture of the FDA, so you simply comply with the request. If you find the nature of the problem uncovered in the phone call is persistent or chronic, then you may approach it from a Quadrant II mentality in an effort to prevent such problems in the future. This again would require considerable proactivity to seize the opportunity to transform the quality of the relationship with the FDA or to work on the problems in a preventive way.

LUNCH WITH THE GENERAL MANAGER.   You might see having lunch with the general manager as a rare opportunity to discuss some longer-range, Quadrant II matters in a fairly informal atmosphere. This may also take thirty to sixty minutes in the morning to adequately prepare for, or you may simply decide to have a good social interaction and listen carefully, perhaps without any plan at all. Either possibility may present a good opportunity to build your relationship with the general manager.

PREPARING THE MEDIA BUDGET.   Regarding item number two, you might call in two or three of your associates most directly connected to media budget preparation and ask them to bring their recommendations in the form of "completed staff work" (which may only require your initials to finally approve) or perhaps to outline two or three well-thought-out options you can choose from and identify the consequences of each option. This may take a full hour sometime during the day—to go over desired results, guidelines, resources, accountability, and consequences. But by investing this one hour, you tap the best thinking of concerned people who may have different points of view. If you haven't taken this approach before, you may need to spend more time to train them in what this approach involves, what "completed staff work" means, how to synergize around differences and what identifying alternative options and consequences involves.

THE "IN" BASKET AND CORRESPONDENCE.    Instead of diving into the "IN" basket, you would spend some time, perhaps thirty to sixty minutes, beginning a training process with your secretary so that he or she could gradually become empowered to handle the "IN" basket as well as the correspondence under item number five. This training program might go on for several weeks, even months, until your secretary or assistant is really capable of being results-minded rather than methods-minded.

Your secretary could be trained to go through all correspondence items and all "IN" basket items, to analyze them and to handle as many as possible. Items that could not be handled with confidence could be carefully organized, prioritized, and brought to you with a recommendation or a note for your own action. In this way, within a few months your secretary or executive assistant could handle 80 to 90 percent of all of the "IN" basket items and correspondence, often much better than you could handle them yourself, simply because your mind is so focused on Quadrant II opportunities instead of buried in Quadrant I problems.

THE SALES MANAGER AND LAST MONTH'S SALES.    A possible Quadrant II approach to item number four would be to think through the entire relationship and performance agreement with that sales manager to see if the Quadrant II approach is being used. The exercise doesn't indicate what you need to talk to the sales manager about, but assuming it's a Quadrant I item, you could take the Quadrant II approach and work on the chronic nature of the problem as well as the Quadrant I approach to solve the immediate need.

Possibly you could train your secretary to handle the matter without your involvement and bring to your attention only that which you need to be aware of. This may involve some Quadrant II activity with your sales manager and others reporting to you so they understand that your primary function is leadership rather than management. They can begin to understand that they can actually solve the problem better with your secretary than with you, and free you for Quadrant II leadership activity.

If you feel that the sales manager might be offended by having your secretary make the contact, then you could begin the process of building that relationship so that you can eventually win the confidence of the sales manager toward your both taking a more beneficial Quadrant II approach.

CATCHING UP ON MEDICAL JOURNALS.  Reading medical journals is a Quadrant II item you may want to procrastinate. But your own long-term professional competence and confidence may largely be a function of staying abreast of this literature. So, you may decide to put the subject on the agenda for your own staff meeting, where you could suggest that a systematic approach to reading the medical journals be set up among your staff. Members of the staff could study different journals and teach the rest the essence of what they learn at future staff meetings. In addition, they could supply others with key articles or excerpts which everyone really needs to read and understand.

PREPARING FOR NEXT MONTH'S SALES MEETING.  Regarding item number seven, a possible Quadrant II approach might be to call together a small group of the people who report to you and charge them to make a thorough analysis of the needs of the salespeople. You could assign them to bring a completed staff work recommendation to you by a specified date within a week or ten days, giving you enough time to adapt it and have it implemented. This may involve their interviewing each of the salespeople to discover their real concerns and needs, or it might involve sampling the sales group so that the sales meeting agenda is relevant and is sent out in plenty of time so that the salespeople can prepare and get involved in it in appropriate ways.

Rather than prepare the sales meeting yourself, you could delegate that task to a small group of people who represent different points of view and different kinds of sales problems. Let them interact constructively and creatively and bring to you a finished recommendation. If they are not used to this kind of assignment, you may spend some of that meeting challenging and training them, teaching them why you are using this approach and how it will benefit them as well. In doing so, you are beginning to train your people to think long-term, to be responsible for completing staff work or other desired results, to creatively interact with each other in interdependent ways, and to do a quality job within specified deadlines.

PRODUCT "X" AND QUALITY CONTROL.   Now let's look at item number eight regarding product "X," which didn't pass quality control. The Quadrant II approach would be to study that problem to see if it has a chronic or persistent dimension to it. If so, you could delegate to others the careful analysis of that chronic problem with instructions to bring to you a recommendation, or perhaps simply to implement what they come up with and inform you of the results.

The net effect of this Quadrant II day at the office is that you are spending most of your time delegating, training, preparing a board presentation, making one phone call, and having a productive lunch. By taking a long-term PC approach, hopefully in a matter of a few weeks, perhaps months, you won't face such a Quadrant I scheduling problem again.

As you go through this analysis, you may be thinking this approach seems idealistic. You may be wondering if Quadrant II managers ever work in Quadrant I.

I admit it is idealistic. This book is not about the habits of highly *ineffective* people; it's about habits of highly *effective* people. And to be highly effective is an ideal to work toward.

Of course you'll need to spend time in Quadrant I. Even the best laid plans in Quadrant II sometimes aren't realized. But Quadrant I can be significantly reduced into more manageable proportions so that you're not always into the stressful crisis atmosphere that negatively affects your judgment as well as your health.

Undoubtedly it will take considerable patience and persistence, and you may not be able to take a Quadrant II approach to all or even most of these items at this time. But if you can begin to make some headway on a few of them and help create more of a Quadrant II mind-set in other people as well as yourself, then downstream there will be quantum improvements in performance.

Again, I acknowledge that in a family setting or a small business setting, such delegation may not be possible. But this does not preclude a Quadrant II mind-set which would produce interesting and creative ways within your Circle of Influence to reduce the size of Quadrant I crises through the exercise of Quadrant II initiative.

# A Final Interview with Stephen R. Covey

IN THE 25 YEARS AFTER THE PUBLICATION *of* The 7 Habits, *Dr. Stephen R. Covey's "circle of influence" grew to encompass the entire globe. He consulted with kings and presidents and taught millions of people through every imaginable channel the principles of effective living. By the time of his death in 2012, he had been named one of the most influential people in the world and* The 7 Habits *the most significant book on self-improvement in a century.*

*He continued to teach* The 7 Habits *all his life. Additionally, the radically changing times called forth even deeper wisdom from Dr. Covey, some of which we'd like to share with you now.*

*The following is a synthesis of the responses Dr. Covey gave near the close of his life to vital questions he was often asked in interviews or during speeches. We have done our best to bring together his final thoughts in his own words into what might be considered his "final interview."*

### What has changed since *The 7 Habits* first appeared?

Change itself has changed. It's accelerated beyond anything any of us ever imagined. Technological revolutions seem to occur hourly. We grapple with economic uncertainty. Global power relations shift dramatically and overnight. And much of the world is terror-stricken, both psychologically and literally.

Our personal lives have radically changed too. The pace of life is now light speed. We are connected to work 24/7. We used to try to do more with less; now many of us are trying on our own to do everything at once.

But one thing hasn't changed and never will change—the only thing you can rely on—the fact that there are timeless and universal principles. They never change. They apply everywhere in the world at all times. Principles like fairness, honesty, respect, vision, accountability, and initiative govern our lives in the same way that natural laws like gravity dictate the consequences of falling off a building. If you go over the edge, you fall. It's a natural principle.

And that's why I am fundamentally optimistic. I am an optimist because I believe in changeless principles. I know that if we live by them, they will work for us.

Unlike a rock that falls if dropped from a building, we are capable of choosing whether to jump or not. We are not unconscious beings to be merely pulled or pushed around by impersonal forces. As humans, we are endowed with the gifts of conscience, imagination, self-awareness, and independent will. These are amazing gifts that animals do not possess. We can sense right from wrong. We can stand apart from ourselves and evaluate our own behavior. We can live out of our imagination, the future we wish to create, instead of being held hostage by the memory of our past. And the more we exercise these endowments the greater becomes our freedom to choose. We can choose to make principles work for us or against us. I revel in that ability to choose.

To live with change, we need principles that don't change.

But there's a problem. Too many of us—more than ever, I'm afraid—are trying to take a shortcut around the principles of life. We want love but not commitment. We want success without paying the price. We want thin bodies and our cake too. In other words, we want something we can never have—the rewards of good character without good character.

That's why I wrote *The 7 Habits of Highly Effective People*. I believe that our culture is drifting from its anchor in those principles, and I want to point to the consequences—that neglecting principles can only result in the shipwreck of our lives. In like manner, I promise you that in the long run, if you will live in alignment with principles you will prosper, personally and professionally.

### Are the 7 Habits still relevant?

I believe the 7 Habits are more relevant than ever.

No one has been more surprised, humbled, and thrilled by the influence of *The 7 Habits* than I have. I'm continually amazed at the effect the book has had on so many people in so many countries. I am so grateful that so many of my associates and friends have taken up the challenge to live and teach the Habits.

Of course, I am just like everyone else who struggles to practice the 7 Habits every day. It's not easy, but it's a challenge. I have found it deeply inspiring to wake up each day and think through my mission in life and my important goals and make small steps toward those things that are most meaningful. I have found it most difficult to live by Habit 5: Seek First to Understand, Then to Be Understood. I have worked at trying to become more patient and a better listener, and I think I have made some progress.

But I can tell you that living the 7 Habits is an exhilarating life-long challenge. That's why I worry when people say they've read the book. I'm afraid they might see something in me that doesn't line up with what I've written. I'm also afraid they will think that reading the book makes them effective overnight—I hope people take seriously the message that you are never done with the 7 Habits.

I'm thrilled to see that more and more people around the world are being trained in the 7 Habits and that thousands have been certified to teach the 7 Habits inside their own organizations. People are attending 7 Habits classes online and in traditional classrooms in more than 140 countries. Even more exciting to me is that tens of thousands of schoolchildren are learning the 7 Habits. In some settings, entire corporations, government agencies, universities, and school systems have adopted the 7 Habits as an organizational philosophy and are finding great success with it.

Why do the 7 Habits continue to influence lives? I think it is because the 7 Habits help people identify their best selves and live accordingly. People, particularly the young, instinctively feel the power of the principles embodied in the 7 Habits and deep down they want more than shortcuts through life. People losing themselves in the hyperactivity of the world want to regain control of their own destinies.

The 7 Habits give people their lives back. They get back the power to choose. They explore and discover their deepest, most cherished purposes. They gain the tools to create and control their own future.

We hear a lot today about identity theft. The greatest identity theft is not when someone takes your wallet or steals your credit card. The greater theft happens when we forget who we really are, when we begin to believe that our worth and identify come from how well we stack up compared to others, instead of recognizing that each of us has immeasurable worth and potential, independent of any comparison. This kind of theft comes from being immersed in a culture of shortcuts where people are unwilling to pay the price for true success. In our families, among friends, at work, we are constantly in the service of an artificial self-image. When man found the mirror, he began to lose his soul. He became more concerned with his image than with his true self; he became a product of the social mirror. His center of identity and worth moved outside of himself.

The 7 Habits bring you back to yourself. The 7 Habits remind you of your true nature. They remind you that *you* are in charge of your life. You are responsible—no one else—for your choices. No one outside yourself can make you think, do, or feel anything you do not choose for yourself. They remind you that you are the programmer and can write the program for your own future. They teach us that life is a team sport, and that interdependence, working cooperatively with others, is a higher state of being than independence.

### Change is hard. How can I change?

I suggest two practices for making changes in your life. The first is to follow your conscience. I speak a lot about the idea that between stimulus (what happens to us) and response (what we do about it) is a space to choose, and what we do with that space ultimately determines our growth and happiness. In this space lie the four human endowments of conscience, imagination, self-awareness, and independent will. Of the four, conscience is the governing one. Often, when we are not at peace in our lives, it is because we are living lives in violation of our conscience and deep down we know it. We can tap into conscience simply by asking ourselves questions and pausing to "hear" the answer. For example, try asking yourself the following questions: What is the most important thing I need to start doing in my personal life that would have the greatest positive impact? Think deeply. What comes to mind? Now, ask yourself another question: What is the most important thing that I need to start doing in my professional life that would have the greatest positive impact? Again, pause, think, and go deep inside yourself to find the answer. If you're like me, you'll recognize those most important things by listening to your conscience—that voice of wisdom, self-awareness, and common sense within you.

Another great question to ask yourself is: What is life now asking of me? Pause. Think carefully. You may sense that you've been unfocused and need to be far more careful with the way you spend your time. Or you may decide that you need to start eating better and exercising because you're constantly tired. Or you may sense that there is a key relationship you need to repair. Whatever it is, there is great strength and power in following through with a change that is endorsed by your conscience. Without deep conviction, you won't have the strength to follow through with your goals when the going gets tough. And conviction comes through conscience.

We all have three different lives: a public life, a private life, and an inner life. Our public life is what others observe. Our private life is what we do when we are alone. Our inner life is that place we go to when we really want to examine our motives and our deepest desires. I highly recommend developing this inner life. This is the place where our conscience can be most instructive because while here we are in the best frame of mind to listen.

A second key to change is to change your role. As I've always said, if you want to make incremental changes in your life, change your behaviors. But if you want to make significant change, work on your paradigms, the way in which you see and interpret the world. And the best way to change your paradigm is to change your role. You may get promoted to be a new project manager at work. You may become a new mother or a new grandfather. You may take on a new community responsibility. Suddenly your role has changed and you see the world differently and better behaviors naturally flow out of the changed perspective.

Sometimes role changes are external events, such as a change in a job responsibility. But other times we can change our role just by changing our mindset or our perception of a situation. Let's say, for example, that you are seen as a control freak at work and that you know you need to start trusting others and letting go. Well, perhaps you could see yourself differently and redefine your role from one of "supervisor" to one of "advisor." With this change of role, this mental shift, you would start to see yourself as an advisor to your team members who are empowered to make decisions and seek your counsel when doing so instead of being the one who has to own everything and constantly follow up.

I'm often asked, Which of the 7 Habits is the most important? My answer is: The most important habit is the one you are having the most difficult time living. Use your endowments of self-awareness and conscience to help you sense which habit you may need to focus on. Often the best way to change is to pick the one thing, the single habit, and to make small commitments to yourself related to that habit and keep them. Little by little your discipline and self-confidence will increase.

**I see what the 7 Habits can do for me personally, but what if my company or organization doesn't practice the 7 Habits?**

Everything starts with the individual because all meaningful change comes from the inside out. When you start the personal process of change, you will soon find that you are also changing your environment, as your influence expands and your example of integrity impresses others. Only after you have successfully begun working on yourself can you start working on the organization.

My great focus is to build the 7 Habits into the culture at large, to help us move on from the Industrial-Age mindset of top-down command and control.

That Industrial Age is still with us mentally. It treats people as things to be controlled. It's the mindset that people are interchangeable things, that one person is the same as another when we all know that every person has unique gifts and is capable of making a contribution no one else can make. On financial statements, people are treated as expenses rather than as the highest-leveraged asset we have. Even if you're a benevolent autocrat, you're still controlling. This is the key flaw of most organizations today.

The 7 Habits can change all that. A 7 Habits culture is deeply empowering to everyone involved in it. In such a culture every person has tremendous value. Complementary teams are carefully designed to leverage the productive strengths of all team members and render their weaknesses irrelevant, as in a singing group where the alto doesn't try to take the place of the tenor or the soprano. All are needed. The key is to unleash them to find their own voices, to aim what they love to do and what they do well at the human needs they serve.

I am so humbled to see how the 7 Habits have helped transform teams and organizations around the world.

For instance, the 7 Habits are the creed of a great mining company in Mexico. Everyone from the CEO to the coal miner is trained in the 7 Habits. Everyone is valued. Productivity skyrocketed while accident rates plunged as everyone took responsibility for results. Spouses started calling up the company, asking, "What have you done with my husband or wife? They are completely changed!" And now whole families are being trained.

I have learned that it takes more than great individuals to make a great company. An organization must also live by the 7 Habits *as an organization*. This means taking initiative, having a crystal-clear mission and strategy, consistently executing on priorities, thinking win-win with all stakeholders, and synergistically innovating for the future. Thinking within the framework of the 7 Habits is crucial to the success of any organization. Building a 7 Habits culture is not just the CEO's job—it's everyone's job. In such a culture, all are leaders.

In the end, my passion has been to build principle-centered leadership into the culture of organizations everywhere. That kind of leadership is for everyone, not just the CEO. All true leadership is based on moral authority, not formal authority. Gandhi never held a formal position. Suu Kyi and Nelson Mandela gained their moral authority from years of imprisonment for the sake of conscience.

All my life I've been a teacher. I've never held a position of high responsibility, but I've felt highly responsible for fulfilling my own mission. Anyone who takes the 7 Habits seriously becomes a leader.

**You've always taught that people should think about the legacy they leave. What will be your legacy?**

On a personal basis, I hope my greatest legacy is with my family, in their happiness and the quality of the lives they lead. Nothing has brought me more happiness and satisfaction than my family. It is what is most important to me. I agree with the observation of a wise leader who once said that "no other success can compensate for failure in the home." Truly, the work you do within your own home is the greatest work you'll ever do. The family is of supreme importance and deserves more time and attention than we traditionally give it. People will spend hundreds of hours thinking through a detailed strategy at work but then won't bother to spend a few hours planning how to build a stronger family.

That said, I don't believe in the false dichotomy that to be successful at home you have to less successful at work. It is not an either-or. With careful planning, you can do both. In fact, success in one will breed success in the other. As well, it is never too late to start anew with your family if you have neglected them in the past.

On a professional basis, when I'm asked what I want to be known for, my answer is simple: My work with children. I believe that every child is a leader and should be seen as such.

When it comes to children, don't define them by their behaviors. Visualize and affirm them as leaders. Leadership is affirming people's worth and potential so clearly that they are inspired to see it in themselves.

We can raise a generation of leaders by teaching the children their innate worth and goodness, by helping them see within themselves the great power and potential they have.

I am so pleased to see that thousands of schools around the world are now teaching the 7 Habits to children, teaching them who they really are and what they are capable of. We're teaching them integrity, resourcefulness, self-discipline, the win-win way of life. We're teaching them to welcome instead of distrust people who are different from them. We're teaching them how to "sharpen the saw," to never stop growing and improving and learning.

This is being done through our *The Leader in Me* program that is being implemented in thousands of schools around the world. In these schools they learn that everyone is a leader, not just a few popular ones. They learn the difference between primary success that comes from real, honest achievement and secondary success— worldly recognition—and they learn to value primary success. They learn that they have this marvelous gift of choice, that they don't have to be discouraged victims or cogs in a machine.

Imagine the future if children grow up deeply connected to these principles, banishing victimism and dependency, suspicion and defensiveness—as fully responsible citizens who take very seriously their obligations to others. That future is possible.

That's what I want to be remembered for.

**What does the future hold for your body of work?**

In my heart of hearts, I am a teacher. After receiving my formal education, I became a professor, a job that I loved. As I began to detect my own mission, it became clear that this idea of principle-centered leadership, as embodied in the 7 Habits and my other works, was far bigger than me. I knew that unless I built an organization to steward and institutionalize this message, its importance and relevance might fade after I was gone.

With that in mind, I decided to start a business, to build an organization that was devoted to spreading principle-centered leadership throughout the world. It started with Covey Leadership Center, which later merged with FranklinQuest to become FranklinCovey. The mission of our company is to enable greatness in people, organizations, and societies everywhere through the application of principle-centered leadership. We now operate in over 140 countries around the world. I am proud of the mission, vision, values, and performance of the organization. It is doing exactly what I hoped it would do. Perhaps most important, FranklinCovey is not dependent upon me, whatsoever, and will continue this work long after I am gone.

**You have said that your most important final message is to "live life in crescendo." What does that mean?**

It means that the most important work you will ever do is always ahead of you. It is never behind you. You should always be expanding and deepening your commitment to that work. Retirement is a false concept. You may retire from a job, but never retire from meaningful projects and contributions.

"Crescendo" is a musical term. It means to play music with ever greater energy and volume, with strength and striving. The opposite is "diminuendo," which means to "lower the volume," to back off, to play it safe, to become passive, to whimper away your life.

So live life in crescendo. It's essential to live with that thought. Regardless of what you have or haven't accomplished, you have important contributions to make. Avoid the temptation to keep looking in the rearview mirror at what you have done and instead look ahead with optimism. I am excited about my forthcoming book called *Life in Crescendo* which I am writing with my daughter Cynthia.

No matter what your age or position in life, if you live by the 7 Habits, you are never finished contributing. You are always seeking something higher and better from life—the next fascinating challenge, greater understanding, more intense romance, more meaningful love. You may get satisfaction from past accomplishments, but the next great contribution is always on the horizon. You have relationships to build, a community to serve, a family to strengthen, problems to solve, knowledge to gain, and great works to create.

One of my daughters once asked me if I had finished impacting the world when I wrote *The 7 Habits of Highly Effective People*. I think I startled her with my answer: This is not to overvalue myself, but I truly *believe* my best work is ahead of me.

*Stephen R. Covey died July 16, 2012, at the age of 79, still fully engaged in about ten different writing projects. He never retired in the traditional sense but lived "in crescendo" right up to the end. As the influence of his thinking continues to spread around the world at a faster and faster rate, transforming the lives of schoolchildren and executives and ordinary people everywhere, we believe with him that his best work is still ahead of him.*

# Problem/Opportunity Index

This index should not be interpreted as an attempt to provide "quick fix" solutions to deep concerns. It is, rather, a reference to material in this book that specifically deals with these concerns and, hopefully, will provide insight and help in working on them. These references reflect parts of the holistic, integrated approach of the 7 Habits and are most effective when understood and used in context.

## PERSONAL EFFECTIVENESS

### Growth and Change

*Can you really create change in your life?*
If you can change *seeing*, you can change *being*, 23–52
Gravity to pull to you, 54–56
From "you" to "I" to "we," 56–61
Your companion in change, 67–68
Opening your "gate of change," 69–70
Being in charge of change, 73–101
Becoming your own first creator, 110–13
Using your head, 140–43
Onward and upward, 317–18

*When change is unsettling*
Creating a changeless core, 115

*When you've been handed a bad script*
Changing it, 110–13, 140–53
Passing a new script on to others, 327–29

*"But it's too hard to change!"*
The power of independent will, 156–58
When to say "yes!" and what it takes to say "no!," 159–67

*Trying to be something you're not*
You can't get the fruits without the roots, 29–30
Symbol without substance, 43–44

*When you're burned out on setting goals*
Putting yourself in control immediately, 99–100
Goals that grow out of mission and roles, 143–45
Making it happen each week, 171–73

### Personal Leadership

*When you don't know if you're being effective or not*
What is "effectiveness" anyway?, 61–67
You're "really busy"—so what?, 105–6

*If you're "successful"—and miserable*
Primary and secondary greatness, 29–30
Symbol without substance, 43–44
Outside-in, 51–52
When your "ladder of success" is leaning against the wrong wall, 105–6

*When what you're doing doesn't work*
Inside-Out, 23–52

*Living a facade*
You can only pretend for so long, 44–46

*When you don't have a solid core*
You can't make a lighthouse move, 40–43
Creating a "principle center," 130–36

# INDEX

# About the Author

**Stephen R.** Covey was an internationally respected leadership authority, family expert, teacher, organizational consultant, and author who dedicated his life to teaching principle-centered living and leadership to build both families and organizations. He earned an M.B.A. from Harvard University and a doctorate from Brigham Young University, where he was a professor of organizational behavior and business management and also served as director of university relations and assistant to the president.

Dr. Covey was the author of several acclaimed books, including the international bestseller, *The 7 Habits of Highly Effective People*, which was named the #1 Most Influential Business Book of the Twentieth Century and one of the top-ten most influential management books ever. It has sold more than 20 million copies in thirty-eight languages throughout the world. Other bestsellers include *First Things First, Principle-Centered Leadership*, and *The 7 Habits of Highly Effective Families*, bringing the combined total to more than 25 million books sold.

As a father of nine and grandfather of forty-three, he received the 2003 Fatherhood Award from the National Fatherhood Initiative, which he said was the most meaningful award he ever received. Other awards given to Dr. Covey include the Thomas More College Medallion for continuing service to humanity, Speaker of the Year in 1999, the Sikh's 1998 International Man of Peace Award, the 1994 International Entrepreneur of the Year Award, and the National Entrepreneur of the Year Lifetime Achievement Award for Entrepreneurial Leadership. Dr. Covey was recognized as one of *Time* magazine's 25 Most Influential Americans and received seven honorary doctorate degrees.

Dr. Covey was the cofounder and vice chairman of Franklin-Covey Company, the leading global professional services firm, with offices in 123 countries. They share Dr. Covey's vision, discipline, and passion to inspire, lift, and provide tools for change and growth of individuals and organizations throughout the world.

# LEARN MORE

Want to learn more about how to develop yourself personally, lead your team, or transform your organization? There are three ways you can engage with FranklinCovey to learn more about how to apply these principles personally and professionally:

- Take the 7 Habits PEQ (Personal Effectiveness Quotient).
- Experience FranklinCovey's award-winning training.
- Read Stephen R. Covey's other bestselling books.

## 1. Take the Personal Effectiveness Quotient (PEQ)

To see how effective you are—where your strengths lie and how you can improve—take the Personal Effectiveness Quotient (PEQ) at **www.7HabitsPEQ.com.**

## 2. Award-Winning Training

Attend a live or live-online three-day *The 7 Habits of Highly Effective People* training. In this dynamic, principle-based program, you will learn how to take initiative, balance key priorities, improve interpersonal communication, leverage creative collaboration, and apply principles for achieving a balanced life.

Are you a leader? Would you like to lead using the 7 Habits paradigms, principles, and tools? Attend this live or live-online two-day training to learn how to be a more effective leader and manager.

You can be an 8th Habit leader. FranklinCovey's *Leadership: Great Leaders, Great Teams, Great Results* program builds on the powerful principles of *The 7 Habits of Highly Effective People* and helps you find your voice and helps others find theirs. This three-day program is offered live or live-online.

**Certify to Teach FranklinCovey Curriculum.** You can certify to become a licensed FranklinCovey facilitator within your organization.

For addition information on any of these training offerings or to become a FranklinCovey facilitator, please visit us at **franklincovey.com/leadership**.

## 3. Bestselling Books by Dr. Stephen R. Covey

*The 8th Habit: From Effectiveness to Greatness*
Discover the 8th Habit and how to be a more effective leader in all parts of your life.

*The Leader in Me*
See how schools around the world are transformed by the 7 Habits principles.

*The 3rd Alternative*
Learn how to solve conflicts and create synergistic solutions by building 3rd Alternatives.

*First Things First*
Discover how to Put First Things First in your personal and professional life.

*Living The 7 Habits*
Read stories by people whose lives have been changed by living the 7 Habits.

*Principle-Centered Leadership*
Learn the core principles of leadership effectiveness in this practical handbook for leaders.

*The 7 Habits of Highly Effective Families*
Learn how to apply the 7 Habits to strengthen your family.

*Great Work, Great Career*
Apply the 7 Habits principles to your work and career to create meaningful and lasting impact.

---

**FranklinCovey.**
THE ULTIMATE COMPETITIVE ADVANTAGE

Franklin Covey Co. (NYSE: FC) is a global company specializing in performance improvement. We help organizations achieve results that require a change in human behavior. Our expertise is in seven areas: leadership, execution, productivity, trust, sales performance, customer loyalty, and education. Franklin Covey clients have included 90 percent of the Fortune 100, more than 75 percent of the Fortune 500, thousands of small- and mid-sized businesses, as well as numerous government entities and educational institutions. Franklin Covey has more than 40 direct and licensee offices providing professional services in over 140 countries. For more information, visit www.franklincovey.com.

# FranklinCovey offices worldwide

**FranklinCovey Angola**
Integrated Solutions Angola, SA
Rua Joaquim Rodrigues da Graça
# 151
Bairro Azul. Luanda - Angola,
C.P. 6185,
ANGOLA
Tel: +244 227 210 108 / +244 227
210 109 (Office Phone)
*msuega@franklincovey.co.ao*

**FranklinCovey Argentina**
LFCA S.A.
Cerrito 774, Piso 11
Ciudad de Buenos Aires, CP
Argentina C1010AAP
Tel: +54 11 4372 5820
Fax: +54 11 4372 5648
*info@franklincovey.com.ar*
*www.franklincovey.com.ar*

**FranklinCovey Pty Ltd
Australia**
Level 1, 139 Coronation Drive
Milton, QLD 4064
Australia
Tel: +61 (7) 3318 9700
*info@franklincovey.com.au*

**FranklinCovey Austria**
Leadership Institut GmbH
Kaasgrabengasse 52/1/10
A-1190 Wien
Tel: +43 1 320 16 22
Fax: +43 1 320 16 23
*info@franklincovey.at*
*www.franklincovey.at*

**FranklinCovey Belgium**
Airport Plaza
Da Vincilaan 19
1831 Diegem/Brussels
Belgium
Tel: +32 2 719 02 15
*jolanda@franklincovey.be*

**FranklinCovey Botswana**
Event Ventures (Pty) Ltd
Private Bag 262
Gaborone
Botswana
Tel: +267 318 4706
*adam@eventventures.co.bw*

**FranklinCovey Bermuda**
Effective Leadership Bermuda
4 Dunscombe Rd.
Warwick, Wk08 Bermuda
Tel: +441 236 0383
Fax: +441 236 0383
*franklincoveybda@logic.bm*

**FranklinCovey Brasil**
Rua Florida 1568
Brooklin - São Paulo – SP
CEP 04565-001
Brazil
Tel: +55 11 5105 4400
Fax: +55 11 5506 6965
*info@franklincovey.com.br*
*www.franklincovey.com.br*

**FranklinCovey Central Eastern**
Europe
FC PL Sp z o o
Ul. Wlodarzewska 33
02-384 Warszawa
Poland
Tel: +48 22 824 11 28
Fax: +48 22 824 11 29
*office@franklincovey.pl*
*www.franklincovey.pl*

**FranklinCovey Colombia**
FranklinCovey Organization
Services (Colombia & Peru)
Av. Carrera 45 (autopista norte
costado oriental)
# 103–34 oficina 202
Edificio Logic 2
Bogotá
Colombia
Tel: +57 1 610 2657
*amesa@franklincovey.com.co*

**FranklinCovey Czech and
Slovacs**
Ohradni 1424/2b
140 00 Praha 4
Czeska Republika
Tel: +420 261 099 341
Fax: +420 261 099 343
*info@franklincovey.cz*
*www.franklincovey.cz*

**FranklinCovey Denmark**
FranklinCovey Nordic Approach
Langebrogade 5
1411 København K
Denmark
Tel: +45 7022 6612
*kin@franklincovey.dk*

**FranklinCovey Dominican**
Republic
Human C x A
Ave. Abraham Lincoln esq. Mejía
Ricart
Torre Piantini, Suite 904
Piantini, Santo Domingo, D.N.
REPUBLICA DOMINICANA
Tel: +1 (809) 922-8677
*ney.diaz@franklincoveydr.com*

**FranklinCovey Ecuador**
Covey Leadership Center
Ecuador
Finlandia 192 y Suecia
Edif. Escandinavia
Loft Of. 5D
Ecuador
Tel: +593 02 333 120
*mfcorral@franklincoveyecuador.com*

**FranklinCovey Egypt**
Leadership Training Center
Villa 7, 1st Touristic District
P.O. Box 27
Mena Garden City
Postal Code 12582
City of 6 October
Egypt
Tel: +20 2 38 37 17 21/23/29
*eman.yassin@franklincoveyegypt.com*

**FranklinCovey Germany**
Leadership Institut GmbH
Bavariafilmplatz 3
D-82031 Grünwald bei München
Tel: +49 89 45 21 48 0
Fax: +49 89 45 21 48 48
*info@franklincovey.de*
*www.franklincovey.de*

**FranklinCovey Gibraltar**
24/10 Crutchetts Ramp
Gibraltar
Tel: +350 58008143
*info@pro-tivity.com*

**FranklinCovey Middle East**
Qiyada Consultants
PO Box 53703
Dubai, UAE
Tel: +971 4 33 222 44
Fax: +971 4 33 222 82
*info@franklincoveyme.com*
*www.franklincoveyme.com*

**FranklinCovey Hellas**
DMS / FranklinCovey Hellas
Group
SA 36
P.S. Stathmou Str.
546 27 Thessaloniki
Greece
Tel: +30 (231) 02 73 979
*antoniadis@franklincovey.gr*

**FranklinCovey Hong Kong**
Right Management
Suite 1401
Dorset House
Taikoo Place
979 King's Road
Quarry Bay
Hong Kong
Tel: +852 2290 0168
*vicky.bui@right.com*

**FranklinCovey Hungary**
FCCoL Hungary Management
Consulting and Training Ltd.
1124 Budapest
Némervölgyi út 64
Hungary
Tel: +36 1 202 0448
*brigitta.bessenyei@franklincovey.bu*

**FranklinCovey India & South Asia**
JIL Tower A
Institutional Area
Ground Floor
Plot No. 78
Sector 18
Gurgaon 122 001
India
Tel: +91 124 4782222
*lavleen@franklincovey.co.in*

**FranklinCovey Indonesia**
P.T. Dunamis Intermaster
Jl. Bendungan Jatiluhur 56
Pusat, Jakarta 12440
Indonesia
Tel: +62 21 572 0761
Fax: +62 21 572 0762
*info@dunamis.co.id*
*www.dunamis.co.id*

**FranklinCovey Israel**
Momentum Training Ltd
9 Rehov Haomanut
Poleg Park
Natanya
Building A1 Entrance
East Iris, Second Floor
Israel
Tel: +97 (2) 986 56226
*roni@momentum.org.il*

**FranklinCovey Italy**
Centro Direzionale Milanofiori
Strada 1 Palazzo F3
20090 Assago
Milano
Italy
Tel. +39 02 80 6721
*chiara.barbieri@cegos.it*

**FranklinCovey Japan**
Seito-kaikan, 7F, 5-7, Sanban-cho
Tokyo, Chiyoda-ku 102-0075
Japan
Tel: +81 3 3237 7711
*training@franklincovey.co.jp*

**FranklinCovey Kenya**
Raiser Resource Group
Ground Floor
Jumuia Place
Lenana Rd.
Nairobi
Kenya
Tel: +254 (0) 20 271 2164/5/7
*ian.ngethe@raiser.co.ke*

**FranklinCovey Lebanon**
Starmanship & Associates
Badaro Street, Beirut,
Lebanon
Tel: +961 1 393494
Fax: +961 1 486451
*starman@cyberia.net.lb*
*www.starmanship.com*

**FranklinCovey Luxembourg**
13 rue de Folschette
L-8613 Pratz
Luxembourg
Tel: +352 (266) 244 60
*sebastian.eberwein@franklincovey.lu*

**FranklinCovey Malaysia & Brunei**
Leadership Resources (Malaysia)
Sdn. Bhd.
D4-1-8
Solaris Dutamas 1
Jalan Dutamas 1 50480
Kuala Lumpur
Malaysia
Tel: +6 03 62055550
*sitham@leadershipresources.my*

**FranklinCovey M.....a**
Achieve Business Consulting and
Training
Know Now Ltd
44/7, Dingli Circus,
Sliema
SLM1912
Malta
Tel: +356 3550 0345
*j.naudi@franklincovey.com.mt*

**FranklinCovey Maroc (Morocco, Libya & Tunisia)**
Zenith Millenium I
Etage 5, Bureau 511 –
Lotissement Attaoufik
Sidi Maarouf
20190
Casablanca
Morocco
Tel: +212 5 22 789 833/832
*meriem@franklincoveymaroc.com*

**FranklinCovey Mauritius**
Seven H Ltd
105 Avenue Roches Brunes
Beau Bassin
Mauritius
Tel: +(230) 454-8743
*cyrilckl@intnet.mu*

**FranklinCovey Mexico/CAC/Chile**
Leadership Technologies, Inc.
Edificio Alfaro – 1er piso Bella
Vista
Avenida Federico Boyd
Ciudad de Panama,
Panama
Tel: +507 264 8899
*jmiralles@franklincoveyla.com*

**FranklinCovey Mozambique**
FranklinCovey Brasil, Ltda
Rua Flórida 1568 - Brooklin
São Paulo - SP
Brazil 04565-001
Tel: +267 318 4706
*jarrais@franklincovey.com.br*

**FranklinCovey Namibia**
Chase & Associates CC
Unit no. 4 no. 6 Luther Street
Windhoek
Namibia
Tel: +264 61 255 492
*afras@chase.com.na*

**FranklinCovey Netherlands**
F&UB. V.
Daam Fockemalaan 10
3818 KG Amersfoort
The Netherlands
Tel: +31 (33) 45 30 627
*j.kuipers@franklincovey.nl*

**FranklinCovey Nigeria**
ReStraL Ltd
12th Floor, St. Nicholas House
Catholic Mission Street
Lagos
Nigeria
Tel: +234 1 264 5885
Fax: +234 1 2635090
*enquiries@restral.com*
*www.franklincoveynig.com*

**FranklinCovey Philippines**
Center for Leadership & Change,
Inc.
4/F Ateneo Professional Schools
130 HV Dela Costa St.
Salcedo Village, Makati City
Philippines
Tel: +632 817 2726
*elaine.rodriquez@franklincoveyphilip pines.com*
*www.franklincovey.ph*

**FranklinCovey Portugal**
Avenida 25 de Abril
Edificio Grei No 184
Piso 1
2750-511 Cascais
Portugal
Tel: +351 214 820 258
*maria.pantaleao@franklincovey.com.pt*

**FranklinCovey Puerto Rico**
Urb. Eleanor Roosevelt
501 Calle Alfredo Carbonell
Hato Rey, PR 00918
Puerto Rico
Tel: +787 977 4065
*iarroyo@franklincoveypr.com*

**FranklinCovey Reunion Island**
J2L
ZAC Les Celestins
12 Rue des Cypris
97 434 La Saline Les Bains
Reunion Island
Tel: + 262 (0) 692 320162
*julien.lescs@j2l.re*

**FranklinCovey Russia**
Management Training
International Ltd (MTI)
5 Kosmonavta Volkova Street
Building 1
125229
Moscow
Russia
Tel: +7495 9981 0272
*a.oleynik@franklincovey.ru*

**FranklinCovey Singapore &
China**
Right Management Singapore Pte
Ltd
10 Hoe Chiang Road
#21–06 Keppel Towers
Singapore 089315
Tel: +65 6532 4100
*zulinah.mooksan@right.com*

**FranklinCovey South Africa**
5 Bauhinia Street
Unit 32 Cambridge Office Park
Highveld Techno Park
Centurion 0157
South Africa
Tel: +27 12 940 0658
*marlinie@franklincoveysa.co.za*

**FranklinCovey South Korea**
Korea Leadership Center
312–4 Gijwa-ri
Bogae-Myun
Anseong City 456-871
South Korea
Tel: +82 (2) 2106 4000
*shkim@eklc.co.kr*

**FranklinCovey Spain**
TEA-CEGOS FranklinCovey
C/ Fray Bernardino de Sahagún,
24, 28036 Madrid
Spain
Tel: +34-912 705 000
Fax: +34-912 705 001
*franklincovey@tea-cegos.es*
*www.tea-cegos-franklincovey.com*

**FranklinCovey Switzerland**
Leadership Institut GmbH
Bogenstrasse 7
CH-9001 St. Gallen
Switzerland
Tel: +41 71 277 19 33
Fax: +41 71 277 19 64
*info@franklincovey.ch*
*www.franklincovey.ch*

**FranklinCovey Tanzania**
NFT CONSULT (TANZANIA)
LTD
Plot 304 Ring Street
Mikocheni Area
P.O.Box 13395
Dar-es Salam
Tanzania
Tel: +255 22(2)773 237 588
*badru.ntege@nftconsult.com*

**FranklinCovey Thailand**
PacRim Leadership Center Co.
Ltd
59/387-389 Moo 4
Ramkhamhaeng Road
Sapansoong, Bangkok 10240
Thailand
Tel: +662 728 0200
Fax: +62 728 0210
*plc@pacrimgroup.com*
*www.pacrimgroup.com*

**FranklinCovey Trinidad &
Tobago**
Leadership Consulting Group
Ltd.
4–6 Chancery Lane
San Fernando
Trinidad & Tobago
Tel: +1 (868) 652 6805
curtis.manchoon@lcg.co.tt

**FranklinCovey Turkey**
FranklinCovey / ProVista
Management Consulting Ltd
Polcenter
Büyükdere Cad. Eczac Ali Kaya
Sk.
No.4 Kat.-2
34394 Levent
Istanbul
Turkey
Tel: +90 212 705 62 30
*suresh.gunaratnam@franklincovey.*
*com.tr*

**FranklinCovey Uganda**
CEMM Group
20 Dewington Rise (Madhvani
Building)
Kampala
Uganda
Tel: +256 7124 25617
*egbusonfe@cemmgroup.com*

**FranklinCovey UK & Ireland**
Grimsbury Manor,
Grimsbury Green,
Banbury
Oxfordshire OX16 3JQ
UK
Tel: +44 (0)1295 274 100
*info@franklincovey.co.uk*
*www.franklincovey.co.uk*

**FranklinCovey Zambia**
Mac Recruitment Ltd
Private Bag E835
Post Net No 84
386 Independence Avenue
Lusaka, 10101
Zambia
Tel: +260-211-266247
*mubanga@mac.co.zm*